MONEY, POLITICS, AND THE FIRST AMENDMENT

MONEY, POLITICS, AND THE FIRST AMENDMENT

FIFTY YEARS OF SUPREME COURT DECISIONS AND CAMPAIGN FINANCE REFORMS

Edited by

LEE C. BOLLINGER

AND

GEOFFREY R. STONE

OXFORD
UNIVERSITY PRESS

OXFORD
UNIVERSITY PRESS

Oxford University Press is a department of the University of Oxford.
It furthers the University's objective of excellence in research, scholarship,
and education by publishing worldwide. Oxford is a registered trade mark of
Oxford University Press in the UK and in certain other countries.

Published in the United States of America by Oxford University Press
198 Madison Avenue, New York, NY 10016, United States of America.

© Oxford University Press 2026

All rights reserved. No part of this publication may be reproduced, stored in a retrieval system, transmitted, used for text and data mining, or used for training artificial intelligence, in any form or by any means, without the prior permission in writing of Oxford University Press, or as expressly permitted by law, by license or under terms agreed with the appropriate reprographics rights organization. Inquiries concerning reproduction outside the scope of the above should be sent to the Rights Department, Oxford University Press, at the address above.

You must not circulate this work in any other form
and you must impose this same condition on any acquirer.

CIP data is on file at the Library of Congress.

ISBN 9780197821916

ISBN 9780197821909 (hbk.)

DOI: 10.1093/9780197821947.001.0001

The manufacturer's authorized representative in the EU for product safety is
Oxford University Press España S.A. of Parque Empresarial San Fernando de Henares,
Avenida de Castilla, 2 – 28830 Madrid (www.oup.es/en or product.safety@oup.com).
OUP España S.A. also acts as importer into Spain of products made by the manufacturer.

*To Jean and Jane
and the next generation:
Emma, Colin, Katelyn, Cooper, and Sawyer
Leni, Julie, Mollie, Maddie, Jackson, and Amaya*

Contents

Acknowledgments	xi
List of Contributors	xiii

    Opening Dialogue   1
    Lee C. Bollinger and Geoffrey R. Stone

PART I: INTRODUCTION TO THE SUPREME COURT: DECISIONS ON CAMPAIGN FINANCE REGULATION

1. *Buckley v. Valeo*'s Dubious yet Durable Contribution–Expenditure Distinction   13
   Richard Briffault

2. How *Buckley v. Valeo* Led Us Astray   35
   Paul M. Smith

PART II: CRITIQUES AND A DEFENSE OF THE MAJOR DECISIONS

3. Getting It Wrong: The Supreme Court and Campaign Finance   51
   Erwin Chemerinsky and Alex Chemerinsky

4. *Citizens United*: Cracks in the Façade   69
   Diane P. Wood

5. A Defense of *Buckley v. Valeo* and *Citizens United v. FEC*   85
   Floyd Abrams

PART III: CAMPAIGN FINANCE AND RACE

6. Race and Campaign Finance Deregulation   93
   Abby K. Wood

PART IV: RECOMMENDATIONS FOR LEGISLATION ON CAMPAIGN FINANCE REFORM

7. Money Talks, Dark Money Whispers: How Anonymous, Unlimited Political Spending Is Corrupting American Democracy 113
   Sheldon Whitehouse

8. Elections in the Age of A.I. 121
   Amy Klobuchar and Stephen Spaulding

PART V: ARGUMENTS INTERPRETING THE "CORRUPTION" RATIONALE

9. Corruption, Campaign Finance, and Criminal Law: *Buckley*'s Legacy 143
   Deborah Hellman

10. Campaign Finance and "Real" Corruption 159
    Nicholas O. Stephanopoulos

11. *Buckley* at 50: By What Right? 179
    Lawrence Lessig

PART VI: THE EFFECT OF CAMPAIGN FINANCE: ON POLITICAL INSTITUTIONS

12. *Buckley v. Valeo*: Doctrinal Difficulties and Institutional Failure 195
    Samuel Issacharoff

13. Campaign Finance and Political Polarization 211
    Richard H. Pildes

14. Party Campaign Finance: From FECA To Modern Hyperpartisanship 227
    Michael S. Kang

15. Plutocratic Democracy, Elon Musk, and the Limits of Campaign Finance Reform 243
    Farris Peale and Guy-Uriel E. Charles

PART VII: THE RELATIONSHIP BETWEEN CAMPAIGN FINANCE AND THE STATE OF AMERICAN DEMOCRACY

16. A Political Question?: Partisan Gerrymandering, Campaign Finance Regulation, and the Supreme Court — 267
    David A. Strauss

17. Without *Buckley*, Would American Democracy Really Be All That Different? — 283
    Pamela S. Karlan

18. Campaign Finance and Contemporary Political Dysfunction — 293
    Nathaniel Persily

PART VIII: A COMPARATIVE APPROACH TO CAMPAIGN FINANCE

19. Leveling The Playing Field: Insights from Comparative Constitutional Law — 315
    Mark Tushnet

    Closing Statement — 331
    Lee C. Bollinger and Geoffrey R. Stone

Other Books by Bollinger & Stone — 335
Notes — 337
Index — 417

Acknowledgments

We would like to express our sincere gratitude to the many people who contributed to this special volume.

First, there are the distinguished scholars and experts who have written the primary essays. They are the heart of this project. Collectively, their deep knowledge and public-spiritedness in dealing with the issue of money in American elections and the fundamental constitutional questions raised make what they have to say profoundly impressive and worthy of close attention by experts and nonexperts alike. We're grateful to each and every one.

In addition, we thank Oxford University Press and OUP editor Dave McBride for being our close partner in these multiple projects (this being our eighth together). No authors could be better served. We also recognize that both Columbia University and the University of Chicago have provided us with the very foundation upon which we can do this work. At Columbia, the Executive Director of the Office of the President Emeritus, Evelyn Schwalb, deserves enormous credit for managing the administration of the project, and Michael Hristakopoulos, the Editorial Manager, skillfully executed the extraordinarily difficult process of turning everything into an actual manuscript, with excellent assistance from Susie Emerson, the primary Research Assistant.

Finally, as always, we thank our spouses most of all, Jean Magnano Bollinger and Jane Dailey. Nothing is possible without them, a fact of life we acknowledge with steadfast appreciation.

List of Contributors

Floyd Abrams, Senior Counsel at Cahill Gordon & Reindel LLP

Lee C. Bollinger, President Emeritus and Seth Low Professor of the University, Columbia University

Richard Briffault, Joseph P. Chamberlain Professor of Legislation, Columbia Law School

Guy-Uriel E. Charles, Charles J. Ogletree, Jr., Professor of Law, Harvard Law School

Alex Chemerinsky, Associate at Greines, Martin, Stein & Richland LLP

Erwin Chemerinsky, Dean and Jesse H. Choper Distinguished Professor of Law, Berkeley School of Law

Deborah Hellman, Robert E. Scott Distinguished Professor of Law and Director of the Center for Law & Philosophy, University of Virginia School of Law

Samuel Issacharoff, Bonnie and Richard Reiss Professor of Constitutional Law, NYU School of Law

Michael S. Kang, William G. and Virginia K. Karnes Research Professor, Northwestern Pritzker School of Law

Pamela S. Karlan, Kenneth and Harle Montgomery Professor of Public Interest Law and Co-Director of the Supreme Court Litigation Clinic, Stanford Law School

Amy Klobuchar, US Senator for Minnesota

Lawrence Lessig, Roy L. Furman Professor of Law and Leadership, Harvard Law School

Farris Peale, 2024 Graduate of Harvard Law School and former clerk with the US Court of Appeals for the District of Columbia

Nathaniel Persily, James B. McClatchy Professor of Law, Stanford Law School

Richard H. Pildes, Sudler Family Professor of Constitutional Law, New York University School of Law

Paul M. Smith, Vice President of Litigation and Strategy, Campaign Legal Center; Visiting Professor from Practice, Georgetown University Law Center

Stephen Spaulding, Former Policy Director, US Senate Committee on Rules & Administration

Nicholas O. Stephanopoulos, Kirkland & Ellis Professor of Law, Harvard Law School

Geoffrey R. Stone, Edward H. Levi Distinguished Service Professor of Law, The University of Chicago

David A. Strauss, Gerald Ratner Distinguished Service Professor of Law, University of Chicago Law School

Mark Tushnet, William Nelson Cromwell Professor of Law, Emeritus, Harvard Law School

Sheldon Whitehouse, US Senator for Rhode Island

Abby K. Wood, Professor of Law, Political Science and Public Policy, University of Southern California Gould School of Law

Diane P. Wood, Retired Circuit Judge of the US Court of Appeals for the Seventh Circuit and Senior Lecturer in Law, University of Chicago Law School

Opening Dialogue

Lee C. Bollinger and Geoffrey R. Stone

Bollinger: This will be our eighth book-length project together. (A complete list of those volumes is provided at the end of this book.) Our general format has been to mark a half-century or century anniversary and reflect on how the jurisprudence surrounding an issue has evolved to the present, on how the nation more generally has dealt with the issue, and on how we might go forward into the future. Such major anniversaries naturally prompt us to look both backward and forward in time.

To do this we offer our own assessments and judgments, but, more importantly, we usually invite the views of twenty or so diverse and leading experts in the field. Our belief is that this provides interested readers of a range of background knowledge and expertise with a unique opportunity for an immersive intellectual experience into the intricacies, debates, and contending perspectives that necessarily characterize any critically important and controversial area of constitutional law and public policy.

Most of our experts have been constitutional scholars, but we also draw on the thinking of scholars from other areas, as well as practitioners from the fields of law, public service, and business. Using this framework, we have, for example, addressed the First Amendment on the 100th anniversary of the first Supreme Court decisions on the issue; the 50th anniversary of the *Pentagon Papers* case, *New York Times Co. v. United States*, 403 U.S. 713 (1971), and the issues surrounding publication by the press (and others) of classified national secrets; the dilemmas in considering "bad speech" on the Internet, primarily on social-media platforms, and the consequences for democracy and what might be done about it; the rise and fall of affirmative action in Supreme Court decisions; the 50th anniversary of *Roe v. Wade*, 410 U.S. 113 (1973), which had just met its demise in *Dobbs v. Jackson Women's Health Organization*, 597 U.S. 215 (2022); and the future generally of free speech in America.

Now, in this volume, we embrace the same tradition in examining the 50th anniversary of the Supreme Court's 1976 decision in *Buckley v. Valeo*, 424 U.S. 1 (1976), which set the First Amendment guidelines for government regulation of money in the context of political campaigns. This is both a vastly complex area and a matter of utmost importance to American democracy. It would be fair to say that in any serious discussion of dangers to democratic self-government in the United States looking to the future, the role of money—of wealth and its uses in politics and political campaigns—would be near the top of the list.

Indeed, in this area the most foundational principles of a free society will be invoked: the basic idea of one person, one vote and what that should mean in practice as well as theory; the importance of minimizing the risks of improper influence, of corruption and of the appearance of corruption; the simple idea that a political official should spend his or her time dealing with the peoples' needs rather than with chasing dollars or fending off opposing dollars; the problems inherent in any government intervention into the way citizens choose to participate in the public forum or in the marketplace of ideas; the fact that the ability and the capacity of citizens to participate in the political process will always be affected by matters extraneous to the merits of their ideas, and that striving for "equality" will arguably be a hopeless, potentially counterproductive, and even dangerous mission; and so on. In short, these issues deal with a complex clash of values and legislative realities.

Still, whether the Supreme Court has embraced the best framework for dealing with this area of public life remains a reasonable and important question. Fifty years ago, in *Buckley*, the Court embraced a dichotomy for thinking about the principle of free speech and the role of money—namely, that of money in the form of "contributions" and in the form of "expenditures"—and a single acceptable rationale for any constitutionally permissible regulation—namely, preventing "corruption," but in a narrowly defined form—that remains with us to this day. Some think that this was the best constitutional resolution possible, while others believe that this framework over the last half century produced a terrible system for the regulation of campaign finance—one that poses a serious threat to the well-being of our democracy. Where would you start?

Stone: Thanks for that great introduction, Lee. Let me offer a bit of historical context. At the time the First Amendment was adopted, no individuals or entities dominated public discourse. At that time, the most common means of communication were public speeches, leaflets, small local newspapers, and so on. Certainly, there were some individuals like Jefferson, Madison, and Adams who, because of their prestige, had a substantial impact on public discourse, but everyone was free to speak more or less freely. With time, though, and with changes in communicative technology and ever-increasing numbers of extraordinarily wealthy and therefore politically influential individuals and corporations, there were growing concerns about the potentially distorting effects of those changes on our democratic process.

The first federal legislative action addressing this concern involved the invention of radio and television. Because there were few airwaves available in any given location, if these powerful new means of communication could be owned and controlled by a handful of very wealthy individuals, they could dominate public discourse in a way that could seriously distort public discourse and understanding. To address this concern, Congress enacted the Communications Act of 1934. Based on the assumption that the government rather than private individuals owned the airwaves, Congress established the Federal Communications Commission and gave it the power to license and regulate radio and television. In 1949, the FCC adopted the Fairness Doctrine, which required the holders of radio and television licenses to cover issues of public importance and to do so in a manner that fairly reflected a range of differing viewpoints. In its 1969 decision in *Red Lion Broadcasting Co. v. FCC*, 395 U.S. 367 (1969), the Supreme Court unanimously held that the Fairness Doctrine did not violate the First Amendment.

But as money came to play an increasingly impactful and potentially distorting role in public discourse and democratic politics, Congress began imposing limitations on political expenditures and contributions. In the Tillman Act of 1907, for example, Congress prohibited corporations from making political contributions to federal political candidates and officeholders. As concerns over the impact of money in politics continued to grow over time, in 1971 Congress, in an overwhelmingly bipartisan vote, enacted the Federal Election Campaign Act, which was signed into law by President Richard Nixon and which, among other things, placed a limit on the amount of their own money that federal political candidates could spend on their campaigns and required candidates to disclose publicly both the expenditures they made and the contributions they received.

Then, in 1974, in legislation signed into law by President Gerald Ford, Congress amended the FECA to set limits on political contributions and expenditures by individuals, political candidates, political parties, and political action committees (PACs), created public-disclosure requirements, and authorized the public financing of political campaigns. The FECA also established the bipartisan Federal Election Commission to oversee the enforcement of the legislation.

In its 1976 decision in *Buckley*, the Supreme Court, in a sharply divided set of opinions, upheld the constitutionality of the contribution limits, the disclosure and reporting provisions, and the public-financing scheme, but held that the limitation on independent campaign expenditures by individuals, political candidates, and PACs violated the First Amendment. In a per curiam opinion, the majority explained that the limitation on the amount that individuals could contribute to a political candidate was constitutional because Congress "could legitimately conclude that the avoidance of the appearance of improper influence [is] critical [if] confidence in the system of representative Government is not to be [eroded]."

On the other hand, the majority held that the government's interest in preventing corruption or the appearance of corruption was of insufficient importance to justify limitations on independent expenditures, as opposed to contributions, to support the election of specific candidates. The majority maintained that the ceiling on independent expenditures imposed "a substantial restraint on the ability of persons to engage in protected First Amendment expression"; and that because the money is not given *directly* to the candidate, this "alleviates the danger" that such "expenditures will be given as a quid pro quo for improper commitments."

Moreover, the majority rejected the argument that the "governmental interest in equalizing the relative ability of individuals [to] influence the outcome of elections [justifies the] expenditure ceiling." In short, the majority maintained that "the concept that the government may restrict the speech of some [in] order to enhance the relative voice of others is wholly foreign to the First Amendment, which was designed 'to secure the widest possible dissemination of information from diverse and antagonistic sources.'" For similar reasons, the majority invalidated the provisions limiting expenditures by candidates from their own personal resources and limiting the total amount that candidates could spend in support of their own election.

Among the justices who disagreed with the majority's reasoning, Justice Byron White's argument is most representative. In short, White argued that there was "no sound basis for invalidating the expenditure limitations, so long as the purposes they serve are legitimate and sufficiently substantial." White maintained that, in enacting this legislation, Congress recognized that it was critical to restore "public confidence in federal elections" and "to obviate [the] impression that federal elections are purely and simply a function of money." This was not, however, the view of the majority.

Bollinger: As you know, Geof, *Buckley* was a fateful moment in American constitutional and political history. The decision set the framework for regulating money in electoral politics that endures to this day, albeit with some important ebbs and flows within that framework that we'll take up in a moment. The majority's decision points were of immense significance and have been highly controversial ever since: that "money" will be treated as "speech," which means in practice that the government's justification for any particular regulation must satisfy the same standard as that applicable for any direct regulation of "speech" alone; that "corruption" will be the only constitutionally acceptable rationale for regulation; and that "corruption" for these purposes will be defined narrowly, closer to a *quid pro quo* than to a general concern about how political candidates and public officials actually think when money is deployed in any way for or against them.

I will want to come back later to your important observation about the potentially analogous treatment of wealth in the context of broadcast media, and how the government intervened to limit that power, and how the Supreme Court wholeheartedly gave constitutional approval to that system. But here's another parallel to consider: When life or property are at stake in judicial proceedings, we routinely accept all kinds of limits on what the parties may say or present to the jury. And, more to the point, it would be treated as both dangerous and preposterous for one side to use wealth, in any way, to enhance its capacity to persuade the jury or court to judge in its favor. Yet with elections, the ultimate manifestation of democracy, exactly the opposite is true.

In the decades after *Buckley*, the role of money in politics grew exponentially, to the point where the circumstances that prompted Congress to enact the Federal Election Campaign Act in 1974 seem innocent and quaint by comparison. By 1990 the Supreme Court was giving indications that it was prepared to reformulate the *Buckley* approach. In *Austin v. Michigan State Chamber of Commerce*, 494 U.S. 652 (1990), the Court considered a Michigan law that forbade corporations to draw on corporate treasury funds to support or oppose candidates for office. In an opinion authored by Justice Marshall, a majority upheld the law, noting that the First Amendment should not stand in the way of legislative efforts to limit the potentially "distorting" effects of massive corporate wealth in the context of elections. Two important changes were set in motion by *Austin*: the special allowance for regulation of corporations in electoral politics, and, more importantly, the introduction of "distortion" as a viable government justification for campaign finance regulation.

The next critical stage in this saga was an act of Congress known as the Bipartisan Campaign Reform Act of 2002 (BCRA), or more colloquially as the McCain-Feingold Act, representing the bipartisan sponsors John McCain and Russ Feingold. This was an amendment to the Federal Election Campaign Act of 1971. It did many things, of course, but for the purposes here it accomplished two very important changes. The first was to address the so-called "soft money" problem that had arisen in the decades after *Buckley*. And the second was to prohibit "electioneering communication" by corporations and unions within certain specified periods around primary and general elections.

After *Buckley*, the Federal Elections Commission allowed political parties to receive unlimited donations to spend in support of or opposition to candidates and for "party building activities," such as get-out-the-vote efforts related to campaigns and elections. The BCRA closed those "loopholes."

And, with respect to corporations and unions, the BCRA embraced the opportunity opened up by *Austin* to limit the role of those organizations in using their corporate funds for supporting or opposing federal candidates for office.

In 2003, the Supreme Court upheld these amendments in the case of *McConnell v. FEC*, 540 U.S. 93 (2003). Justices Stevens and O'Connor delivered the Court's decision, with dissents from Justices Scalia, Thomas, Kennedy, and Rehnquist. The fact that the opinions took up nearly 300 pages in the official report is a testament to the labyrinthine nature of campaign finance law and the extensive analyses and differences among the justices.

But the Court's favorable turn in permitting the legislative branch to put a framework around elections, with a more expansive notion of the public interest in avoiding corruption and the appearance of corruption, and with a more positive reception to regulations reining in the potentially distorting effects of enormous wealth on public debate, especially when it is concentrated in the coffers of corporations and unions, was to turn out to be a momentary ebb in the Court's interventions.

Stone: As you note, in the years since *McConnell*, with the appointment of ever-more Republican—"conservative"—oriented justices, the Court has shifted dramatically in its analysis of campaign finance regulation.

Only four years after *McConnell*, after Justice Samuel Alito replaced Justice Sandra Day O'Connor, the Court, in a five-to-four decision in *Federal Election Commission v. Wisconsin Right to Life*, 551 U.S. 449 (2007), held § 203 of the BCRA unconstitutional as applied to Wisconsin Right to Life's televised political advertisements that criticized Wisconsin's senators for participating in a filibuster to block the confirmation of several of President Bush's judicial nominees. Justice Souter, joined by Justices Stevens, Ginsburg, and Breyer, dissented.

The next year, in *Davis v. Federal Election Commission*, 554 U.S. 724 (2008), in another five-to-four decision, once again with Roberts, Thomas, Scalia, Kennedy, and Alito in the majority, the Court held unconstitutional § 319(a) of BCRA, the so-called "Millionaire's Amendment," which provided that, if a candidate for Congress spent $350,000 or more of his own money in order to secure his own election, the opposing candidate was then permitted to accept individual campaign contributions up to three times larger than would otherwise be allowed. In his opinion for the Court, Justice Alito maintained that "in *Buckley*, we soundly rejected a cap on a candidate's expenditure of personal funds to finance campaign speech," and although the challenged law "does not impose a cap on a candidate's expenditure of personal funds, it imposes [a] penalty on any candidate who robustly exercises that First Amendment right." Alito concluded that because the challenged law imposed "a substantial burden on the exercise of the First Amendment right to use personal funds for campaign speech, [it] cannot stand unless it is 'justified by a compelling state interest.'" "No such justification," he concluded, "is present here."

Justice Stevens, joined by Justices Souter, Ginsburg, and Breyer, dissented: "The Millionaire's Amendment [is] the product of a congressional judgment that candidates who are willing and able to spend over $350,000 of their own money in seeking election to Congress enjoy an advantage over opponents who must rely on contributions to finance their campaigns. To reduce that advantage, and to combat the perception that congressional seats are for sale to the highest bidder, Congress has relaxed the amount of contributions that the opponents of self-funding candidates may accept from their supporters. [Because] the Millionaire's Amendment does not impose any burden [on] the self-funding candidate's freedom to speak [and] because it does no more than diminish the unequal strength of the self-funding candidate, it does not violate the [Constitution]." That, however, was a dissent.

In a series of subsequent decisions, the increasingly Republican-dominated Roberts Court continued to cut back on the authority of government to address the potentially distorting impact of money on the democratic electoral process. In *Arizona Free Enterprise Club's Freedom Club PAC v. Bennett*, 564 U.S. 721 (2011), for example, in another five-to-four decision, the Court held unconstitutional a state law that provided additional state funds to candidates who were being substantially outspent by their political opponents. In her dissenting opinion, Justice Kagan argued that "Arizona's statute does not impose a 'restriction,' or 'substantia[l] burde[n],' on expression. The law," she maintained, "has quite the opposite effect: It subsidizes and so produces *more* political speech. . . . Except in a world gone topsy-turvy, additional campaign speech and electoral competition is not a First Amendment injury."

Three years later, in *McCutcheon v. Federal Election Commission*, 572 U.S. 185 (2014), the same five-justice majority invalidated a provision of the BCRA that limited the total amount of money a donor could contribute to all candidates or committees. In *Buckley* the Court had upheld the constitutionality of contribution limits to individual candidates, but in *McCutcheon* the majority held unconstitutional the law's aggregate contribution limits, maintaining that there was not a sufficient government interest to justify the challenged provision.

The dissenters, in an opinion by Justice Breyer, disagreed, arguing that, "in the absence of limits on aggregate political contributions, donors can and likely will find ways to channel millions of dollars to parties and to individual candidates, [producing] 'corruption' or 'appearance of corruption.'" Breyer maintained that the majority, in substituting its understanding "of how the political process works for the understanding of Congress [creates] huge loopholes in the law [and] undermines, perhaps devastates, what remains of campaign finance reform." *See also Federal Elections Commission v. Ted Cruz for Senate*, 596 U.S. 289 (2022).

And then there is the question of the expenditure of money by non-media corporations to influence democratic elections. As you noted above, the Court first addressed this issue in 1990, fourteen years after *Buckley* and well before the Roberts Court decisions mentioned above. *Austin v. Michigan Chamber of Commerce* involved the constitutionality of the Michigan Campaign Finance Act, which prohibited non-media corporations from using treasury money to make independent expenditures to support or oppose candidates in political elections. The Court, in a six-to-three decision, held that, although private individuals could not constitutionally be prohibited from spending their money independently to support the election of political candidates, it was constitutional for government to restrict corporations from doing so.

In an opinion by Justice Thurgood Marshall, the Court recognized a state's compelling interest in combating "the corrosive and distorting effects of immense aggregations of wealth that are accumulated with the help of the corporate form and that have little or no correlation to the public's support for the corporation's political ideas." In short, he noted, in a democracy, just as corporations do not have a right to vote, they do not have the same First Amendment rights as private individuals. Interestingly, four of the six justices in the majority had been appointed by Republican presidents, although that was before the appointments process became so politicized.

Twenty years later, in *Citizens United v. Federal Elections Commission*, 558 U.S. 310 (2010), the Roberts Court, in a five-to-four decision, overruled *Austin* and held, in an opinion by Justice Anthony Kennedy, that the First Amendment prohibits government from restricting independent corporate expenditures for political campaigns, and that § 203 of the McCain-Feingold Bipartisan Campaign Reform Act was unconstitutional as applied to corporations as well as to individual citizens. In short, the Court held that corporations, like individual citizens, have the same First Amendment right to spend as much money as they like in order to support the election of their favored candidates.

Justice Stevens, in an opinion joined by Justices Ginsburg, Breyer, and Sotomayor, dissented. Corporations, Stevens wrote, are not "We the People" for whom our Constitution was established. Stevens argued that the Court's decision "threatens to undermine the integrity of elected institutions across the Nation." "A democracy," he added, "cannot function effectively when its constituent members believe laws are being bought and sold." In the end, Stevens argued, "the Court's rejection of *Austin* and *McConnell* comes down to nothing more than its disagreement with their results." Indeed, he noted, virtually every one of the majority's arguments "was made and rejected in those cases, and the majority opinion is essentially an amalgamation of resuscitated dissents." "The only relevant thing that has changed since *Austin* and *McConnell*," Stevens observed, "is the composition of this Court." The decision in *Citizens United*, he maintained, thus strikes at the vitals of *stare decisis*.

Moreover, embracing an "originalist" argument, Stevens insisted that "there is not a scintilla of evidence to support the notion that anyone believed [that the

First Amendment] would preclude regulatory distinctions based on the corporate form. To the extent that the Framers' views are discernible and relevant to the disposition of this case, they would appear to cut strongly against the majority's position. [T]he Framers [held] very different views [than the majority does today] about the nature of the First Amendment right and the role of corporations in society." The Framers, he insisted, "took it as a given that corporations could be comprehensively regulated in the service of the public welfare. Unlike our colleagues, [the Framers] had little trouble distinguishing corporations from human beings, and when they constitutionalized the right to free speech in the First Amendment, it was the free speech of individual Americans that they had in mind."

In short, whatever criticisms individuals might have had about *Buckley*, we have come a long way from *Buckley* to the present. The central question is whether such dramatic protection of the rights of billionaires and corporations to influence the democratic process is, in fact, required by the First Amendment.

Bollinger: We can leave it to our authors to recount the Court's decisions from *Citizens United* to the present. For our purposes, it suffices to say that the recent majority of Republican-appointed justices has continued to narrow the scope of permissible congressional and legislative reforms in the realm of campaign finance, even beginning to cast doubts on imposing limits on direct contributions. Increasingly, it seems that only disclosure requirements are open for consideration.

At the end of the essays, we will have further comments on the state of First Amendment analysis in this area of campaign finance regulation and on the larger implications for the nation. For now, let's turn our attention to the views of our authors.

PART I

Introduction to the Supreme Court

Decisions on Campaign Finance Regulation

I

Buckley v. Valeo's Dubious yet Durable Contribution–Expenditure Distinction

Richard Briffault

Introduction

At the heart of the campaign finance jurisprudence inaugurated by *Buckley v. Valeo* is the distinction between contributions and expenditures.[1] Although the Supreme Court held that both contributions and expenditures are expressive and associational activity protected by the First Amendment, it determined that contributions and expenditures are different orders of speech that receive different degrees of constitutional protection. Coupled with its findings that campaign money could be limited to prevent corruption and the appearance of corruption but not to promote political equality, and that contributions but not expenditures pose a danger of corruption, the Court sustained the contribution limits in the Federal Election Campaign Act Amendments of 1974 (FECA) but struck down FECA's expenditure limits.

By drawing the contribution–expenditure distinction, *Buckley* produced a campaign finance law that Congress never enacted and set the stage for many of the pathologies that have marked the campaign finance system ever since. The combination of unlimited spending to be funded by limited contributions led directly to our world of endless fundraising,[2] the rise of PACs and other fundraising intermediaries,[3] the explosion of independent spending, and the invention of a host of devices—soft money, issue advocacy, super PACs, dark money—used by candidates and their supporters to overcome the distinction in practice while giving recognition to it in form.

This contribution–expenditure distinction has been criticized since its inception.[4] Three of the eight justices who participated in *Buckley* rejected the distinction, with Chief Justice Burger and Justice Blackmun writing that neither form of campaign money can be regulated[5] and Justice White urging that both contribution and expenditure limits are constitutional.[6] Subsequently, other justices have questioned the distinction, and even justices who agreed with the distinction have disagreed over how to apply it.[7] Commentators have regularly denounced it as "implausible,"[8] "anomalous,"[9] "untenable,"[10] and "doomed."[11] Indeed, in the early 2000s, it appeared that a majority of the justices had rejected the distinction, albeit without a consensus as to how to replace it. More recently, the Court has hinted that the distinction may be up for reconsideration and has eroded it by intensifying its review of contribution restrictions. Yet, a half-century after *Buckley*, the contribution–expenditure distinction remains a central tenet of campaign finance doctrine.

This chapter will assess the contribution–expenditure distinction: the justification for it, the difficulties the Court has had in applying it, and the division within the Court over its soundness. It will also consider why a doctrine so problematic in both theory and practice continues to be a basic principle of campaign finance law, and what the prospects of campaign finance law look like going forward.

Establishing the Distinction

In *Buckley*, the Supreme Court held that there is a fundamental constitutional distinction between campaign expenditures and campaign contributions. Although the First Amendment protects both forms of campaign money, the Court determined that FECA's expenditure limitations "impose significantly more severe restrictions on protected freedoms of political expression and association than do its limitations on financial contributions."[12] In the Court's view, expenditures are essential to campaign speech "because virtually every means of communicating ideas in today's mass society requires the expenditure of money," and thus limiting spending "necessarily reduces the quantity of expression by restricting the number of issues discussed, the depth of their exploration, and the size of the audience reached."[13] Limiting spending by candidates or political groups was tantamount to limiting electioneering itself, so the Act's spending limits could be sustained only if "the governmental interests advanced in [their] support satisfy the exacting scrutiny applicable to limitations on core First Amendment rights of political expression."[14] The Court then went on to strike down three types of expenditure restrictions imposed by FECA: on a candidate's total campaign spending, on a candidate's use of personal or family funds, and on spending by non-candidate individuals or groups in support of or opposition to a candidate. For each restriction, the Court determined that the government's proffered justifications did not satisfy "exacting" review.

Contributions, by contrast, were characterized as a lesser order of speech, and contribution limitations were held to be less of a burden on First Amendment rights. "A contribution serves as a general expression of support for the candidate and his views but does not communicate the underlying basis for the support."[15] It is essentially a "symbolic expression of support," so a limitation on the size of the donation a contributor may make is "only a marginal restriction upon the contributor's ability to engage in free communication."[16] To be sure, donations provide the funds for candidates or political groups to communicate with the voters, but "the transformation of contributions into political debate involves speech by someone other than the contributor."[17] The Court would subsequently label contributions as "speech by proxy."[18] Though very low contribution limits could prevent candidates and political committees "from amassing the resources necessary for effective advocacy," the Court saw no evidence that FECA's contribution limits would have "any dramatic adverse effect" on the funding of campaigns.[19] Applying what it referred to as a "rigorous standard of review," the Court concluded that the "weighty interests" advanced by the government in preventing corruption and the appearance of corruption justified the Act's dollar limits on contributions by individuals to candidates.[20] The Court also sustained the Act's limits on donations by political committees to candidates and on an individual's aggregate campaign contributions in an election cycle as acceptable means of preventing evasion of the basic limit on individual donations to candidates.[21]

The contribution–expenditure distinction was fundamental to *Buckley*. The Court turned to it immediately after its opening determination that, for purposes of the First Amendment, campaign finance restrictions address speech, not conduct, and cannot be dismissed as mere regulations of time, place, and manner. The distinction was essential to the Court's determination that the interest in preventing corruption and the appearance of corruption justified contribution restrictions—notwithstanding plaintiff's arguments that disclosure and antibribery laws are less restrictive means of accomplishing the same goals[22]—but that anticorruption concerns are insufficient to justify the greater First Amendment burden posed by limits on spending by noncandidate groups expressly advocating the election or defeat of candidates or on total candidate spending. The same anti-circumvention arguments that the Court deemed sufficient to justify limits on contributions to committees and aggregate donations were rejected when applied to campaign money that took the form of expenditures. To be sure, the difference in the Court's treatment of contributions and expenditures limits was connected to the Court's narrow definition of corruption in terms of a donor–candidate *quid pro quo* relationship, its pseudo-empirical determination that spending by groups not prearranged or coordinated with a candidate "may well provide little assistance to the candidate's campaign and indeed may prove counterproductive,"[23] and its rejection of political equality as a justification for campaign finance regulation.[24] But the Court clearly framed its analysis in terms of the different constitutional status of contributions and expenditures and the resulting difference in the standard of review.

The contribution–expenditure distinction immediately raised at least three questions. First, how clear is that distinction? The Court never defined either term, and the distinction has proven to be blurry both in theory and in practice. Second, what exactly is the difference in the degree of constitutional review between contributions and expenditures? *Buckley* subjected contribution limits to a "rigorous standard of review"; expenditure limits received "exacting scrutiny."[25] Although the Court clearly viewed expenditure limits as presenting a far more substantial First Amendment problem than contribution limits, the difference in the degree of scrutiny required by "rigorous" versus "exacting" is, to say the least, not obvious. Were these even two different standards of review, or something more like points on a sliding scale? Third, how persuasive is the distinction? Three of the eight Justices who participated in the case[26] rejected the idea that contributions and expenditures should receive different First Amendment treatment, and in the decades since then another half-dozen justices have either questioned the distinction or rejected it outright. In the early 2000s, it appeared that a majority of the Court was poised to reject the distinction, but there was no majority for a rule to replace it. These issues will be taken up in the next three sections.

Contribution or Expenditure?

Buckley assumes that contributions and expenditures are different campaign activities, but the distinction is not so clear either in law or in practice. FECA uses closely overlapping definitions for these key concepts. A "contribution" is "a gift, subscription, loan, advance, deposit or gift of money or anything of value . . . made for the purpose of influencing the nomination for election, or election, of any person to Federal office."[27] An "expenditure" is "a purchase, payment, distribution, loan, advance, deposit, or gift of money or anything of value . . . made for the purpose of influencing the nomination for election, or election, of any person to Federal office."[28] There is some slight variation between the two definitions, but what is more striking is how similar they are. For both, the central focus is the use of money or anything of value for the purpose of influencing a federal election, rather than the specific technique of how the money is so used.

Candidate Self-Funding

In *Buckley* itself, the Court divided over whether a specific campaign practice should be treated as a contribution or an expenditure. Justice Thurgood Marshall joined the *Buckley* majority in agreeing that contribution and expenditure restrictions should receive different constitutional treatment but dissented with respect to the Court's invalidation of FECA's limits on a candidate's use of personal or family funds. The opinion for the Court treated this provision as an expenditure limitation that imposed "a substantial restraint on the ability of persons to engage in protected First Amendment expression."[29] But for Justice Marshall this was simply a limit on the contribution the candidate makes to his own campaign.[30] In Marshall's view, the limit was justified in part by an interest in "providing some regulatory symmetry" in a system that limits large contributions to the non-wealthy but would otherwise allow the wealthy to contribute without limit to themselves.[31]

Coordinated and Independent Expenditures

More significantly, *Buckley* also recognized that some expenditures—those "coordinated" with a candidate—are the functional equivalent of contributions and may be constitutionally treated as such. The Court noted that FECA treated expenditures by third parties that are "controlled by or coordinated with the candidate and his campaign" as contributions and agreed that such "prearranged or coordinated expenditures amount[] to disguised contributions."[32] In the *Colorado Federal Republican Committee* cases in 1996 and 2001, the Court underscored the constitutional difference between coordinated expenditures and what came to be known as "independent" expenditures.

In *Colorado Republican I*,[33] the Court determined that expenditures by a political party in support of its candidate undertaken without any direct contact between the party committee's decision-makers and the candidate benefited by the expenditure were "independent," and so could not be limited. Subsequently, in *Colorado Republican II*,[34] the Court held that a party's expenditures coordinated with its candidate could be treated as contributions to the candidate and subject to FECA's limit on a party's donation to a candidate. In neither case, however, did the Court articulate a standard defining what makes an expenditure truly independent or, instead, a quasi-contribution. In *Colorado Republican I*, the FEC argued simply that a party committee's spending is, as a matter of law, necessarily coordinated with its candidate. The Court, in a plurality opinion, rejected that position, requiring that the party's expenditure be coordinated in fact with the candidate in order to receive the constitutional treatment of a contribution.[35] This would have been difficult, if not impossible, in that case, as the Republican committee's expenditures criticizing the Democratic incumbent were undertaken so early in the election cycle that the Republicans had not yet selected their candidate.[36] As a result, *Colorado Republican I* gives no guidance for determining whether a party's spending is independent or coordinated when the party has a candidate in the race.

In *Colorado Republican II*, the party committee mounted a facial attack on the application of coordinated spending limits to parties, contending that, given the close connection between a party and its candidate, the spending limit imposes a "unique First Amendment burden" on the party.[37] The Court rejected that argument, citing evidence that donors give to parties "with the tacit understanding that specific candidates" will benefit,[38] so that the party coordinated spending limit served to backstop the limits on individual donor-to-candidate contributions. Again, though, as the case was brought as a facial challenge to the spending limit, the Court had no occasion to consider when a party's—or any entity's—expenditure should be considered independent and when it should be considered coordinated with the benefited candidate.

The coordinated–independent distinction—a direct outgrowth of the contribution–expenditure distinction—has bedeviled campaign finance law for decades. The Supreme Court has never addressed how to draw that distinction. The leading lower-court decision held that in the absence of an express request or suggestion from a candidate, an otherwise independent expenditure becomes coordinated only when "there has been substantial discussion or negotiation between the campaign and the spender" over the communication's contents; its timing; its location, mode, or intended audience; or its extent.[39] The discussion or negotiation between the candidate and the spender must be sufficiently substantial that the two "emerge as partners or joint venturers."[40]

Congress, in the Bipartisan Campaign Reform Act of 2002 (BCRA), adopted a definition of "independent expenditure" that excludes any expenditure made "in concert or cooperation with or at the request or suggestion of such candidate, the candidate's authorized political committee, or their agents, or a political party committee or its agents."[41] The BCRA also directed the FEC to adopt new regulations on coordinated communications "that shall not require agreement or formal collaboration to establish coordination" and cover "payments for communications made by a person after substantial discussion about the communication with a candidate of a political party."[42] The FEC, in turn, has promulgated a complex multipart rule that considers both the content of the communication and the conduct of the spender and the candidate or party. The rule focuses on whether the spending is "at the request or suggestion" of the candidate's campaign or a party committee; whether the candidate's campaign or party was "materially involved" in the communication's development; or whether there has been "substantial discussion" between the candidate's campaign or party and the spender about the creation, production, or distribution of the communication.[43]

Although the FEC's rule confirms that coordination does not require any agreement or formalized collaboration between the candidate's campaign and the spender, it has been utterly unable to prevent the massive amount of de facto coordination between candidates and "independent" spenders that is characteristic of contemporary election campaigns. Candidates may fundraise for "independent" spenders;[44] and "independent committees can canvass voters[45] and pay many of the campaign's non-communications expenses."[46] Through what is known as "redboxing," candidates can ask outside groups to fund particular campaign messages that target particular groups of voters through specifically indicated media formats.[47] Yet, none of these actions has been found to turn the "independent" expenditures into coordinated quasi-contributions. Still, if coordination turns an expenditure into a contribution, then billions of dollars of expenditures are actually contributions, albeit not legally recognized as such.

The public understands that most so-called independent expenditures are really contributions. When the media reports on the major "donors" to the candidates, they are largely tracking the funding of supportive super PACs and other nominally independent committees.[48] But the law continues to treat such expenditures as constitutionally distinct from contributions.

Occasionally, reality breaks through even for the Supreme Court. In *Caperton v. A. T. Massey Coal Co.*,[49] the Court held that an elected justice of the West Virginia Supreme Court of Appeals violated the Due Process Clause when he refused to recuse from participating in a case in which the chairman and principal officer of one of the parties had spent $3 million supporting the justice in his recent election campaign. Only $1,000 of that $3 million was actually a contribution to the justice's campaign committee; the remainder consisted entirely of independent expenditures or contributions to an independent committee, accounting for more than two-thirds of that committee's total funds. Yet, the Court, in an opinion by Justice Kennedy, consistently referred to those expenditures as "contributions" to the West Virginia justice, which, like other contributions but not like independent expenditures, would cause the justice to "feel a debt of gratitude . . . for [the] extraordinary efforts to get him elected."[50] *Caperton* was not a campaign spending case and did not deal with any law that might have limited the spending in that election, but its discussion of the campaign spending that triggered the Due Process Clause violation revealed more clearly than any campaign finance case the difficulty of distinguishing between contributions and expenditures.

Contribution Limits Treated as Expenditure Limits, and Vice Versa

Buckley indicated that contribution limits would be subject to a less "exacting" review than expenditure limits, but in *Citizens Against Rent Control ("CARC") v. City of Berkeley*[51] and *Davis v. FEC*,[52] the Court treated a contribution limit as if it were an expenditure limit. *CARC* addressed the limits Berkeley had imposed on donations to ballot proposition committees. Although the case primarily turned on the Court's conclusion that *Buckley*'s anticorruption justification for contribution limits was available only for contributions to candidates,[53] the Court also determined that the limit should be subject to the "exacting judicial scrutiny" applicable to spending limits, because the contribution limit "automatically affects expenditures, and limits on expenditures operate as a direct restraint on the freedom of expression of a group or committee."[54] In *Davis*, the Court considered a challenge to the constitutionality of the so-called Millionaire's Amendment, a provision added to the BCRA that raised the limits on contributions to a candidate who was being outspent by a high-spending self-financing candidate. Although the amendment did not address spending at all, the Court treated the liberalized contribution limit as a burden on the expenditures of the self-financing candidate, applied the standard of review applicable to expenditure limits,[55] and struck it down.

By the same token, the Court in *McConnell v. FEC* subjected the restrictions the BCRA placed on the ability of national parties and state party committees to spend soft money to the standard of review applicable to contribution restrictions.[56] The Court prefaced its treatment of the constitutional challenge to the BCRA's soft-money provisions by restating and reaffirming *Buckley's* distinction between contributions and expenditures and the concomitant difference in the standard of review.[57] But it determined that the restrictions on soft-money spending had been "adopted to implement the contribution limit, or to prevent circumvention of that limit" and so should be treated as contribution—and not expenditure—restrictions.

Standard(s) of Review

Buckley indicated that contribution limits and expenditure limits are subject to different standards of review, but the sharpness of that distinction has varied considerably over time. In an early post-*Buckley* case, *California Medical Ass'n v. FEC*,[58] decided in 1981, Justice Blackmun, who had provided the pivotal fifth vote for the Court's decision sustaining FECA's limit on how much an association is allowed to donate to its own political action committee, denied that "the test to be applied to contribution limitations is different from the test applicable to expenditure limitations."[59] He urged that the standard of review should be the same for both types of restriction, although he found that the government had shown that the restriction at issue was closely drawn to address the threat of actual or potential corruption.[60] The following year, in *FEC v. National Right to Work Committee* (*NRWC*),[61] the Court sustained a limitation on the ability of a corporation to solicit donations to its PAC without referring to the standard of review it was applying. In 1985, in *FEC v. National Conservative Political Action Committee* (*NCPAC*),[62] the

Court struck down the limit on PAC independent spending with respect to a presidential candidate who had chosen to accept public funding. The *NCPAC* decision distinguished itself from the *NRWC* case by noting that the earlier decision involved contributions and that the Court had "concluded in *Buckley* that there was a fundamental constitutional difference between money spent to advance one's views independently of the candidate's campaign and money contributed to the candidate to be spent on his campaign."[63] But then the Court stated that it was applying a "rigorous" standard of review to the *expenditure* restriction, citing *Buckley*'s invocation of the "rigorous" standard[64]—which *Buckley* had applied to FECA's *contribution* restrictions.

Subsequently, the distinction in the treatment of contributions and expenditures and in the standards of review became clearer and more consistently applied. In *FEC v. Massachusetts Citizens for Life, Inc. (MCFL)*,[65] an independent-spending case, the Court emphasized that any independent expenditures "constitute expression 'at the core of our electoral process and of the First Amendment freedoms,'" and thus any limit on such spending must be "justified by a compelling state interest";[66] the Justices further claimed that they "have consistently held that restrictions on contributions require less compelling justification than restrictions on independent spending."[67] In *Austin v. Michigan Chamber of Commerce*, the Court sustained Michigan's ban on the expenditure of corporate treasury funds in support of or opposition to a candidate, but in so doing the Court reiterated *MCFL*'s holding that strict scrutiny applies to an expenditure restriction, testing "whether it is narrowly tailored to serve a compelling interest."[68] *Nixon v. Shrink Missouri Government PAC*,[69] in 2000, clarified the lower standard of review for contribution restrictions, holding that a contribution restriction would pass constitutional muster if the "regulation was 'closely drawn' to match a 'sufficiently important interest.'"[70] The Court confirmed that contribution limits would require a less compelling justification than expenditure limits, and that, compared with expenditure limits, contribution limits "would more readily clear the hurdles before them."[71] More specifically, the "quantum of empirical evidence needed to satisfy heightened judicial scrutiny"[72] of legislative judgments setting contribution limits was relatively modest: "[T]here is little reason to doubt that sometimes large contributions will work corruption of our political system, and no reason to question the existence of a corresponding suspicion among voters."[73]

In a series of campaign finance cases that followed over the next three years, the Court stuck with *Shrink Missouri*'s "closely drawn" test and its highly deferential approach to contribution restrictions, invoking it in *Colorado Republican II*,[74] *FEC v. Beaumont*,[75] and *McConnell v. FEC*.[76] The *Beaumont* decision is particularly striking, as the Court relied on *Shrink Missouri*'s more deferential standard of review of contribution restrictions to sustain not just a contribution limit but the century-old federal ban on contributions by corporations in federal elections. As the Court explained, "the level of scrutiny" of a campaign finance restriction was based "on the importance of the 'political activity at issue' to effective speech or political association," and "contributions lie closer to the edges than to the core of political expression," thus supporting "relatively complaisant review under the First Amendment."[77]

But just a few short years later, in 2006, the Court began to move away from *Shrink Missouri*'s highly deferential standard. In *Randall v. Sorrell*,[78] the Court struck down Vermont's limits on contributions to candidates for state office. The plurality opinion by Justice Breyer—joined only by Chief Justice Roberts and Justice Alito, both of whom had been only recently appointed to the Court—purported to apply the "closely drawn" standard and to be more deferential to legislative judgments concerning contribution limits than to those concerning expenditure limits.[79] But the plurality undertook a probing assessment of multiple provisions of the law, compared Vermont's restrictions with those of other states, and closely reviewed statistics concerning the funds raised and spent in multiple state legislative campaigns—a far closer scrutiny of a contribution restriction law and its potential effects than the Court had ever undertaken before. The plurality concluded that Vermont's limits were so low that they restricted the ability of candidates, especially challengers, to mount competitive campaigns, and so were unconstitutional.[80] Three justices who had been in the *Shrink Missouri* majority, including Justice Souter, the author of the Court's opinion in that case, dissented.[81]

Since *Randall*, the Court has invalidated the contribution restriction before it in every case it has fully considered. As previously discussed, in *Davis v. FEC* the Court struck down the Millionaire's Amendment's differential contribution limits. In *Thompson v. Hebdon*,[82] the Court vacated and remanded the court of appeals' decision sustaining Alaska's contribution restrictions for failure to follow the "closer review" of the law required by *Randall*.[83] More significantly, in *McCutcheon v. FEC*,[84] the Court invalidated the federal aggregate contribution limits—that is, the overall cap that federal law placed on the total amount of money an individual could donate to all candidates, parties, and political committees in an election cycle. In so doing, the Court for the first time rejected a part of *Buckley*, setting aside *Buckley*'s validation of the constitutionality of FECA's aggregate contribution limit.

Chief Justice Roberts's plurality opinion in *McCutcheon* expressed considerable doubt that the aggregate limit was needed to prevent donors from circumventing the limit on donations to a particular candidate—what he referred to as the "base limit." Moreover, it put new teeth into the "closely drawn" requirement by finding the law "poorly tailored" to the government's interest in preventing the circumvention of the base limit. Roberts spun out "multiple alternative" means by which Congress might prevent circumvention of the base limit, although he was careful to avoid "opin[ing]" on the constitutionality of the proffered alternatives.[85] He also pointed to disclosure as a "less restrictive alternative" to the aggregate contribution limit—the first time in the post-*Buckley* era that the Court raised disclosure as the constitutionally preferred means of regulating campaign finance in a contribution—not an expenditure—case.[86]

The 2022 decision in *FEC v. Ted Cruz for Senate*[87] further tightened up the Court's review of contribution restrictions. *Cruz* addressed a federal rule that limits the ability of a candidate's committee to repay a loan the candidate made to the committee by capping the amount of money the committee can repay the candidate from post-election contributions. There was no limit on repayment to the candidate from contributions made to the committee prior to the election, only on post-election donations. As Justice Kagan explained in her dissent, "The theory of the legislation is easy to grasp. Political contributions that will line a candidate's own pocket, given after his election to office, pose a special danger of corruption."[88] The Court, however, invalidated the measure. In his opinion for the Court, Chief Justice Roberts urged that limiting the repayment of loans to a candidate deters candidates from lending to their campaigns, thus burdening their electoral speech.[89] He determined that the government had failed to provide hard evidence that post-election contributions to repay candidate loans have been a source of corruption.[90] Neither the "common sense" assessment of post-election loan-repayment contributions as effectively gifts to winners nor statements by members of Congress to that effect provided sufficient evidence of a danger of corruption or its appearance to satisfy the toughened "closely drawn" standard.

To be sure, the Court has continued to cite the centrality of the contribution–expenditure distinction, but only in cases involving expenditure restrictions, such as *Citizens United v. FEC*,[91] or the supplemental funding supplied to publicly funded candidates facing high-spending opponents that the Court in *Arizona Free Enterprise Club's Freedom Club PAC v. FEC* treated as tantamount to a spending limit.[92] Contribution restrictions remain on the books and continue to have some prospect of withstanding a constitutional challenge, while expenditures are constitutionally immune from limitation. But the lower standard of review for contribution restrictions has been ratcheted upward. The two standards have not yet converged, but they are closer than ever before.

Division Within the Court

From the very beginning, the question of whether there is any difference in the degree of constitutional protection for contributions in contrast to expenditures has divided the Court. Three of the eight justices who participated in *Buckley* rejected any distinction. Chief Justice Burger, joined by Justice Blackmun, would have given contributions the same constitutional status as expenditures. They emphasized both that limiting contributions would constrain candidate spending and that the restrictions burden the ability of donors to engage in political communication much as a spending limit does: "[P]eople—candidates and contributors—spend money on political activity because they wish to communicate ideas, and their constitutional interest in doing so is precisely the same whether they or someone else utters the words."[93] Moreover, the Chief Justice urged, the distinction is "unworkable" in practice, presciently writing that "it is not too much to predict that the Court's holding will invite avoidance, if not evasion, of the intent of the Act, with 'independent' committees undertaking 'unauthorized' activities in order to escape the limits on contributions."[94]

Justice White also rejected the contribution–expenditure distinction, but he would have sustained FECA's restrictions on expenditures as well as the contribution limits. He did not see expenditures enjoying any greater constitutional protection than contributions, determined that the expenditure limits reinforced the contribution limits, and would have deferred to "the considered judgment of Congress" that both sets of limits were needed to address corruption and "restore and maintain public confidence in elections."[95] Like the other dissenters—although reaching a very different conclusion—he also challenged the practicability of the distinction: "It would make little sense to me, and apparently made none to Congress, to limit the amounts an individual may give to a candidate or spend with his approval but fail to limit the amounts that could be spent on his behalf."[96]

In the decades since *Buckley*, the equivalent of almost an entire Supreme Court has either expressed an openness to reconsidering the distinction or has rejected it outright. But, as in *Buckley*, with some Justices wanting to make it easier to regulate expenditures and others wanting to strike down contribution restrictions, there has not yet been a majority to reject the distinction.

In 1985, Justice Marshall became the first—and only—Justice who had joined the *Buckley* per curiam to subsequently embrace Justice White's dissenting view, announcing that he was "now unpersuaded by the distinction established in *Buckley*" and voting, in dissent, to sustain a limitation on independent spending by political committees.[97] Justice Stevens repeatedly stated that he would overturn the contribution–expenditure distinction and permit regulation of expenditures.[98] Justices Souter, Ginsburg, and Breyer at various times indicated a willingness to reconsider the constitutionality of certain types of spending restrictions, such as those on the personal funds of "independently wealthy candidates,"[99] or to consider arguments for spending restrictions, such as addressing "the time burdens of fundraising," which *Buckley* had not directly considered.[100]

On the deregulatory side, Justice Thomas has consistently called for the repudiation of *Buckley*'s contribution–expenditure distinction, beginning with *Colorado Republican I*, the first campaign finance case to come before the Court after his appointment. He would accord contributions the same First Amendment protection as expenditures, and would apply strict judicial scrutiny to contribution limits.[101] Justice Scalia joined Justice Thomas's rejection of the contribution–expenditure distinction in *Nixon v. Shrink Missouri*,[102] *Colorado Republican II*,[103] and *Randall v. Sorrell*.[104] Justice Kennedy joined Justices Thomas and Scalia in *Colorado Republican II*,[105] and wrote his own separate opinions in *Shrink Missouri*, voicing his doubts about "the existing distortion of speech caused by the halfway house we created in *Buckley*"[106] and in *Randall*, expressing "my own skepticism" about the campaign finance "legal universe we have ratified and helped create."[107]

Justice Thomas's opinions have repeatedly rejected the second-tier constitutional status of contributions, dismissed the "speech by proxy" label, and emphasized that "[c]ontributions to political campaigns, no less than direct expenditures, 'generate essential political speech' by fostering discussion of public issues and candidate qualifications."[108] Although the Court in *McCutcheon* struck down the federal aggregate contribution limits, Justice Thomas did not join Chief Justice Roberts's plurality opinion, but wrote separately to underscore his ongoing view that *Buckley* should be overruled and strict scrutiny applied to contribution limits.[109]

Justice Kennedy's opinions put primary weight on the "serious distortion" of the campaign finance system that followed from *Buckley*—the rise of PACs, soft money, and issue advocacy "as contributors and candidates devise ever more elaborate methods of avoiding contribution limits"[110]—that is "confusing if not dispiriting to the voter."[111] He seemed less committed to enhancing the constitutional protection of contributions, noting in his *Shrink Missouri* dissent that he "would leave open the possibility that Congress, or a state legislature, might devise a system in which there are some limits on both expenditures and contributions."[112] Nonetheless, in these cases, Justice Kennedy joined Justice Thomas in voting to strike down the challenged contribution restrictions.

The Court's growing disenchantment with the contribution–expenditure distinction, but its inability to reach a consensus on how to replace it, were on display in *Randall v. Sorrell*. That case considered a Vermont law that imposed both expenditure and contribution limits in state elections. The US Court of Appeals for the Second Circuit not only sustained the contribution limits but, apparently emboldened by the Supreme Court's recent run of cases sustaining campaign finance restrictions, and especially the separate opinions in *Shrink Missouri* indicating a possible reconsideration of the constitutionality of spending limits, also held that the Vermont expenditure limits might be constitutional and remanded the case for trial.[113] Justice Breyer, no longer open to permitting expenditure limits, sought to write an opinion that would reaffirm as *stare decisis Buckley*'s contribution–expenditure distinction, albeit with a more probing review of the burden the contribution restrictions placed on First Amendment interests. However, only two justices were willing to join him, and only one—Chief Justice Roberts—was willing to do so as a matter of *stare decisis*.[114] Three justices voted to strike down both the contribution and expenditure limits, while three justices voted to sustain or to be willing to sustain both sets of limits. Though endorsed by only a third of the Court, the contribution–expenditure distinction survived.

In the two most recent campaign finance cases, the Court has hinted that the distinction may be up for reconsideration. In *McCutcheon*, Chief Justice Roberts opened his analysis by referring to the "significant energy" spent by the parties and *amici* "debating whether the line that *Buckley* drew between contributions and expenditures should remain the law."[115] Rather than reaffirm *Buckley*, the plurality opinion determined there was "no need" to revisit the contribution–expenditure distinction, as under its "rigorous" application of the "closely drawn" test the aggregate contribution restriction was unconstitutional.[116] Similarly, in *Cruz* the Court mused about the debate between the parties over whether to apply strict scrutiny or "closely drawn" review before deciding that there was no need to resolve the issue—or reaffirm to *Buckley* on this point—because the challenged law failed both standards.[117]

A Dubious but Durable Compromise

As a matter of principle, the contribution–expenditure distinction has little to recommend it. As Justice Marshall wrote in recanting his prior support for the doctrine, both contributions and expenditures implicate the same First Amendment rights of speech and association and "in both cases the regulation is of the same form: It concerns the amount of money that can be spent for political activity."[118]

Contributions are a crucial form of political participation. Candidates and organizations depend on contributions in order to get their messages out to the voters, and for many voters making a contribution is an important means of participating in the electoral process. Few voters have the time or money to take out ads or campaign for candidates on their own. Rather, for most voters the most realistic means of supporting a candidate is through a contribution. Contributions may do more than just signal the fact of support. When contributed through a PAC or bundled together with those of other ideologically compatible donors, they can communicate the positions on issues the donors support.[119] As for "speech by proxy," much political-association speech is speech by proxy for the association's members, and, as the Court's freedom-of-association cases indicate, that activity enjoys full constitutional protection.

By the same token, not all expenditures are pure speech. Campaign finance law treats as expenditures a host of activities—hiring staff, renting office space, buying equipment, transportation, renting hotel rooms, polling, opposition research, assembling focus groups, and more—that involve preparing for communications to voters but are not communications themselves. It is hard to see why these "back office" activities are speech at all, let alone a higher order of speech than the contributions that fund these expenses. And, of course, even without formal coordination and prearrangement, candidates' pursuit of massive sums of supportive independent expenditures is as potentially corrupting as the solicitation and acceptance of donations to the candidate's own campaign committee.[120]

To be sure, there are differences between contributions and expenditures. Contributions involve a direct connection between the donor and the recipient. To that extent, donations to candidates more closely resemble the gifts to public officials that are typically subject to conflict-of-interest regulation.[121] Even skeptics of campaign finance reform have acknowledged that there is a "plausible case under the First Amendment" for limiting contributions to prevent corruption.[122] And, as the Court has emphasized, contribution limits leave open other avenues for political participation and provide an incentive to candidates to seek a broader base of financial support. Unlike contributions, expenditures do underwrite direct communications of facts and arguments to the voters to mobilize voter engagement. Some independent expenditures may enable the expression of political ideas separate from clear support of political candidates, while limits on total campaign expenditures raise the risk of limiting effective electoral competition and protecting incumbents.

But these distinctions are differences of degree, not kind. Contributions often have the same First Amendment value as expenditures, and expenditures can pose the same dangers of corruption and the appearance of corruption, which the Court has recognized as compelling governmental interests justifying restriction. Contributions and expenditures are interconnected, with expenditures both dependent on contributions and substituting for them when contributions are restricted. Indeed, the campaign finance world created by the Court has promoted the proliferation of political committees and practices that mock the idea that we have a regulated campaign finance system and contribute to the public's cynicism about our elections and the government that results from them. In the absence of a principled distinction between the two forms of campaign money, it would make more sense both in theory and in practice to treat specific campaign practices as falling along a continuum of First Amendment–protected activity and regulable threats to the integrity of the political system[123] rather than to draw a sharp constitutional dichotomy between contributions and expenditures.

Candidly, there is not much new in the criticisms just voiced. Critics—and justices—have pointed to the conceptual flaws and deleterious practical effects of the contribution–expenditure distinction ever since *Buckley* was first handed down five decades ago. Instead of defending the distinction, most observers have simply explained it as part of the *Buckley* "compromise," the effort to find a middle path between viewing campaign finance regulation as a means of promoting the integrity of the political process and enabling the expressive and associational activities protected by the First Amendment.[124] Because the distinction lacks a coherent conceptual core, critics have long predicted its "demise."[125] As Professor Burt Neuborne once put it, "Give it a good, hard push and, like a rotten tree, *Buckley* will keel over."[126] Yet twenty-seven years after Neuborne pronounced the distinction "doomed," it is still with us.

What accounts for the durability of such an unsatisfactory doctrine? First, it has proven to be somewhat flexible in application. The Court has varied its standard of review of contribution restrictions, allowed some expenditures to be regulated as if they were contributions, and protected some contributions because of their close connection to expenditures. Second, and probably more importantly, the doctrine has survived because, at least until now, neither candidate for replacing it—protecting contributions as much as expenditures, or permitting regulation of expenditures like regulation of contributions—has commanded support from a majority of the justices. This was most apparent in the mid-2000s, when it seemed that the doctrine was especially ripe for replacement and the justices split into three nearly equal camps over the proper constitutional treatment of expenditure and contribution restrictions. *Randall v. Sorrell* underscored the depth of the division within the Court over the proper framework for addressing campaign finance regulations. Until that divide is bridged and a majority emerges favoring one position or the other, the contribution–expenditure distinction is likely to persist.

After the Contribution–Expenditure Distinction?

We may finally be at that point where there is a majority on the Court in favor of replacing the contribution–expenditure distinction. In every single campaign finance case the Court has decided in the nearly two decades after *Randall*, the challenge to a regulation—whether federal or state, and whether affecting expenditures, contributions, or public funding—has prevailed.[127] In *McCutcheon* and *Cruz*, the Court applied its most stringent review of a contribution restriction to date and hinted at the possibility of reopening the standard of review applicable to contributions. With a clear anti-regulatory majority in command of the Court, the end of the contribution–expenditure distinction may at last be at hand.

What would that look like, and how would it affect campaign financing? Given the current composition of the Supreme Court, it would almost certainly entail strict scrutiny of limitations on contributions and coordinated expenditures. The prevention of corruption would likely continue to be a compelling government interest,[128] but restrictions would have to be narrowly tailored to advancing that interest. The Court would likely require more evidence that campaign contributions have been used to accomplish *quid pro quo* corruption, closely scrutinize the fit between the restriction in question and the prevention of corruption, and consider the possibility of less burdensome alternatives to contribution limits for achieving that goal.

The Court would likely come down especially hard on restrictions justified as necessary to prevent circumvention of the basic donor-to-candidate contribution limit. An early casualty could be the long-standing federal ban—and similar bans on the books in many states—on corporate contributions to candidates. Those bans have survived *Citizens United*'s repudiation of the idea that corporations pose a special danger of corruption only because of *Buckley*'s more deferential standard of review of contribution restrictions—*Citizens United* addressed only a ban on expenditures—and the concern that donors might use corporations to circumvent the limits on individual donations to candidates.[129] With the end of deferential review and the Court's increased skepticism of the anti-circumvention argument, these restrictions, and similar ones on union donations, are likely to fall.

Similarly, limits on political-party donations to and coordinated expenditures with candidates would be prime targets for constitutional challenge. These restrictions were sustained by the Supreme Court in *Colorado Republican II* on the theory that donors could use parties as conduits for contributions to candidates, and thus limits on such direct political-party support for candidates are justified to prevent circumvention of the individual-to-candidate limits. Though *Colorado Republican II* found sufficient evidence of a circumvention danger in the record to sustain the federal limit on coordinated expenditures, a future Court applying strict scrutiny and a narrow tailoring requirement is unlikely to do so. Indeed, in summer 2024 a substantial majority of the US Court of Appeals for the Sixth Circuit, sitting en banc, intimated that in light of the Supreme Court's more recent decisions *Colorado Republican II* is no longer good law, although the circuit court considered itself still bound by that older decision until the Supreme Court overturns it.[130] Post-*McCutcheon* and post-*Cruz*, other courts have likewise been doubtful about whether state law restrictions on contributions to or between intermediary organizations[131] are sufficiently "closely drawn"—let alone "narrowly tailored"—to be justified as preventing circumvention of the base contribution limits.[132]

More significantly, a post-*Buckley* Court could invalidate the basic individual-to-candidate and PAC-to-candidate restrictions sustained by *Buckley* that have been a keystone of federal campaign finance law for five decades and central to the campaign finance laws of forty states as well.[133] At the very least, elimination of the contribution–expenditure distinction would mean that courts would very likely conduct a more searching review of the specific terms of contribution restrictions, such as the dollar level of any limit, whether limits are uniform across all offices in a jurisdiction, whether limits are on a per-election or annual basis, or whether there are different limits for different campaign participants (individuals, political committees, and political parties). States with relatively low limits or more restrictive laws overall would probably have a hard time showing that their limits are "narrowly tailored" to prevent corruption when other states have made do with less restrictive limits. More generally, states, local governments, and Congress might be required to provide hard evidence of a connection between campaign contributions and *quid pro quo* corruption—something that would likely be difficult to do.

Of course, it could be argued that even the invalidation of contribution limits would have little effect on campaign finance in practice, as the proliferation of super PACs, independent spending, unrestricted social-media spending, and other campaign finance developments have made the contribution limits on the books largely irrelevant.[134] From this perspective, contribution limits have been no more effective than King Canute in beating back the waves of campaign money flowing from wealthy individuals and interest groups. Indeed, eliminating the limits could have the beneficial effect of redirecting the flow of funds back to candidates and parties and away from the less politically accountable super PACs and independent groups.

It is, however, far from clear that contribution limits have become irrelevant or that removing them would improve the political process. Both candidates and donors prefer contributions to independent committees and super PACs over direct donations to a campaign. Candidates have more direct control over the contributions than independent spending, and can much more easily and quickly redirect the use of funds in their own campaign committee coffers in light of campaign developments than they can affect the actions of allied committees and super PACs.[135] Candidate spending—funded by contributions—is also more efficient than super-PAC or independent spending, as candidates benefit from the federal law requiring television and radio broadcasters in the preelection period to charge candidates' ads the "lowest unit rate" they charge all other advertisers, and noncandidate committees have to pay more for their advertising. In other words, independent spending is a "second-best strategy for candidates,"[136] not a first-best one. Wealthy individuals also seem eager to make direct contributions to candidates to the extent permitted. They regularly "max out" on their contributions to federal and state candidates rather than directing all their campaign funds to super PACs and independent committees.[137] With both candidates and larger donors preferring direct individual-to-candidate contributions, lifting or eliminating contribution limits would surely result in a surge of contributions to candidates.

Nor is it clear that removing contribution limits would be a good thing. Studies of state contribution limits that analyze the differences in limits from state to state, and within individual states over time, have found that contribution limits promote electoral competition,[138] reduce both the financial advantages of incumbents[139] and their margins of victory,[140] better align candidate preferences with those of the voters,[141] and correlate with more redistributive public welfare spending.[142] Contribution limits affect the mix of sources of campaign funds—small donors, wealthy individuals, special interests—and the politics and policies that result from elections.[143] And, of course, the symbolic significance of the end of contribution limits—whether seen as a vindication of the First Amendment or the elimination of the last restraint on the power of wealth to influence elections and officeholders—would be enormous.

This is not the place for a thorough discussion of the benefits and costs of contribution limits. The only point to be made here is that, notwithstanding the emergence of campaign finance practices designed to outflank those limits, the limits continue to matter, and their elimination would likely matter as well.

Conclusion

Still, the doom of the contribution–expenditure distinction has been predicted, inaccurately, before. The Court's recent, more probing review of contribution restrictions may enable it to give protection to contributions comparable to the protection accorded expenditures—or to adopt some intermediate standard of review that allows some contribution restrictions to survive—without formally reconsidering the doctrine. In other words, we may be witnessing a quiet erosion of the contribution–expenditure distinction that will give the Court greater room to take a hard line on contribution restrictions while making a formal overruling of *Buckley* unnecessary. For a Court that has drawn criticism for its willingness to overturn precedents, preserving the doctrine in form while ignoring it in substance may be the preferred solution.

2
How *Buckley v. Valeo* Led Us Astray

Paul M. Smith

Looking back over the past fifty years, *Buckley v. Valeo*[1] clearly has been one of the two or three most consequential Supreme Court decisions governing the operation of America's democracy. All of the subsequent cases addressing money and politics—and there have been many—have been structured and constrained by the core choices the Court made in *Buckley*.

What were those core choices? First, the Court decided that the only asserted governmental interest that was legitimate and could potentially justify regulation in this sensitive area was the prevention of corruption.[2] The Court rejected as wholly foreign to American law any notion that the government could legitimately seek to prevent monopolistic dominance of the marketplace of ideas by a few voices.[3] That was a major error. That error was then compounded by a second one: The Court ruled that, while aggressive regulation of campaign contributions was constitutionally justified to serve anti-corruption concerns, no regulation of independent *expenditures* could be justified because (it said) such independent expenditures cannot by their very nature buy the spender undue influence over officeholders.[4] That conclusion was doubly mistaken. Even if the relevant governmental interests justifying regulation are limited to the prevention of corruption (and they should not be), it still should be obvious that a very large independent expenditure in support of a candidate can motivate that candidate to do the bidding of the spender once he or she is in office. And if the relevant interests are broadened to include the prevention of monopolization of the debate, then the regulation of independent expenditures naturally becomes even more important.

Because the Court made these fundamental missteps and then decided to leave in place the parts of the law that survived its constitutional analysis, we ended up with an incomplete system of campaign finance regulation that carried with it the seeds of its own destruction. True, the system worked tolerably well for a while. Most campaign spending was done by official campaigns that had to collect funds subject to campaign contribution limits. But then several things happened. First, considerable sums began to be directed to political parties in the form of unlimited "soft money" contributions because, it was thought (following *Buckley*'s lead), only contributions to specific individual candidates can cause those candidates, when they win office, to do the bidding of donors. This proved wrong when the two main political parties developed systems for using soft-money contributions to bid for valuable access to important officeholders. That phenomenon necessitated the passage of the soft-money ban that was a key part of the McCain–Feingold Act passed in 2002.

The more important development was an outgrowth of the *Buckley* Court's decision to give nearly absolute protection to independent expenditures. Once the Court made that move, eventually it was going to be difficult to justify preventing *corporations* from engaging in such speech, and even more difficult to prevent rich individuals and corporations from magnifying the impact of their speech by pooling their funds into what became known as super PACs. And that, of course, is what happened. We now have a campaign finance system awash in expenditures by super PACs funded by billionaires and corporations.

What are the consequences of that reality? First, at least for a time, it meant that the marketplace of political ideas during political campaigns could be dominated, even monopolized, by a few big spenders with views unlikely to reflect those of the bulk of the electorate. But that concern may be fading, because technological changes have at least begun to ameliorate that problem.

First, especially in high-profile races like presidential elections, the Internet has made it possible for popular candidates to raise vast sums of money in the form of small donations to their campaigns and to friendly super PACs. When that happens, the super-rich and corporations lose their near-monopoly position in the political marketplace. Still, it should be emphasized that, in lower-profile races like many congressional contests, it remains possible for an injection of concentrated wealth—whether it be from a rich challenger or an aggressive super PAC—to have an oversized influence on the outcome.

Second, there has been a very recent but very pronounced shift in television viewing habits away from the outlets that carry campaign commercials and to streaming services with few or no ads. This shift has the potential to dissuade campaigns from continuing to spend a large percentage of campaign funds on television commercials, and to move instead to social-media-based strategies. Thus, streaming media may provide an additional mechanism for defusing the impact of super PACs funded by the wealthy.

But even if concerns about monopolization of the marketplace of ideas may now be moderating, that does little to address the problem of corruption that can result from massive individual or corporate contributions to candidates' favorite super PACs. Campaigns will always need money (absent public financing), and it will always be easier to collect money in big chunks from megadonors than in small amounts from a broader public. Those megadonors, in turn, can rest assured that their phone calls will be answered and their concerns will be given generous consideration when candidates become officeholders making public policy.

How, in an ideal world, should regulation respond to this central problem? If current law could be disregarded or changed, the ideal solution would be a higher limit on campaign contributions combined with a comparably lower limit on independent expenditures. The expenditure cap would need to be high enough to allow a person with means to become an effective participant in the political debate, but low enough to prevent domination by such participants and serious corruption effects. The cap would also require some clear definitional lines about what constitutes independent spending advocating the election or defeat of a given federal candidate. As a first cut, the definition could look something like: "all expenditures for the production or display of advertisements reasonably understood as primarily intended to influence the outcome of a federal election." But more work is clearly needed on that definitional issue.

The First Mistake

When faced with a First Amendment challenge to a new federal law that capped both contributions to federal campaigns and independent spending by third parties supporting or opposing federal candidates, the Supreme Court first had to decide whether regulating the contribution and spending of *money* creates serious concerns under a constitutional provision that protects freedom of *speech*. Much ink was spilled by advocates and even Justices arguing that money is not speech and that the First Amendment therefore is categorically irrelevant.

But the *Buckley* majority was right to reject that simplistic notion. *Of course* First Amendment concerns may be raised when the government limits the contribution and spending of money intended to fund core political speech. At a minimum, it would violate the First Amendment if the government were to discriminate, directly or indirectly, in its regulation of campaign contributions or independent expenditures in favor of a given individual, regulating contributions or spending so as to favor one party's candidates and not another's.

Moreover, even nondiscriminatory caps on contributions and spending limit the ability of the affected person to participate in a political campaign. If you feel very strongly that a given candidate is the most wonderful person to come along in our lifetime and you want to pay for a massive ad campaign to help that person, a law capping how much you can spend certainly inhibits your core political speech. That cannot be denied.

But despite its absolute-sounding language, the First Amendment is not absolute. Sometimes, sufficiently important governmental interests can justify laws that burden speech. And that is particularly true when the law does not discriminate based on the viewpoint of the speaker or the content of the speech, as the campaign finance laws reviewed in *Buckley* did not. In such a case, a court need not apply the strictest form of First Amendment scrutiny, demanding that the law serve a compelling state interest in the least restrictive possible way. It should be enough if the law serves an important or substantial state interest that outweighs its impact on speech.

In fact, that is the standard the Court applied in *Buckley* in reviewing, and ultimately upholding, the caps on campaign contributions. It used a watered-down version of strict scrutiny, asking only whether the contribution limitation served a sufficiently "important" (not "compelling") governmental interest and whether it was "closely drawn" to avoid unnecessary infringements on First Amendment rights. Using that standard, the Court upheld contribution limits as serving the purpose of preventing corruption of the recipient candidates who might otherwise make decisions when in office under the influence of large contributors.

But the Court's first error was in limiting the relevant governmental interests to the prevention of corruption. Since corruption concerns were a sufficient justification for limiting payments directly to candidates' campaigns, the Court did not need to address any additional interests in upholding contribution limits.

But the existence of other legitimate government interests became central in the later section of the opinion addressing expenditure limits. Once the Court had held that large independent expenditures by supporters cannot be corrupting (see more on that *infra*), the next argument by the government was that expenditure limits serve a governmental interest in "equalizing the relative ability of individuals and groups to influence the outcome of elections."[5] Put differently, the government claimed a legitimate interest in preventing monopolization of the marketplace of ideas by a few speakers, at least regarding speech directly advocating the victory or defeat of federal candidates.

That claim was dispatched in probably the most celebrated sentence in the long *Buckley* opinion: "the concept that government may restrict the speech of some elements of our society in order to enhance the relative voice of others is wholly foreign to the First Amendment, which was designed 'to secure the widest possible dissemination of information from diverse and antagonistic sources,' and 'to assure unfettered interchange of ideas for the bringing about of political and social changes desired by the people.'"[6]

But this sentence contains its own refutation. The Court argues that the First Amendment aims to promote the wide dissemination of information from "diverse and antagonistic sources." Yet if the airwaves and other forms of political expression are dominated by a few people who share one key characteristic—great wealth—then that aim of the First Amendment is not served. The speakers who can be heard will not be diverse and may not be antagonistic either.

Given that reality, there should be nothing strange about arguing that governmental efforts to improve the diversity of voices reaching large audiences can be justified as *serving* First Amendment interests and should not be seen as "wholly foreign" to our constitutional scheme. Indeed, in the 1990 decision in *Austin v. Michigan Chamber of Commerce*, a majority of the Justices agreed with this point, at least with regard to corporate-funded speech.[7] There, the Court upheld a state ban on corporate expenditures to influence candidate elections, reasoning that the huge sums of money accumulated in corporate general treasuries give corporations "'an unfair advantage in the political marketplace.'"

Ten years later, in a concurrence defending a state contribution limit applicable to individuals, Justice Breyer noted that there were First Amendment concerns on both sides of the constitutional ledger and argued that the "Constitution often permits restrictions on the speech of some in order to prevent a few from drowning out the many."[8]

An even more recent and thoughtful exploration of this idea came in 2014 in Justice Breyer's dissent in *McCutcheon v. FEC*.[9] This case involved contributions rather than expenditures—specifically the constitutionality of an overall annual cap on contributions to federal candidates and committees. And Justice Breyer tried to wedge the antimonopoly point under the rubric of anticorruption, because that was the only interest the Court had left standing since *Buckley*. But even with those differences noted, Justice Breyer's dissent stands as a strong defense of affirmative government action to protect the viability of the marketplace of political speech:

> Consider at least one reason why the First Amendment protects political speech. Speech does not exist in a vacuum. Rather, political communication seeks to secure government action. A politically oriented 'marketplace of ideas' seeks to form a public opinion that can and will influence elected representatives. . . . Corruption breaks the constitutionally necessary 'chain of communications' between the people and their representatives. . . . It derails the essential speech-to-government tie. *That is one reason why the Court has stressed the constitutional importance of Congress' concern that a few large donations not drown out the voices of the many.*[10]

Even outside the area of campaign finance regulation, the Court long ago recognized the legitimacy and importance of the governmental interest in assuring that the information and advocacy communicated to the public are not dominated by a single point of view. This issue arose in the context of regulation of private broadcaster licensees during an era when broadcast radio and television utilizing a limited spectrum was the only electronic form of mass communication. Although the regulatory system granted considerable discretion to those licensees to make editorial judgments about the programming they would distribute, that system also included the Fairness Doctrine, which obligated the licensees to present diverse points of view. The Supreme Court unanimously upheld that Doctrine in the landmark *Red Lion Broadcasting*[11] case. It recognized that while the editorial judgments of broadcasters merit some limited protection under the First Amendment, the right of viewers and listeners to receive diverse points of view was paramount.

Concomitantly, in a subsequent case, *CBS v. DNC*, the Court upheld a decision by the Federal Communications Commission to allow a licensee to refuse all paid editorial advertising. A key part of its reasoning was the concern about monopolization by a few speakers. The Court explained:

> The Commission was justified in concluding that the public interest in providing access to the marketplace of "ideas and experiences" *would scarcely be served by a system so heavily weighted in favor of the financially affluent, or those with access to wealth.* . . . Even under a first come, first served system proposed by

the dissenting Commissioner in these cases, *the views of the affluent could well prevail over those of others*, since they would have it within their power to purchase time more frequently. Moreover, there is the substantial danger, as the Court of Appeals acknowledged, . . . that the time allotted for editorial advertising could be monopolized by those of one political persuasion.[12]

As the broadcast-regulation analogy suggests, the key in such situations is achieving the right balance. Just as the Commission balanced the free-speech rights of the broadcasters against the right of the public to receive diverse and valuable programming, an "antitrust" regime regulating campaign speech must be carefully designed so that it does not go too far—particularly if it is being used to justify limits on expenditures rather than just contributions. Expenditures do, after all, often go directly to the funding of political speech. The limits on spending must not overly constrict the rough-and-tumble of the free marketplace of ideas.

But at a minimum, it should be clear that the government has a legitimate interest in providing public funding on a nondiscriminatory basis, in order to more evenly assist candidates in running serious campaigns. Moreover, as will be discussed below, it should also be seen as legitimate for the law to cap (at a fairly high level) the amount that any one person or corporation (or group of corporate affiliates) can spend or donate to influence a given federal campaign. Doing that would not prevent anyone from participating robustly in the arguments over who should win a given election. And it would serve to prevent the kind of de facto censorship that occurs when a few wealthy people or corporations so dominate the discussion that it is futile for anyone else to try to be heard.

The argument that it is un-American to do anything to protect the political marketplace of ideas from monopolization ultimately makes no constitutional or historical sense. Such protection can lead to a better form of political debate and ultimately a better form of democracy. Lack of it threatens to skew American democracy in a way that is hard to defend. The *Buckley* Court, unfortunately, made precisely this error.

The Second Mistake

Things got worse when the Court in *Buckley* made a second glaring error. After limiting the legitimate government interests that can justify regulation in this area to just one—preventing corruption—the Court categorically forbade regulation of independent campaign expenditures. It did so on the theory that such expenditures by individuals unaffiliated with a candidate cannot by their very nature cause serious corruption. That is, they can never allow the spender to gain undue influence over the policy decisions of the candidate being supported, once that candidate takes office.

To summarize that conclusion is to understand why it makes no sense. Who is more likely to buy undue influence—a direct contributor who exceeds the current legal limit by a couple of thousand dollars or an independent spender who buys $50 million in television commercials supporting the same candidate? It is hard to see any plausible basis for saying that relatively small contributions raise legitimate corruption concerns but massive spending to pay for campaign ads do not.

In concluding that the risk of corruption goes away as regulation shifts from contribution limits to expenditure limits, the *Buckley* Court emphasized that it was only giving absolute constitutional protection to *independent* expenditures, those not coordinated with the candidate. It then speculated that "such independent expenditures may well provide little assistance to the candidate's campaign and indeed may prove counterproductive."[13] The notion seemed to be that the big spender's message might be off point and might step on the messages the campaign was trying to send. But is that really likely? A spender intent on buying undue influence would make every effort to avoid such interference, and she could do so easily, even while maintaining total independence from the campaign, simply by choosing topics that complemented the messages the campaign was sending out.

The Court also explained that a truly independent expenditure, by definition, could not be part of a *quid pro quo* bribery arrangement. After all, if it were, the expenditure would have to be coordinated with the candidate in some sense. But that is no answer. Bribery is not the only evil that campaign laws seek to forestall; they also target a much broader and less explicit form of influence purchasing.

The *Buckley* Court knew this. In upholding contribution limits, the same Court recognized that bribery was only the most "blatant and specific"[14] method of using money to influence government action, and that the government's anticorruption interests extended far more broadly. What it meant was that the government has a legitimate interest in avoiding buying and selling of influence that can be exercised after the fact. No one should be able to contribute so much that, after the campaign, an elected leader will always take the donor's call—and will nearly always do his bidding. When that occurs, money has caused a form of corruption, even without any form of *quid pro quo* deal. Thus, as the Court would later explain in *McConnell v. FEC*, "In speaking of 'improper influence' and 'opportunities for abuse' in addition to '*quid pro quo* arrangements,' we [have] recognized a concern not confined to bribery of public officials, but extending to the broader threat from politicians too compliant with the wishes of large contributors."[15]

The *Buckley* Court also noted that the goal of avoiding even the *appearance* of corruption was "[o]f almost equal concern."[16] As the *McConnell* Court later explained: "Take away Congress' authority to regulate the appearance of undue influence and 'the cynical assumption that large donors call the tune could jeopardize the willingness of voters to take part in democratic governance.'"[17] And in analyzing how to prevent such an appearance, it certainly would not make sense to limit concern to *quid pro quo* arrangements. If a candidate is largely funded by a few wealthy donors and then, when in office, pursues policies that benefit those few at the expense of the majority of voters, it will of course be widely assumed that these two facts are causally linked. And cynicism will be the result.

A full understanding of the concerns that underlie campaign finance regulation thus makes clear that the government has a strong reason to seek to prevent wealthy individuals from laying out huge sums in the form of independent expenditures, knowing they will reap the benefit later in the form of special access to, and deference from, officeholders. None of this should be controversial. But the *Buckley* Court simply denied this obvious reality.

The Consequences of These Errors

Having found its way to the conclusion that the contribution limits were constitutional and the expenditure limits were not, the Court had a further choice: whether to allow the constitutional portions of the Act to take effect or to invalidate the whole and send the issue back to Congress to be sorted out. It opted for severability, leaving in place the portions of the law it had found constitutional. That left us with a system of campaign finance regulation that severely limited contributions to campaigns and other political committees, but that completely deregulated spending by wealthy candidates on their own campaigns (because those were seen as expenditures) and also completely deregulated expenditures by other individuals as long as they were not coordinated with campaigns.

That essentially accidental set of regulatory arrangements worked reasonably well for a while. Presidential campaigns were publicly financed. And most other federal candidates raised money for their campaigns in the limited increments the law allowed. Independent expenditures were not very frequent and substantial. But that meant that candidates did not have all the money to spend that they wished they had, and wealthy individuals and corporations were looking for ways to participate more fully.

Such individuals and corporations gravitated over time to making contributions to political parties in the form of "soft money." This was money donated to the political parties ostensibly for "party building" activities. Over time, the scope of what parties could do with their funds broadened, and soft-money contributions consequently grew in value. The parties expanded this category of donations by creating giving programs in which various levels of donations earned the donor specific forms of access to party leaders in Congress. As the *McConnell* Court made clear, it was a pure money-for-access arrangement, which persisted until soft-money contributions were banned in 2002.

That ban sharply limited giving to political parties. But the *Buckley* Court had granted absolute First Amendment protection to independent campaign expenditures, and now potential donors cast about in search of a replacement for parties as the primary destination for their campaign donations. Thus, it was inevitable that sooner or later someone would propose the idea of a pool of donations that could be spent only on collective independent expenditures. That occurred in 2010, and the idea was, unsurprisingly, upheld by the D.C. Circuit Court of Appeals in the *SpeechNow*[18] case. The super PAC was born.

What kind of campaign finance system did that leave us with? Today, contributions to the official campaigns of federal candidates, as well as to political parties and other political committees, remain quite limited. But virtually every candidate now has his or her "own" super PAC—meaning that the candidate was involved in its creation and has found ways to indicate that it is the endorsed destination for the contributions of would-be donors. In many cases, candidates probably also violate the law by directly coordinating campaign strategy with their favorite super PAC. Given how easy it is to do so out of sight, it is difficult for the FEC to enforce the non-coordination requirement, and it is fair to say that many of the FEC's commissioners in recent years have been less than enthusiastic about such enforcement.

But even when there is no coordination between the candidate and a supportive super PAC, candidates are certainly aware of major donations to their super PACs. It follows that we have arrived at a system that allows would-be purchasers of undue influence to contribute unlimited amounts of money, so long as most of their contributions are not directed to the candidate's official campaign. With such a system in place, it is hard to say that the central goals of regulation endorsed as legitimate by the *Buckley* Court—preventing corruption and the appearance of corruption—are being achieved consistently.

What of the goal that *Buckley* disclaimed? The current system is just as badly designed to prevent the voices of the few from drowning out the voices of the many. That is hardly surprising given the Court's complete deregulation of independent expenditures, including those by rich self-funding candidates, by wealthy individual spenders, and, more commonly, by wealthy donors to super PACs. And so we see individual self-funders continuing to get themselves elected, and we see super PACs like AIPAC targeting individual candidates for Congress, with sometimes devastating effects.

But despite these monopolization concerns, there are signs of hope for the future. For two reasons, each related to technological evolution, the dominance of a few voices in our political debates is not going unchallenged now and likely will be diminished going forward.

First, there is the fact that, by using the Internet, some candidates can raise almost unlimited amounts of money in the form of legal, small-dollar contributions to their campaigns. This was first demonstrated by Barack Obama, who in his first presidential run in 2008 raised so much money that he repudiated public funding (with its attendant spending limits) and ended up far outspending his general-election opponent, John McCain. More recent presidential candidates who raised vast sums in small chunks have included Bernie Sanders, Donald Trump, and Kamala Harris. And this phenomenon is not limited to presidential elections; think of Beto O'Rourke's Senate race in Texas in 2018, or John Fetterman's in Pennsylvania in 2022.

This phenomenon means that, in electoral contests, the marketplace of ideas need not be dominated by megadonors. Indeed, a popular candidate funded mainly by smaller donations to his or her campaign has an extra advantage: under current law, ads purchased by candidates' own campaigns are priced at the lowest rate available. An ad of the same length paid for by a super PAC would cost multiples of that rate. Thus, the dollars contributed to campaigns by small donors are much more valuable than the dollars contributed by mega-donors to super PACs. So some candidates' ability to raise large sums from many small donors, and to spend those dollars more efficiently, can sometimes blunt concerns about dominance by the few in the political marketplace.

Of course, such candidates are more the exception than the rule. In many important election contests, neither major-party candidate has the ability to raise money from small donors to an extent that would allow them to match the impact of a very wealthy opponent or a super PAC funded by rich donors. We see examples of this continued reality frequently in House races. A prime example is the way the American Israel Public Affairs Committee (AIPAC) and affiliated super PACs have targeted progressive Democratic House members who are viewed as insufficiently supportive of Israel. They have been able to take down quite a few.

The other relevant technological change involves how people watch television and whether they are even exposed to televised advertising. We have recently reached the point in the United States where the occupants of more than half of the homes do not watch television using traditional cable and focus instead on streaming services, which tend to be subscription-based and commercial-free. For that reason, there is reason to believe that by far the largest single budget item for campaigns—paid broadcast advertising—is becoming less useful and less important. As that occurs, it may lessen the impact of large infusions of cash into campaigns and thereby reduce concerns about monopolization of the political marketplace. To be sure, campaigns and PACs will still try to reach voters with their messages through social media and other means. But those alternatives should cost considerably less.

Where Should Regulatory Policy Go Now?

In an ideal world, and freed of the constraints imposed by *Buckley*, what would be the best public policy going forward in this area of the law? Clearly, there needs to be some limit on the ability of megarich people and corporations to spend money on campaigns. Without that, it will be impossible to impose any meaningful check on the ability of those large spenders to buy influence over officeholders. At the same time, the current limits on campaign contributions seem far too low if the goal is to prevent corruption. In a world where independent expenditures may total in the millions, candidates are not going to be overly influenced by a contribution in the range of $5,000.

So, I would advocate doubling or tripling the contribution limit, while reimposing a commensurate limit on the amount of money any one individual spends on independent expenditures. This project will be tricky for a couple of reasons. First, the law would need to develop some sort of workable definition of the expenditures we are seeking to limit. Second, the actual amount of money that would constitute the lowest constitutionally permissible cap on these contributions and expenditures would need to be determined.

Turning first to the definitional problem, I do not propose solving it completely here, but it is possible to make a start. An expenditure cap would need to apply to all spending on the production and distribution of any message reasonably understood as primarily intended to influence the outcome of a federal election. It would also include, of course, contributions to organizations that make such expenditures. Legislation could include a series of factors to be considered in deciding whether a given message was primarily designed to influence an election—including the timing, the competitiveness of the election contest, and the extent to which the message references the election itself.

It would be a mistake, in this ideal world unconstrained by current law, to adopt the Supreme Court's rule, first enunciated in *Buckley*, that only express advocacy for the victory or defeat of a candidate can be considered to fall into the regulated category. As hard experience with corporate "issue ads" has demonstrated, a cap limited in that way would be close to useless. This was the problem that led to McCain–Feingold's ban on corporate "electioneering communications" in the weeks leading up to an election—the ban struck down in *Citizens United v. Federal Elections Commission*.[19] But legally speaking, we would be starting afresh here.

As for where to draw the constitutional line on expenditure caps, such questions are always awkward in constitutional decision-making. A good example is the question of when state *contribution* limits are too low to be acceptable under the First Amendment. The Supreme Court answered that question in *Randall v. Sorrell*[20] by saying that Vermont had gone too far, without really explaining how it had drawn that constitutional line.

A good argument can be made that expenditure limits should be allowed down to the level of the somewhat elevated contribution cap. In current dollars, I might set both caps at around $20,000 per election contest. In *Buckley*, the Court was concerned that the expenditure limit at issue there would prevent any entities except campaigns, political parties, and the institutional press from using the most effective means of communication of views about an election to the general public. But paradoxically, the emergence of the super PAC has ameliorated that concern. Just as an individual's campaign contributions get pooled with other supporters' contributions to pay for advertising and other forms of communication, super PACs pool contributions and make expenditures in the same way, thus allowing each contributor to play a part in facilitating expression about a given political contest.

Setting the limit high enough to allow any one person to pay the full cost of creating and distributing advertising might be viewed by some as desirable, but in reality that would require a limit so high that it would serve little or no purpose. An advertising campaign can cost millions of dollars; if we set a limit that allows a single person to pay for such a campaign, the corruption concerns raised by our current system would return with a vengeance. Such a limit might as well not exist.

But I see no reason the First Amendment should not be interpreted as protecting the right to make contributions or expenditures up to a point where the amounts of money at issue cause other competing concerns about corruption and monopolization to come to the fore. That kind of balanced system would be far preferable to the system of regulation we have now, a system that permits a few large donors to exercise excessive influence not just on the outcome of the election but also on the governing decisions of those elected to public office.

PART II

Critiques and a Defense of the Major Decisions

3
Getting It Wrong
The Supreme Court and Campaign Finance
Erwin Chemerinsky and Alex Chemerinsky

Introduction

Buckley v. Valeo was a terrible decision.[1] In *Buckley*, the Supreme Court began to treat the act of spending money as if it were speech worthy of protection under the First Amendment. In a series of subsequent decisions, the Court reaffirmed and applied its conclusion that spending money in a campaign equals speech. But spending money isn't speech. And that fiction has contributed to the serious crisis facing American democracy. The Court has compounded this error by holding that political expenditures by corporations are of equal value to speech by actual humans. On the whole, the Court's campaign finance case law has created an election system that gives enormous and disproportionate influence to those with money: rich individuals and corporate treasuries.[2]

Buckley and its progeny must be understood from a political perspective. Conservative justices have created a campaign finance system that is widely seen as favoring Republicans.

The fiction that money is speech has no basis in the history of the First Amendment or the Court's prior First Amendment jurisprudence. And the false equivalency drawn between speech by a human and an expenditure by a corporation is unjustified and dangerous in a democracy.

This essay has three parts. First, we identify what we think the goals of a campaign finance system should be. Second, we examine the Court's campaign finance decisions. We argue that beginning with *Buckley v. Valeo*, the Court has consistently gotten it wrong in interpreting the First Amendment, and the result has been to create a system that gives far too much influence in elections to those with money, and which at a minimum risks corruption and the appearance of corruption. Finally, we offer thoughts as to why this has occurred. The decisions cannot be explained by originalism or by precedent. They must be seen through a partisan political lens. They are rulings by Republican justices to help Republican candidates and they have created an edifice of campaign finance law that undermines American democracy.

The Goals of a Campaign Finance System

In order to assess the Supreme Court's campaign finance decisions, it is necessary to have clear goals for what is to be accomplished. We identify five objectives:

Preventing corruption and appearance of corruption

The electorate has an undeniable interest in ensuring that elected officials are not corrupt. And there is justifiably a widespread sense that an elected official is beholden to those who spent significant sums to get him or her elected. The government thus must be able to regulate political spending to some degree to prevent corruption in order to vindicate this interest of the electorate and to enhance confidence in the election process. As we discuss below, this should include the power to prevent both corruption that could arise from contributions directly to candidates and expenditures independently made in the candidate's favor.

The Supreme Court has repeatedly recognized the compelling government interest in preventing corruption and the appearance of corruption.[3] But the Court has also held that preventing corruption and the appearance of corruption is the *only* legitimate objective for regulating campaign spending.[4] And it has defined corruption far too narrowly.[5] For example, under *Citizens United*, money given directly to a candidate is treated as a risk, but money spent in favor of a candidate with a candidate's knowledge and approval is not. There is no meaningful difference in terms of the danger of corruption and the perception of corruption.

There is no doubt that preventing corruption and the appearance of corruption is a crucial objective. As the Supreme Court has explained: "The importance of the governmental interest in preventing [corruption through the creation of political debts] has never been doubted."[6] Justice Elena Kagan correctly stated: "Our campaign finance precedents leave no doubt: Preventing corruption or the appearance of corruption is a compelling government interest."[7]

But we disagree that this is the only permissible goal of campaign finance regulation. A good campaign finance system must have other objectives, which we discuss below, beyond stopping corruption.

Allowing people to express support or opposition to a candidate

A republican system of government literally cannot work without the freedom to express support or opposition to candidates. Creating a system that protects such expression ought to be of paramount importance. There are myriad ways of conveying support, including endorsement, attending rallies, door-to-door canvassing, and, yes, spending money. Each of these holds an important place in our political culture and should be encouraged.

A campaign finance system therefore must sustain a difficult equilibrium. On one hand, political spending should be regulated to ensure the confidence of the electorate and the functioning of the electoral system—for example, by preventing corruption. But on the other hand, there should also be the right to express support to candidates by contributing toward their election. As we explain in Part II, we think this balance can be managed by according a modicum of constitutional protection to expressive spending—but less than under the Court's current jurisprudence. The Court's post-*Buckley* case law leaves almost no room for the necessary regulation that must exist to enable the system we imagine.

Preventing some voices from drowning out others

In elections, especially lower-visibility elections, the side that spends the most tends to win.[8] Occasionally, that side wins by spending so heavily that it effectively drowns out its opponent.[9] While the best candidate may indeed be the best-financed, we worry that good candidates can too easily be priced out of office. It is impossible to even measure how many individuals are discouraged from running because of the amount they would need to raise for a campaign.

According to a 2023 poll by Pew Research Center, 72% of Americans think there should be a limit on political expenditures, and 85% think that the cost of political campaigns makes it hard for good people to run for office.[10] Only 11% of respondents supported unlimited spending.[11]

Ideally, a campaign finance system ought to regulate the amount of money spent in an election to ensure that voters hear all sides of an issue, and not just the side with money. But unlike some other objectives that we have identified, on which there is universal acceptance, we recognize that this goal is very much in dispute (even though it polls well). In the past, the Supreme Court upheld restrictions on corporate contributions and expenditures on the ground that there was a sufficiently compelling state interest in restricting corporate political spending to limit distortions caused by political wealth.[12] But the Roberts Court changed its mind and now flatly rejects the notion that there is ever an interest in leveling the playing field.[13] As we explain in Part II, we disagree with the Roberts Court. The Supreme Court had it right before: "Corporate wealth can unfairly influence elections."[14]

We also think it important to note that restrictions of political spending are not the only way to avoid drowning out voices. One good (but currently unconstitutional) way to level the playing field would be to offer public funding to candidates if they are up against a high-spending, privately funded opponent. It doesn't need to be dollar for dollar, so long as it prevents worthwhile candidates and issues from being drowned out by a well-funded opposition.

Providing sufficient funds so that candidates can inform and persuade voters

Relatedly, an election system should strive to ensure that candidates have enough money to get their message out. Voters can't be persuaded by messaging that they don't hear. And the reality is that most forms of communication cost money. Holding rallies, buying advertising, sending mailers, and managing campaign staff are expensive.[15] We want a campaign finance system that will ensure that candidates have sufficient funds, via either public financing or lawful private contribution, to be able to get their messages across.

Providing disclosure of who is spending so as to allow informed reactions

Finally, an electoral system should provide voters with enough information to make an informed decision. Disclosure requirements are crucial because they ensure that voters have important information regarding candidates and candidate expenditures, and because disclosing that information deters corruption.

This is an area where the Court has gotten it right, at least to a degree. The Court has said that "disclosure provides the electorate with information 'as to where political campaign money comes from' . . . in order to aid the voters in evaluating those who seek federal office."[16] The Court also observed that "the disclosure requirements discourage corruption and the appearance of corruption because of the light of publicity."[17] Finally, the Court explained that "such requirements are an essential means of gathering the data necessary to detect violations of the contribution limitations."[18] Although disclosure requirements are compelled speech, they are justified by an important state interest and should be constitutional if appropriately tailored.

How the Supreme Court Has Gotten It Wrong

We identify five major errors the Court has made in its campaign finance decisions:

By treating spending money as "pure speech"—and thus requiring that regulations of campaign spending meet strict scrutiny—rather than as conduct that communicates

Many cases over the last half-century have raised the question whether, and to what extent, political spending is worthy of First Amendment protection. The Court has been consistent that political spending is First Amendment activity, but for a while it was unclear whether spending money should be thought of as "pure speech" or as "conduct" that communicates a message. Pure speech receives the most protection. A law that abridges speech on the basis of content or viewpoint must survive strict scrutiny—that is, it must be the least restrictive way of achieving a compelling government interest. By contrast, a law that restricts communicative conduct need only survive intermediate scrutiny under *United States v. O'Brien*, which held that draft-card burning was not protected by the First Amendment. Under *O'Brien*, a restriction of communicative conduct is constitutional if the law is tailored to a sufficiently important government interest that is unrelated to the suppression of the message.[19]

In *Buckley v. Valeo*, the US Court of Appeals for the District of Columbia Circuit, in an en banc decision, held that political spending should be treated as communicative conduct, not pure speech.[20] The DC Circuit thus applied intermediate scrutiny under *O'Brien*, largely upholding the Federal Election Campaign Act and its amendments.[21]

But the Supreme Court reversed the DC Circuit and held that spending money in elections should be treated as speech, not conduct, so regulations that restrict political spending must meet strict scrutiny, not intermediate scrutiny.[22] The Court began a lengthy per curiam opinion by noting that the "Act's contribution and expenditure limitations operate in an area of the most fundamental First Amendment activities. Discussion of public issues and debate on the qualifications of candidates are integral to the operation of the system of government established by our Constitution."[23] Because of the importance of money in elections, the Court expressly refused to apply the *O'Brien* test, used for conduct that communicates. The Court said that "[t]he expenditure of money simply cannot be equated with such conduct as destruction of a draft card. Some forms of communication made possible by the giving and spending of money involve speech alone, some involve conduct primarily, and some involve a combination of the two."[24] In any event, the Court said that even if *O'Brien* were the proper inquiry, it wouldn't apply because the Act would be treated as a law designed to suppress speech and therefore could not benefit from the more lenient test of *O'Brien*. Instead, the Act would have to meet strict scrutiny.

Thus, *Buckley* clearly treats spending money in a political campaign as a form of political speech. The Court said that "[a] restriction on the amount of money a person or group can spend on political communication during a campaign necessarily reduces the quantity of expression by restricting the number of issues discussed, the depth of their exploration, and the size of the audience reached. This is because virtually every means of communicating ideas in today's mass society requires the expenditure of money."[25]

We strongly disagree with this conclusion. Spending is a way of expressing support for a candidate, but it is not in itself speech. Rather, it is conduct that facilitates speech. As Judge J. Skelly Wright explained: "Money, in other words, may be related to speech, but money *itself is not speech*."[26] Justice John Paul Stevens also expressed this well: "Money is property; it is not speech. Speech has the power to inspire volunteers to perform a multitude of tasks on a campaign trail, on a battleground, or even on a football field. Money, meanwhile, has the power to pay hired laborers to perform the same tasks. It does not follow, however, that the First Amendment provides the same measure of protection to the use of money to accomplish such goals as it provides to the use of ideas to achieve the same result."[27] Simply put, conduct which merely facilitates speech should not be treated as if it were as sacrosanct as the speech itself. Education also facilitates speech, yet the Court has rejected the claim that there is a fundamental right to education.[28]

But that doesn't mean that political spending should remain entirely outside of the First Amendment. We still support robust protection for political spending. Indeed, enabling political support through money is encompassed in three of the five objectives we discussed in Part I: allowing expression of support, preventing voices from being drowned out, and providing sufficient funds to get the message out. But because money is not speech, it shouldn't receive the extremely challenging strict-scrutiny test. Instead, it should be tested under intermediate scrutiny, as in *O'Brien*. This inquiry will still put the burden on the government to justify the law.[29] But it will better reflect that campaign finance *should* be subject to reasonable and sufficiently tailored regulation—something that has not really been possible since *Buckley*.

It could be argued that *O'Brien* is different from the campaign finance context because in *O'Brien* the federal law was not directed at speech—the effect on expression was only incidental—while restrictions on contributions and expenditures are directed at activities that are inherently expressive. We disagree with this characterization. The federal law in *O'Brien* that prohibits the destruction of draft cards was adopted for the very purpose of stopping a method of communication: Men were burning their draft cards to express opposition to the Vietnam War. In other words, the effect on speech was direct, not incidental. Nonetheless, because it was conduct that communicates, the Court used a test less than strict scrutiny and much like what came to be developed as intermediate scrutiny. Similarly, in the context of restrictions on campaign finance, unless one starts with the assumption that spending money is inherently expressive (a premise we reject), the effect on communication is at least as incidental as in *O'Brien*.

The consequence of *Buckley* is to make it far more difficult for the government to impose restrictions on campaign spending because of the need for the government to meet strict scrutiny. It is the foundation for the law of campaign finance that has developed over the last half century.

Drawing a distinction between contributions and expenditures and not allowing expenditure limits

Having decided that strict scrutiny must be met, the Court in *Buckley v. Valeo* then drew a distinction between contributions (money given directly to a candidate or a committee for a candidate) and expenditures (money that a person spends independently). The Court concluded that contribution limits are permissible but expenditure limits are unconstitutional. The distinction was based in part on the way in which each affected speech. The Court saw expenditure limits as restricting the nature and quantity of speech that would occur, but saw little direct effect on speech through contribution limits. The Court explained that

> [t]he expenditure limitations contained in the Act represent substantial rather than merely theoretical restraints on the quantity and diversity of political speech.... By contrast, ... a limitation on the amount of money a person may give to a candidate or campaign organization [involves] little direct restraint on his political communication, for it permits the symbolic expression of support evidenced by a contribution but does not in any way infringe the contributor's freedom to discuss candidates and issues.[30]

In part, too, the Court's distinction was based on its belief that campaign contributions—money given directly to a candidate or campaign—bear a greater risk of corruption than independent expenditures. The Court said that restrictions on the amount that a person or group could contribute to any particular candidate were justified to prevent "the actuality and appearance of corruption resulting from large individual financial contributions."[31] The Court explained that

> [t]o the extent that large contributions are given to secure a political quid pro quo from current and potential office holders, the integrity of our system of representative democracy is undermined.... Of almost equal concern as the danger of actual quid pro quo arrangements is the impact of the appearance of corruption stemming from public awareness of the opportunities for abuse inherent in a regime of large individual financial contributions.[32]

In other words, even if large contributions were not given to inappropriately curry a candidate's favor, the electorate might infer otherwise, which would diminish confidence in the government.

But the Court said that independent expenditures to support a candidate do not entail the same risk of corruption or the appearance of corruption. It has since built on this. For example, in *Citizens United*, the Court said that although large direct contributions can be regulated to prevent *quid pro quo* corruption, "an independent expenditure is political speech" that cannot be restricted under the First Amendment.[33]

The distinction between contributions and expenditures makes little sense.[34] Large expenditures risk corruption or the appearance of corruption in the same way as large contributions. If a candidate knows that someone has spent a significant amount of money to get him or her elected, there will be exactly the same effects as when the money comes through contributions.[35] At the end of the day, the money all goes to roughly the same place; we doubt it matters much to candidates whether they buy their own ads or whether someone else does it for them. Elected officials can be influenced by who spends money on their behalf, just as they can be influenced by who directly contributes money to them. The perception of corruption might be generated by large expenditures for a candidate, just as it can be caused by large contributions. As Justice Stevens explained, "even technically independent expenditures can be corrupting in much the same way as direct contributions."[36]

Moreover, if spending more money in an election is a form of communicating greater support, there is no reason to draw a distinction between contributions and expenditures. Demonstrating support by contributing directly to a campaign or issue committee is no less expressive than independently spending money to support that candidate or ballot issue. Justice Clarence Thomas has expressed this in arguing that both contribution and expenditure limits should be unconstitutional: "I would reject the framework established by *Buckley v. Valeo*. . . . Instead, I begin with the premise that there is no constitutionally significant difference between campaign contributions and expenditures: both forms of speech are central to the First Amendment."[37]

We agree with Justice Thomas that campaign contributions and expenditures *should* be treated the same in constitutional analysis. But unlike Justice Thomas, we think that means that both contributions and expenditures should be subject to regulation, because both are equally expressive and both carry an identical risk of corruption or the appearance of corruption. The Court's wholesale rejection of restrictions on independent expenditure was therefore wrong.

According corporations the same rights as individuals to spend money in election campaigns

Until 1978, the Court never accorded corporations First Amendment rights. This changed in *First National Bank of Boston v. Bellotti*, where the Supreme Court declared unconstitutional a Massachusetts law that prohibited banks or businesses from making contributions or expenditures in connection with ballot initiatives and referenda.[38] The law provided for an exception if the initiative materially affected the property, business, or assets of the corporation. Justice Powell, writing for the Court, concluded that the value of speech is in informing the audience, and that any restriction on speech, regardless of its source, therefore undermines the First Amendment. Powell explained:

> The speech proposed by appellants is at the heart of the First Amendment's protection.... If the speakers here were not corporations, no one would suggest that the State could silence their proposed speech. It is the type of speech indispensable to decisionmaking in a democracy, and this is no less true because the speech comes from a corporation rather than an individual. The inherent worth of the speech in terms of its capacity for informing the public does not depend upon the identity of its source, whether corporation, association, union, or individual.[39]

The Court's rationale for protecting expenditures by corporations was not about the rights of corporations. Rather, it was an instrumental argument: More speech by corporations is desirable because it adds more expression to the marketplace of ideas. The danger, of course, is that spending by corporations directly out of their corporate treasuries can distort election campaigns and drown out other voices.[40] The simple truth is that although elections require money, worthwhile positions are not always adequately financed. When the field is saturated by corporate expenditure, it inevitably gives dominance to certain perspectives and limits what voters learn. Ironically, Justice Powell's reasoning had the right idea but got it backward. If the First Amendment is about the audience, then there may be a greater justification in regulating speech to ensure that the audience can hear what it wants to hear, not just what corporations think it should hear.

But even if we focus on the speaker rather than the audience, there is still less justification for allowing corporations a broad right to speak. As the Court recognized in *FEC v. Beaumont*,

> corporate contributions are furthest from the core of political expression because corporations' First Amendment speech and association interests are derived largely from those of their members and of the public in receiving information. A ban on direct corporate contributions leaves individual members of corporations free to make their own contributions, and deprives the public of little or no material information.[41]

Protection of human speech is also justified in part by more intangible interests in self-realization and individual liberty that are less applicable to nonhuman entities like corporations.[42] As Justice Stevens stated in his *Citizens United* dissent:

> In the context of election to public office, the distinction between corporate and human speakers is significant. Although they make enormous contributions to our society, corporations are not actually members of it. They cannot vote or run for office. Because they may be managed and controlled by nonresidents, their interests may conflict in fundamental respects with the interests of eligible voters.[43]

We think it is particularly important that there be some limits on corporate political expenditures, in addition to contributions. But we don't think it's necessary to distinguish between corporate and individual expenditures. If the Court were to revise its case law to permit reasonable limits on independent expenditures—as we have argued it should—that would also adequately limit the distorting effects of corporate spending via expenditures.

The Court's broad, constitutionally imposed deregulatory agenda has removed political control over politics from the voters. Professor Mark Tushnet has explained:

> The First Amendment has replaced the due process clause as the primary guarantor of the privileged. Indeed, it protects the privileges more perniciously than the due process clause ever did.... Today, in contrast, the First Amendment stands as a general obstruction to all progressive legislative efforts.... Under [*Buckley*] and [*Bellotti*], however, [corporate] investments in politics—or politicians—cannot be regulated significantly.[44]

Nothing in the Constitution compelled this deregulation. It was a policy choice that is politically advantageous for those with money.

Rejecting the ability to restrict spending to prevent some voices from drowning out others

Relatedly, we disagree with the Court's categorical rejection of the government interest in leveling the playing field. Many have criticized the Court for giving inadequate weight to the value of equality of influence in political campaigns.[45] Allowing unlimited expenditures allows the wealthy to drown out the voices of those with less money. It thus permits those with money to have much more influence in election campaigns and ultimately with elected officials.[46] Ensuring that important voices are not totally drowned out, so that voters get a full picture, is a compelling interest that justifies the limits on expenditures, especially by corporations, that the Court has invalidated. It also justifies partial subsidization of less well-funded candidates to ensure that voters learn of minority positions as well.

As mentioned earlier, there was a time when the Court allowed restrictions on corporate expenditures to prevent the distortion of the electoral system. In *Austin v. Michigan Chamber of Commerce*, the Court upheld a restriction on corporate contributions or expenditures, expressly relying on the ability of the state to limit corporate speech so as to limit the distortions caused by corporate wealth.[47] A Michigan law prohibited corporations from using their revenues to contribute to candidates or to make expenditures for or against candidates. The corporations, however, could create a separate fund to solicit contributions and could spend money from this segregated fund.

Justice Thurgood Marshall's majority opinion said that the Michigan law was directed at

> the corrosive and distorting effects of immense aggregations of wealth that are accumulated with the help of the corporate form and that have little or no correlation to the public's support for the corporation's political ideals. The Act does not attempt "to equalize the relative influence of speakers on elections"; rather, it ensures that expenditures reflect actual public support for the political ideas espoused by the corporations.[48]

Thus, the Court concluded that the government was justified in restricting both corporate expenditures and contributions. The Court emphasized that the corporation still could spend money; it just had to be raised separately from corporate funds.

The Court followed this in *McConnell v. Federal Election Commission* by upholding a provision of the Bipartisan Campaign Finance Reform Act that prohibited corporations and unions from engaging in independent expenditures for broadcast advertising, for or against identifiable candidates, thirty days before a primary or sixty days before a general election.[49] The Court, citing to *Austin*, upheld these restrictions and reaffirmed the ability of the government to limit corporate spending in election campaigns, so as to prevent distortions of the marketplace of ideas.

But in *Citizens United v. Federal Election Commission*, the Court expressly overruled *Austin* and this aspect of *McConnell* and held that restrictions on independent expenditures from corporate treasuries (and, by implication, by unions) violate the First Amendment.[50] The key difference from seven years earlier, when the Court decided *McConnell*, was that Justice O'Connor, who had been in the five-Justice majority in that case, had been replaced by Justice Alito, who joined the *McConnell* dissenters and Chief Justice Roberts (who took the same position as Chief Justice Rehnquist).

The Court rejected *Austin*'s concern with preventing corporate wealth from distorting elections, concluding that the restrictions on independent expenditures by corporations and unions violated the First Amendment. The Court stated:

> The censorship we now confront is vast in its reach. The Government has "muffle[d] the voices that best represent the most significant segments of the economy." And "the electorate [has been] deprived of information, knowledge and opinion vital to its function." By suppressing the speech of manifold corporations, both for-profit and nonprofit, the Government prevents their voices and viewpoints from reaching the public and advising voters on which persons or entities are hostile to their interests.[51]

Justice Stevens wrote a lengthy and vehement dissent, which was joined by Justices Ginsburg, Breyer, and Sotomayor. The dissent rejected the majority's premise that wealthy corporations are entitled to the same First Amendment rights as individuals. As Justice Stevens stated:

> The financial resources, legal structure, and instrumental orientation of corporations raise legitimate concerns about their role in the electoral process. Our lawmakers have a compelling constitutional basis, if not also a democratic duty, to take measures designed to guard against the potentially deleterious effects of corporate spending in local and national races.[52]

The Court erred in overruling its decisions that had recognized a compelling interest in preventing corporate expenditures from distorting our election system. The Court's decision in *Citizens United* has already had a profound effect on our democracy, as corporations can now spend unlimited money to get candidates elected or defeated. As one report noted:

> It has also become a growing problem as each respective election cycle has seen record-breaking amounts of spending. Campaign spending by corporations and other outside groups increased by nearly 900% between 2008 and 2016. In 2020, total election spending was $14.4 billion, up from $5.7 billion in 2018, and more than $1 billion in dark money was spent.[53]

Dark money is money spent by organizations without the need to disclose their donors. As election-law expert Professor Richard Hasen stated: *Citizens United* "helped to usher in a sea change in American elections, and its influence on the decade that followed is hard to overstate."[54] There has been an explosion of undisclosed money, super PACs, and foreign influence in American elections.

Declaring unconstitutional public funding systems that lead to more speech

One way to combat the evils of the campaign finance system is public funding of elections. But the Court significantly limited public funding systems in its decision in *Arizona Free Enterprise Club's Freedom Club PAC v. Bennett*.[55] The case involved an Arizona voter-passed initiative law, adopted after a major political scandal, which provided for public funding of elections for state offices. Under the Arizona Citizens Clean Elections Act, no candidate was required to accept public funding for his or her election. A candidate wishing to receive such money could qualify for receiving public funds by obtaining a specified amount of donations. Candidates choosing to take public funds had to agree, among other things, to limit their expenditure of personal funds to $500, to participate in at least one public debate, to adhere to an overall expenditure cap, and to return all unspent public money to the state.

The concern, though, was that if the amount of public funds was fixed, it could be exceeded by an opponent who did not take public funds. The Arizona law said that if an opponent not taking public funds spends more than a designated sum, a publicly financed candidate receives roughly one additional dollar for every dollar spent by the opposing privately financed candidate. The publicly financed candidate also receives roughly one dollar for every dollar spent by independent expenditure groups to support the privately financed candidate or to oppose the publicly financed candidate. But there was a cap on these additional funds; matching funds top out at two times the initial authorized grant of public funding to the publicly financed candidate.

The Supreme Court, in a 5–4 decision, declared this law unconstitutional. The Court said that the Arizona law was unconstitutional because it penalized candidates who spent their own money in elections. The "penalty" was that their increased spending would be met with greater public funds for an opponent accepting such money. The Court said that the Arizona law violated the First Amendment because it would discourage candidates, and their supporters, from spending money in elections.

But this is just wrong: the Arizona law in no way restricted or regulated any speech. The sole effect of the Arizona Citizens Clean Election Act was to increase money for candidates taking public funds. Justice Kagan in dissent explained that, although the majority opinion repeatedly characterizes the Act as limiting speech, "Arizona's matching funds provision does not restrict, but instead subsidizes, speech."[56] If one accepts that spending money in elections is a form of speech protected by the First Amendment, then the Arizona law actually *increased* speech.

What Explains the Decisions?

It is important to see that the Court's decisions on campaign finance are entirely based on value choices by the conservative justices to protect the ability of those with wealth, including corporations, to influence the outcome of elections. It is absurd to say that the original meaning of the First Amendment was to safeguard the right of corporations to spend unlimited amounts of money in election campaigns. Those who drafted and ratified the First Amendment could not have imagined campaign spending as it exists in the 21st century, let alone the wealth of modern corporations and their ability to influence the outcome of elections through spending.

Justice Stevens made exactly this point in his dissenting opinion in *Citizens United*, noting that the majority

> makes only a perfunctory attempt to ground its analysis in the principles or understandings of those who drafted and ratified the Amendment. Perhaps this is because there is not a scintilla of evidence to support the notion that

anyone believed it would preclude regulatory distinctions based on the corporate form. To the extent that the Framers' views are discernible and relevant to the disposition of this case, they would appear to cut strongly against the majority's position.[57]

Justice Scalia, in his response, stressed that there is no exclusion in the First Amendment for corporations. He wrote:

> The lack of a textual exception for speech by corporations cannot be explained on the ground that such organizations did not exist or did not speak. To the contrary, colleges, towns and cities, religious institutions, and guilds had long been organized as corporations at common law and under the King's charter . . . both corporations and voluntary associations actively petitioned the Government and expressed their views in newspapers and pamphlets.[58]

But corporations as they exist today were not known in 1791. Far more important, corporate campaign spending in elections was unknown. Nor is it possible to think of an analogous form of expression that existed then to justify an originalist finding that it deserves constitutional protection. Justice Scalia suggests nothing to the contrary. Nor can he or anyone else justify the conclusion in *Citizens United* based on the original understanding of free speech when the First Amendment was ratified. The Constitution is simply silent on the question of whether corporate political expenditure should get constitutional protection. Prior to *Buckley* and *Belotti*, there was little basis in the Court's precedents to assume that corporate spending would be treated as equivalent to individual speech. It does not logically flow from the First Amendment's text. And it is impossible to say that the original understanding of the First Amendment was that spending money in elections is speech; that a distinction should be drawn between contributions and expenditures; that the government cannot regulate campaign spending to prevent distortion; that corporations have the right to spend unlimited amounts of money from corporate treasuries; or that public-funding schemes are unconstitutional. None of the Court's holdings with regard to campaign finance can be justified based on the original meaning and understanding of the First Amendment.

The Court's conclusion that spending money in a campaign is speech is similarly specious.[59] Spending money *can* be expressive, but so can a lot of conduct. Flag burning, for example, is highly expressive—it conveys a clear criticism of the entity associated with the flag—and is worthy of First Amendment protection. But burning a flag isn't speech and it doesn't receive strict scrutiny; it's expressive conduct and is therefore evaluated under intermediate scrutiny.⁶⁰ Ditto for other forms of expressive conduct, like burning draft cards or hanging a flag upside down.⁶¹ And the same should be true of the expenditure of money.

The Court's campaign finance decisions must be understood from an ideological perspective. It is the only possible explanation for the pervasive illogic and consistently partisan outcomes of those decisions. There has long been a perception that corporations and the wealthy tend to favor conservatives in the interest of lower taxes and less regulation. It thus made sense from a conservative perspective to deregulate corporate political spending: deregulation would benefit Republicans. But when Congress and state legislatures enacted limits on political spending, it threatened to cut off conservatives' perceived advantage. The Court has held unconstitutional most attempts to regulate campaign finance.

Protecting the right of citizens to support their preferred candidates, including by spending money, is a laudable objective—indeed, it is one of the five we suggested in Part I. But it is an objective that should be approached with caution and nuance. Since *Buckley*, however, the Court has thrown caution to the wind. Everything other than individual contribution limits, the Court (incorrectly) says, is unconstitutional because it isn't narrowly tailored to preventing *quid pro quo* corruption. That incredibly rigid approach to election regulation is impracticable and undesirable to everyone except those who believe they are likely to benefit. In this context, Republicans stand to gain greatly from the conservative Court's bending of law and reason.

For example, as we explained above, the public-financing law in *Arizona Free Enterprise Club* provided a dollar to a publicly funded candidate for every dollar their opponent spent, up to a point—this cannot possibly be explained on the basis of prior First Amendment theory or doctrine. The law in no way restricted privately funded candidates' speech. The Arizona law was viewpoint- and content-neutral; the public funding was available without regard to a candidate's or opponent's political affiliation, so long as they complied with the statutory restrictions. The Court's decision to strike down the law can only be explained by the fact that the law threatened to chip away at the monetary advantage possessed by the Court's preferred candidates. It should not be surprising that the plaintiff in many of the Court's campaign finance decisions—*Arizona Free Enterprise, Citizens United, McConnell v. FEC, McCutcheon v. FEC, Davis v. FEC*, and many others—was a conservative organization or candidate.

Conclusion

Beginning with *Buckley*, the Supreme Court has entertained the fiction that political spending is as worthy of First Amendment protection as pure political speech by a citizen. Nothing in the text or history of the First Amendment required that conclusion. And it is stunning in its illogic when extended to corporations. Corporations are unthinking, unfeeling, nonvoting, nonhuman, and potentially foreign-controlled entities that now exert outsized influence in American politics. There is little reason to permit their unrestricted influence—except if it is politically advantageous to do so. The thought that such spending will control the direction of this country and the future of the planet should make us deeply uncomfortable with the last half century of campaign finance decisions by the Supreme Court.

4

Citizens United

Cracks in the Façade

Diane P. Wood

The Supreme Court's *Citizens United* decision burst on the scene in 2010[1] with a sweeping set of legal propositions based on a view of the world that was, at a minimum, contestable. Readers walked away with a breathtaking set of constitutional postulates: corporations are the same as any other kind of voluntary association; the electoral process may not be regulated (perhaps at all), because in the final analysis it is just speech—indeed, an especially favored type of speech; brazen *quid pro quo* corruption is the only abuse that Congress may address; and measures designed to respond to the more pervasive sale and purchase of influence and legislation touch too closely on First Amendment interests to be permissible. And those are just the headliners—the opinion contains much more along similar lines.

The Court's opinion is an amalgam of legal propositions and untested empirical points. One thing, however, is unmistakable: to the extent that the Court anticipated in 2010 that its opinion would have little effect on the status quo, it must by now know that it was sorely mistaken. One number is enough to make the point: By October 9, 2024, according to the *New York Times*, Vice President Kamala Harris had raised $1 billion since she entered the presidential race in mid-July and quickly became the Democratic Party's nominee—an unprecedented amount over such a short period.[2] The money raised in support of President-elect Donald Trump was equally impressive.[3] In short, political campaigns have become a multibillion-dollar industry in the United States. Yet at the same time, it is unclear how such vast pools of cash have actually affected ultimate outcomes. A comparison to mutually assured destruction comes to mind.

Whether or not the ends have justified the means, *Citizens United* is primarily troublesome for the dubious legal propositions on which it rests, including its equation of money with speech and its assumption that corporations are exactly the same as flesh-and-blood human beings for purposes of elections. Both of those moves were too facile. The assumptions, both empirical and legal, on which they were based have not stood the test of time. Thanks largely to the tsunami of money *Citizens United* unleashed into the political system, the days of one person, one vote envisioned by such cases as *Reynolds v. Sims*[4] have given way to a regime of one dollar, one vote.[5] Why legislators are entitled to represent dollars, when they cannot represent "trees or acres,"[6] demands a more serious answer than the Court gave in *Citizens United* or has offered since then.

If every word of *Citizens United* really were etched into constitutional stone, the prospects for our democracy would be troubling. But a careful look at the assumptions shows that there is room for reform. For example, even if it appears that the two major political parties have equal access to funding, the public's interest in disclosure remains powerful. During the primary season, people are exposed to many candidates; some may not have deep pockets, and others may be independents or third-party adherents. More than that, if elections are to be bought and sold, then there is a powerful case for allowing the American public to know the identities of the buyers and sellers, no matter what formal party affiliation a candidate has. This need is particularly compelling if the immediate source of funds is a corporation. In that case, people often will know only such unilluminating facts as that State X's pension fund holds a large bloc of shares, or that Able & Baker, LLP, is a shareholder. If Congress really wants to ensure that voters know whose advice they are being asked to take (and also, not inconsequentially, whether foreign interests lie behind an apparent US entity[7]), a more robust disclosure regime is a sensible and constitutional first step.

It is not too late to correct the errors embedded in the *Citizens United* framework. We have taken comparable steps before. The constitutional error perpetuated in *Plessy v. Ferguson*[8] lasted for fifty-eight years, from 1896 until 1954, when *Brown v. Board of Education* was decided.[9] *Citizens United* has been on the books for less than half that time; there is no reason to think that it has achieved the status of a "super-precedent,"[10] a judicial decision that has become almost untouchable.

Such a reconsideration would not be an exercise in futility. The Constitution expressly confers on Congress the power to regulate federal elections through the Election Clause of Article I, section 4.[11] And it cannot be too surprising that such regulation occasionally needs to be reconciled with important First Amendment interests. So what? No part of the Constitution stands alone, free from the constraints imposed by other provisions. No less an authority than Chief Justice William H. Rehnquist made this point in his book *All the Laws But One*.[12] Pertinent here are the constitutional rights to vote, to equal protection of the laws, and to "a Republican Form of Government";[13] all must be given effect, along with the freedoms of speech, association, and petition for redress of grievances that are commonly implicated by the electoral process.

With that in mind, I begin with a few words about the background against which *Citizens United* was decided, before turning to the case itself. Next, I look at the reception *Citizens United* has had since its release. Finally, I offer some thoughts about how campaign finance regulations and the First Amendment may be able to coexist with sensible regulations designed to cabin the adverse effects that have made politics a "pay to play" enterprise.

Citizens United: Antecedents and Holdings

The *Citizens United* decision did not, Athena-like, emerge full-grown and armed from the head of Zeus, or, for that matter, from the pen of Justice Kennedy. The Court had visited the area of election regulation before. Until 1976, it had generally upheld reasonable limitations on the electoral process as the price one pays to protect the fundamental right to vote, to ensure integrity (broadly construed—not limited to overt criminal corruption[14]) in the electoral system, and ultimately to live in a democratic society.[15]

All that changed when the Court handed down its pivotal decision in *Buckley v. Valeo*, which addressed "constitutional challenges to the key provisions of the Federal Election Campaign Act of 1971 (the FECA)."[16] Three of the targets of that law have proven to be of enduring importance: (1) its limitations on individual contributions, both to candidates and cumulatively; (2) its limitations on expenditures, particularly those related to specific candidates; and (3) its public-disclosure requirements. The Court approached all of these provisions with a skeptical eye, working from the premise that "[t]he Act's contribution and expenditure limitations operate in an area of the most fundamental First Amendment activities."[17] Critically, it rejected the argument that restrictions on "the giving and spending of money" related to conduct, not speech, and thus did not have to satisfy the strictures of the First Amendment.[18] Instead, it embraced the conclusion that the FECA's contribution and expenditure provisions "impose[d] direct quantity restrictions on political communication"[19] and thus that a restriction on money was itself a restriction on speech. It was unmoved by the practical reality that those with fewer dollars to spend will be unable to speak as effectively as those with substantial resources.[20] Nor did it appear to recognize that a dollar bill itself is not doing any speaking (other than perhaps revealing what country issued the currency and how much that piece of paper is worth), but instead represents an input into the speech that the holder of that dollar bill wants to disseminate.

That is odd, coming from a court that only thirteen years earlier had entertained a case brought by the owner of a newspaper, the Minneapolis Star and Tribune Company, challenging a state tax that specifically targeted "paper and ink products consumed in the production of a publication."[21] The Court struck down that tax, which applied only to publications protected by the First Amendment and discriminated against the press in other ways, but it acknowledged that a nondiscriminatory tax, such as a general sales tax, on paper and ink would have been permissible.[22] Note in this connection that the tax was not assessed against the published newspaper; it was directed to the inputs that go into the newspaper's production. Just so with the money used to finance political campaigns. Those funds are just the content-neutral "ink and paper" needed to create the ads through which various members of the population speak.

It is meaningless to say, as the *Buckley* Court did and the *Citizens United* Court repeated, that restrictions on money "necessarily reduce[] the quantity of expression by restricting the number of issues discussed, the depth of their exploration, and the size of the audience reached."[23] That is a truism. Any time there is less money to spend on an item or an activity (at least in a capitalist economy), less of that item or activity will be produced. If less money goes to the pharmaceutical industry, fewer new drugs will be developed; if libraries receive less money, their book purchases will diminish; if a major factory in an area shuts its doors, the people who lost their jobs will not have as much to invest in political campaigns. Yet no one thinks that the First Amendment has anything to say about these possibilities. Justice White made this point at greater length in his separate opinion in *Buckley*.[24]

The Court did not engage seriously with this argument. Instead, it jumped straight to the justifications that had been advanced in support of the FECA, acknowledging as it did so that the prevention of both corruption and the appearance of corruption were legitimate interests. For purposes of the contribution restrictions, it found that these goals justified what it saw as "the limited effect upon First Amendment freedoms" caused by the contribution ceiling.[25] It also rejected the argument that the contribution provisions were overbroad and invidiously discriminated in favor of incumbents and against challengers.[26]

The behavioral assumptions on which the Court relied appear to be nothing but intuitions. Their source is unclear, but perhaps they reflect the modesty of the specific contribution limitations found in the Act: for individuals, $1,000 to any single candidate per election and an overall annual limit of $25,000, and for individuals and for groups focusing on a particular candidate, $1,000 a year. Perhaps at those levels it made sense to say that the First Amendment was not heavily implicated by contribution levels. What the Court did not answer is whether the elimination of these caps would change the communicative aspects of contributions.

The *Buckley* Court took a less forgiving view of expenditure limitations, because they imposed "direct and substantial restraints on the *quantity* of political speech."[27] It found that these provisions "limit[ed] political expression at the core of our electoral process and of the First Amendment freedoms,"[28] based exclusively on the truism that campaign ads cost money, and a candidate with a tight budget will not be able to purchase as much coverage. Proceeding from this "money is speech" premise, the Court held that a cap on expenditures limiting each individual to $1,000 per year per candidate translated directly into a limitation on political expression. It also postulated that these "expenditure limitations impose[d] far greater restraints on the freedom of speech and association than [did] [the Act's] contribution limitations."[29]

The next logical question was whether the government's asserted justifications for the law were enough to save it. No, was the reply, for several reasons. First, the FECA's prohibitions were too easy to evade, simply by refraining from mentioning a candidate's name. Second, the Court accepted as fact that "the independent advocacy restricted by the provision does not presently appear to pose dangers of real or apparent corruption."[30] At the same time, it dismissed the salience of any government interest in "equalizing the relative ability of individuals and groups to influence the outcome of elections."³¹ If Billionaire X can purchase thousands of ads, and Worker Q can afford only a $10 contribution to a campaign, that's just the way it is. The Court found the alternative of permitting "government [to] restrict the speech of some elements of our society in order to enhance the relative voice of others . . . wholly foreign to the First Amendment."³²

While there is much more to *Buckley*, the only additional point worth highlighting is its treatment of the FECA's reporting and disclosure requirements. Such laws have been in place since at least 1910,³³ and that is where matters stood until Congress enacted the FECA in 1971. While acknowledging that there are cases in which "compelled disclosure, in itself, can seriously infringe on privacy of association and belief,"³⁴ the *Buckley* Court held that such a finding should be made only after careful analysis. The state's interest in disclosure must survive "exacting" scrutiny,³⁵ and there must be "a relevant correlation or substantial relation between the governmental interest and the information required to be disclosed."³⁶

The Court offered three reasons why the reporting and disclosure requirements of the FECA met that demanding standard: first, they inform the electorate about the sources and use of money; second, they deter both actual and apparent corruption; and third, they facilitate the collection of data necessary to detect violations of the contribution limitations.³⁷ Sunshine, as the saying goes, is the best disinfectant, and the Court concluded that Congress had not run afoul of the First Amendment by requiring more rather than less information in the public domain.

More than thirty years elapsed between *Buckley* and *Citizens United*, but nothing in the interim period undermined *Buckley*'s key rulings. The most important change during that time was Congress's enactment in 2002 of the Bipartisan Campaign Reform Act (BCRA).³⁸ Pursuant to that Act, corporations and unions were forbidden to use general treasury funds to make independent expenditures for so-called electioneering communications or for anything that expressly advocated for the election or defeat of a particular candidate. The year after BCRA took effect, the Supreme Court upheld its provisions in the case of *McConnell v. Federal Election Commission*,³⁹ which itself relied on *Austin v. Michigan Chamber of Commerce*.⁴⁰ *Austin* upheld a Michigan statute prohibiting corporations from using general treasury funds for *independent* campaign expenditures for or against a specified candidate. The Court in *Austin* conceded that the law impinged on expressive rights, but the majority found that it was narrowly tailored to address a compelling state interest—averting the enhanced risk of corruption or the appearance thereof. This risk was especially concerning given certain aspects of the corporate form: its perpetual nature, the fact that stockholders do not generally associate with corporations for expressive purposes, and the ability of corporations to amass significant wealth.[41] The following passage captures the essence of the *Austin* Court's reasoning:

> [T]he [Michigan statute] is precisely targeted to eliminate the distortion caused by corporate spending while also allowing corporations to express their political views.... [T]he Act does not impose an *absolute* ban on all forms of corporate political spending but permits corporations to make independent political expenditures through separate segregated funds. Because persons contributing to such funds understand that their money will be used solely for political purposes, the speech generated accurately reflects contributors' support for the corporations' political views.

In other words, corporations can serve as the organizing mechanism for likeminded people to associate and express their views, through the vehicle of a special fund (usually called a Political Action Committee, or PAC); shareholders with a different perspective are not compelled to face the unpleasant choice between paying for someone else's speech and selling their shares, potentially on unfavorable terms.

Recognizing the difficult choice that would be faced by dissenting shareholders if general treasury funds *could* be used, the *Austin* Court drew some important distinctions between unincorporated unions and business corporations:

> [L]abor unions differ from corporations in that union members who disagree with a union's political activities need not give up full membership in the organization to avoid supporting its political activities.... [A] union may not compel those employees to support financially "union activities beyond those germane to collective bargaining, contract administration, and grievance adjustment."[42] An employee who objects to a union's political activities thus can decline to contribute to those activities, while continuing to enjoy the benefits derived from the union's performance of its duties as the exclusive representative of the bargaining unit on labor-management issues. As a result, the funds available for a union's political activities more accurately reflects members' support for the organization's political views than does a corporation's general treasury.[43]

In essence, *Austin* assured that the union and the corporation would end up in the same place. The union takes political positions only for workers who have not exercised their *Beck* rights, and the corporation does no more than funnel political contributions made by willing shareholders to a PAC whose viewpoint is known to all. Both types of entity—union and corporation—thus work through a voluntarily constituted subgroup that shares a particular political view.

Twenty years after *Austin* was decided, the Court noted probable jurisdiction in *Citizens United* and sought reargument on the question whether it should overrule *Austin*, along with relevant parts of *McConnell*.[44] Sweeping *Austin* out of the way would allow the Court again to consider whether corporations could be forbidden by law from using their general treasury funds to make direct contributions or "independent expenditures" urging the election of clearly identified candidates.

The underlying facts of the case were simple. *Citizens United*, a small nonprofit corporation with an annual budget of $12 million, prepared and in January 2008 released a film called *Hillary: The Movie*, which (to put it mildly) portrayed then-Senator Hillary Clinton in an unfavorable light. As she was at the time a candidate for the Democratic Party's nomination for President, the campaign-finance laws came into play. The dispute concerned the way that *Citizens United* would be permitted to pay for "video-on-demand" distribution of the film within thirty days of the primary elections. The company wanted to use its general treasury funds for that purpose, rather than only funds from its PAC. BCRA, however, forbade that choice, and so the issue was joined: could BCRA survive First Amendment scrutiny?

The Court, speaking through a majority opinion authored by Justice Kennedy, said no. After brushing off an argument that the film did not qualify as an electioneering communication,[45] as well as a contention that video-on-demand is sufficiently different from television ads that BCRA did not apply to that format,[46] the Court began by refusing to draw distinctions among different types of corporations—nonprofits, those funded by individuals, those with certain corporate purposes, and so on.[47] It then confirmed that *Citizens United* had not waived its facial First Amendment challenge to the statute.[48]

On the merits, the Court emphasized that BCRA made it a *felony* either expressly to advocate for the election or defeat of candidates or to disseminate electioneering materials within specified periods (thirty days of a primary or sixty days of a general election). In short, this was a ban on speech.[49] Citing *Buckley*, it reiterated that "a restriction on the amount of money" someone can spend on political communication at a specified time necessarily reduces the quantity of expression.⁵⁰ Laws such as BCRA "that burden political speech," it said, "are subject to strict scrutiny, which requires the Government to prove that the restriction furthers a compelling interest and is narrowly tailored to achieve that interest."⁵¹ The Court also relied on the general rule that prohibits restrictions based on the identity of a speaker,⁵² on the theory that BCRA singled out corporate speech for regulation.

The Court then portrayed the doomed *Austin* decision as a radical change from the past—one that "identified a new governmental interest in limiting political speech: an antidistortion interest."⁵³ Faced with these supposedly conflicting lines of precedent—one that forbade restrictions on political speech based on corporate identity and one that permitted them—the Court chose the former. In doing so, it not only rejected the risk of distorting the electoral process as a permissible rationale for election regulations, but it also threw cold water on the idea that BCRA could be supported by the anti-corruption interest on which the Court had relied so often. Its language is worth repeating: "[W]e now conclude that independent expenditures, including those made by corporations, do not give rise to corruption or the appearance of corruption."⁵⁴ *Who says?*, the reader is tempted to ask. *Why not?*, another may wonder. What amounts to corruption—only direct bribery, or more subtle forms of selling influence? The Court never answered those questions; instead, it brushed off "the interest of dissenting shareholders from being compelled to fund corporate speech" as inconsequential.⁵⁵ That interest, it asserted, could be stretched to support censorship of a *New York Times* or Fox News editorial.⁵⁶

All of this provided the backdrop for the Court's decision to overrule *Austin*. It offered several reasons in support of its ruling. First, it complained that "speakers find ways to circumvent campaign finance laws."⁵⁷ Second, it observed that rapid changes in communicative technology counseled in favor of the abandonment of any regulation of corporate speech.⁵⁸ Third, it announced that "[n]o serious reliance interests are at stake."⁵⁹ Without a sufficiently compelling interest in support of BCRA's restriction on corporate speech, the law facially violated the First Amendment.

The opinion did leave a few narrow areas for continued regulation, however. The Court took pains to say that it was not addressing the validity of measures designed to prevent foreign individuals or legal entities from "influencing our Nation's political process."⁶⁰ Last, and of potentially greater importance, the Court rejected *Citizens United*'s challenge to BCRA's disclaimer and disclosure provisions. The statute required televised electioneering communications funded by anyone other than the candidate to include a disclaimer stating that "Person or Entity X is responsible for the content of this advertising,"[61] among other things. In addition, it required any person who spends more than a modest $10,000 to file a statement with the Federal Election Commission identifying "the person making the expenditure, the amount of the expenditure, the election to which the expenditure was directed, and the names of certain contributors."[62]

As it had done in *Buckley*, the Court found that disclaimer and disclosure requirements do not prevent anyone from speaking, and that—at least as a facial matter—they do not conflict with the First Amendment. In coming to this conclusion, the Court subjected these requirements to "exacting scrutiny," which it signaled is slightly more deferential than "strict scrutiny."[63] Exacting scrutiny, it explained, "requires a substantial relation between the disclosure requirement and a sufficiently important governmental interest."[64] It left the door open to an as-applied challenge, if the person could show "a reasonable probability that disclosure of its contributors' names [would] subject them to threats, harassment, or reprisals from either Governmental officials or private parties."[65]

Several Justices wrote separately, but the opinions pertinent here are those of Justice Stevens and Justice Thomas. Justice Stevens pointed out the lack of empirical support showing what the actual effects of BCRA had been on all kinds of organizations, including corporations and unions. Alluding to the legislative history of BCRA, he wrote that "Congress crafted BCRA in response to a virtual mountain of research on the corruption that previous legislation had failed to avert."[66] He made much the same point about one of the justifications for overruling *Austin*: the majority's insistence that the decision had been "undermined by experience since its announcement."[67] As he put it, "[t]his is a curious claim to make in a case that lacks a developed record."[68] It is equally curious, he argued, given the fact that "not a single for-profit corporation, union, or State" had asked the Court to overrule *Austin*.[69]

Justice Stevens also challenged other aspects of the majority opinion: its characterization of the restriction on the use of treasury funds as a "ban" on corporate speech; the idea that BCRA was guilty of drawing an identity-based distinction; and the lack of any evidence in the historical record supporting the idea that the drafters of the First Amendment thought that they were precluding regulatory distinctions based on the corporate form. Indeed, in

1791 corporations were nothing like today's entities, as Justice Stevens pointed out.[70] They were holders of specific charters granted by the legislature for specifically described purposes.[71]

The remainder of his points were more institutional. Congress, he contended, not the Court, is better suited to assess and implement the anticorruption, antidistortion, and shareholder-protection concerns that underlay BCRA. Justice Stevens ended with a lament: "While American democracy is imperfect, few outside the majority of this Court would have thought its flaws included a dearth of corporate money in politics."[72]

The Court's opus ended with a partial dissent from Justice Thomas. While he agreed with the majority's overruling of *Austin* and its position on the First Amendment and corporate speech, he took exception to its decision to uphold the Act's disclosure, disclaimer, and reporting requirements.[73] He was particularly influenced by an *amicus curiae* brief that recounted the experience of the advocates of California's Proposition 8 in the 2008 general election. That measure, which the voters approved, restricted the definition of marriage to an arrangement between one man and one woman.[74] Opponents of the measure, according to the *amicus*, had engaged in serious acts of harassment against its proponents, including property damage and threats of physical violence or death. Such threats of retaliation chill speech and, the *amicus* contended, are enabled by the public-disclosure requirements. Justice Thomas found this to be a persuasive argument and urged that the First Amendment does not require people to suffer this kind of mistreatment. As-applied actions, he feared, would not be effective in the face of such conduct.

Citizens United, Fifteen Years Later

As I noted at the outset, those who predicted that *Citizens United* would unleash a torrent of money into the electoral system, and that the result would be a host of undesirable outcomes, were right. Worse, the most important measures the *Citizens United* opinion left on the table to ensure election integrity—the disclosure, disclaimer, and reporting requirements—would be diluted in the Court's 2021 decision in *Americans for Prosperity Foundation v. Bonta*.[75] That case tested the validity of a California regulation that required tax-exempt charities to file copies of their IRS disclosure forms, plus all relevant schedules, with the state attorney general. These documents include information about the names and addresses of donors who had contributed more than $5,000 to the organization in a given tax year. Petitioners objected that Schedule B, one of the required forms, contained information that was so sensitive that the forced disclosure violated their First Amendment rights. The idea was that potential donors, knowing about the loss of privacy entailed by this disclosure, would be less likely to contribute to them and that any contributions would subject them to possible reprisals.

Apparently reviewing the California system under the "exacting scrutiny" standard,[76] the Court found it incompatible with the First Amendment. Narrow tailoring, the Court said, is necessary no matter what level of scrutiny applies to a case, and this law flunked that test. The Court conceded that the state had "an important interest in preventing wrongdoing by charitable organizations,"[77] but it found the mismatch between that interest and the scope of the required disclosure to be fatal. Moreover, there was little to no evidence that the state had ever used this detailed information, and the record indicated that it had never even considered less restrictive alternatives.[78] The net result of the decision was to underscore that even disclosure and reporting requirements do not get a free pass—they are subject to strict review.

If *Bonta* proves nothing else, it is a signal that the debate launched by *Buckley* and *Citizens United* is still very much with us. And if that is the case, then it is not too late to suggest some changes that would restore the balance between legitimate regulation of the election process and the First Amendment rights of all who participate in it.

The first, and most glaring, error that should be corrected is the direct equation between speech and money. As Justice White trenchantly put it in his *Buckley* dissent, money is merely an input to speech, just as is ownership of a computer, access to a WiFi network, a pen and paper, a smartphone, and any other tools for communication. The regulation of money is content-neutral. It is no different, for First Amendment purposes, from content-neutral signage regulations, such as the billboard rule at issue in *City of Austin, Texas v. Reagan National Advertising of Austin, LLC.*[79] In that case, a city regulation regulated off-premises billboards more stringently than signs advertising activities conducted on the property where they were placed. The Supreme Court upheld the regulation, reasoning that

> [u]nlike the regulations at issue in *Reed* [*v. Gilbert*, 576 U.S. 155 (2015)], the City's off-premises distinction requires an examination of speech only in service

of drawing neutral, location-based lines. It is agnostic as to content. Thus, absent a content-based purpose or justification, the City's distinction is content-neutral and does not warrant the application of strict scrutiny.[80]

With that demanding standard of review out of the way, the Court saw no First Amendment impediment to the validity of the ordinance.

Note, in this connection, what the Court was saying. It did not blindly follow a "more billboards are better" approach to the ordinance, because if it had done so, it would have struck down the limitations on off-premises billboards and comparable displays. It did not insist that the recipient don blindfolds and ignore the fact that there was some speech associated with the regulated structures. Instead, it expressly rejected "the view that *any* examination of speech or expression inherently triggers heightened First Amendment concern."[81] Only measures that "discriminate based on the topic discussed or the idea or message expressed" are forbidden as content-based.[82]

The fact that money can be used to purchase campaign ads also proves too much, for all the reasons noted above. Taken to its extreme, the "money equals speech" equation would require the deletion of such well-known laws as the prohibition against bribery of a public official,[83] the prohibition against kickbacks in government contracting,[84] and restrictions on expenditures by charitable organizations (which lose their preferred tax status if they overcompensate executives or engage in other forms of waste). People who own a property that has been designated as a historical landmark are forbidden from spending their own money to raze the property and build a modern replacement, but no one thinks that the First Amendment has anything to say about such rules, even if the owner asserts that the decision to raze is a comment on the architectural style of the original structure.

With the equation between money and speech gone, we can return to an era in which the electoral process can be regulated in a way that does not exclude so many voices from meaningful participation. Over the years, concern has mounted about the ways in which money can distort the electoral process. In ways that were unimaginable even when *Citizens United* was handed down, people with control over huge resources can flood the Internet, the airwaves, social media, and any other forms of communication so completely that they can drown out the voices of those with lesser resources. It is odd, to say the least, that the Court is willing to leave the political process vulnerable to these kinds of distortions during the period leading up to an election, while at the same time it is so solicitous of elections held in a workplace for the purpose of deciding whether to unionize. In the latter case, the law calls for "laboratory conditions"—that is, an environment in which all employees will feel free to exercise their vote without fear of interference from either the union or the employer.[85] No such requirement exists for normal political elections.

Another area that remains open to regulatory intervention even after *Citizens United* relates to the stunning advances in generative artificial intelligence, and in particular to the false, inaccurate, or misleading contributions it may insert into the "marketplace of ideas." *United States v. Alvarez*[86] holds that a blatantly false statement that the speaker had been awarded the Congressional Medal of Honor is protected under the First Amendment.[87] But how far should this principle be extended, if the "speaker" is ChatGPT, Claude, Copilot, or Bard? It seems likely that regulation of those platforms is still possible. US patent law, for example, has refused to equate natural persons with AI.[88] For purposes of campaign finance regulation, why not apply the same standard to the use of deepfakes and AI hallucinations. The *Alvarez* Court did acknowledge that the falsity of speech might be a factor that can be addressed in an independent claim, such as one for libel, impersonating a federal officer, or perjury.[89] It does not require too much imagination to conjure up similar examples of redressable harm through AI, whether through *ex ante* regulation or *ex post* tort actions.

Next, it is time to jettison the core assumption of *Citizens United* that corporations are exactly the same as groups for all purposes, including election activities. That is far from true; in fact, it is easy to distinguish even among different kinds of corporations. It is ironic at best that the Court made its sweeping ruling against the factual backdrop of a small, ideologically homogeneous entity whose raison d'être appears to have been to urge a certain viewpoint in an election (and possibly more generally). Close, family-held corporations may also demand separate analysis.[90] It is hard to imagine a devoted Hillary supporter wanting to purchase stock in *Citizens United*, which operated more like a voluntary association such as Habitat for Humanity, the World Wildlife Foundation, or the National Rifle Association. The distinction between its general treasury funds and its PAC money was therefore thin, if not nonexistent.

Even if we were to lump all entities using the corporate form together, important distinctions between them and unions nevertheless remain. The Court in its *Citizens United* opinion relied heavily on an assumption that unions and corporations are just two different forms of association, but in so doing it elided dispositive differences. The most important, as noted above, is the fact that while unions are permitted to spend the equivalent of their own general treasury funds on political activities, they are required by law to allow any member who does not share their political views to opt out. Indeed, for public unions, the Supreme Court has held that even an agency-fee arrangement violates the First Amendment rights of the employees.[91] An agency-fee arrangement has the effect of compelling a person "to *subsidize* the speech of other private speakers," and therefore "raises . . . First Amendment concerns."[92] Those First Amendment concerns were serious enough that the Court ruled that state and public-sector employers are forbidden from collecting agency fees from nonconsenting employees.[93] Thereafter, only the willing would be required to take part in any political activities.

The situation of those in the private sector is comparable. As noted earlier, under *Communication Workers of America v. Beck*,[94] bargaining-unit employees who do not wish to be union members are entitled to limit their agency fees to core collective-bargaining purposes. Put otherwise, they are entitled not to pay fees for the union's political activities. That puts them roughly in the same position as public-sector employees. The group that contributes to political speech is limited to those who agree with the message that is being delivered.

The role of PACs in this picture is also worth a mention. The *Citizens United* Court assumed that the PAC alternative is impermissibly burdensome, and so it was not enough to tell the company that it could finance the distribution of the *Hillary* film exclusively through the PAC. More recent experience does not bear out the Court's gloomy assessment. PACs abound in the political space. Data from the Federal Election Commission indicate that even before the 2024 races were over, PACs had raised $7.3 billion and spent $6 billion.[95] That is not a picture of a cumbersome, non-user-friendly device. Surely the time has come to knock aside that support beam from the *Buckley/Citizens United* edifice. Indeed, looking at the political landscape today, it is hard to think of a less realistic, more Ivory Tower statement.

Another area that cries out for reform is more empirical. How would *Citizens United* and similar cases have turned out if, instead of brushing off concerns about corruption both in the electoral process and in the subsequent job of governing, the Court had recognized the seriousness of this concern. It would be possible to study who gets to meet with congresspersons or executive-branch decisionmakers, how quickly telephone calls get returned, whose lobbyists' drafts make their way through committees and legislative counsel—and whose concerns never see the light of day. The role of money in our polity has become so huge that many politicians complain that all they ever do is raise funds—funds to support current campaigns, funds to pay off old campaign debts, funds to plan for future campaigns, funds for their parties, ad nauseam. Greater regulation of funds in the system would restore some time for genuine governing, to everyone's benefit.

On another note, it is regrettable that the Court gave such little weight to the equality costs of the *Citizens United* regime. It is hard to believe that the voice of someone who lacks the disposable income to make a political contribution, or whose budget permits only a modest donation of $100, will command the same attention from a candidate or a sponsor of an issue as the voice of someone who contributes millions. The Court was worried about somehow being required to "equalize" voices, but that may be exactly what the one person, one vote fundamental right requires. Or maybe, if the wealthy person wants to donate to support a cause and forgo the *quo* of a *quid pro quo*, one could imagine a mode of giving that creates a wall of anonymity between the donor and the campaign. If the money is given anonymously, the troublesome later influence, access, and even corruption would be far less likely.

Conclusion

The *Citizens United* decision did no favors for the integrity and effectiveness of the US electoral system. Its empirical assumptions remain shaky at best, and its legal foundation is full of holes. Campaign finance regulation that does not depend on content should satisfy any First Amendment test. Measures designed to assure equality of voice and absence of any tinge of corruption have passed scrutiny before, and they should pass scrutiny in this context. Disclosure—that is, "more speech"—has always been a favored way of reconciling First Amendment interests with others. Even without a constitutional earthquake, it should be possible to reform the campaign finance system along the lines discussed here. The work cannot begin too soon.

5

A Defense of *Buckley v. Valeo* and *Citizens United v. FEC*

Floyd Abrams

Q. Thank you, Floyd, for letting us ask you a question for this volume on campaign finance regulation and the First Amendment. This is a subject you know well, having been intimately involved with it at the level of litigation and at the level of overall analysis. We would like to invite you to reflect on that and on the other essays in this book. Perhaps it's best to put the question this way: Should the Supreme Court reaffirm its rulings in *Buckley v. Valeo* and *Citizens United v. Federal Election Commission*?

A. My short answer is that both are landmark First Amendment rulings to be celebrated as enduring protections of the First Amendment. The distinguished contributors to this book seem to disagree. Reading their submissions as a whole, they seem to me not to support adequate, let alone robust, First Amendment protection in the sensitive area of speech about elections and, indeed, public issues more generally. I do not think I am unfair in concluding that they view the First Amendment not as a protector of speech but as a problem to be overcome, since what they view as a too-protective reading of the First Amendment—the reading applied in both cases—would preclude the limitations on speech that were held unconstitutional in both cases.

My own views about the topic were formed many years ago. My experience began in 1972 with a statute limiting the funding of speech during a political campaign. I was a young partner then at Cahill Gordon & Reindel. The year before, our firm, working with Yale Law School Professor Alexander Bickel, had represented the *New York Times* in *New York Times Co. v. United States*,[1] informally known as the *Pentagon Papers* case. Bickel was the chief counsel to the *Times*, and I led a team of lawyers who worked with him defending the case. When it ended with our victory in the Supreme Court, we were retained by the *Times* to handle the bulk of pending and, we hoped, future constitutional litigation against it.

In May of the following year, I received a call from a lawyer at the *Times*. The paper had published a two-page paid advertisement urging the impeachment of then-President Richard Nixon based on the US bombing of Cambodia. The advertisement praised several members of Congress who had criticized the bombing. The *Times* had not been subpoenaed, I was told, but the entity that had placed the ad, the National Committee for Impeachment, had been, based on the then-new Federal Election Campaign Act of 1971. The government's theory was that the advertisement mentioned people who were running for office and who therefore might be viewed as a "political committee" subject to various limitations under the statute. The *Times* had not received any communication from the government, and so the questions I was asked were speculative: Might the *Times* itself be charged with an offense? How strong would a First Amendment defense be in such a case?

My responses, as I recall or imagine them now, were reassuring about the *Times*'s own exposure to legal risk. The notion that the newspaper could be held criminally liable for publishing the advertisement seemed fanciful even under the Nixon administration. More broadly, I opined that even a hostile Congress would not support doing so. Ultimately, the Second Circuit ruled in favor of the accused organization, concluding that the government's interpretation of the law "would be incompatible with the First Amendment."[2]

The following year, the ACLU sought injunctive and declaratory relief against the clerk of the House of Representatives challenging sections of the statute which imposed spending limits on candidates for federal office in the communications media. The case arose after the ACLU submitted a paid advertisement to the *Times* against the Nixon administration's opposition to court-imposed busing. The advertisement listed in an "honor roll" the names of 102 members of Congress who had previously opposed the Administration's anti-busing policy. Under the Federal Election Campaign Act of 1971, a publication could not lawfully publish an advertisement on behalf of a candidate without a certification from the candidate that the advertisement did not exceed statutorily established spending limits.

The ACLU refused to provide any such certification to the *Times*, which published the advertisement without it. The *Times* agreed that the ACLU could not be required to provide the certification, and I drafted an *amicus* brief saying so. In *ACLU v. Jennings*,[3] the Court held that the requirement of such certifications would violate the First Amendment and exempted the ACLU and other affected organizations from its scope.

These cases from half a century ago are not relics from a forgotten past. They greatly influenced the decision of the ACLU to support First Amendment challenges to the constitutionality of the statutes at issue in both *Buckley* and *Citizens United*—statutes that limited spending in elections and were held unconstitutional under the First Amendment for doing so. They also greatly influenced my own views on the topic and the brief I wrote and filed in the Supreme Court in *Citizens United* on behalf of Senator Mitch McConnell.

Both *Buckley* and *Citizens United* are firmly rooted in First Amendment principles. The Federal Election Campaign Act of 1971, as amended in 1974, significantly limited overall expenditures, limited what a candidate could spend on his or her campaign, and placed ultimate decision-making power in a governmental agency. The law was challenged in *Buckley* by an extraordinarily diverse collection of individuals and organizations: the New York Civil Liberties Union and the American Conservative Union, the Mississippi Republican Party and the Libertarian Party, individuals holding the most inconsistent views ranging from conservative Senator James Buckley to liberal Senator Eugene McCarthy. All wished to be heard saying that without adequate funding—the funding that Congress had criminalized—they could not be heard.

It is worth recalling what the much-criticized *Buckley* opinion said about the limitation on expenditures that Congress had enacted. Speaking broadly, as rulings protecting First Amendment rights tend to do, the Court concluded that a "restriction on the amount of money a person or group can spend on political communication during a campaign necessarily reduces the quantity of expression by restricting the number of issues discussed, the depth of their exploration, and the size of the audience reached."[4] That statement seems to me self-evidently correct. So, I think, is the more often quoted language that followed, and that I think critics of the Court's opinions on this topic should bear in mind. "[T]he concept," the opinion states,

> that government may restrict the speech of some elements in our society in order to enhance the relative voice of others is wholly foreign to the First Amendment, which was designed "to secure 'the widest possible dissemination of information from diverse and antagonistic sources,'" and "'to assure unfettered interchange of ideas for the bringing about of political and social changes desired by the people.'"[5]

The wisdom of that conclusion became even clearer when I began to devote a great deal of time to representing NBC. In doing so, I saw first-hand how the First Amendment is always at risk when the government is deeply involved in decision-making about what speech may be voiced and what not. Consider one of the most ambitious and ultimately dangerous efforts at equalizing the marketplace of speech: the brilliantly named but no less dangerous "fairness doctrine" formerly applicable to radio and television.

On its face, it had considerable appeal. How could it be anything but "fair" to require radio and television stations "to provide coverage of vitally important controversial issues of interest to the community served by [radio and TV] and to provide a reasonable opportunity for the presentation of contrasting viewpoints on such issues"?[6]

Yet after those requirements had been in effect for a number of years, the Federal Communications Commission summed up their impact by saying: "In sum, the fairness doctrine in operation disserves both the public's right to diverse sources of information and the broadcaster's interest in free expression. Its chilling effect thwarts its intended purposes, and it results in excessive and unnecessary governmental intervention into the editorial processes of broadcast journalists."[7]

I bear personal witness to that conclusion. For a number of years while I was a partner at Cahill Gordon, I saw the baleful effects of the doctrine on our client, NBC. As a journalistic enterprise, it sought conflicting views on a wide range of newsworthy events. But with the requirement to do so imposed by law and subject to constant overview by the FCC, a decision had to be made for each newscast about one story or another, always taking into account that the price of an interview with Senator C might be an interview with Senator Y, regardless of Senator Y's genuine newsworthiness.

Only years after the "fairness doctrine" was abandoned did we learn just how politicized its implementation had become. We now know that President Kennedy "approved a plan to coordinate fairness doctrine complaints to target radio stations that aired right wing editorials" and that President Nixon "worked with a conservative media watchdog group, Accuracy in Media, to bring fairness doctrine complaints against programs" critical of his administration.[8] Accuracy in Media was the very organization I had litigated against at NBC's expense for a number of years.

There is a lesson in this, and it sweeps well beyond the fairness doctrine. Government cannot be trusted to pass judgment on what speech shall be permitted and what not. The language in *Buckley* warning about allowing government to play the role of restricting "the speech of some elements in our society in order to enhance the relative voice of others" was prescient.[9] The language in *Citizens United* that the First Amendment was "premised on mistrust of government power" rings as true as when Justice Kennedy wrote it.[10]

PART III

Campaign Finance and Race

6
Race and Campaign Finance Deregulation

Abby K. Wood

Introduction

As the Supreme Court has deregulated campaign finance, white people have become even more overrepresented among political donors in the United States.[1] The racial wealth gap is widening, and campaign contributions—91% of which are from white people—have soared. All of this combines to create a situation in which voters of color suffer harm to their descriptive and political representation.[2]

Part of the Court's deregulation has opened the door to anonymous donating and spending in our elections. Voters suffer informational harms from this anonymity, and it is compounded by a general failure to require more transparency in online advertising. Some of these harms fall more heavily on voters of color, especially Black voters.

In this chapter, I summarize the disparate *representational* and *informational* harms from the Supreme Court's deregulation and the elected branches' failure to regulate in its wake. After describing the harms, I analyze the limited solutions that equality-minded reformers could attempt within our cramped campaign finance jurisprudence. Finally, I explain how changes to our jurisprudence could open the door to a more equitable campaign finance system.

Campaign Finance Deregulation Favors White People

To understand how campaign finance deregulation has systematically favored white people, one must understand its history. Congress started to regulate campaign finance with the Tillman Act in 1907, which banned corporate contributions. Over the next sixty-five years, regulations slowly accrued, restricting the uses of money in politics and requiring disclosure. But enforcement lagged until the Federal Election Campaigns Act (FECA) was amended in the wake of the Watergate scandal and President Nixon's resignation. FECA reformed campaign finance in two ways. First, it restricted campaign financing by setting limits on spending and contributions, requiring disclosure of donations and expenditures, and creating a fund for public financing of presidential campaigns. Second, it created an enforcement body, the Federal Elections Commission. As the ink dried on FECA, the Supreme Court decided *Buckley v. Valeo*,[3] which famously "constitutionalized" campaign finance in the United States, ruling that limits on campaign financing burden our First Amendment rights and are therefore reviewed under constitutional tiers of scrutiny. This decision called into question all restrictions on campaign financing everywhere in the country. Unsurprisingly, after holding that First Amendment scrutiny applies, *Buckley* struck down several of FECA's limits.

In the ensuing fifty years, deregulation by the courts has continued, despite periodic attempts by elected officials and state voters to refine campaign finance statutes to eliminate some of the biggest abuses of our largely private system. The most important decision of the last fifteen years was *Citizens United v. FEC*, which allowed corporations to make independent expenditures directly from their general treasuries. *Citizens United* was followed quickly by *SpeechNow v. FEC*, which ruled that limits on the amounts of donations to groups who make only independent expenditures were unconstitutional. There have been several other important deregulation decisions in the years since, related to public financing regimes, candidate loan reimbursement, and aggregate spending limits. The Supreme Court did not have to constitutionalize campaign finance jurisprudence; by declaring money in politics to be protected "speech" and "association," the Court set up decades of court-mandated deregulation.[4]

All of this deregulation favors white people. On average, white households hold more wealth than non-white households. The typical white household has nearly ten times more wealth than the typical Black household.[5] Therefore, the people who are most likely to enjoy the benefits of deregulation established in *Buckley* are overwhelmingly wealthy—and white. In fact, non-Latino white people donate 91% of all campaign contributions.[6] The flood of white money to campaigns creates *representational harms* for voters of color, who are less likely to be represented either descriptively (by candidates or incumbents of color) or politically (by having their policies advanced by elected officials).

The gaps in the disclosure regime that are a byproduct of the deregulation described above create *informational harms.* Informational harms reduce a voter's knowledge about a candidate. These harms come from so-called "dark money," as I will describe below. Dark money is probably also associated with disinformation, which creates separate (and very direct) informational harms. Disinformation is disproportionately targeted to Black people, in particular. Finally, failure to require disclosure of targeting criteria for political ads run on social media deprives all voters of important information. It may likewise hurt Black voters—those most likely to be targeted with disinformation—more than other groups of voters. In the next part, I explain the representational and informational harms.

Campaign Finance Deregulation and Representational Harms

Buckley's legacy of deregulation exacerbates racial inequality by advantaging the white and wealthy, while setting up structural challenges to representation for voters of color. These racial inequities in campaign contributions create certain *representational harms.*

Figure 6.1, from Aneja et al. (2022), illustrates how the racial wealth gap grows over time, as each cycle of unlimited campaign financing by wealthy (white) people leads to white-dominated politics and reduced descriptive and substantive representation for people of color. We observe a sizable gap in campaign contributions along racial lines. Donors tend to give, and candidates to receive, within their racial group.[7] Because early money matters in campaigns,[8] the dominance of white donors means that white candidates are more likely to be selected as the party's candidate in the primary stage, or, absent a primary, for the general election. That fact (combined with gerrymandering resulting in vote dilution for voters of color) helps explain the relative paucity of elected officials of color, a problem of descriptive representation for voters of color.

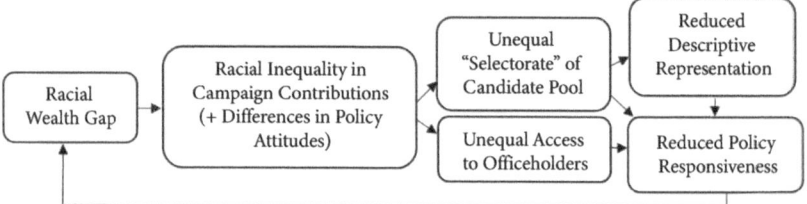

Figure 6.1 The flow of racial wealth inequality through our campaign finance, electoral, and policymaking systems. Donating, running for office, voting, making claims on elected officials, and influencing policymaking are all forms of political participation.

In addition to the inherent benefits of a diverse and representative congressional pool, descriptive representation has been linked by existing political-science scholarship to substantive representation of policy interests in Congress.[9] Americans hold differing preferences over policy issues, some of which follow racial lines (*see* Figure 6.2). We also know that incumbents tend to grant meetings to donors over non-donors, *and*—unsurprisingly, given access differentials—that incumbents tend to misapprehend their donors' preferences to be their constituents' preferences. Misalignment between the interests of candidates and constituents occurs when outsize access and influence over candidate policy decisions from a wealthy, white minority can bias policy choices away from the median voter of a district.[10] Risk of misalignment is especially salient when donors contribute to campaigns for seats they themselves cannot vote for.[11] When policies are skewed in favor of (white) donor preferences, they exacerbate the wealth gap, perpetuating the cycle depicted in Figure 6.1.

Donation inequality along racial lines far outstrips even the underrepresentation of minority populations in Congress and outstrips gaps in voter-participation rates. Racial disparities in the donor class of the same relative magnitude exist in federal and state races. They are also replicated in donations to "outside groups" such as PACs and super PACs.[12] Across the campaign finance landscape, racial inequality is pervasive and endemic.

Despite these representational harms, the Courts reject the government's interest in "leveling the playing field" between rich and poor candidates—even outside of the racial context—as insufficiently compelling to survive constitutional scrutiny.[13] At this point, the only state interest in limits or bans

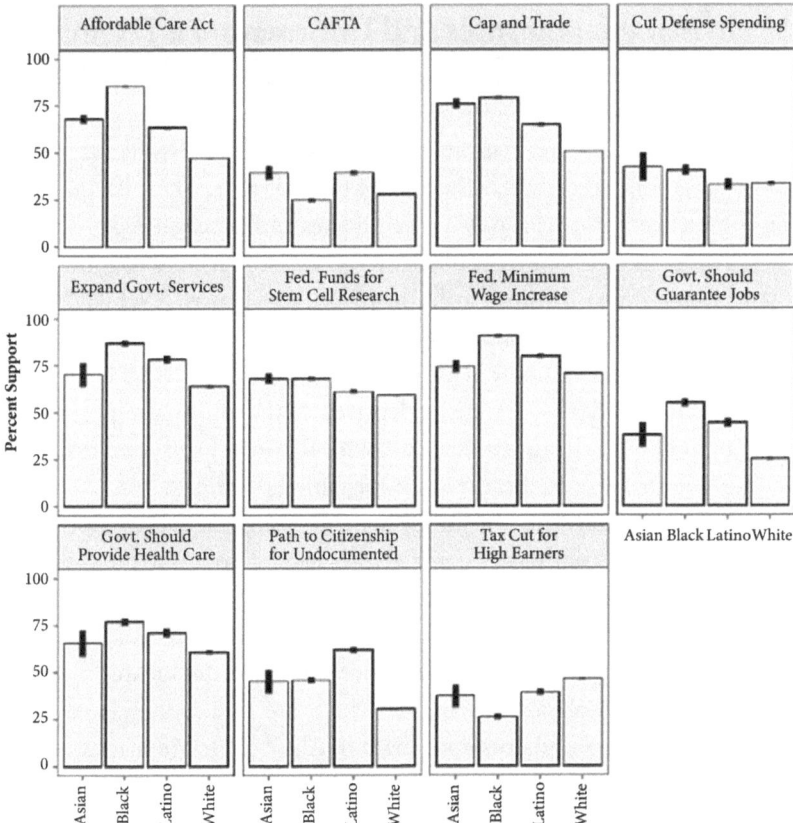

Figure 6.2 Policy attitudes vary significantly by race. Plot shows average support for policies by racial group, along with 95% confidence intervals. Government job guarantee, government health care, and expanded government services questions are from the American National Election Study (1992–2016). All other questions are from the Collaborative Congressional Election Study (2006–2014).

Source: Aneja et al. (2022). Across all policies, the difference in policy support from Black and white Americans is statistically significant ($p < 0.05$).

in campaign finance that the court deems compelling is the interest in reducing *quid pro quo* corruption or its appearance—in other words, preventing bribery. This is a cramped view of the compelling reasons that governments and voters might want to limit campaign financing in their jurisdictions. The Supreme Court's rejection of the equality rationale has exacerbated representational harms for voters of color *and* exacerbated the racial wealth gap.

Missing Disclosures and Informational Harms

Informational harms from missing disclosures result from the combination of campaign finance deregulation and the political branches' failure to fully mandate disclosure even where the court would allow it. These harms deprive voters of relevant information about candidates and issues on the ballot.

In the years since *Buckley*, the Supreme Court has upheld disclosure laws in most opinions, even those that strike down limits and bans.[14] While *Buckley v. Valeo* upheld FECA's disclosure provisions, the opinion expresses concern that certain groups might be more harmed by disclosure than others. The Court has recognized that, under FECA, being deprived of the information provided in campaign finance disclosures is a legally cognizable injury sufficient to establish standing. In other words, it causes an informational harm.[15]

The Court is correct that the public benefits from campaign finance disclosure. Empirical research shows that the information contained in disclosures helps predict how an elected official will vote,[16] that voters use campaign finance information revealed in disclosures as a heuristic to guide their vote choice,[17] that voters react to information contained in disclosures,[18] and that campaign finance violations (many of which are disclosure-related), when made public, cost incumbents vote share.[19] All of these are measures of the *informational benefit* of campaign finance disclosure.[20]

Informational harms result when voters are deprived of the informational benefits they should expect in a well-ordered democracy. Yet these harms are everywhere today. Gaps in campaign finance disclosure regulations reduce the transparency and accountability of our political campaigns, making it more difficult for voters to make informed choices.[21] In this Part, I focus on three informational harms from regulatory gaps. One is "dark money," which emerged with the failure to regulate disclosure after the Court eliminated a ban on corporate independent spending in *Citizens United* and *SpeechNow*. The second concerns the absence of mandated disclosure of campaign advertising targets on social media. This second informational harm, unlike dark money, is not a direct result of the court's deregulatory opinions. However, the constitutionalization of campaign finance jurisprudence and the deregulation that has followed probably complicate states' efforts to make targeting more transparent (like broadcast advertising). The third harm is related to both dark money and the lack of targeting disclosure: disinformation. Disinformation causes direct informational harms to voters.

To discuss these harms, I first describe the court's creation of dark money. I then return to the focus on disproportionate racial harms, explaining how informational harms intersect with targeting. Informational harms are probably worse for voters of color—especially Black voters—who we know are more likely to be targeted with disinformation messaging, much of which is created and spread using anonymous donors' money.

Citizens United and *SpeechNow* created the conditions for a vast flood of anonymous money into our politics. They allowed a new category of donors—corporations—to make expenditures directly from their treasuries. Those corporations claimed that they were not required to disclose their donors, and they have not suffered legal consequences for not disclosing them. This phenomenon is called "dark money." Dark money leads to "gray money" when groups that are required to disclose their donors, such as super PACs, receive donations from dark-money groups, obscuring the sources of some (or most) of the gray-money groups' donations.

Today, a lot of the money in our election campaigns, along with almost all the money spent on issue ads, is fully or partly anonymous. In the 2024 federal election campaign, outside groups spent over $4.5 billion, and over half of that money was from dark-money or gray-money sources.[22] Only 37.1% of outside money spent to support or oppose candidates was from fully disclosed donors.[23] Outside money is a major factor in our campaigns: In 2024, outside spending surpassed combined campaign spending in fifty-six races—or nearly 12% of the 469 federal seats that Americans voted on.[24]

It doesn't have to be this way, of course. The persistence of dark money and gray money is a policy choice. In the wake of *Citizens United*, several agencies, including the FEC, the SEC, and even the IRS, could have regulated disclosure of the new political spending by corporations (including LLCs and 501(c)(4) social-welfare organizations). Senate Republicans placed a rider in the FY 2016 appropriations bill requiring that the SEC and IRS not use their appropriations to mandate transparency of campaign financing spent by corporations.[25] It has been continuously included in our omnibus bills since 2016, even when Democrats had control of both houses.[26] There is now a quiet bipartisan agreement to maintain anonymity for corporate campaign speech.[27]

Dark money and disclosed money are different in terms of donors and speech. Due to the hidden data problem inherent in dark money, it is difficult to quantify how different the politics are between people contributing anonymously and those giving disclosed contributions. One recent study used data that had been revealed during litigation in California to show that people who opt into dark-money avenues of political donations do so in ways that are, indeed, different from their disclosed donations.[28]

Differences also exist on the expenditure side. Expenditures by dark-money groups are qualitatively different from expenditures from groups that disclose their donors. Jain and Wood found that political advertising in the 2018 US election cycle sponsored by dark money was more negative than ads with disclosed donors.[29] We also know that there is a link between negative political advertisements and disinformation, ads with disinformation tending to be more negative.

Dark Money and Disinformation

Disinformation lies to or misleads the voter. This is a separate informational harm, which is unlikely to be remedied by law, given restrictions on content-based regulation.[30] Dark money and disinformation share commonalities. Dark-money advertising is more negative than transparent advertising. Disinformation tends to be more negative than truthful advertising. Together, these facts suggest that disinformation is most likely to emanate from non-disclosed sources, since dark-money ads are more negative than ads with disclosed donors. Because of data limitations, however, scholars have not yet established a link between dark money and disinformation.

Social-Media Advertising: Target Secrecy

We now turn to another form of nondisclosure as an informational harm: social-media targeting nondisclosure. This harm, unlike informational harms from dark money, does not flow directly from *Citizens United* and *SpeechNow*; however, the deregulatory environment has made it difficult to convince lawmakers and regulators to require targeting disclosure.

It is no secret that campaigns want to target their messages to particular audiences. Targets are typically based on various demographic and consumer information. Before the era of social media, most targeted campaign messages were aimed at broad swaths of voters. For example, when campaigns have run ads on broadcast radio or television, they target all viewers or listeners of the shows during which the ads air. And those targets are public knowledge, since the FCC requires disclosure in its publicly available Political File.

Enter social media, microtargeted ads, and target secrecy. Microtargeting allows advertisers to target vanishingly small portions of social media users. Microtargeting is, of course, cost-effective for the advertiser. Some uses are quite benign, but others carry unique risks of political divisiveness.[31] No law requires that targets for political ads on social media be disclosed or otherwise identifiable, no matter how large or small the targeted audience.

The democratic risks from the status quo of social-media political advertising are twofold. First, where microtargeting is used, accountability for toxic or divisive speech is minimized because the audience is so small.[32] The second risk of microtargeted political advertising is related: if disinformation is spread and its targets are not publicly identifiable, there is no chance to reach the recipients of disinformation to correct the record. Counterspeech—the court's preferred remedy for disinformation[33]—is impossible.

Decision-makers of all political stripes may be reluctant to regulate themselves out of a useful tool or to force disclosure of their social-media advertising targets.[34] But disclosure of those targets would mitigate informational harms. First, voters would learn whether campaigns speak differently to different audiences, perhaps revealing that campaigns contradict themselves when they think no one will notice. Second, having targets available would allow for the correction of disinformation (another informational harm) via counterspeech.

To summarize: the informational benefits of campaign finance are well established in the literature, and so-called dark money creates informational harms by depriving voters of that information. Dark-money ads are more negative than ads that have disclosed donors, and ads containing disinformation are more negative than factually accurate ads.[35] Political advertising on social media, with its microtargeting and target secrecy, creates additional harms. These harms affect all voters.

I now turn to discuss the ways these harms disproportionately burden voters of color.

Informational Harms Burden Voters of Color Disproportionately

After political party, race is the most important widely available or inferable criterion for voter outreach. In some cases, it actually surpasses party identification in importance. This is especially true for Black voters, who traditionally favor the Democratic Party by large margins.[36] Black voters are therefore targets for both turnout efforts (from Democrats) and suppression efforts (from their opponents).

Targeting voters by race is easy. Though most platforms claim that they do not allow targeting by race, they do allow "look-alike" targeting, which asks the platform to target people whose data and use patterns look like those on a list provided by the advertiser. Similarly, advertisers can target users of consumer goods associated with Black hair, alumni of HBCUs, and individuals identifiable by similar indicators.

Race-based targeting is not necessarily a problem for democracy. Some messages and messengers appeal more to audiences of certain races, so finding those audiences can be an efficient way for a campaign to shore up support.[37] Targeting by language group makes sense, too, for campaigns that want to reach communities in languages other than English. However, as I will discuss next, targeting along racial lines is all too often used to spread disinformation, suppress votes, and harass people of color, especially Black people.

In 2016, Russian disinformation was disproportionately targeted to Black voters, who, at only 12.7% of the population, "accounted for over 38% of US-focused Facebook ads purchased by the Russian Internet Research Agency and almost half of the user clicks."[38] The Senate Intelligence Committee concluded that Black voters were the group most frequently targeted by "Russian operatives and troll farms." They received messages like "Our Votes Don't Matter" and "Why Would We Be Voting"[39] often from users in so-called "digital Blackface."[40] In addition to the voter-suppression harms, these are clear informational harms suffered disproportionately by Black voters. Similar messages also emanated from dark-money sources, compounding the informational harm.[41]

Black Americans are not alone in being targeted by disinformation. Targeting immigrants with disinformation is another common tactic.[42] According to a founder of the Spanish-language fact-checking group Factchequeado, "disinformation efforts often hinge on topics most important to each community, whether that is public safety, immigration, abortion, education, inflation or alleged extramarital affairs."[43] In the United States, this disinformation operates as a voter-suppression tactic, feeding into "justifiable concerns that the system is stacked against" communities of color.[44]

We can now view the representational and informational harms from deregulating campaign finance using a racial lens. As discussed above, white people are overrepresented in the donor class. If these white donors are disproportionately "speaking" in ads that are targeted to Black voters and immigrant communities, the representational harms discussed above exacerbate the informational harms just discussed if any of the following is true: (1) the ads are funded by dark money (the white donors are anonymous), (2) the ads contain disinformation, or (3) the targets are not disclosed.

Legal Recourse to Address These Harms Under the Current System

In this brief section, I explain why some of these harms are hard to address under the current system.

Remedying representational harms

Despite the clear relationships between deregulation, inequality in donations, and representational harms, legal recourse through the courts has proved difficult, though not impossible. One approach focuses on leveraging existing Equal Protection doctrine, an uphill battle with a narrow path to success. Another approach, likely to be slightly more fruitful, would require a novel argument under the Voting Rights Act (VRA). But the best bet would be legislative: a strong and generous public-financing program would be upheld by the courts as long as it didn't run afoul of existing jurisprudence. All these arguments are covered at length in my 2022 article with Abhay Aneja and Jake Grumbach,[45] but I will summarize them very briefly here.

Equal Protection—The Equal Protection clause of the 14th Amendment guarantees equal protection under the law. This includes the equal right to vote, and scholars' opinions are divided on whether it also includes equal right to participate (including via campaign finance).[46] The Supreme Court has struck down several laws that erect barriers to the act of voting, such as poll taxes,[47] high candidate-filing fees,[48] and vote dilution.[49] The vote-dilution case that is closest to our set of concerns is *White v. Regester*, in which a large voting district in Texas was ruled unconstitutional because it diluted the Mexican American vote. The Court, in language that resonates with our argument, said that "economic realities of the [minority] community" prevented plaintiffs from "effective participation in political life."[50] The district-court opinion is even more in line with our concerns, saying that "[t]he lower court readily acknowledged the resource disadvantage faced by Black and Latino voters, and the existence of 'radically unequal expense' problems for minority candidates. A change in Texas's electoral system was thus necessary to provide minority votes with 'the opportunity to participate effectively in the political process.'"[51]

Successful Equal Protection challenges require a finding of state action. While the canonical modes of state action are legislation and regulation, there are cases that have taken a more creative approach.[52] *Terry v. Adams*, a challenge to the so-called "white primary" in Texas, lacked a majority rationale but contained language from Justice Clark that "any 'part of the machinery for choosing officials' becomes subject to the constitution's restraints."[53] Scholars have posited that another route to an Equal Protection claim is grounded in "state neglect" having ripened into action.[54] This argument has had limited success before the courts.[55]

VRA—Litigants might also bring a claim under Section 2 of the VRA for vote denial or vote dilution. These are, again, unlikely to succeed under current jurisprudence, even though the VRA is based in discriminatory results rather than discriminatory intent. The VRA has twin goals of equal participation and fair and effective representation. States cannot achieve these goals if the court takes a narrow view of participation and representation as only involving voting, ignoring the financing and nominating of candidates that determine our vote choices.[56]

The Court approaches Section 2 in two phases. First, it requires that some preconditions be met.[57] Then, the Court conducts a "totality of the circumstances" test based on nine factors in a Senate report.[58] We focus in our argument on Factors Four and Nine. Under Factor Four, plaintiffs could argue that deregulated campaign finance excludes minorities from the candidate-slating process, because candidates of color are unable to participate in the "wealth primary." Under Factor Nine, plaintiffs could argue that deregulated campaign finance schemes reduce political responsiveness by elected officials to the particularized needs of members of the minority group. These arguments are closely tied to the descriptive-representation and political-representation harms described above.

Public Financing—Public-financing programs can help equalize campaign financing along wealth and racial lines. While several types exist, it is voucher programs, in which each registered voter receives a certain number of vouchers to assign to candidates, that align best with states' equality goals. Public-financing programs are relatively rare and change over time, so they are difficult to study. Nevertheless, available studies suggest that public financing can increase the number of donors to campaigns,[59] the number of candidates running for office,[60] and political competition.[61] The potential of these programs to increase financial inclusion for donors (and possibly candidates) along racial lines, as the programs in New York City and Seattle have apparently done, seems promising.[62] To succeed, these programs must be generous enough to encourage all, or almost all, candidates to opt in to using them.

Public-financing programs have been challenged, sometimes successfully, on constitutional grounds. To stay on the constitutional side of public-financing design, such programs should observe a few rules of thumb. First, they should be entirely voluntary. Second, they should not refer to equality as a driving purpose, but should instead focus on reducing *quid pro quo* corruption or its appearance. Third, they should not boost campaigns with fewer resources against campaigns with more resources or even outside group support. Fourth, if they require candidates to voluntarily agree to spending and contribution limits, as most do, the programs seem to be allowed to have "escape hatches" from those limits in the case of massive independent expenditures against the publicly funded candidates.[63]

Informing Candidates of Constituency Preferences—One of the representational harms we observe is that access to donors leads elected officials to misunderstand their constituencies' preferences. Elmendorf and Wood have brainstormed ways to solve this informational problem. One solution is providing them constituency-level voting preferences. Another is a twist on the public-financing voucher programs in which donations themselves are both anonymous (to reduce subsequent microtargeting) and geographically geocoded (to help inform overall constituency preferences).[64]

Remedying Informational Harms

The informational harms from donor anonymity and failure to disclose advertising targets can be resolved with either legislation or regulation (or both). All we need for donor disclosure is for Congress to remove the appropriations rider that both parties have maintained for around a decade—a tall order! The entities running campaign ads paid for by non-disclosed donors should be required to register with the FEC and disclose donor information.

When it comes to informational harms from disinformation, the government's hands are rightly tied in terms of content regulation.[65] Where registered groups produce ads containing disinformation, the government cannot censor or require platforms to censor. That is why advertising target disclosure is crucial to our democratic discourse: we can't counterspeak without knowing who received the message in the first place. All registered entities running ads on social media should be required to either disclose their targeting criteria or make their lists of targets re-targetable (anonymously so) for the purposes of counterspeech.[66]

Where ads or speech exist outside the reach of campaign finance regulators, the solutions become more difficult. In the case of foreign meddling, a government solution related to campaign finance is unlikely, and proposals for our government security apparatus are beyond the scope of this chapter. Where disinformative speech is unpaid—for example, speech by an online influencer with a large following—campaign finance regulation is no help. Private solutions for informational harms from disinformation include innovations such as X's Community Notes to combat disinformation and options to report abuse and threats, where relevant.

Sometimes the initial speech is created outside the reach of regulators, but is then amplified with paid bots. California now requires disclosure of the use of bots for political speech, and the payments themselves can bring a campaign under the jurisdiction of a regulator. When paid bots violate platforms' terms of service, the platforms should enforce their terms of service against those users.

Table 6.1 summarizes the deregulations discussed, the phenomena and harms that result, whether those harms fall along racial lines, and whether we can solve the harms under the current jurisprudence.

In a Perfect World

Let us now imagine that our silly state of jurisprudential affairs does not exist, and that instead we live in a world in which the people and their elected officials can regulate campaign finance with fewer judicial constraints. In this perfect world, the court has either abandoned its insistence that money in politics is protected by the First Amendment or broadened its view into what state interests are compelling enough to justify campaign finance regulation and survive First Amendment scrutiny.

If the court had never "constitutionalized" campaign finance, the money in campaigns could simply be considered property and regulated as such.

Table 6.1 Description of deregulatory actions, the phenomena and harms that result, whether harms burden voters of color, and whether we can resolve them under current jurisprudence.

Deregulation/Failure to regulate	Phenomenon	Harm	Does harm fall more heavily on people of color?	Solvable under current jurisprudence?
SCOTUS lifts limits on spending and outside-group donations, says equality is not a compelling reason to regulate	Age of big money, in which white donors dominate and candidates of color are less likely to be nominated	Descriptive representation Political representation/alignment	Yes	Only with (1) an aggressive reading of VRA or (2) a nationwide public financing program so attractive that all campaigns opt in.
SCOTUS rules that access and influence are not corruption (and therefore not compelling reasons to regulate).	Donors get more access to elected officials than non-donors; elected officials' sense of constituent preferences aligns more closely to donor than constituent preferences.	Political representation/alignment	Yes	Probably not, though informing elected officials of constituency-level policy preferences can correct this.
SCOTUS decides Citizens United, then Congress blocks disclosure regulations.	Dark money and gray money enter the campaign finance system.	Informational harm (knowing who donates to campaigns matters)	Not clear. We don't know whether voters of color see disproportionate amounts of dark-money ads.	Yes, by lifting appropriations rider and requiring disclosure.

continued

Table 6.1 *continued*

Deregulation/Failure to regulate	Phenomenon	Harm	Does harm fall more heavily on people of color?	Solvable under current jurisprudence?
Regulators fail to require disclosure of targets for social-media ads.	Microtargeting continues.	Informational harm (knowing how campaigns target subgroups would inform voters)	Yes, insofar as Black voters are probably most likely to be targeted by race	Yes
Dark money plus nondisclosure of targeting probably encourage disinformation to flourish.	It's multicausal, but disinformation flourishes.	Informational harm (being served direct disinformation, even when not seeking information, is harmful)	Yes, especially for Black voters, who are disproportionately targeted	If dark money is disclosed and targets are transparent, disinformation may decrease. Disinformation from non-registered speakers remains.

Campaign finance laws would have a much higher chance of surviving judicial review. Of course, incumbents might write laws to protect themselves from challengers, and courts would have to develop doctrines to help prevent such incumbency-protection regimes. But courts have long handled situations like this, including in a line of cases aimed at ensuring that contribution limits are not too low.[67]

Even in the world in which campaign financing is a First Amendment matter, the Court has wrongly rejected the equality rationale. States had cited that rationale for decades in their campaign finance laws. Despite what a handful of Supreme Court justices believe, equality is important in a democracy, and working toward it is a compelling governmental interest. Similarly, preventing distortions of politics by corporations is a compelling interest. Constraining undue influence over politicians and policy from wealthy donors is another. Ensuring political alignment between elected officials and voters is similarly compelling. The Court's cramped view that the only compelling interest for limits and bans is the prevention of a single kind of corruption is, frankly, absurd.

Either of these changes would have made it likely that the challenged campaign finance laws would survive judicial scrutiny. The massive growth in independent expenditures would not have occurred. Dark money would not exist. Corporations would be restricted to limited amounts of disclosed spending via separate segregated funds.

From a policy perspective, public-financing programs, which are already available, could be strengthened. Under the current jurisprudence, they would have to be voluntary. In many countries, public financing is mandatory and is channeled through strong party systems. A comparison of the relative merits of voluntary versus mandatory public financing is beyond the scope of this brief chapter; however, several countries with mandatory public financing enjoy vibrant speech environments, so it seems possible to achieve both.[68]

Disclosure would be strengthened through elimination of dark money and disclosure of large contributions for issue ads. Any advertising targets would be disclosed and available for counterspeech. And that counterspeech would undoubtedly be needed, because a perfect world does not involve content restrictions from government! Disinformation would continue to exist.

Conclusion

The perfect world sounds nice. Reviving the equality rationale would allow policies such as public financing and limits on campaign financing to persist. With equality as a goal and campaign finance regulations written to support that goal, the flow of events described in Figure 6.1 would become less extreme over time, policy and descriptive representation for voters of color would improve, and informational harms would be reduced for all voters. This suggests a much better place to live than the one described in this chapter. The unraveling of *Buckley v. Valeo* could lead to improved racial equality in our politics.

PART IV

Recommendations for Legislation on Campaign Finance Reform

7

Money Talks, Dark Money Whispers
How Anonymous, Unlimited Political Spending Is Corrupting American Democracy

Sheldon Whitehouse

"Campaign finance" is such a bland term, so bland it practically turns off the brain. But that bland term describes the mechanism that defines America's balance of political power—who gets listened to in American elections. In just two decades, far-right billionaires and polluters have disrupted that balance of power, secretively, to their great advantage and to the peril of a democracy that is supposed to hear regular voters.

When I first ran for the Senate, the best a billionaire or corporate CEO could do for a candidate was to "max out" with a $5,000 contribution from an ordinary corporate PAC whose donors were disclosed, "max out" personally with a disclosed donation, and host a fundraiser that "bundled" limited individual and PAC checks from employees and friends, all also disclosed. It was very difficult to get the total number raised into the hundreds of thousands of dollars. Candidates would of course be grateful, but in a race that cost millions of dollars such donations would not be determinative.

Today, a billionaire or a corporate entity can make a political donation in any amount; launder it through one or more 501(c)(4)s, which don't have to disclose donors; and land it in a super PAC that only discloses the identity of the final intermediary group. Now, with its identity hidden, the special interest can launch the super PAC with $10 million or $50 million or $100 million dollars into an advertising campaign to attack the candidate's opponent or support the candidate (usually the former). In supporting a candidate, they can even use film clips that candidates have posted for that purpose on the candidate's

Sheldon Whitehouse, *Money Talks, Dark Money Whispers*. In: *Money, Politics, and the First Amendment.*
Edited by: Lee C. Bollinger and Geoffrey R. Stone, Oxford University Press. © Oxford University Press (2026).
DOI: 10.1093/9780197821947.003.0008

own campaign website. How much attention from the political class do you think goes to someone willing and able to trigger that kind of massive political artillery to elect or defeat a candidate?

It's a whole new world. It also concentrates power in party leaders. Rather than go to the trouble of setting up a super PAC, big donors can go to super PACs already set up by party leaders in Congress, drop in $50 million (with the donor's identity laundered away), and let the party leader deploy the funding in key battleground races. Members of the House or Senate who think of crossing a big donor can expect a call from leadership: "I need you not to do that. It would interfere with our ability to defend our incumbents and defeat our opponents. You'd be hurting your colleagues and condemning us to the minority. We need that money."

One solution is my DISCLOSE Act, which would require disclosure of the identity of the true donor behind any spending over $10,000 in a political race.[1] Republicans block that bill every time we try to pass it,[2] so Democrats have to play by these horrible rules as well, making both parties participants in the corroded system. Without that kind of disclosure, we're left to the worst kind of world, in which those who seek the most from the political system and have the most to spend to achieve their goals get even more power. The greediest and most powerful get more power to slake their greed, and it's all hidden from view. Big interests that want deregulation, polluters with a pollute-for-free business model, billionaires who want to pay no taxes—all of them can come and feast anonymously.

For those at the feast, it's a bargain. The Trump tax cuts sent over a trillion dollars to the richest individuals and the biggest corporations.[3] Republicans blocking climate legislation protect a fossil-fuel industry subsidy running over $600 billion dollars a year, just in the United States.[4] For billionaires and big polluters, their most profitable investments are now their investments in politics.

This disruption of the balance of power has largely been hidden. The special-interest–fueled attack and realignment came through three main vectors. One was to disable the Federal Election Commission by stacking it with a bloc of appointees dedicated to frustrating its mission by stopping its work.[5] Don't authorize investigations; don't bring cases; don't update rules; prevent anything from happening. No repeal of FEC authorities by Congress occurred, no new legislation was debated and passed, no policy change from Congress was required: just quiet and deliberate evisceration of the agency from the inside.

The shell remains intact; the life of the agency has died. A regular voter could visit Washington, see the FEC building still there, and imagine an agency at work protecting our elections, but the joke would be on them.

The second vector has been the long campaign to capture and control the Supreme Court, similar to the capture and control by 19th-century railroad barons of the commissions that set their rates. There's a whole body of economic and administrative-law scholarship on "regulatory capture" (sometimes called "agency capture"), so I won't dwell on it.[6] Plus, I've written a book on the scheme through which the capture of the Court was accomplished.[7] Suffice it to say here that the new dark turn was accomplished by billionaires and polluters using well-known tactics to capture not just administrative agencies but courts themselves, even the Supreme Court.

The third vector was to open our elections to unlimited dark money and create an enormous archipelago of entities designed to facilitate hiding who was behind that money flow: 501(c)(4)s, now usually twinned with virtually indistinguishable 501(c)(3)s; entities like Donors Trust that exist entirely to launder away donor identities; super PACs, foul beasts that didn't exist when I was first elected to the Senate but now stalk every major election; and a vast array of performative front groups that broadcast to the public the message of the special-interest billionaire elite. The front groups commonly have benign and happy-sounding names—lots of "Freedom" and "Heritage," "Heartland" and "Enterprise," and much unauthorized arrogating of proud names from our American political history.

That vast archipelago of corrupting infrastructure was created as a direct result of the *Citizens United* decision,[8] a decision which was itself a product of the Court-capture scheme. Each year since that January 2010 decision, elections have become more expensive and less transparent. Dark-money groups have poured more than $2.6 billion into federal elections since *Citizens United*.[9] Billionaire political spending has increased by a factor of seventy, from $17 million for the 2008 election to $1.2 billion for 2020.[10] They didn't spend that money for nothing. A massive political power shift to secretive, creepy billionaires has resulted, a shift that also of course empowered all their phony front groups.

Citizens United shows a Court bending over backward to reach that result, a signal of intent that is in turn a signal of influence. The signals were several.

First was the appalling sloppiness of equating money with speech. The two are not the same. Money can certainly be used to amplify the effectiveness and impact of speech, but that doesn't make it speech. Gunfire can be used to amplify the effectiveness and impact of speech, but that doesn't mean you can reasonably call gunfire "speech" and forbid regulating it. To say "Give me your purse" to someone is one thing; to say "Give me your purse" while holding a gun to someone's head is completely different.

The Declaration of Independence was definitely speech, but it likely would not have accomplished independence on its own. The effectiveness and impact of that incident of speech was definitely amplified by revolutionary cannons and muskets, but it would be insane to say that cannon fire and rifle fire represent protected First Amendment speech that Congress can't regulate. Similarly, while money can amplify the effectiveness and impact of speech, it can also bribe, corrupt, improperly influence, bully, silence, drown out, and distort, among a host of evil results.

Second was the avoidance of any originalist discussion by the right-wing majority—supposedly avowed originalists—when equating corporations with people, a result that would have astounded the Founding Fathers. It took the minority dissent to point out that corporations are not equal to people in the Constitution for purposes of political speech, and that the Founders would have been horrified at unlimited corporate spending against We, the actual People.[11] At the Founding, corporations were few, rare, and regarded with grave suspicion. But for the right-wing Justices, originalism is a doctrine of convenience, employed selectively to achieve their desired result, and this was not a moment for originalism.

Third, as I wrote in a recent law review article, was the way *Citizens United* reached its desired result by making up its own facts.[12] That's not the proper role of any appellate court in our system of justice. Facts are found at the trial court. The adversary process between contesting parties—conducted in an open and potentially lengthy trial and motions process, supervised by a neutral judge, and with possible review to correct error—is designed to winnow out falsehoods. In *Citizens United*, the majority didn't just break the rule about where facts should be found; they also outright ignored robust lower court and congressional factual records that were available to them in the places where facts *should* be found. Congress in particular had compiled a voluminous record of evidence about the corrupting effects of money in elections, as had various courts.[13] The Court ignored all that, making up its own facts in secret as it prepared the decision. Worst of all, the facts the *Citizens United* majority made up through this improper exercise are demonstrably false.

Two false facts stand out. First, the Court asserted that there was no risk of corruption, or even appearance of corruption, because all this new corporate spending would be "independent" from campaigns.[14] We know that's a joke, as has been well documented by Campaign Legal Center and others.[15] Second, and even worse, the Court claimed that all this new political spending would also be "transparent," so voters would know who is speaking to them and could evaluate the source.[16] Billions of dollars in dark money spent in the years since are galling proof of that being false.

These false facts were not idle; they were essential to the logic of the decision. To keep Congress away from regulating the massive new spending that the majority had unleashed, the majority had to pretend that the unlimited spending would not be corrupting (if it were corrupting, Congress could obviously regulate it). "Independence" and "transparency" were the two false predicates that got them across that bar as they crafted the decision.

If the *Citizens United* majority didn't know those facts were false back then, they knew it soon thereafter. In *American Tradition Partnership, Inc. v. Bullock*, Senator John McCain and I wrote an *amicus* brief pointing out to the justices that both their "independence" and "transparency" predicates were plainly (and by then indisputably) false.[17] But the justices didn't care; indeed, they didn't even allow argument. The false facts had gotten them to the result they wanted, and those were not to be disturbed. It was one of the saddest, darkest moments in my public life when I heard that decision. My heart fell; the Court's refusal even to hear argument in the case brought me to the horrified conclusion that what I was seeing was a deliberate scheme, not an innocent error.

As evidence mounts daily of more and more corrupting dark money pouring into our elections, the Supreme Court has stubbornly refused to reexamine the false facts upon which it propped *Citizens United*, despite ample opportunity to do so. I would add that there is an unpleasant correlation between the dark money that the decision unleashed and the dark-money forces that got so many Federalist Society justices onto the Court.[18]

Indeed, if you want a specific example of corruption, look at how fossil-fuel dark money stopped Congress from passing any serious bipartisan climate legislation. I was in the Senate in 2007, 2008, and 2009, before *Citizens United*, when the Senate was working on several strong, bipartisan climate bills.[19] John McCain ran for president as the Republican nominee in 2008 with a serious climate platform.[20] Then in January 2010 came *Citizens United*, and that bipartisan work all died instantly. No Republican has joined a serious climate bill since *Citizens United*, as the fossil-fuel industry became the party's go-to funder, putting to work its unlimited resources and its archipelago of front groups and identity-laundering outfits purpose-built for that effort. We are now in the jaws of a climate crisis caused by fossil-fuel dark money, and it was *Citizens United* that ensured that there would be no meaningful response.

One accurate finding of *Citizens United* was that unlimited spending would be corrupting if it were not transparent.[21] But rather than treat its own finding about this corrupting danger seriously, the right-wing justices are now embarked on a mission to make dark money a constitutional right. Look no further than *Americans for Prosperity Foundation v. Bonta*, protecting the identities of the secret funders of the Americans for Prosperity Foundation, the corporate sibling of Americans for Prosperity, which is the main creature in the Koch brothers' vast bestiary of political-influence entities.[22] The present state of the art in secretive political influence is to twin a 501(c)(4) entity, which is allowed to spend money politically, with a 501(c)(3) entity, which is allowed tax deductibility of donations in addition to donor secrecy. There is virtually zero enforcement of whatever "corporate veil" should separate the entities, which often share offices, staff, donors, and board members. Some spawn further front groups, operating as "fictitious names" of the original front group.[23] In the *Bonta* case, where as many as fifty front groups showed up as *amici curiae* to recommend that result, the majority turned a blind eye to all of that.[24]

In addition to the conceded problem of dark money causing political corruption, it is deeply undemocratic to hide from citizens the most basic information about who's who on America's political playing fields—and it's frustrating for citizens to be bombarded with ads by phony front groups that sell no product or service and serve only to mask special-interest influence. In Rhode Island politics, if you're being fooled, the colloquial phrase is that you don't "get the joke." For regular voters, the dark-money influence joke is on them.

Worse still, once impenetrably secret avenues exist for dark money to influence our elections, there is nothing to prevent foreign actors from interfering in American elections through those same dark-money avenues. Secret is secret. And don't expect the media companies running the advertisements to protect us. Facebook has posted paid political advertisements whose payment came denominated in rubles.[25] You don't have to be a genius to see that as a red flag—but Facebook pocketed the money and ran the ads.

As a matter of corporate governance, because leaders of for-profit corporations are given great latitude in deciding what is in the best interest of the corporation, it is anomalous to allow corporate *officers* to engage in dark-money corporate political spending out of the corporate *treasury* (including potentially self-dealing political spending out of that corporate treasury) that corporate *shareholders* aren't even told about or given any say in.

Whether it's selective principles, tortured analysis, false facts, foreign shareholder influence, or improper secrecy from shareholders, there are plenty of flaws in the *Citizens United* decision. But the problems are not confined to the flawed decision. This is not an academic exercise. This decision's fundamental indecencies are that it denies ordinary citizens basic information about who's doing what to whom on the political playing field—a playing field that in our democracy those citizens ultimately oversee. And, oh yes, its dark-money flood is corrupting, by the decision's own terms.

To solve these problems, I've proposed several solutions. One, the DISCLOSE Act mentioned above, would require the actual, original donors of any campaign spending over $10,000 in a race to disclose their identities—no front groups, shell corporations, or identity-laundering intermediaries. The second, my Supreme Court Ethics, Recusal, and Transparency Act, would put the Justices under the same rules that apply to all other federal judges.[26] It's not for nothing that the billionaire donors behind the huge, undisclosed gifts to certain Justices and their families are politically active in right-wing circles and in advocacy groups whose purpose is to influence the Court.[27] My third bill, the Supreme Court Biennial Appointments and Term Limits Act, creates Supreme Court term limits, so that justices would move on and off the Court in orderly fashion.[28] No timed departures to put seats on the Court in your party's hands; no quest for youth, to win more decades of influence for your nominee. Sitting justices would rotate off after eighteen years of service, when they could choose to retire or to instead await "original jurisdiction" cases conferred on the Court by the Constitution, while their new replacements took up the appellate workload the Constitution declares is to be "regulated" by Congress. A final theory, recognizing that it is the role of the Supreme Court to say "what the law is" but not what the facts are, would be to withhold deference to Supreme Court decisions predicated on false facts.[29]

This is for real. An entire massive multibillion-dollar industry of dark-money influence has emerged, using literally hundreds of sham entities to bamboozle the American public and acquire secret influence over politicians and political parties, and through them to control our American institutions of democracy. Behind that foul and fake array lurk a handful of creepy billionaires and polluting industries, who now hold the reins of those institutions, all invisibly to the average voter.[30]

"Campaign finance?" This is about a lot more than "campaign finance." This is the means of a slow and steady corruption of the greatest democracy the world has ever known, a corruption at the hands of those whom that democracy has treated the best.

8

Elections in the Age of A.I.

Amy Klobuchar and Stephen Spaulding

On a cold January day in New Hampshire, two days before the first-in-the-nation presidential primary, thousands of voters in the Granite State got an unexpected phone call from someone who sounded just like the then-President of the United States, Joe Biden, who was at the time running for reelection.[1]

"What a bunch of malarkey," said the voice on the other end of the line, using a favorite phrase of former President Biden. "You know the value of voting Democratic. Our votes count. It's important that you save your vote for the November election. We'll need your help in electing Democrats up and down the ticket. Voting this Tuesday only helps Republicans in their quest to elect Donald Trump again. Your vote makes a difference in November, not this Tuesday."[2] It was not actually President Biden telling people not to vote. It was a deepfake—a fraudulent and realistic misrepresentation of someone's voice or likeness—created by artificial-intelligence technology to make the voice on the phone sound like the president.

The story gets weirder. The deepfake was created by a magician, a self-described "digital nomad" who was paid $150 by a political consultant who had worked for one of President Biden's rival candidates who was not involved in the scam in any way.[3] The magician created the deepfake in twenty minutes and it only cost him a dollar.[4] He told a reporter afterward that "it's so scary that it's this easy to do. People aren't ready for it."[5]

Five months later, New Hampshire's Republican attorney general secured an indictment against the political consultant who paid the magician for the deepfake and charged him under state law with thirteen felony counts of voter suppression and thirteen misdemeanor counts of impersonating a candidate under state law.⁶ The Federal Communications Commission also proposed a $6 million fine, including for spoofing a caller-identification number that falsely said it was coming from a number belonging to a former chair of the New Hampshire Democratic Party.⁷

The deepfake robocall is one of many examples that have affected candidates from both parties. What they show is how artificial intelligence can be used to cheaply and effectively create realistic video or audio of a candidate doing something or saying something they never did. Days after Vice President Kamala Harris became the presumptive Democratic nominee for president, Elon Musk, owner of the social-media platform X, shared a deepfake video of Harris saying some things she never said.⁸ Florida Governor Ron DeSantis's presidential campaign used artificial-intelligence–generated deepfake photos in a video that showed former President Trump hugging Dr. Anthony Fauci.⁹ A super PAC ran radio ads using artificial-intelligence–generated audio of the voices of Governor Nikki Haley and Senator Tim Scott, making it sound like they said things they never did.¹⁰ An artificial-intelligence–generated video that appeared to show Senator Elizabeth Warren saying that Republicans should not vote was viewed more than 200,000 times.¹¹ She never said that. One month before the 2024 general election, a gubernatorial candidate in Indiana aired an ad with a picture of his opponent at a supposed rally to ban gas stoves, but in reality it was a digitally altered photo of her actual campaign kick-off in which the digitally-altered version replaced signs showing her campaign logo with fake ones that read "No gas stoves."¹²

Advances in technology often have the capacity to disrupt the status quo while solving problems, and artificial intelligence brings tremendous potential to make people's lives better. It is already doing that. But artificial intelligence also has the capacity to supercharge disinformation and sow chaos. David Brooks put it well when he wrote that people in artificial intelligence "seem to be experiencing radically different brain states all at once," and that "it is literally unknowable whether this technology is leading us to heaven or hell."¹³

When it comes to how artificial intelligence will impact elections, it is important that the law be as sophisticated as those trying to use AI to influence voters. It is critical to put guardrails in place at both the state and federal levels to address the most pernicious deepfakes that intentionally deceive voters about candidates running for election. Disclosure when artificial intelligence is used in political ads is another tool for ensuring that voters know if what they are seeing is real. Agencies charged with protecting the integrity of our elections—like the Federal Election Commission and the Election Assistance Commission—could also provide guidance to state and local election officials on how artificial intelligence can impact their work.

The emergence of artificial-intelligence technology and its impact on elections, the pervasive spread of disinformation, and the increasing prevalence of dark money that can fund it in secret—these are the threats that require policymakers to act and update laws that regulate the influence of money in politics. *Buckley v. Valeo*, decided in 1976 after Congress overhauled campaign finance laws in the wake of the Watergate scandal, provides a sturdy foundation for further legislation by Congress and the states. Today, in cases implicating *Buckley*'s legal framework—which hinges on curbing corruption—courts need to build on *Buckley* to confront these technological advancements and their impact on our democracy.

Election Laws Must Be Updated to Account for New Risks Undermining Democracy

The ease with which cheaply produced and highly realistic deepfakes of candidates can spread was not foreseeable when Congress overhauled election law after Watergate, or even when, led by Senators John McCain and Russ Feingold, it later passed the Bipartisan Campaign Reform Act in 2002. Technology simply did not exist at the scale and level of sophistication that it does today.

Social-media platforms like Facebook were not around, either. Apps on our phones are now how many people connect with their friends and family and share photos of their vacations and grandchildren, but they are a lot more than that. They are central sources of information about news and politics, and in many cases they keep people siloed off from what they might otherwise see outside of the algorithms that keep feeding users with new content. Especially after *Citizens United* and the resulting explosion of campaign spending and dark money, we are seeing the persistence of disinformation on these platforms. And social-media companies are embedding artificial intelligence in their products which will yield even more risks if the worst foreseeable consequences are not mitigated.

There are other problems that plague elections, too. Some states have made it harder to vote. In North Carolina in 2016, for example, the conservative

Fourth Circuit Court of Appeals ruled that one of the state's newly passed laws was designed with "almost surgical precision" to stop African Americans from voting.[14] One year after the 2020 election, when Americans voted in record numbers in the middle of a global pandemic, state legislators introduced more than 440 bills to restrict voting, with thirty-four becoming law in nineteen states.[15] As discussed later in this chapter, it is well within Congress's power to pass legislation—like the Freedom to Vote Act—to combat these kinds of state laws and put in place basic national standards to ensure that every American can cast a ballot.

This is happening as Americans' trust in institutions is slipping and as extremism and polarization are pushing people into separate corners.[16] Trust is a bedrock value in a democracy, because it bolsters people's confidence that, when they vote, they have a voice in their government. The need to take action on these issues has only become more urgent.

To the extent that Congress has passed election-related legislation since *Buckley* in 1976, it has done so in several discrete areas. When Congress passed the Bipartisan Campaign Reform Act in 2002, it focused on campaign finance laws to reduce the undue influence of money in our elections. It set baseline standards for some aspects of election administration like the National Voter Registration Act in 1993, known as the "motor voter" law, which enabled people to register to vote at state departments of motor vehicles, and the Help America Vote Act in 2002, after the contested recount in Florida that led to *Bush v. Gore*. Congress also repeatedly reauthorized the Voting Rights Act to fight racial discrimination in voting, most recently in 2006 by an overwhelming bipartisan margin. However, the Supreme Court later struck down a key provision of this law in *Shelby County v. Holder*, and despite many efforts, Republicans have not joined Democrats in working to repair the law in light of ongoing efforts to make it harder to vote. In 2022 Congress again came together in a bipartisan way to revise the antiquated Electoral Count Act that governs how Congress counts electoral votes for president, closing loopholes in the wake of the invasion of the Capitol on January 6, 2021, by supporters of Donald Trump.

Of course, the emergence of artificial intelligence and how it can be used in elections presents new and urgent challenges. Laws regulating how campaigns and political advertisements are financed, including how the public knows who is trying to influence its views, were crafted for an analog world of television and radio, billboards and newspaper advertising, phone banks and door-knocking. It was not until 2024, for instance, that the Federal Election Commission removed "telegrams" and "typewriters" from its regulations.[17]

But while television and radio advertising is an effective way for candidates to get their message out, today there are many more tools to reach voters in more sophisticated ways, especially online. Most Americans—86%—get their news on the Internet, through their phones, tablets, or computers.[18] Younger people especially are getting their news—and targeted advertising—on apps like TikTok.[19] Much of this content is not traditional paid advertising but instead organic content or information created by paid influencers with massive followings. It is produced cheaply and can easily go viral.

Laws that regulate what voters see and how they are targeted are in large part tied to the spending of money in elections. These are the laws that require candidates to say they approve the messages they pay for, that limit how much a person can give to a political candidate, and that are supposed to, in theory, let voters follow the money to know who is influencing their views.

A long line of Supreme Court cases starting with *Buckley* has affirmed that the only government interest that can support these laws under the First Amendment is the government's interest in curbing corruption and its appearance. But in the fifty years since the Supreme Court decided *Buckley*, the nature of campaigning and the way that voters are influenced have changed significantly. It is important to consider how well equipped our laws are to continue to protect our free and fair elections and how they should be updated.

From Watergate to *Buckley*

Congress has acted in response to big threats to the integrity of our democracy before, with one of the most prominent examples coming after the Watergate scandal.

Watergate was a lot of things besides a third-rate burglary at the Democratic National Committee headquarters. It was an abuse of power, an obstruction of justice, and an assault on ethics in government. Watergate was also a campaign finance scandal.[20] President Richard Nixon's counsel, John Dean, told the president that it was going to cost a million dollars in hush money to pay off some of the Watergate burglars for the blackmail they were demanding. President Nixon told Dean that "you could get a million dollars. And you could get it in cash. I know where it could be gotten. I mean, it's not easy, but it could be done."[21]

Congress acted in 1974 to take on the need for accountability in government by passing one of the most sweeping campaign finance laws in American history. The Federal Election Campaign Act Amendments of 1974 created strict spending limits in elections, set contribution limits for how much candidates could accept from donors, and established an independent agency—the bipartisan, six-member Federal Election Commission—to enforce the law.[22]

James Buckley, the senator from New York who went on to serve in the Reagan administration and later as a judge on the US Court of Appeals for the District of Columbia Circuit, filed suit to challenge the law's constitutionality.

When the Supreme Court decided *Buckley* two years after the law's passage, it created a framework that has shaped election law for decades. Using the First Amendment to analyze campaign finance limits, the Court held that "virtually every means of communicating ideas in today's mass society requires the expenditure of money."[23] It distinguished between limits on how much money a person can give directly to candidates (contribution limits) and limits on how much money a person can spend to influence an election in ways other than giving to a candidate (expenditure limits). The Court upheld contribution limits—emphasizing that these limits on giving money directly to candidates protect the integrity of our democracy and guard against corruption—while striking down the law's expenditure limits, which the Court interpreted as unduly restricting political speech under the First Amendment and—since the money does not go directly to a candidate—as unnecessary to guard against corruption.[24] This dichotomy between upholding contribution limits while striking down expenditure limits has been fundamental to the Court's approach to campaign finance law in the decades since the decision.

In limiting the government's interest solely to curbing corruption, the Court rejected other rationales for limits on spending in elections, particularly what it called in *Buckley* "equalizing" the ability of people and interest groups to make their voices heard in our democracy.[25] As Congress and state legislatures consider new laws in light of the emergence of artificial intelligence and turbocharged disinformation, there are additional reasons to support measures to protect our free and fair elections, including the need to strengthen the public's trust and confidence in democracy, protect truth and facts, and safeguard the integrity of the democratic process.

Judicial Interpretation of Congress's Power to Regulate Campaigns

McConnell v. Federal Election Commission (2003)—Over the five decades since *Buckley* was decided, political scandals involving money have come and gone, but the Court has repeatedly affirmed curbing corruption and its appearance as the major—and only—justification for campaign finance laws. The Court has both expanded and narrowed what types of corruption can be addressed by campaign finance laws. In *McConnell v. Federal Election Commission*, the Court took a broad approach in upholding most of the Bipartisan Campaign Reform Act (McCain-Feingold), the law that shut down the ability of corporations and others to give unlimited money to political parties.[26] The bill, introduced by Senators John McCain of Arizona and Russ Feingold of Wisconsin, passed with bipartisan support in the House and Senate and was signed into law by President George W. Bush.

A key provision of McCain-Feingold prohibited corporate spending on campaign ads masquerading as issue ads—the type of ad that calls out candidates in the days before an election but falls short of expressly advocating for a candidate's election or defeat.[27] These ads allowed corporations to circumvent a long-standing federal ban on corporate campaign spending (other than through a corporation's political action committee) because they did not expressly call for the election or defeat of a candidate, even though for practical purposes they had the same impact as political ads.[28]

A case challenging the law filed by Senator Mitch McConnell eventually made its way to the Supreme Court. Justices John Paul Stevens and Sandra Day O'Connor jointly authored the part of the opinion that upheld the law's ban on corporate spending on campaign ads and its prohibition on certain unlimited contributions to political parties. Justice O'Connor was the only member of the Court, at the time and since, who had once held elected office herself, as the first woman to serve as the Arizona Senate's majority leader. She had firsthand experience with the role of money in elections, which some have suggested informed her practical perspective on the issue. The Court would take a decidedly deregulatory turn after she retired.[29]

Echoing its reasoning in *Buckley*, the Court wrote in *McConnell* that Congress's anti-corruption interests in passing McCain-Feingold "directly implicate the integrity of our electoral process," which the ruling went on to describe as "the very means through which a free society democratically translates political speech into concrete governmental action."[30] Put more plainly, the Court in *McConnell* made clear that curbing corruption and its appearance goes beyond what it called "cash-for-votes" to include "curbing undue influence."[31] The decision also affirmed language from earlier precedent in *Nixon v. Shrink Missouri Government PAC* in 2000, in which it deemed efforts to curb corruption as necessary to respond to "the broader threat from politicians too compliant with the wishes of large contributors."[32]

Citizens United v. Federal Election Commission (2010)—Seven years after *McConnell*, the Court decided *Citizens United v. Federal Election Commission*. By then, Justice O'Connor, a pivotal vote to uphold campaign finance laws, had been replaced by Justice Samuel Alito, who would vote with the Court's new Chief Justice, John Roberts, to reshape campaign finance jurisprudence.[33] The question originally before the Court in *Citizens United* was a narrow one pertaining to whether a ninety-minute video critical of then-Senator Hillary Clinton was in fact a political advertisement funded by a corporation, implicating provisions of McCain-Feingold.[34] After oral argument, the Court did something that it very rarely does: it ordered reargument, in a maneuver that greatly expanded the question before it.[35] It asked the parties to reargue the case with a focus on whether to overrule part of *McConnell* and also *Austin v. Michigan Chamber of Commerce*, a 1990 case that upheld prohibitions on corporate campaign spending if the funds were spent independently of campaigns.[36]

In its five-to-four decision, Justice Anthony Kennedy's opinion in *Citizens United* overruled a crucial holding of *McConnell* and *Austin* and struck down core provisions of McCain-Feingold, holding for the first time that corporations enjoy a First Amendment right to spend an unlimited amount of their general treasury funds to influence elections.[37] The decision immediately gave corporations a new and powerful tool to spend directly on political campaigns to influence public policy: direct spending from their profits, not just their PACs.

Citizens United significantly limited the type of corruption that Congress could tackle. Justice Kennedy wrote that "[w]hen *Buckley* identified a sufficiently important governmental interest in preventing corruption or the appearance of corruption, that interest was limited to *quid pro quo* corruption."[38] This was a blanket rejection of earlier cases, including *McConnell* and *Shrink Missouri PAC*, which explicitly noted that corruption goes beyond "cash-for-votes."[39] Going further, and without much of a factual record before it (unlike the 100,000-page record in *McConnell*), the Court declared that the "[t]he appearance of influence or access, furthermore, will not cause the electorate to lose faith in our democracy."[40] Ultimately the Court ruled that "independent expenditures, including those made by corporations, do not give rise to corruption or the appearance of corruption."[41]

Justice Stevens's powerful dissent, joined by Justices Ruth Bader Ginsburg, Stephen Breyer, and Sonia Sotomayor, said that "[w]hile it is true that we have not always spoken about corruption in a clear or consistent voice, the approach taken by the majority cannot be right. . . . Corruption operates along a spectrum, and the majority's apparent belief that *quid pro quo* arrangements can be neatly demarcated from other improper influences does not accord with the theory or reality of politics."[42]

In other words, four Justices agreed that Congress, when it passed McCain-Feingold, had ample authority to put guardrails in place to protect against the type of influence that comes with money in politics that the Court's majority had upheld just seven years earlier in *McConnell*: a ban on campaign spending by corporations out of their general treasury funds. The results? In the decade and a half since the decision, it unleashed a flood of money in elections, at least $2.6 billion of it undisclosed, despite the part of the opinion upholding disclosure requirements that had the support of eight Justices.[43] The ruling led to the creation of super PACs and dark-money groups that could accept unlimited money from donors—including from corporations—and drown out Americans' voices at the ballot box.

McCutcheon v. Federal Election Commission (2014)—The Court's most recent high-profile case on Congress's power to regulate spending in elections came in *McCutcheon v. FEC* in 2014. The decision marked the first time that a federal contribution limit put in place by Congress was struck down as unconstitutional, going even further than the *Buckley* decision that struck down expenditure limits. At issue was the overall limit that a donor could contribute in support of candidates, political parties, and PACs combined. At the time, that overall limit was $123,200, or more than twice the then-median household income.[44] After the decision, individual donors were allowed to contribute up to $3.6 million to one party and its candidates, an amount Justice Elena Kagan noted would secure donors "a very, very special place at the table."[45] As the FEC adjusts contribution limits every two years, today the overall limit exceeds $6 million.

Doubling down on the narrow view of corruption that the Court articulated in *Citizens United*, Chief Justice Roberts wrote in *McCutcheon* that "Congress may target only a specific type of corruption—*quid pro quo* corruption," which he described as "[t]hat Latin phrase [that] captures the notion of a direct exchange of an official act for money."[46] This appeared to be an effort to respond to what Justice Stevens wrote in his dissent to *Citizens United* about how much authority Congress has to take on the threat of corruption in elections. Evaluating the $123,200 overall contribution limit that a person could give to federal candidates, political parties, and PACs in a two-year period, Chief Justice Roberts wrote in *McCutcheon* that

> spending large sums of money in connection with elections, but not in connection with an effort to control the exercise of an officeholder's duties, does not give rise to . . . *quid pro quo* corruption. Nor does the possibility that an individual who spends large sums may garner influence over or access to elected officials.[47]

He also called the "ingratiation and access" that candidates have with supporters—implicitly including major campaign spenders—a "central feature of democracy."[48]

Having set up the question on such narrow grounds, Chief Justice Roberts struck down the overall contribution limit, creating a new path for donors to give multimillion-dollar contributions in support of political campaigns in a two-year cycle. It further eroded the regulatory framework intended to mitigate the increasing influence of money in politics and, combined with *Citizens United*, dismantled foundational protections that Congress put in place to provide for accountability in our democracy.

Disclosure and Transparency

One positive aspect of this line of cases is that the Court has consistently upheld transparency and disclosure laws when it comes to citizens' right to know who is attempting to influence their vote.

Buckley cited three reasons to uphold campaign finance disclosure laws. First, disclosure gives the public information it can use in assessing candidates for office. The Court held in *Buckley* that the "sources of a candidate's financial support . . . alert the voter to the interests to which a candidate is most likely to be responsive and thus facilitate predictions of future performance in office."⁴⁹ Second, it shines a light on who is giving money in the first place, as the Court noted that "exposure may discourage those who would use money for improper purposes either before or after the election."⁵⁰ Third, disclosure is necessary to enforce the law and is an efficient way to detect violations of campaign finance limits.⁵¹ In sum, disclosure allows the public, constituents, and the press to follow the money.

The Court has repeatedly affirmed the importance of disclosure, including in broader terms than it did in *Buckley*. In the only portion of *Citizens United* to have the support of eight justices (with Justice Clarence Thomas taking an opposing view), Justice Kennedy wrote that "disclosure . . . enables the electorate to make informed decisions and give proper weight to different speakers and messages."⁵² Given the context of the Court's decision to allow corporations to spend directly on elections, the same eight justices agreed that disclosure laws let shareholders "determine whether their corporation's political speech advances the corporation's interest in making profits, and citizens can see whether elected officials are in the pocket of so-called moneyed interests."⁵³ And notably the Court held that disclosure advances the First Amendment's interest in an informed electorate because disclosure "permits citizens and shareholders to react to the speech of corporate entities in a proper way," so that voters can "make informed choices in the political marketplace."⁵⁴

In his opinion in *McCutcheon*, four years after *Citizens United* was decided, Chief Justice Roberts wrote that "[t]oday, given the Internet, disclosure offers much more robust protections against corruption. . . . Because massive quantities of information can be accessed at the click of a mouse, disclosure is effective to a degree not possible at the time *Buckley*, or even *McConnell*, was decided"— and the Court affirmed that disclosure requirements "do not impose a ceiling on speech."⁵⁵

In fact, Justice Antonin Scalia specifically emphasized the essential value of disclosure in 2010, writing in *Doe v. Reed* that

> requiring people to stand up for their political acts fosters civic courage, without which democracy is doomed. For my part, I do not look forward to a society which, thanks to the Supreme Court, campaigns anonymously . . . hidden from public scrutiny and protected from the accountability of criticism. This does not resemble the home of the brave.⁵⁶

Ongoing and Emerging Threats to the Integrity of Our Democracy

The Court's decision in *Buckley* and those that followed provide some guidance for new laws to advance democratic principles of accountability and transparency in elections. Some of the problems we must confront to protect democracy have been around for a long time, like the influence of money in politics. But new ways to influence elections, such as artificial intelligence, present unprecedented challenges that Congress and state legislatures must address. And while at least nineteen states have passed legislation to regulate artificial intelligence in elections, including at least seventeen states that have required a minimum of labeling for digitally altered ads, with a smaller number banning certain ads generated by artificial intelligence, Congress has yet to act.

Dark Money—Despite efforts to improve disclosure laws in Congress and strong support from the American people for doing so—with overwhelming majorities consistently supporting transparency in campaign spending—the law has not kept pace, and disclosure is not as readily or easily available as Chief Justice Roberts assumed it would be in *McCutcheon*.[57] We have seen the rise of "dark money," a term used to describe money that influences elections but that comes from secret sources.[58] In 2015 Merriam-Webster added the phrase to its dictionary.[59]

Since *Citizens United*, more than $2.6 billion in federal campaign spending and contributions has come from secret sources.[60] Researchers at OpenSecrets, a nonpartisan research group that analyzes campaign spending trends, found that between 2010 and 2023, "at least $3 out of every $10 in outside spending reported to the FEC since *Citizens United* can be traced to dark money groups."[61]

Dark money deprives the public of the transparency that is critical to the functioning of a democracy. Without transparency in campaign spending, voters are unable to see who is behind funding political campaigns, and that makes it difficult to hold public officials accountable.

Congress was on the cusp of solving the problem soon after *Citizens United* when it was close to sending the DISCLOSE Act, led by Senator Sheldon Whitehouse, to the President's desk. The bill requires major campaign spenders to disclose their contributors of $10,000 or more to outside spending groups. It passed the House in 2010 and received 59 votes for cloture in the Senate, falling one vote short of the 60 required to defeat a filibuster.[62] The measure has since passed Democratically-run Houses multiple times, including as part of the Freedom to Vote Act, and the bill again came within two votes of making it through a procedural hurdle in the Senate when the chamber considered needed changes to the Senate rules to pass the Freedom to Vote Act in 2022.[63] While all Democratic Senators supported the bill, two would not vote for creating a filibuster exemption for passing it.

Some dismiss dark money as an abstract concept that, while corrosive to democracy, is not a front-burner issue for most Americans. The reality, though, is that dark money can put the agenda of special interests ahead of the public interest without voters having any idea who is paying to influence their votes.

An example in Ohio illustrates the point. In 2023 a former speaker of the Ohio House of Representatives, Larry Householder, and a former chairman of the Ohio Republican Party, Matthew Borges, were convicted in a federal racketeering trial involving $60 million in bribes—some of which involved secret campaign spending—so that a power company on the verge of bankruptcy could get some of the funds from a $1.3 billion nuclear-power-plant bailout.[64] The power company's money was funneled through a web of consultants and nonprofits—including one controlled by former Representative Householder—to elect the Speaker and his allies so that they could later support the power company's bailout.[65] In a deferred prosecution agreement, the company admitted that it had steered money through dark-money groups specifically to "conceal payments for the benefit of public officials and in return for official action."[66] Though the bailout was eventually repealed, this scandal—one of the largest in Ohio's history—shows how secret spenders can secure sweetheart deals if disclosure laws do not keep pace with the reality of how campaigns are run and won, especially after *Citizens United*.

Another example comes from Wisconsin, where an out-of-state Texas billionaire—the CEO of a lead-paint manufacturer—steered $750,000 in dark money from his company and his own bank account to support state legislators and Wisconsin's former Governor Scott Walker, who were in the midst of high-profile recall elections in 2011 and 2012.[67] Governor Walker was ultimately not recalled. In the ensuing year, the Wisconsin legislature passed a bill signed into law by then-Governor Walker shielding lead manufacturers from liability in then-pending lawsuits that had been filed on behalf of children poisoned by lead.[68] The law was pushed by lobbyists for the same company's owner that pumped three-quarters of a million undisclosed dollars into the effort to defend the governor and certain legislators from recall.[69] The spending remained secret until 2016—four years after the last recall—when it came to light as a result of a separate investigation into campaign activities related to the recall effort.[70]

Artificial Intelligence and Disinformation—The 2024 election cycle marked the first time that artificial intelligence captured the public's attention as an emerging threat to elections. The technology has the ability to accelerate the spread of disinformation and to do so cheaply, making people believe candidates are doing or saying things they never did or said.[71] As it becomes increasingly difficult to discern authentic content from content generated by artificial intelligence, Americans become more likely to question the reality of what they are seeing.[72] Additionally, the technology also has the capacity to sow confusion about when, where, and how to cast a ballot.[73]

In 2023, when I led the US Senate Committee on Rules and Administration, we held the first Congressional hearing on the impact of artificial intelligence in elections.[74] At that hearing, all of the witnesses agreed that artificial intelligence posed a threat to our elections, and witnesses from both parties testified in support of federal legislation to ban the use of deepfakes to mislead voters.[75]

The concern is of course not unique to the United States. At least fifty countries representing more than half of the world's population held elections in 2024, and deepfakes now have been used to influence elections from Taiwan to India to Slovakia to Argentina.[76] It is a continuation and escalation in disinformation tactics that can cross international borders. Yet while some countries have recently passed laws on this subject, the United States—with the exception of a smattering of state laws—has done nothing.

The alarms about disinformation in elections have been sounding for some time in the United States. After the 2016 election, our intelligence agencies confirmed that Russia worked to undermine public trust in the democratic process through influence campaigns and cyberattacks.[77] A bipartisan Senate investigation confirmed how Russian disinformation efforts targeted the United States with bots and fake accounts on platforms like Facebook and Twitter to pose as Americans and sow division and distrust in democracy.[78] The technology that facilitates this has only gotten more sophisticated and cheaper to produce since then.

Though security officials from administrations under presidents of both parties have repeatedly affirmed the security of recent elections, intelligence officials continue to warn about foreign attempts to interfere in our elections.[79] In 2024 FBI Director Christopher Wray remarked that

> advances in generative [artificial intelligence], for instance, are lowering the barrier to entry, making it easier to engage in malign influence while making foreign influence efforts by players both old and new, more realistic and more difficult to detect . . . this election cycle, the US will face more adversaries moving at a faster pace enabled by new technology.[80]

Throughout the 2024 election, the Department of Homeland Security issued bulletins warning state and local officials about how artificial intelligence provides "enhanced opportunities for interference."[81] One of the most damaging effects of deepfakes and other disinformation is how they can lead voters to assume that even the authentic content that they are seeing is fake.[82] It blurs reality. Voters will look at content and question the truth of what they see and hear. This undermines one of the most important values in democracy: the truth. Voting—the choices that determine our country's future—depends on an informed electorate.

Ongoing Concerns with Money in Politics—The continuing impact of secret spending in elections and the rise of artificial intelligence are happening at a time when voters' concerns about money in politics persist. *Citizens United* paved the way to super PACs, with more than $9 billion in outside spending since the decision, and that is just at the federal level.[83] An analysis of campaign spending a decade after the decision found that just ten donors and their spouses spent $1.2 billion in federal elections.[84] And while money does not guarantee success in elections, candidates face steep odds without it. In 2022 the top-spending candidate won 94% of House races and 82% of Senate races.[85]

Americans have made their frustrations clear in poll after poll, with broad majorities of Republicans, Democrats, and independents fed up with a campaign finance system that they believe favors special interests who are using campaign contributions to push aside the priorities of everyday Americans.[86] Too many people think that their voices are being drowned out by a system flooded with contributions that sets the agenda and gives those who can afford it access and influence over decisions of government.

While most people do not run for office to do the bidding of their wealthiest campaign contributors, there is no question that powerful special interests can make progress difficult on the issues most important to voters, and one of the biggest obstacles to that progress is the role of money in politics, including the billions of dollars in dark money. It undermines trust and confidence in a democracy that is based on the idea of one person, one vote.

Proposals to Modernize Election Laws

There is some good news here, with solutions that have strong support among the American people and growing momentum to take on the threats that we are seeing. Policymakers are tackling these issues head-on with new laws and proposals to uphold trust in elections and our democracy. Nineteen states have passed laws to address the impact of artificial intelligence in elections,[87] and these laws are passing in states across the political spectrum, from Minnesota and Colorado to Texas, from Utah and Alabama to California and New York. These states used different tactics, from banning election-related deepfakes to requiring that AI-related content have disclaimers.[88] Some companies have taken voluntary steps to rein in the use of their products to spread disinformation, barring some of their tools from being used to influence elections or requiring disclaimers when artificial intelligence is used.[89]

But a patchwork approach is not enough to deal with the scope and severity of the risk. It will also take Congress to pass federal law that clearly governs federal campaigns.

One step should be to ban—within the framework of the Constitution—the fraudulent deepfakes of candidates in political ads and robocalls that are actually intended to deceive voters and influence elections, with exceptions to cover uses like parody, satire, and news reporting. States like Minnesota and Texas have passed laws to do this, which are squarely aimed at protecting the integrity of the democratic process from efforts to defraud voters about candidates on the ballot.[90]

An additional way to bolster our democracy against deceptive AI-generated content is to require disclaimers on political ads when artificial intelligence is used in ways that might not rise to the level of being materially deceptive deepfakes of candidates. Disclosure gives voters information to evaluate what they are seeing and hearing in political ads so that they can make decisions about how to vote. The Supreme Court has repeatedly affirmed measures to require disclosure, including in *Citizens United* and *McCutcheon*. To ensure that such disclaimers are effective, and so that viewers do not tune them out, legislation can be carefully crafted to require disclaimers only when political ads are substantially generated by artificial intelligence but not when it is used in minor ways, including to adjust colors and make other insignificant cosmetic changes. Just as other regulations require candidates to "stand by" their ads, this proposal would require political advertisers who use artificial intelligence in substantial ways to do the same thing, so that voters can make their own judgment on whether to rely on the ad when deciding how to vote.

Given deliberate efforts to make it harder to vote in some states across the country in recent years, there are other ideas to consider. Basic national standards, like those in the Freedom to Vote Act, for reforms such as a minimum number of days of early voting, voting by mail for those who want it, and same-day and automatic voter registration are commonsense policies that in many cases are based on laws that have long been on the books in red, blue, and purple states alike.

The Freedom to Vote Act also includes provisions to counter the influence of money in politics, including dark money, the growing issue of super PACs working as arms of political campaigns, and loopholes that can allow foreign interference in elections. The Freedom to Vote Act incorporates the DISCLOSE Act to shine a light on dark money so that voters know who is influencing our elections, and it would also make improvements to the bipartisan Federal Election Commission so that it can better enforce laws and regulations that are already in effect. Finally, the bill would reduce the influence of money in politics by shutting down the types of super PACs that have popped up since *Citizens United* and that work closely with candidates in a way that circumvents the purpose of contribution limits because the spending is not truly independent of campaigns.

Constitutional Interests

As Congress and states pass these types of proposals into law, the Court may be faced with the need to recognize additional constitutional justifications that go beyond its past approach. Some leading scholars have noted that *Buckley*'s reliance on corruption was unduly narrow. For example, Justice John Paul Stevens testified in the Senate in 2014 after retiring from the bench that "the Court's campaign finance jurisprudence has been incorrectly predicated on the assumption that avoiding corruption or the appearance of corruption is the only justification for regulating campaign speech and the financing of political campaigns," and that "[e]lections are contests between rival candidates for public office. Like rules that govern athletic contests or adversary litigation, those rules should create a level playing field."[91]

As policymakers pass new laws to combat threats to elections, one reason courts should uphold them is the protection of the democratic process itself. Ensuring that elections are free from undue influence and manipulation—whether from fraudulent deepfakes, untraceable dark money, or disinformation—is crucial to maintaining the legitimacy and stability of democratic governance and the principle of one person, one vote. Alternatively, or in addition, new arguments can be made that allowing unlimited dark money, election-influencing artificial intelligence, and the resulting disinformation actually do spur corruption and that the Court should reexamine how narrowly it has interpreted the concept of corruption in previous cases.

Strengthening confidence in democracy itself is also essential, and doing so will require new measures to keep up with how campaigns are run so that elections remain free, fair, and transparent. Laws that confront the harm that artificial intelligence and dark money can do to elections, including how both can fuel disinformation, will help rebuild trust.

Ultimately, in addition to curbing corruption and its appearance, our laws should ensure that Americans have a meaningful chance to make their voices heard. Underlying all of this must be the public's right to be informed when people make their voices heard at the ballot box as engaged citizens.

Conclusion

Since *Buckley*, the central question in the Court's approach to laws that regulate spending in elections hinges on whether they curb corruption and its appearance. Later cases like *Citizens United* and *McCutcheon* redefined that concept so narrowly that unlimited money in elections from corporations, dark-money groups, and other special interests is now allowed.

But we are not powerless to respond. Democracy suffers if we do not account for the right of voters to have a meaningful and informed voice at the ballot box to chart the future of our country. That is why we must continue to take action in light of new threats that impact the integrity of our elections that were not anticipated when these cases were decided, like the potential for artificial intelligence to spread disinformation and deceive voters.

The way that campaigns are run, financed, and executed to reach voters has changed dramatically in recent decades, but the continued need to protect the democratic process remains paramount. Doing so will enhance public confidence in the institutions of government that represent the people, which is essential for the future of our country. Democracy is resilient. But to deliver on its promise, we must continue to work to protect it.

PART V

Arguments Interpreting The "Corruption" Rationale

9
Corruption, Campaign Finance, and Criminal Law
Buckley's Legacy
Deborah Hellman

The legacy and importance of *Buckley v. Valeo*[1] can be captured in different ways, many of which are described in the other chapters of this volume. A crucially important dimension of that legacy is the fact that the Supreme Court, in deciding that giving and spending money in connection with elections raised First Amendment concerns, arrogated *to itself* the task of defining what the corruption of democracy involves.[2] A constitutional law of "corruption" begins in *Buckley* and develops in the fifty years since because the Court identified "corruption and the appearance of corruption"[3] as the only interests that are sufficiently compelling to justify the burdens on speech imposed by campaign finance restrictions.

In the years since *Buckley*, the Court has moved from a broader understanding of corruption to a more narrow and constrained account. For example, in the 1990 case *Austin v. Michigan Chamber of Commerce*,[4] the Court upheld restrictions on corporate expenditures on the grounds that "the corrosive and distorting effects of immense aggregations of wealth that are accumulated with the help of the corporate form and that have little or no correlation to the public's support for the corporation's political ideas"[5] constitute a form of corruption. In addition, in the 2003 case *McConnell v. FEC*,[6] the Court defined "corruption" to include both a *quid pro quo* exchange and a situation in which a legislator counts the preferences of wealthy contributors more heavily than the preferences of others.[7]

Today, by contrast, the Court defines corruption narrowly. In *Citizens United v. FEC*,[8] the Court declared that only *"quid pro quo* corruption" can justify restrictions on speech.[9] Justice Kennedy, writing for the Court, stressed that "[i]ngratiation and access, in any event, are not corruption."[10] Because corruption is limited to *quid pro quo* exchanges, wealthy candidates who spend their personal wealth on their own campaigns are immune from being corrupted, and the fact that they do so is not now viewed by the Court as a form of corruption.[11]

Whether the Court defines "corruption" broadly, as in *Austin* and *McConnell*, or narrowly, as in *Citizens United*, the important point to stress is what it is, precisely, that the Court is defining in each of these cases. The Court is not defining what genuine corruption actually is. Rather, it is opining about what conception or facet of genuine corruption is, in its view, sufficiently compelling to justify restrictions on political contributions and expenditures. The first objective of this chapter is to emphasize the distinctness of these inquiries and to describe the ways in which they are often confused or conflated.

This observation gives rise to an opportunity. Legislatures, at both the federal and state levels, have an important role to play in articulating what they find genuine corruption to be. They can do so using ordinary criminal law. For example, while the Supreme Court said in *Citizens United* that "[i]ngratiation and access ... are not corruption,"[12] legislatures can enact laws that expressly forbid the exchange of money or other value for access to governmental officials. Doing so would have several potential benefits. First, it might allow ordinary criminal law to influence the way the Court defines "corruption" in campaign finance cases, reversing a trend in which the Court's campaign finance holdings may be exerting influence on its interpretation of federal criminal law.

Second, the enactment of statutes asserting alternative views of the nature of corruption would help clarify and emphasize the difference between what the Court is doing when it defines "corruption" in the context of assessing the constitutionality of campaign finance regulations and what legislatures are doing when they prohibit certain conduct. Put simply, while the Court's role is to define what interests are sufficiently compelling to justify restrictions on giving and spending money on elections, it has no special role to play in defining "corruption" when constitutional issues are not in play. This is an important point to emphasize in its own right. But, in addition, it turns out that the very logic of the Court's own understanding of corruption as a *quid pro quo* exchange would make the fact that legislatures criminalize additional exchanges relevant to the *constitutional* question raised in the campaign finance context, as I explain below.

Corruption as a Constitutional Concept and as a Political Concept

When the Supreme Court defines "corruption" in the context of evaluating the constitutionality of campaign finance restrictions, we should remember what–exactly–the Court is defining in these cases. The Court is not defining—indeed, *could* not define—what genuine corruption actually is, as the Supreme Court has no entitlement, nor expertise, to pronounce on that question. While it may be the "province and duty of the judicial department to say what the law is,"[13] it is not within its bailiwick to opine about political theory.[14] What the Court is defining in these cases is the form of corruption that is, in its view, sufficiently compelling to justify the burdens on speech that campaign finance laws involve. Call this concept *Compelling-Interest Corruption*. In order to distinguish *Compelling-Interest Corruption* from genuine corruption, whatever that includes, call the latter concept CORRUPTION. By emphasizing that these two things are conceptually distinct, I am not asserting that CORRUPTION is necessarily different from *Compelling-Interest Corruption*. Perhaps the Court's understanding of *Compelling-Interest Corruption* exactly mirrors genuine CORRUPTION. But perhaps it does not. My point is simply that by opining on the *legal* question of what interest is sufficiently compelling to justify the burdens on speech involved in campaign finance laws, the Court can only pronounce on that legal question. It cannot determine what CORRUPTION truly includes.

It is also important to remember the sort of constitutional judgment the Court is making when it defines *Compelling-Interest Corruption*. The Court is not interpreting constitutional text.[15] Rather it is opining about the sorts of *interests* that are weighty enough to provide a justification for the burdens on speech that various campaign finance laws involve. (As an aside, we might note that the Court recently rejected this approach to assessing when a constitutional right has been violated in the context of the Second Amendment right to bear arms, and so the status of this method of interpreting constitutional rights is currently uncertain.[16]) The Court's definition of *Compelling-Interest*

Corruption is thus an instance of constitutional doctrine, rather than constitutional interpretation, and as such arguably entitled to less deference than its pronouncement on the meaning of the constitutional text.

CORRUPTION, by contrast, is a concept whose meaning derives from the proper functioning of democracy, the role that elections play within a democracy, and the duties that elected officials owe to their constituents and to the body politic as a whole.[17] Of course, people are likely to disagree about the answers to these questions, and so what counts as a corrupting influence on elected officials within a democracy is contested. To some, the fact that legislators are more responsive to the preferences of large donors than to others is a form of corruption.[18] To others, it is not.[19] My aim here is not to defend one view on this question over another, but rather to stress that the Court brings no special expertise to this question of moral or political theory. What genuine CORRUPTION entails is a question that each of us individually, or all collectively, must answer.

The way in which the people can express their view about the nature of CORRUPTION includes not only campaign finance laws but also, importantly, other laws, including criminal law. Familiar examples of such laws include both federal and state laws that prohibit bribery, the acceptance of gifts over designated amounts, and those that define proscribed conflicts of interest, among others. Legislatures must do so in ways that do not run afoul of constitutional prohibitions, to be sure. Because campaign finance restrictions implicate First Amendment free-speech protections, legislatures may be limited in how they can give voice to their own views about the nature of CORRUPTION using that vehicle. But there are other options. For example, legislatures can use criminal law to make illegal certain exchanges that they view as corrupt. In so doing, a legislature would be expressing its view about the nature of CORRUPTION.

This suggestion highlights the bifurcation of the legal task allotted to courts and the political task reserved to legislatures. One might wonder whether defining "corruption" is special or different from other constitutional questions such that these two tasks can be separated in this context but not others. It is not. When addressing questions of constitutional law, courts answer constitutional questions, and this requires them to define constitutional concepts—such as *Compelling-Interest Corruption*. These constitutional concepts are often related to ordinary concepts but not necessarily coextensive with them. Sometimes the limits on what the Court is doing are obvious. When the Court defines "procedural due process," which is clearly a term that has a special constitutional meaning, we easily recognize that although "procedural due process" is related to fairness, the Court is not providing and cannot provide the last word about what fairness truly requires in the procedural context. When the Court defines terms like "corruption," however, this feature of its task can be overlooked because the constitutional concept is so easily confused with the ordinary concept. Avoiding this confusion is the reason I propose using the term *Compelling-Interest Corruption* to refer to the result of the Court's work.

An example, admittedly far-fetched, will help to illustrate the point. Imagine that the Court had said that safeguarding democracy (rather than avoiding corruption) is the only interest that is sufficiently compelling to justify restrictions on speech in the context of elections—and then, in later cases, had gone on to define "democracy" to mean rule by property owners. The upshot of this line of cases would be that protecting rule by property owners would be the only interest that is sufficiently compelling to justify restrictions on speech in the context of elections. But it would not mean that genuine democracy is equivalent to rule by property owners. Moreover, legislatures could express their own views about what genuine DEMOCRACY consists of by means of laws that do not conflict with this hypothetical Court's pronouncements about what interests justify speech restrictions in the context of elections. For example, a state might enact a law that granted suffrage to non-property owners. In doing so, the state would be in dialogue with the Court about the nature of DEMOCRACY. Analogously, were a state today to enact laws that forbid the exchange of money for access to elected officials, the state would be in dialogue with the Court about the nature of CORRUPTION.

Not only can citizens express their views about what genuine CORRUPTION consists of by enacting laws prohibiting various conduct, the enactment of such anti-corruption statutes may also have a meaningful impact on the legal doctrine of *Compelling-Interest Corruption*. How so? First, to the extent that courts continue to conflate *Compelling-Interest Corruption* and genuine CORRUPTION, the enactment of laws criminalizing the exchange of access for something of value, for example, may influence how the Court defines *Compelling-Interest Corruption*. Second, and alternatively, the enactment of such laws may serve to clarify the distinction between *Compelling-Interest Corruption* and genuine CORRUPTION. This clarification may put internal pressure on the Court's conception of *Compelling-Interest Corruption*, perhaps ironically, by drawing the people's views of what exchanges are forbidden within the Court's view that *Compelling-Interest Corruption* requires *quid pro quo* exchange. Both mechanisms of influence provide a means by which the people can be in conversation with the Court about the nature of *Compelling-Interest Corruption*. In so doing, they may be able to resist *Buckley*'s legacy of arrogating to the Court the role of defining CORRUPTION and to take back some agency in defining it for ourselves.

Conflation and Cross-Pollination

Legislators should enact laws that assert their own views about what actions by governmental officials are genuinely CORRUPT. When they do so in contexts that do not involve restrictions on First Amendment rights, they can assert their prerogative to define genuine CORRUPTION while also complying with their obligations to defer to the Court's determinations about the meaning of the Constitution. In what follows, I use the example of the exchange of something of value for access to an elected official as an exemplar of such a law, because the Court, in *Citizens United*, so baldly asserted that "[i]ngratiation and access . . . are not corruption"—a claim I find normatively flawed. But this is merely an example. The point that bears emphasis is that *Buckley* began the tradition of the Court defining "corruption." But once we remember that what it defines is *Compelling-Interest Corruption*, rather than genuine CORRUPTION, there is room—and opportunity—for legislatures to define CORRUPTION themselves.

When the Court defines *Compelling-Interest Corruption*, it is articulating the interest that it judges to be sufficiently compelling to justify restricting speech. It is not, as I have just emphasized, actually opining about what CORRUPTION truly is. So how might a newly enacted law criminalizing the exchange of money for access—a statement about actual CORRUPTION—influence how the Supreme Court defines *Compelling-Interest Corruption*? The answer lies in the fact that the Court has shown little appreciation for the distinction between these two concepts, and this conflation invites slippage between these ideas and confusion about what precisely the Court is doing. Such cross-pollination has, to date, arguably allowed the Court's campaign finance cases to influence its interpretations of federal criminal law. But the direction of that influence could be reversed so that clearly drafted criminal-law statutes (at either the federal or state level) could induce changes in campaign finance doctrine.

Citizens United v. FEC invalidated a ban on corporate and union spending on elections during the preelection period.[20] In reaching this result, the Court makes the statement that "[i]ngratiation and access . . . are not corruption,"[21] in the context of rebutting the argument that if corporations spend large sums of money supporting particular candidates, those candidates may feel indebted (ingratiation) to the corporations or will give the corporations special opportunities to present arguments for their positions (access). The statement appears to say that such ingratiation and access are not CORRUPTION. But that is not in fact what it does say. Indeed, the Court acknowledges that ingratiation and access are "cause for concern":

> If elected officials succumb to improper influences from independent expenditures, if they surrender their best judgment, and if they put expediency before principle, then surely there is cause for concern. We must give weight to attempts by Congress to seek to dispel either the appearance or the reality of these influences. The remedies enacted by law, however, must comply with the First Amendment; and it is our law and our tradition that more speech, not less, is the governing rule. An outright ban on corporate political speech during the critical preelection period is not a permissible remedy. Here Congress has created categorical bans on speech that are asymmetrical to preventing *quid pro quo* corruption.[22]

What this passage actually claims is that while ingratiation and access may be CORRUPTING, such a concern is not weighty enough to constitute *Compelling-Interest Corruption* under the Court's First Amendment doctrine. But that nuance is obscured by language that asserts that "[i]ngratiation and access . . . are not corruption."

Citizens United was decided in 2010. In 2016, the Court decided the criminal case *McDonnell v. United States*.[23] In *McDonnell*, the Court overturned the conviction on bribery charges of former Virginia Governor Robert McDonnell because the jury instructions allowed for conviction if the jury found that the governor had accepted money and other valuable items in exchange for merely setting up meetings for and making phone calls on behalf of a businessman who hoped to have his product evaluated by Virginia universities. The relevant statute[24] provided that it is illegal to "corruptly" accept "anything of value" for "an official act."[25] There was ample evidence that Governor McDonnell had accepted money and other valuable items (a Rolex watch, for example) in exchange for setting up meetings and making calls. The problem, according to the Court, was that merely setting up meetings or making calls for someone fails to qualify as an "official" act.[26] This interpretive judgment is, largely, a matter of statutory interpretation,[27] but one has to wonder whether *Citizens United*'s view that granting access is not sufficiently corrupting to raise constitutional concerns influenced the Court in *McDonnell* in concluding that granting access is not an "official act."

Indeed, what else could the act of setting up a meeting of this kind be? Actions by public officials that are not "official" are personal. For example, suppose Robert McDonnell paid someone to cut his lawn or was paid by someone to cut their lawn (unlikely, to be sure, but the hypothetical is useful). These actions would not be official actions. McDonnell would be doing them in his personal, rather than official, capacity. It is for this reason that the person who pays McDonnell for McDonnell to cut that person's lawn (hypothetically) would be *paying* McDonnell, not *bribing* him.[28] By contrast, when the governor called people at Virginia universities to set up meetings for the person who gave him money to do so, the governor called as governor, not in his personal capacity. It is for this reason that the people he called took his call and took the meeting (even if they ultimately did not do what the businessman who paid McDonnell had hoped). These factors make the governor's action official rather than personal.[29]

We cannot know whether *Citizens United*'s statement that granting access is not corruption influenced the Court to think that granting access is not an "official act" in *McDonnell*, but the similarities of the views, combined with the timeline, are provocative at the least. And while the opinion in *McDonnell* never directly cites to *Citizens United*, it is noteworthy that the connection between the cases is emphasized by *amici* and in a manner that engages in precisely the slippage between *Compelling-Interest Corruption* and genuine CORRUPTION that I emphasize here.[30]

If the interpretation of criminal-law statutes addressing corruption of governmental officials can be influenced by how the Court delineates *Compelling-Interest Corruption* in campaign finance cases, perhaps the direction of such influence can run in the opposite direction as well. Suppose state or federal criminal-law statutes were drafted to unambiguously prohibit the exchange of money or other things of value for access to governmental officials. The enactment of such laws could affect how courts understand what counts as *Compelling-Interest Corruption* in campaign finance cases. While *McDonnell* held that such an exchange was not covered by the federal bribery statute as currently drafted, a new statute could make clear that such an exchange is forbidden.

The mechanism by which this reverse influence would occur is as follows. As I noted, the Court uses the term "corruption" in *Citizens United*, thereby inviting the confusion about what precisely it is talking about. Is it defining the sort of corruption that is sufficiently bad, in the Court's view, that avoiding it is compelling and thereby justifies burdens on speech? Or is it making a statement about what sort of thing is genuinely corrupting? This slippage between what I call *Compelling-Interest Corruption* and CORRUPTION facilitates the influence of campaign finance law on criminal law, and so could also facilitate the influence of clearly drafted criminal-law statutes defining certain conduct as CORRUPT on campaign finance law by modulating the way courts define *Compelling-Interest Corruption*.

The Potential Impact of Clarifying the Concept

Alternatively, perhaps clear statements by legislatures that the exchange of access for money or something else of value is prohibited would clarify the distinction between CORRUPTION and *Compelling-Interest Corruption*. By enacting such a law, the legislature would be expressing its view about what CORRUPTION includes. The fact that a legislature has asserted what it finds CORRUPTION to be would help to clarify for all (including the Supreme Court itself) that when the Court says that "[i]ngratiation and access ... are not corruption," the Court is not speaking about actual CORRUPTION but instead about the legal concept *Compelling-Interest Corruption*. This clarification would help to make clear that the job of defining what actual CORRUPTION is does not lie with the Court, as it is not a legal question to which the Constitution provides an answer. Such clarification could have two important consequences.

First, a legislature's assertion regarding what it finds actual CORRUPTION to be should give the Court pause about how the Court defines *Compelling-Interest Corruption* because that task depends on a judgment that is a mixed question of fact and law, and the factual part is one about which legislators bring more knowledge and expertise than do judges. To see why, consider what a Court is doing when it applies strict scrutiny and articulates those interests that are sufficiently compelling to outweigh or justify the burden on speech. The Court is pronouncing on what interests are *compelling*: meaning that they are urgent, critical, serious, or exigent. The fact that a legislature saw fit *to criminalize* such exchanges provides evidence that the legislators who enacted the law believe that avoiding this conduct is critical. This fact should matter to the Court. While the judgment that interest X is a "compelling state interest" is a legal judgment, to be sure, it is a legal judgment that depends on a factual judgment about the actual importance of the interest at stake. And legislators have information about that fact that the Court may well lack. Moreover, as a practical matter, it may be harder for the Court to say that avoiding the exchange of money for access is not the sort of corruption that is sufficiently compelling to count as *Compelling-Interest Corruption* when a legislature has made such conduct a crime.[31]

Second, and perhaps more critically, when a legislature criminalizes the exchange of money for access, it makes a particular exchange a forbidden *quid pro quo*. This is important because the Court has already recognized that *Compelling-Interest Corruption* includes forbidden *quid pro quo* exchanges. As a result, when a law makes it a crime to exchange money for access, it effectively, and necessarily, brings that exchange within the scope of the corruption interest already recognized by the Court as compelling.

Let me explain this point in a bit more detail. Current campaign finance doctrine provides that avoiding corruption or its appearance is the interest (perhaps the only interest) that justifies the burdens that restrictions on giving and spending money on elections impose on freedom of speech. The Court has defined "corruption" (i.e., *Compelling-Interest Corruption*) narrowly so that it includes only *quid pro quo* exchanges. But what, precisely, does the Court mean by a "*quid pro quo* exchange?" That term clearly does not encompass *all* exchange of some *quid* for some *quo*, as any ordinary purchase satisfies that definition. And clearly not all purchases are corrupt. A state could not forbid candidates from purchasing newspapers (a protected First Amendment activity) on the grounds that this prohibition is justified by preventing the reality or appearance of a *quid pro quo* exchange, even though the exchange of money for a newspaper literally fits that definition. Rather, what the Court refers to by using the Latin term is a subset of exchanges, those with some sort of negative valence. Which ones are those? It is tempting to say that what is forbidden are "corrupt" exchanges, but that line of argument is question-begging; as the Court says that what is "corrupt" are *quid pro quo* exchanges, so it can hardly then say that the exchanges that count as *quid pro quo* exchanges are those that are corrupt. Instead, what distinguishes a *quid pro quo* exchange from an ordinary purchase (such as buying a newspaper) is that a *quid pro quo* exchange is legally forbidden. That being the case, when a state forbids the exchange of money for access, campaign finance laws aimed at avoiding the reality or appearance of exchanges of value for access would be permissible under existing campaign finance doctrine. In such cases, access (or the exchange of money for access, to be precise) is a *quid pro quo* exchange and thus corruption.

The Exchange of Money for Access Is a Form of Corruption

My main point is that legislatures should define what CORRUPTION is for themselves to the extent that they are permitted to do so within existing law. But given that I am exploring the repercussions of their doing so using the example of a law forbidding the exchange of value for access to governmental officials, one has to wonder whether enacting such a prohibition is a good idea. I turn to that now.

Imagine that Governor McDonnell had decided to supplement his income in a more direct and transparent manner by simply offering spots on his own schedule to the highest bidder for each time slot. By saying that setting up a meeting, without more, is not an "official act" under federal law, the Court would have to conclude that Governor McDonnell has not violated federal bribery law. But he has clearly done something wrong, and something that could and should be made illegal.[32] If we are talking about whether this is a form of CORRUPTION (i.e., the real thing), it is beyond doubt that the answer is yes.

It is remarkable, then, that the Court treats the phenomenon of officials granting special access to contributors and gift-givers as normal politics, with the implication that what is normal cannot be corrupt. In *McDonnell*, the unanimous opinion of Chief Justice Roberts reaches this judgment by conflating paid-for access with normal politics in a disturbing way:

> Section 201 prohibits *quid pro quo* corruption—the exchange of a thing of value for an 'official act.' In the Government's view, nearly anything a public official accepts—from a campaign contribution to lunch—counts as a *quid*; and nearly anything a public official does—from arranging a meeting to inviting a guest to an event—counts as a *quo*. . . . The basic compact underlying representative government *assumes* that public officials will hear from their constituents and act appropriately on their concerns—whether it is the union official worried about

a plant closing or the homeowners who wonder why it took five days to restore power to their neighborhood after a storm. The Government's position could cast a pall of potential prosecution over these relationships if the union had given a campaign contribution in the past or the homeowners had invited the official to join them on their annual outing to the ball game.[33]

The argument contained in this passage appears to be that representative democracy depends on elected officials hearing from their constituents and being responsive to what they hear. If these constituents *happen* to have provided the elected official with an innocuous gift (say, lunch) or to have given a campaign contribution to this official, then both parties will be vulnerable to prosecution. That can't be permissible, or so the argument goes.

But this argument is flawed in two important ways. First, while access may provide the *quid* and lunch or a campaign contribution could provide the *quo*, what is missing in the Court's description of this scenario is any account of the *pro*. That is, the prosecution of either party would need to prove that the thing of value was promised or given *in exchange for* access to the official. In the examples that the Court offers in its parade of horribles, that worry seems seriously misplaced. Would anyone believe that an official granted access to a constituent in exchange for lunch? Would any prosecutor bring such a case? The concern voiced by the Court seems dramatically overblown.

Second, the passage quoted above emphasizes that "[t]he basic compact underlying representative government *assumes* that public officials will hear from their constituents and act appropriately on their concerns." However, the "basic compact underlying representative government" also assumes that elected officials will give approximately equal weight to the interests and concerns of each of their constituents. It is for this reason that each person gets one, and only one, vote, that wealthy individuals cannot buy the votes of others,[34] and that the Constitution demands equal population per elected representative.[35] While the Court has held that First Amendment values resist the idea of equalizing how much each person may speak or equalizing the impact that their expression will have,[36] the basic compact of representative government takes a different view about the significance of equality in the context of political participation. It is perhaps for this reason that the passage above uses the word "appropriately" where it does. The basic compact of representative government does not assume that officeholders will hear from their constituents and merely act. Rather they must respond "appropriately." While the Court does not spell out the normative import of this qualification, it seems reasonable to assume that giving greater time and attention to large donors than to those who lack the financial ability to donate to the representative's campaign is inappropriate. And agreeing to provide access in exchange for such large contributions is worse still.

Qualifications and Counterarguments

Given the argument presented above, why was the *McDonnell* decision—holding that Governor McDonnell cannot be convicted under current federal law for accepting money for merely setting up meetings—a unanimous decision? And why has neither Congress nor any state used its legislative powers to forbid the exchange of value for access?[37]

Let me begin with *McDonnell* and federal law. The decision in *McDonnell* largely rests on grounds of statutory interpretation.[38] That being the case, both Congress and state legislatures should be free to take a different view. In a clearly written statute, either body could prohibit the exchange of value for access to public officials. By "exchange," I mean an explicit or implicit deal in which value is exchanged for access. Whether legislatures should go further in defining conduct they view as CORRUPT might raise more difficult questions, so why not begin with the low-hanging fruit—conduct that is clearly CORRUPT—and explore how the exercise of legislative voice affects campaign finance law?

Beyond statutory interpretation, the Court in *McDonnell* also rests its decision on federalism concerns, expressing the worry that reading the federal law at issue to prohibit the exchange of value for access would involve the "Federal Government in setting standards [of] good government for local and state officials."[39] This concern regarding federal prosecutors setting the ethical standards for state and local officials is a recurring theme.[40] Indeed, the Court draws on similar federalism concerns in its most recent corruption-related decision, *Snyder v. United States*, invalidating the conviction of a local official for violating a different federal anti-corruption law.[41] Justice Jackson, dissenting in *Snyder*, argues that federalism concerns actually are the central reason that the Court invalidates the law.[42]

To the extent that *McDonnell* rests on statutory-interpretation grounds, both Congress and state legislatures are free to adopt a different view and to enact laws that criminalize the exchange of access for money or something else of value. To the extent that *McDonnell* relies on federalism concerns, state legislatures are exempt from this critique and are therefore free—and perhaps encouraged—to use their police powers to set standards of good government for themselves. It is for this reason that it makes sense for states to take the lead in adopting laws that make clear what, in their own views, counts as CORRUPT.[43]

McDonnell also hints at the idea that its decision rests on constitutional considerations. Whether this refers only to the federalism issue, which is obviated in the case of state laws, or something else entirely remains unclear. In some of the cases in which the Supreme Court restricts the application of federal laws aimed at curbing corruption in some form, worries about vagueness or notice implicate the constitutional demands of due process.[44] To the extent that this is the issue, legislatures must take care to carefully draft such new laws and to explicitly specify what exchanges are forbidden. In addition, the Court appears concerned that broadly written anti-corruption laws invite selective prosecution by prosecutors who will choose to use their discretion to pursue political rivals.[45] Again, that concern calls for precise and carefully drafted statutes, but it need not be an impediment to the project of legislatures asserting their views about the nature of CORRUPTION.

So why have no legislatures done this so far? Perhaps because of a lack of political will. Alternatively, perhaps the lack of action is traceable to the conflation between *Compelling-Interest Corruption* and genuine CORRUPTION, which leads legislators to think—wrongly—that they do not have a role to play in defining corruption. A good place to begin would be a state law that prohibits the exchange of something of value for access to public officials.

Buckley's Legacy Fifty Years On

The underappreciated legacy of *Buckley v. Valeo* is its role in anointing the Supreme Court as the branch tasked with defining corruption, a role which the Court has enthusiastically embraced. But the Court's purview in addressing that task has been misunderstood. The Court can define *Compelling-Interest Corruption* but not genuine CORRUPTION. In order to correct this misunderstanding and enable the views of legislatures to have their proper place within both legal doctrine and popular understandings, Congress and state legislatures (especially the latter) should enact clearly drafted statutes that prohibit specific exchanges, or other action, that they see as corrupt. The enactment of such laws will clarify the difference between the task allocated to the Court and the role of the people's representatives. And, in addition, through the different mechanisms described in this chapter, these laws may actually work to transform the legal concept of *Compelling-Interest Corruption* to be more in line with actual CORRUPTION, as the people define it.

10

Campaign Finance and "Real" Corruption

Nicholas O. Stephanopoulos

Introduction

"Yesterday, upon the stair / I met a man who wasn't there," begins Hughes Mearns's poem *Antigonish*. It continues: "He wasn't there again today / I wish, I wish he'd go away."[1] In the Supreme Court's campaign finance cases and the empirical literature on money in politics, corruption sometimes resembles Mearns's absent man. "Real" corruption—*quid pro quo* corruption, the only kind of corruption the Court now recognizes—is almost never present in the records the Court reviews. Over and over, the Court evaluates campaign finance laws aimed at stopping corruption without any evidence that corrupt exchanges are, in fact, occurring. Corruption is also the man who wasn't there in much of the relevant empirical work. These studies tend to find that campaign contributions *aren't* typically traded for legislators' votes: that most politicians are, in this sense, noncorrupt.

Unbeknownst to the Justices or even most scholars, however, an emerging literature identifies an area in which *quid pro quo* corruption is actually rife. This area is government contracting—the state entering into agreements with private parties for services in return for payments—a massive industry with an annual revenue of about $700 billion at the federal level alone. In this context, several recent studies show that firms whose political action committees (PACs) donate to federal officeholders receive more, and larger, federal contracts. The contracts that donating firms obtain also usually have weaker enforcement mechanisms, ensue after more irregular procurement processes, and are awarded by more politicized agencies. These findings replicate at the local level, where, for example, judges in Harris County, Texas, are more likely to assign appointments in indigent defense cases to attorneys who have given money to their campaigns. These findings replicate internationally, too, linking campaign contributions to government contracts in countries including Brazil, Colombia, Croatia, the Czech Republic, and Lithuania.

My primary goal in this chapter is to introduce this novel literature to judges, lawyers, and scholars who may be unaware of it. Contrary to the conventional wisdom in both the Court and (part of) the academy, in at least one major domain, overt swaps of campaign donations for official acts are very much a feature of the present, not a relic of the past. Next, I probe *why quid pro quo* corruption is more prevalent in government contracting than in generic legislating. One reason may be that the *quo* in this context—an agreement channeling money to a particular party—is a more concentrated benefit than a typical law, whose effects are more diffuse. Another explanation may be that a single officeholder (or a few officeholders) can often steer a contract to a favored party, while the efforts of many politicians are generally required to pass a law. One more piece of the puzzle may be that government contracting is low-profile and non-ideological, while (some) legislating is more visible and controversial.

Lastly, I explore the implications of widespread *quid quo pro* corruption existing in government contracting—and existing at all in contemporary politics. Most intuitively, when laws that seek to block exchanges of campaign donations for government contracts are challenged, courts should uphold these measures. The Supreme Court has never ruled on the validity of so-called "pay-to-play" provisions, but they're even better tailored to fighting corruption than are conventional contribution limits. Additionally, since the laws on the books haven't stamped out corruption in government contracting, policymakers should consider further steps. For instance, the federal ban on contractors *themselves* making campaign donations could be extended to contractors' PACs, parent firms, subsidiaries, employees, and family members. Contracting agencies could also institute procurement processes less susceptible to political influence.

At a higher level of abstraction, observers of campaign finance should rethink their assumptions about corruption. *Quid pro quo*s aren't freak occurrences today. In at least one crucial field, they're commonplace. If they arise in government contracting, they might also be found in other areas where individual officeholders can surreptitiously supply concentrated benefits to specific parties. And in that case, campaign finance regulations aren't too broad for their anticorruption mission—"prophylaxis upon prophylaxis," in the Court's mocking words.[2] Instead, they're the dam preventing even more *quid pro quo*s from pouring into our politics.

The Supposed Absence of Corruption

The avoidance of *quid pro quo* corruption (and its appearance) is the principal rationale the current Court recognizes for limiting money in politics. Exaggerating a bit, the Court even sometimes says it "has identified *only* one legitimate interest for restricting campaign finances": the anticorruption interest.[3] Given this interest's centrality, a critical question is how much *quid pro quo* corruption there is in modern American government. The more corruption there is, the more compelling the state interest in combating it becomes. And vice versa: There's less urgent a need to stop corruption if it's relatively rare—to wish a man who isn't there would go away.

Maybe surprisingly, over the last generation the Court has given the same answer to the question about the incidence of *quid pro quo* corruption. Namely, that little, even no, such corruption has been documented.[4] This answer, moreover, has played an important role in the Court's reasoning in, and disposition of, campaign finance cases. Start with the Court's 2003 decision in *McConnell v. FEC*.[5] Addressing the lawfulness of a federal ban on "soft money" contributions, the Court noted the absence of "concrete evidence of an instance in which a federal officeholder has actually switched a vote" because of a soft money donation.[6] In fact, the massive record compiled by Congress didn't include "a single discrete instance of quid pro quo corruption attributable to the donation" of soft money.[7] Of course, the *McConnell* Court nevertheless upheld the federal soft money ban. But to do so, it had to conceive of corruption more generally as donors' undue access to, or influence over, politicians.[8] Under the "crabbed" *quid pro quo* understanding of corruption, the soft money ban would likely have fallen.[9]

Next, consider the Roberts Court's most (in)famous campaign finance decision, *Citizens United v. FEC*.[10] In that 2010 case, the federal government defended its ban on corporate campaign expenditures on (among others) anticorruption grounds. The Court responded that it was unaware of "any direct examples of [Congress members'] votes being exchanged for . . . expenditures."[11] The Court also observed that "26 States do not restrict independent expenditures by for-profit corporations."[12] Yet "[t]he Government does not claim that these expenditures have corrupted the political process in those States."[13] Given this lack of evidence of corporate campaign spending being traded for state action, the Court held that the ban on such spending was poorly tailored to thwarting *quid pro quo*s: "Here Congress has created categorical bans on speech that are asymmetrical to preventing quid pro quo corruption."[14]

Or take the Court's 2022 campaign finance ruling, *FEC v. Cruz*,[15] involving a limit on candidates repaying themselves with post-election contributions for personal loans they had previously made to their campaigns. These donations might seem particularly likely to be elements of *quid pro quo* transactions, being made after an election (when the victor is known) and to repay debts (not to convey political messages). But the Court wanted historical proof, not logical reasoning, on this point. And it didn't find it. "[T]he Government is unable to identify a single case of quid pro quo corruption in this context," the Court complained.[16] Turning to the states' experiences, as in *Citizens United*, the Court remarked that "most States do not impose a limit on the use of post-election contributions to repay candidate loans."[17] Yet at the state level, too, there was no record of a post-election contribution being swapped for an official act. In part for these reasons, the Court concluded that "the Government has not shown that [the law at issue] furthers a permissible anticorruption goal."[18]

There are more cases in which the Roberts Court stressed the absence of *quid pro quo* corruption and relied on this absence to nullify campaign finance regulations. In the interest of space, I relegate these cases to the footnotes.[19] Now, the Roberts Court is a conservative body ideologically hostile to curbs on money in politics. So it's even more striking that a near-consensus exists in a very different community that *quid pro quo* corruption is uncommon: the social-science academy. Over the last few decades, dozens of studies have searched for a causal relationship between campaign contributions and governmental actions. Most of these studies have focused on PAC donations because the firms associated with PACs often command enormous resources and so are natural places to look for *quid pro quo* corruption. Most of these studies have also used Congress members' votes as their dependent variables because these carefully tracked up-or-down choices are the quintessential acts performed by legislators.[20]

The bulk of this work finds that PAC contributions to members of Congress *don't* affect the votes they cast. Here's how the best-known review of this literature puts it: "[T]he evidence that campaign contributions lead to a substantial influence on votes is rather thin."[21] Congress members' votes "depend almost entirely on their own beliefs and the preferences of their voters and their party."[22] Compared to these factors, "[c]ontributions explain a miniscule fraction of the variation in voting behavior."[23] Another literature review zeroes in on "event studies" that examine whether firms thought to be politically connected experience abnormal positive or negative returns after surprise events that strengthen or weaken their connections. This review determines that "[w]ell-designed political event studies do not support the hypothesis that campaign contributions buy political favors."[24] Surveying these and other reviews, a recent article concurs that "there have been few consistently demonstrated effects of money on roll call votes."[25] Accordingly, "the prevailing wisdom in the discipline . . . is that campaign contributions do not influence policy outcomes."[26]

There are, to be sure, dissenting academic voices. One literature review considers the regression coefficients for PAC contributions in hundreds of statistical tests. About one-third of these coefficients are statistically significant, potentially indicating a nonrandom relationship between PAC contributions and Congress members' votes.[27] Another review conducts a meta-analysis of all relevant studies. It rejects the null hypothesis that campaign donations have no impact on voting behavior in Congress.[28] However, these reviews fail to exclude studies whose methodologies prevent them from distinguishing between campaign dollars driving Congress members' votes and the opposite scenario of Congress members' votes driving campaign dollars.[29] Even on their own terms, moreover, these reviews concede that most studies don't find statistically significant effects and that the effects they do find are generally small. So, at most, these reviews require only a modest revision of the conventional wisdom. Maybe *quid pro quo*s are infrequent, not nonexistent, and a weak influence on congressional voting behavior, not no influence at all.

Corruption in Government Contracting

In light of this case law and academic work, the Justices and many scholars would be shocked to learn that *quid pro quo* corruption does occur—regularly and impactfully—in at least one area. This area is government contracting:

the state entering into agreements with private parties to pay them for services with public funds. In stark contrast to the literature on PAC contributions and Congress members' votes, recent studies *unanimously* find that donating firms receive more, and larger, federal contracts. These studies also identify several mechanisms through which campaign dollars yield contracting advantages. The conclusion that the *quid*s of campaign contributions are often exchanged for the *quo*s of government contracts further extends to the local American context. It reaches abroad, too, as studies of foreign government contracting are just as consistent in their results as are their American counterparts.

The 2011 study that spawned this government contracting literature examined all corporate PACs in operation from 1979 to 2006.[30] Controlling for other variables, PAC donations in the previous electoral cycle were strongly linked to federal contracts for PACs' parent firms in the current cycle.[31] Specifically, an additional $200,000 in donations led, on average, to more than a hundred extra contracts worth more than $5,000,000.[32] This finding also held for both earlier (1980–1992) and later (1994–2006) periods and for both defense and nondefense firms.[33] The latest and most methodologically sophisticated study looks at the contributions of individual employees (which dwarf PAC donations) from 2004 to 2015.[34] Aggregating these contributions at the level of the employer, and controlling for other variables, donating firms again receive more revenue from federal government contracts.[35] They do so whether their donations are treated in binary fashion (yes or no), categorically (high, medium, or low), or continuously (by dollar amount).[36]

Other studies tell virtually the same story. From 1993 to 2010, S&P 500 companies whose PACs made contributions were about twice as likely to win federal contracts, and a $500 increase in contributions was associated with roughly $200,000 more in contracting revenue.[37] From 2001 to 2006, over a sample of smaller federal no-bid contracts, a $100 increase in donations from a firm's employees was linked to around $250 more in contracting revenue.[38] From 2001 to 2010, each additional net member of Congress prevailing in a close race to whom a corporate PAC contributed led to the receipt of about two more federal contracts worth over $11,000,000.[39] From 2009 to 2015, companies whose PACs gave more to Barack Obama than to his opponents, and whose executives attended meetings at the White House, obtained an average of over $17,000,000 more in federal contracting revenue.[40] And in the particular contexts of post-war reconstruction in Afghanistan and Iraq,[41] cleanup after Hurricane

Katrina,[42] and the 2009 stimulus package,[43] firms with donating PACs and/or employees were, once again, more likely to be awarded federal contracts.

As interesting as these bottom-line results are the channels through which campaign dollars produce contracting benefits. One of these channels is the clout of the politicians who are given money. By virtue of their positions, some politicians have more ability to sway contracting decisions than do others. A study thus finds that contributions to members of Congress who sit on the Appropriations, Budget, or Transportation and Infrastructure Committees, which are heavily involved in allocating federal spending, have a larger impact on the likelihood of winning federal contracts than do contributions to other legislators.[44] Similarly, donations to the party of the president, the head of the executive branch, breed more favoritism in federal contracting than do donations to the opposing party.[45]

Another path between campaign dollars and contracting benefits runs through the access to, and relationships with, politicians that this money buys. As noted above, firms whose executives attend White House meetings subsequently receive more federal contracting revenue.[46] Why do these executives get White House invitations? In part because of contributions from their firms' PACs: More of these donations lead to a higher probability of a White House visit.[47] Analogously, members of Congress are more likely to own stock in companies whose PACs give to them.[48] Stock ownership is a kind of relationship that merges the financial interests of stockholders and firms. In turn, this ownership relationship has a downstream effect on contracting: Companies with more politician stockholders-donees are awarded more federal contracts.[49]

One more factor that mediates the connection between campaign dollars and contracting benefits is the politicization of federal agencies issuing contracts. More politicized agencies, agency components, and agency procurement processes are more susceptible to pressure from elected officials receiving contributions from would-be contractors, and so more apt to favor these firms. Specifically, compared to independent agencies, executive agencies tend to follow procurement processes that put the government at greater risk of bad outcomes due to lack of notice, nontransparent criteria, single bids, and the like.[50] Components of *all* agencies (even independent ones) also use riskier procurement processes when these offices are staffed by larger numbers of political appointees.[51] And in these cases where riskier procurement processes are employed, significant advantages accrue to donating firms. These firms are especially likely to win noncompetitive contracts and contracts with few bids—the very contracts most prone to political manipulation.[52]

The discussion to this point has dealt only with federal government contracting. But an impressive recent study shows that certain local officeholders—judges in Harris County, Texas—also strongly prefer their campaign donors when they award contracts—indigent defense case assignments. Controlling for other variables, an attorney who contributes to a judge doubles her usual number of case assignments in the month of the contribution.[53] On average, a $1,000 donation leads to extra monthly revenue of about $1,300 for the donor.[54] Notably, the effect of giving money quickly decays, such that six months after a contribution a donor attorney receives no more case assignments than a non-donor, and a year later a donor attorney receives *fewer* case assignments.[55] Also notably, donors to incumbent judges who lose reelection stop obtaining more case assignments after the judges leave office, and donors to successful challengers start getting more case assignments after the victors don their judicial robes.[56]

Abroad, as well, studies find evidence of campaign dollars being traded for government contracts in Brazil,[57] Colombia,[58] Croatia,[59] the Czech Republic,[60] and Lithuania.[61] The Lithuanian study, in my view the most compelling of this group, exploits a ban on corporate contributions to candidates that took effect in 2012. Before the ban, controlling for other variables, donating firms were about five percentage points more likely to be awarded government contracts.[62] This edge began to diminish as soon as the ban was instituted, and within less than two years it disappeared entirely.[63] Moreover, firms that had donated before the ban systematically lowered their contract bids after the ban, and, when they won contracts after the ban, won them by a larger margin than before the ban.[64] These facts imply that, before the ban, money from donating firms bought them leaked information about competitors' bids, which these firms used to make offers just below their rivals' prices.[65]

Now, this literature is persuasive to me, but would it convince the Supreme Court that *quid pro quo* corruption is common in government contracting? The Court *has* been willing to consider academic studies of corruption, commenting on them both in a 2000 case[66] and in *Cruz*. In *Cruz*, however, the Court criticized the article the Federal Election Commission cited as evidence that post-election contributions to repay the loans of members of Congress sway these legislators' subsequent votes. The problem, according to the Court, was that this article didn't establish when "voting pattern changes [are] part of an illicit quid pro quo."[67] That is, the article didn't "pin down a causal link."[68]

Unlike the article in *Cruz*, much of the government contracting scholarship I've summarized *does* pin down (or, at least, strongly suggest) a causal link. Almost all these studies include controls for other variables that might affect contracting decisions (firm size, firm industry, firm contracting revenue in previous years, and so on) as well as firm and year fixed effects.[69] Even more credibly, several studies use research designs that are particularly well suited to demonstrating causation. For example, one study treats the net number of members of Congress winning in close races to which a PAC contributes as its key independent variable, not a PAC's raw contributions.[70] Because it's largely random whether Congress members win or lose in close races, the net number of winners to which a PAC donates is also mostly a matter of chance. If this net number is nevertheless a significant driver of the federal contracts a PAC's parent firm receives, this relationship is plausibly causal. Exogenous variation in the net number has direct contracting consequences.

Likewise, the fine-grained data of the Harris County study—broken down by month and distinguishing between incumbent judges and challengers—enables us to draw causal inferences. What explanation could there possibly be, other than recurring *quid pro quo*s, why donor attorneys *don't* get more indigent case assignments the month before their donations, *do* get more case assignments that month, and then see this benefit ebb unless they give again?[71] By the same token, why else would attorneys who contribute to defeated incumbent judges stop getting more case assignments, and attorneys who contribute to successful challengers start getting them, if not swaps of campaign money for profitable work?[72]

For still more causal evidence of *quid pro quo*s, return to the Lithuanian study of the 2012 ban on corporate contributions to candidates. You might be skeptical of the pre-2012 finding that donating firms were substantially more likely to receive government contracts.[73] Maybe it was some unobserved and uncontrolled-for feature of these firms—not their donations to candidates—that led to their success in the procurement process. But such doubt can't reasonably be maintained given what happened after the ban went into force in 2012. After that date, any mysterious property of previously donating firms would have stayed the same. But their prior success in the procurement process *didn't* stay the same. Instead, it evaporated, soon leaving them with no edge at all over previously nondonating firms. Frequent *quid pro quo*s before the ban, mostly eliminated by the ban, can easily make sense of these developments. Any other account would be farfetched by comparison.

Of course, even the soundest studies might not be enough for the author of *Cruz*, Chief Justice Roberts, who introduced the phrase "sociological gobbledygook" to our lexicon.[74] But the case that *quid pro quo* corruption in government contracting is widespread doesn't rest on statistics alone. It also rests on specific instances—many, many known instances—in which campaign contributions were exchanged for contracting advantages. In 1939, the year before Congress prohibited donations from federal contractors, a scandal flared over contractors buying Democratic Party convention souvenir books, at the inflated price of $250 per book, in proportion to their contracting businesses.[75] In the Watergate era, the Senate Select Committee on Presidential Campaign Activities uncovered "evidence of quid pro quos for the contracts" issued by four cabinet departments and six agencies.[76] "Another notorious pay-to-play scheme" in this period "involved Vice President Spiro Agnew ... accept[ing] bribes (including campaign contributions) in exchange for infrastructure contracts while serving as Baltimore County Executive and Governor of Maryland—and ... continu[ing] to request payments from contractors as Vice President."[77]

In the 1980s, Senator Harrison Williams was convicted on several charges after he "use[d] his position ... to obtain government contracts" for a titanium mine and processing plant.[78] (This facility wasn't actually real; it was invented by undercover agents as part of the "Abscam" investigation.[79]) In the 1990s, Connecticut Treasurer Paul Silvester "collect[ed] campaign contributions in exchange for placing $500 million in state pension investments with certain equity funds."[80] This incident helped prompt the SEC to adopt a rule forbidding firms from managing jurisdictions' pension funds within two years of donating to jurisdictions' elected officials.[81] In the 2000s—a heyday of *quid pro quo* corruption in government contracting—Connecticut, Illinois, and New Jersey all saw pay-to-play scandals engulf high-ranking politicians.[82] Illinois Governor George Ryan, for instance, "steer[ed] state contracts to friendly firms in exchange for financial support for his gubernatorial campaign."[83] The 2000s were also when Representative Randy "Duke" Cunningham "accept[ed] millions of dollars in bribes in exchange for influencing Defense Department contract awards,"[84] and Representative Bob Ney entered into "a series of quid pro quos with the lobbyist Jack Abramoff, including steering a multi-million dollar contract for a[n] ... infrastructure project to one of Abramoff's clients."⁸⁵ More recently, Ohio House Speaker Larry Householder secured a subsidy for a utility company in return for secret funding,⁸⁶ and dozens of New York City Housing Authority officials were indicted for pay-to-play offenses.⁸⁷

As long as this list is, it includes only some of the most prominent cases of campaign contributions being traded for contracting favors. The full record of pay-to-play indictments and convictions (let alone well-founded suspicions) is much more voluminous.⁸⁸ A skeptic of statistics like Chief Justice Roberts, then, could dismiss the empirical evidence of *quid pro quo* corruption in government contracting but still conclude that this evil is pervasive. This conclusion is bolstered by—but in no way requires—statistical analysis.

Explanations

The materials I've surveyed in the last two sections pose a conundrum. They indicate that *quid pro quo* corruption is *rare* in generic legislating but *prevalent* in government contracting. Why would one state function be mostly devoid of—but another rife with—swaps of campaign dollars for official acts? I think there are several solutions to this riddle, several reasons why government contracting is materially different from generic legislating. Together, these reasons start to sketch a general theory of how *quid pro quo* corruption arises.

First, while a typical law benefits many parties, a government contract directly benefits only the contractor. Legislation can be as broad or narrow as legislators want. But most modern legislation is "public" legislation, written in generally applicable terms that are usually satisfied by a range of individuals or entities. In fact, Congress has enacted only five "private" laws, conferring advantages to identified parties, over the last dozen years.⁸⁹ In contrast, essentially all government contracting is "private" contracting. Almost all government contracts, that is, are awarded to specific named parties, who alone are obligated to provide services and, in return, entitled to receive payments. The upshot is that a typical law supplies a *diffuse* benefit, a benefit divided among many beneficiaries. A government contract, on the other hand, channels a *concentrated* benefit to the contractor, a prize no one else can claim.⁹⁰

It should be plain that a private party considering entering into a *quid pro quo* transaction with a politician would prefer a concentrated to a diffuse benefit. The party would capture the entire concentrated benefit, while it would have to share the diffuse benefit with others. Precisely because the *quo* is larger in the case of a concentrated benefit, a private party would be more likely to offer a politician a *quid* to obtain it. Intuitively, it's more attractive to get a big reward for a given investment than a small one. To illustrate this logic, suppose the government can distribute $100 in governmental spending either via legislation equally to ten entities or by contract wholly to one entity. Also suppose a private party can secure either the enactment of the law or the award of the contract for the same $10 campaign contribution. In this hypothetical, the party has no reason to agree to a *quid pro quo* (and thus to commit a felony) for the sake of the law's passage. Here, $10 in will result in just $10 out. But the party has a stronger incentive to trade its donation for the contract's issuance. There, $10 in will yield *$100* out. This is the first reason, then, why government contracting may be especially conducive to *quid pro quo* corruption: the greater potential *quo* for a given *quid* in this context.

The second reason is that a typical law requires the efforts of many officeholders to be enacted, while a single politician can sometimes steer a government contract to a contractor. At the federal and state levels, majorities in two legislative chambers, as well as the assent of the president or the governor, are constitutionally obligatory for bills to be passed. Legislative rules may also necessitate committee approvals, and political norms may demand that a majority of the majority party be in favor.[91] Conversely, elected officials have *no* formal role in most awards of government contracts. When politicians do become involved in the procurement process, they usually operate alone or in conjunction with just a few other politicians. They convey information to and from agencies and bidders. They threaten, cajole, or otherwise induce contracting officers to do their bidding. They *don't* exercise any powers that require the concurrence of other officeholders. The means through which politicians influence contracts are informal—often illegal—and so can be employed unilaterally.

Just as a private party mulling a *quid pro quo* would prefer a concentrated to a diffuse benefit, it would rather contribute to one elected official (or to a handful) than to many. Obviously, making many campaign donations is more expensive, and so more undesirable, than making one donation (or just a few). A private party would be more inclined to offer a *quid* for a given *quo* if the requisite *quid* was smaller. Amending the above hypothetical, imagine that a party can obtain the same $100 in revenue through either a (highly targeted) law or a government contract. Also say that, for the law to be enacted, the party must make ten $10 contributions (to party leaders, committee chairs, and the like), while a single $10 contribution (to a politician with few scruples but much clout) will suffice for the contract to be issued. Again, the party has no reason to agree to a *quid pro quo* for the law ($100 in, $100 out). And again, the party has a stronger incentive to exchange its campaign money for the contract ($10 in, $100 out). Much as a larger *quo* may make *quid pro quo* corruption more likely in the government contracting context, so may a smaller *quid*.

The last contrast between generic legislating and government contracting turns the telescope to look at officeholders' (not donors') interests. Votes on bills are legislators' most public acts. They're tracked by official records, converted into ideology scores by scholars and interest groups, and, in some cases, attacked or lauded in campaigns. Legislators also face many, often conflicting, pressures when deciding how to vote on bills. Their party generally has a position. So do their constituents and (not quite the same) their voters. Legislators may have their own personal views to weigh as well. But none of this is true for government contracts. These agreements are essentially invisible to the public. Very few voters know about them (even when they're fiscally significant), let alone what surreptitious steps legislators may have taken to bring them about. And because of this low salience, legislators have much more freedom to maneuver. Their party almost never has a stance on a particular contract. The same goes for their constituents and voters. Legislators are unlikely to have any personal views either that might interfere with their interventions on behalf of would-be contractors.[92]

Consequently, not only should a private party be more inclined to *offer* a *quid pro quo* in the government contracting context, but a legislator should be more apt to *accept*. The donor's *quid* must compete against many other factors in the case of legislation, but has the procurement field almost all to itself.[93] Revising the running hypothetical one more time, suppose a legislator is presented with two potential $10 contributions, one in return for a vote on a bill, the other for assistance in winning a contract. The second proposition is probably much more appealing to the legislator. It entails behind-the-scenes help, not a public expression of support. It's also less likely to conflict with other drivers of the legislator's actions such as party loyalty, public opinion, and personal ideology. Government contracting may thus be more amenable to *quid pro quos* because, from the perspective of legislators, the *quos* they're asked for are easier for them to give.

Put these pieces together and a general theory of *quid pro quo* corruption begins to emerge. Such corruption may be more common when (1) a private party can secure a concentrated rather than a diffuse benefit; (2) this benefit can be provided by one politician (or just a few); and (3) the activity required to provide the benefit is nonpublic and noncontroversial to the politician's other constituencies. This account makes sense of the seemingly irreconcilable findings of the previous two sections. In the generic legislating context, benefits to private parties are typically diffuse, the consent of many politicians is necessary to supply these benefits, and the expressions of this consent are visible and often contentious. But in the government contracting context, benefits to private parties are concentrated, a single politician can sometimes confer these benefits, and the politician can do so covertly and without irritating her other constituencies. There's a satisfying answer, then, to the question of why *quid pro quo* corruption appears to be rare in generic legislating but prevalent in government contracting. All three potential causes of *quid pro quo*s tend to be absent in the former context but present in the latter.

Might there be other areas where all three potential causes of *quid pro quo*s tend to be present? Certainly, and I explore some of them in the next section. Before venturing beyond government contracting, though, I consider the implications of widespread corruption in this context. One is attitudinal: Judges, lawyers, and scholars should stop assuming that *quid pro quo*s are highly infrequent in modern American politics. Another is legal: Since *quid pro quo* corruption *is* endemic in government contracting, courts should uphold the regulations that try to prevent it. One more implication blends law and policy: Since existing rules haven't stamped out *quid pro quo* corruption in government contracting, policymakers should take more anticorruptive steps and courts should then sustain them.

Implications

Most of the time, when Supreme Court opinions and academic articles say there's little *quid pro quo* corruption in generic legislating, they're careful to limit their remarks to that context. On occasion, however, these defensible statements blur into stronger claims that *quid pro quo*s seldom occur today, period. In *Citizens United*, for example, the Court noted the absence of known cases of "votes being exchanged for . . . expenditures."[94] But the Court accompanied this observation with the broader assertion that "few if any contributions to candidates will involve quid pro quo arrangements" of any kind.[95]

A review of the campaign finance literature similarly opens by describing the "conventional wisdom" that "PAC contributions rarely exert an independent influence on roll call votes."[96] But this position is then conflated with the different, more sweeping view that "the campaign contributions of interest groups have far less influence than commonly thought" over all governmental activity.[97]

It's understandable that commentators sometimes slide from legislation specifically to state action writ large. Again, legislators' votes on bills are their most public and controversial acts. It's understandable, but it's incorrect. The federal government alone spends about $700 billion annually on contracts with private parties.[98] Worldwide, countries redistribute roughly 15% of their gross domestic products through the procurement process.[99] If this enormous state enterprise is rife with *quid pro quo* corruption, then it's simply wrong to suppose that such corruption is mostly nonexistent today. In fact, such corruption is rampant, just not in the first place (legislation) you might think to look for it. This reality, in turn, requires a paradigm shift in the attitudes of judges, lawyers, and scholars about *quid pro quo*s. These individuals should recognize, and internalize, that campaign donations *are* regularly swapped for certain official acts. These individuals should also be receptive to, not dismissive of, efforts to block *quid pro quo* corruption. This anticorruptive project might be overkill—"prophylaxis upon prophylaxis"[100]—if *quid pro quo* corruption were rare. But since it's common, good governance entails trying to stop it.

For the Supreme Court, being receptive to anticorruptive measures should start with sustaining pay-to-play provisions when they reach its docket. At the federal level, a law has prohibited contractors from contributing to candidates or political parties since 1940.[101] Federal agencies have also targeted particular forms of *quid pro quo* corruption. In 1994, the Municipal Securities Rulemaking Board (MSRB) banned brokers and dealers of municipal securities from obtaining contracts to issue securities from jurisdictions to whose officeholders the brokers and dealers had donated over the previous two years.[102] In 2010 and 2016, respectively, the SEC adopted analogous two-year time-outs for investment advisers and placement agents, pegged to their last contributions to jurisdictions' elected officials, during which they may not be involved in managing these jurisdictions' pension funds.[103] Many more pay-to-play provisions exist at the state and local levels. Some of these are narrower than their federal counterparts, for instance, limiting but not forbidding donations from contractors.[104] Others are more aggressive, applying to not just contractors themselves but also their PACs, parent firms, subsidiaries, employees, and/or family members.[105]

As pointed out earlier, the Supreme Court has never addressed the validity of a policy aiming to extirpate *quid pro quo* corruption in government contracting. Lower federal courts, though, have assessed, and approved, all the federal policies flagged in the previous paragraph.[106] Federal and state courts have also mostly[107] (but not universally[108]) upheld state and local pay-to-play provisions. When the Supreme Court ultimately confronts one of these measures, the Court should follow the lead of most other courts. And the Court should do so in an opinion that reaches two key conclusions. One is that *quid pro quo* corruption is, in fact, extensive in government contracting. This judgment is supported by all the empirical and anecdotal evidence cited above, which distinguishes this context from generic legislating. The other conclusion is that a pay-to-play law markedly reduces (even if it doesn't eradicate) *quid pro quo* corruption in government contracting. This is the finding of the Lithuanian study showing that donating firms' advantage in securing government contracts vanished after corporate campaign contributions were prohibited.[109] Likewise, the MSRB's two-year time-out for donating brokers and dealers of municipal securities was "responsible for eliminating at least 99% of the abuses involving pay-to-play" in this sector.[110]

Of course, the Roberts Court is the body that brought us *Citizens United*, *Cruz*, and many other decisions striking down campaign finance regulations. But it's plausible that even this antiregulatory Court would greenlight a pay-to-play law. This Court has rejected state interests *other than* the prevention of *quid pro quo* corruption as legitimate justifications for restricting money in politics. The defense of a pay-to-play law, however, could rest solely on the anticorruption interest. It would be unnecessary to invoke other rationales like the pursuit of political equality or the avoidance of electoral distortion.[111] This Court has also suggested that most limits on campaign contributions are valid, declining to disturb the federal base limits, for example, for two decades.[112] The anticorruption argument for a pay-to-play law is *stronger* than that for a standard contribution limit, because there's much more evidence of *quid pro quo*s in government contracting than in generic legislating. And when this Court faced another campaign finance rule tackling nonlegislative corruption—a canon of judicial conduct banning judicial candidates from soliciting contributions—The Court sustained that rule.[113] The Court thus seems open to the possibility that, even if *quid pro quo* corruption is infrequent in the legislative process, it may be more widespread elsewhere.

I mentioned a moment ago that a typical pay-to-play law doesn't eradicate *quid pro quo* corruption in government contracting. One reason why is that it might not apply to entities and individuals distinct from contractors themselves, but sharing their interests, who could also be motivated to trade campaign donations for government contracts. The federal pay-to-play law, for instance, doesn't reach contractors' PACs, parent firms, subsidiaries, employees, or family members.[114] An intuitive way to block more corrupt exchanges, then, is to expand a pay-to-play law's coverage.[115] If this were done federally, the extension to contractors' PACs should be legally unproblematic. Many studies determine that contributions from contractors' PACs drive extra government deals for contractors and so imply the presence of *quid pro quo*s. On the other hand, I'm unaware of evidence directly linking contributions from contractors' parent firms, subsidiaries, employees, or family members to more government work for contractors. Such ties may well exist, given the overlapping interests between contractors and these entities and individuals, but they haven't yet been proven. Accordingly, proponents of a broader federal pay-to-play law would be well-advised to document that campaign dollars are often swapped for government contracts by firms and persons allied with contractors. A wider law's validity could easily turn on the thoroughness of this documentation.[116]

Another policy recommendation follows from the empirical finding that contractors with donating PACs are even more likely to be awarded government contracts when riskier procurement processes are used.[117] To reiterate, riskier procurement processes are those that raise the probability of bad outcomes for the government due to lack of notice, nontransparent criteria, single bids, and so on. Politically connected contractors enjoy an even greater edge when government contracts are issued in these more clandestine, less competitive ways. To take away this edge, borne of corruption rather than merit, riskier procurement processes should simply be avoided whenever possible.[118] Unless there are extenuating circumstances—a natural disaster, a war, an urgent deadline—advance notice of a contracting opportunity should be provided, terms shouldn't be crafted to favor any bidder, and the contract should go to the qualified firm making the lowest bid.[119] Notably, more open and competitive procurement processes would be legally invulnerable. They're already widely used by governments at all levels. Their even greater use would raise no colorable legal claims.

And another policy suggestion with an empirical basis: Recall that contractors with donating PACs have a particularly large advantage when procurement processes are not just riskier but also more politicized.[120] Greater politicization here means that contracts are awarded by executive rather than by independent agencies; and, within all agencies, by offices with more instead of fewer political appointees. To lessen the politicization of government contracting, some procurement could be shifted from executive agencies to independent agencies with similar substantive responsibilities. To illustrate, certain financial regulation contracts could be issued by the SEC, not the Treasury Department, and certain environmental contracts by the Environmental Protection Agency, not the Interior Department. Additionally, within all agencies, some procurement could be shifted to more politically insulated offices that are home to fewer political appointees.[121] Again, these moves would be entirely unproblematic from a legal standpoint. No law requires contracting to be politicized, so no law could be violated by its partial depoliticization.

As I foreshadowed earlier, the last topic I discuss is whether *quid pro quo* corruption might be common in areas beyond government contracting. Per the theory I previously outlined, (1) *quid pro quo*s may regularly arise when private parties' benefits are concentrated rather than diffuse, (2) these benefits can be provided by a single politician (or just a few), and (3) this provision is covert and noncontroversial to other constituencies. So which other areas might share these features?

One possibility is government licensing: the process by which the state grants permission to entities or individuals to engage in designated businesses. A license is a concentrated benefit whose entire value is gained by the licensee, a single politician can sometimes intervene to secure a license, and this intervention is unlikely to be visible or salient to other audiences. Unsurprisingly, given these attributes, anecdotal evidence exists of *quid pro quo* corruption in government licensing.[122] States have also passed anticorruptive laws barring certain kinds of licensees, like casino and liquor companies, from making campaign contributions.[123] And courts have universally upheld these laws, precisely because of the heightened risk of *quid pro quo*s in this context.[124]

Another area that could be prone to trades of campaign dollars for official acts is regulatory enforcement. The enforcement of laws and rules through inspections, penalties, and bans on doing business is a concentrated *harm* incurred fully by the affected party. The prevention or mitigation of such enforcement is thus a concentrated benefit, which a single politician can sometimes enable through nonpublic, noncontroversial steps. As expected, based on these characteristics, one study finds that financial firms with donating PACs are less likely to be targeted by SEC enforcement actions and receive smaller monetary penalties if prosecuted.[125] Another study shows that corporate executives who give to politicians and are accused of fraud end up with smaller monetary penalties and fewer days banned from serving as officers or directors.[126] According to one more study, nuclear power plants with donating PACs are rewarded by fewer annual hours of plant inspections.[127]

Government bailouts are a final setting in which *quid pro quo*s may frequently occur. A bailout is obviously a concentrated benefit for a firm—often one that makes possible the firm's continued existence. And a single politician can sometimes ensure that a donating firm is bailed out through actions that leave few fingerprints. Sure enough, given these properties, a domestic study finds that, the more firms gave to members of the House Financial Services Committee in 2007–2008, the more likely their applications for capital under the Troubled Asset Relief Program were to be approved.[128] A comparative study similarly shows that, across thirty-five countries, politically connected firms are bailed out more often than are their peers that lack political ties.[129] Of course, these examples of government licensing, regulatory enforcement, and government bailouts are probably far from exhaustive. There may well be other areas, too, where the conditions for *quid pro quo* corruption are habitually satisfied. The point is that government contracting isn't unique in being conducive to corruption. It could even be the tip of a much larger iceberg.

Conclusion

In the second stanza of *Antigonish*, the poem takes a sudden twist: The invisible man materializes. "When I came home last night at three / The man was waiting there for me."[130] The story of Mearns's invisible man, I've argued in this chapter, is akin to that of *quid pro quo* corruption. Long thought to be absent by Supreme Court Justices and scholars alike, it's actually present—pervasive—in the arena of government contracting. This is likely because of the confluence of several factors: *concentrated benefits* being allocated to *private parties* by *individual politicians* through *secretive, nonsalient means*. These recurring *quid pro quo*s mean that policymakers should adopt, and courts should uphold, measures aimed at fighting corruption in government contracting. More generally, observers of money in politics should realize that exchanges of campaign dollars for official acts have hardly been vanquished. The man who wasn't there is, in fact, still here.

11

Buckley at 50

By What Right?

Lawrence Lessig

It is unlikely that the author of *Buckley v. Valeo*—the opinion was per curiam but likely crafted by Justice Brennan—would have recognized just how strange the opinion would seem fifty years after it was delivered. At the time, the logic and approach were ordinary. Over time, at least from the perspective of some, it has become odd. With no clear textual grounding, and no effort to link its proscriptions to the early or original meaning of the First Amendment, *Buckley*, like Athena, seems to spring forth from the mind of the Court fullblown, as if always part of our tradition, and confident that it would define our future as well.

Yet as Justice Thomas has said about *New York Times v. Sullivan*, from the perspective of originalists, *Buckley* is a "policy-driven decision[] masquerading as constitutional law."[1] And as the opinion continues to govern an incredibly important slice of the law of democracy, it is timely and appropriate to ask a foundational question: What is the democratic sanction for this constitutional limit on the power of Congress and the states? When did we, the people, ratify a constitutional norm that would justify so fundamentally displacing the democratic will as expressed through elected representatives?

Because as the work of scholars such as Jud Campbell has evinced, *Buckley*'s rule was no part of the original meaning of the First Amendment. And to the extent one embraces the modern rule that *Buckley, ipse dixit*, announced, it is clear that at least the lower courts have extended *Buckley*'s reach far beyond its own logic. It is time for the Supreme Court to carve back fundamentally on the judicial regulation that *Buckley* has imposed, either by enforcing an interpretation more consistent with its own premises, or, for the originalists at least, narrowing the scope of its reach to be consistent with founding norms.

Lawrence Lessig, Buckley *at 50*. In: *Money, Politics, and the First Amendment*. Edited by: Lee C. Bollinger and Geoffrey R. Stone, Oxford University Press. © Oxford University Press (2026).
DOI: 10.1093/9780197821947.003.0012

This essay will explore that re-crafting in the context of the rule governing contributions to independent political action committees—so-called "super PACs," as Eliza Newlin Carney dubbed them in 2010.[2] *Buckley* didn't address that question directly, but the struggle that courts have had applying *Buckley*'s rule to this important category of political speech shows both the weakness in *Buckley*'s approach and the need for judicial retreat.

Buckley's Origin

Scholars have long noted the gap between the modern and evolved doctrine of the Free Speech and Press Clauses of the First Amendment, and any original meaning of that text.[3] That gap is not surprising. Modern First Amendment law was born long before modern originalism made any self-conscious judicial debut. Early First Amendment cases did little more than recognize the tension between the plain text of the First Amendment and the obvious tradition of Congress making plenty of law regulating speech and the press. Even Justice Black, the Court's proto-originalist, who insisted "I read 'no law . . . abridging' to mean *no law abridging*,"[4] saw no inconsistency in prosecuting symbolic speech or punishing children for disfavored views.[5]

Instead, rather than founding ideals or original understanding, the law of the First Amendment emerged from a felt necessity among Justices that beyond the plain meaning of "Congress shall make no law . . . abridging the freedom of speech," there had to be a principle standing behind those words, and that it, the Court, had a responsibility to enforce that principle in a wide range of law.

In 1976, the Court inserted this principle into two distinct but important regulatory contexts. Over the strong dissent of Justice Rehnquist, the Court extended First Amendment protection to commercial speech.[6] And with a string of qualifications and partial dissents, the Court, per curiam, extended First Amendment protection to campaign finance law.[7] Both doctrines have grown dramatically in the fifty years since. The law of commercial speech has been characterized as *Lochner*'s second coming.[8] The law of campaign finance has radically affected the scope and nature of political campaigns.

Yet both applications flowed naturally from the form of analysis that had emerged by the mid-1970s: A regulation of speech triggered a form of heightened scrutiny. Heightened scrutiny forced courts to determine which state interests were sufficiently strong to justify the regulation. Courts weighed those state interests against an assessment of the free-speech interests at stake in any case and determined which interests would be deemed to prevail.

In the context of campaign finance, *Buckley* recognized "corruption" or the "appearance of corruption" as a sufficiently strong state interest justifying limits on political speech. Regulations that advanced the fight against "corruption" or the "appearance of corruption" had at least a chance of surviving First Amendment review; regulations that did not would likely not.

There's a whole industry of scholarship arguing about whether *Buckley*'s identification of "corruption" was meant to be exclusive or not. Likewise, there's an industry of scholarship arguing about whether the Court's definition of "corruption" was meant to be limited, as the Court has recently insisted, to "*quid pro quo* corruption" or not.

But I want to begin with a point that among First Amendment scholars is just too rarely remarked, but that could become increasingly salient among Justices on the current Supreme Court. It is a point grounded in the birth of the conservative judicial movement, and one that justifies, at least in Justice Scalia's view, the doctrine of originalism.

That point is this: For originalists, it should be extraordinary that we have a doctrine of constitutional law that empowers judges to identify interests that they think sufficiently strong as a means to upholding the legislation of democratic legislatures or not. *Buckley* said "corruption" was sufficiently strong. Why? According to whom? The Court treats it as obvious that it must identify the interests that will suffice to uphold a regulation, without even pretending that its views have any connection to the views either of those who ratified the First Amendment or of a present constitutional majority. Put most starkly, and from the perspective of democratic theory: No one could believe that at any point in American history, we, the people, ratified as part of our Constitution the doctrine that the Court now enforces to constrain the work of legislatures.

That's not to criticize the modern doctrine. It's not to say that the doctrine is not valuable, or productive, or even good for the nation. It is certainly not meant to commend originalism as its replacement.[9] It is simply to note that its contours do not flow from the democratic will of we the people at any point in our history—and that, at least at the birth of modern originalism, this fact would have mattered. The conservative judicial movement placed Alex Bickel's "counter-majoritarian difficulty" at center stage,[10] and it called for an approach to constitutional law that would keep judges to the side. The only sanction, these conservatives insisted, for a court overruling a legislature was a clear commitment in the Constitution that was inconsistent with some law. Absent such a commitment, no court, within a democracy, could legitimately interfere with the laws of a democratic legislature.

Originalism complemented this theory of restraint with a theory of interpretation.[11] To know the commitments of the Constitution, originalists insisted a court should read its words within their framing context. Early originalists sought "the intent" of the framers.[12] Later originalists reformed that standard, focusing instead on the original public meaning of the words the framers used.[13] Either way, the theory of meaning operationalized the theory of restraint. As Charles Fried, Ronald Reagan's second solicitor general, put it,

> [t]he concept of originalism speaks to the most basic legal question: by what authority do judges impose their views on the people, even to the point of striking down laws made by the people's elected representatives?[14]

If you believe, as the most prominent judicial originalists believed, that history constrains (Fried did not[15]), originalism was activism's remedy.[16] As Justice Scalia put it: "[t]he main danger in judicial interpretation of the Constitution ... is that the judges will mistake their own predilections for the law."[17] "Nonoriginalism," he insisted, "plays precisely to this weakness"; originalism fights against it. And though Scalia conceded that that history was "difficult,"

> the question to be decided is not whether the historically focused method is a perfect means of restraining aristocratic judicial Constitution-writing; but whether it is the best means available in an imperfect world.[18]

Originalism today has lost this founding humility. But given its origins, it is fair to ask, how? If the purpose of recurring to founding moments is simply to identify the clear boundaries constraining democratic legislatures, that purpose should itself constrain the scope of judicial discretion and the rule the Court announces to enforce the Constitution. Yet nothing in First Amendment doctrine as it has evolved suggests any desire to constrain judicial discretion. Judges have become the über-regulators for any regulation that might be framed as a regulation of speech. And in the context of the Internet, that increasingly means practically any regulation of that technical platform. Judge Freeman's opinion nullifying the California Age-Appropriate Design Code Act should strike an originalist—of at least the original Scalia mold—as a nightmare of judicial activism.[19]

No doubt, in some cases, a Court can plead interpretive necessity. As John Marshall famously argued in *Marbury v. Madison*,[20] the Constitution's requirement that treason be proven with "the Testimony of two Witnesses" forces the Court to reject convictions supported by the testimony of one witness. "On the Testimony of two Witnesses" could not, given the rules of English grammar, permit convictions on the testimony of one witness. Filling out the ordinary meaning of that clear judicial constraint will always require some judgment.

But the First Amendment doctrine that governs campaign finance law today does not follow as a matter of logic from the words of the First Amendment. The First Amendment does not speak of "corruption." Even if it did, as Justice Breyer brilliantly argued in his dissent in *McCutcheon v. FEC*,[21] there are any number of conceptions of "corruption" that would support any number of different proscriptions on a legislature's freedom to regulate campaign spending or contributions. The Court is not driven to one or another from the very nature of the act of interpreting a Constitution. Instead, the Court is picking one interpretation over another, based, apparently, upon its own judgment of which First Amendment is best for America, or upon the values it thinks best for America. In the rhetoric of the conservative legal movement, in its selecting among the many possible meanings of the word "corruption," the Court is imposing its own political preferences upon we, the people, often conflicting with the actual political judgment of the democratic branches of our Republic.

My point here is not to reject this mode of constitutional reasoning, either in the context of the First Amendment or generally. My point instead is simply to flag its character. Because in other contexts, the Court's originalists are quick to denigrate this method—and reverse it. Yet, except for Justice Thomas, not here. The same justices who voted to overturn *Roe* because that doctrine, they said, has no connection to anything any framer of the Constitution said,[22] nor even to any universal view among a present majority, are perfectly willing to strike laws in the name of the First Amendment, even though that doctrine too has no connection to anything any framer said, nor to any universal view among a present majority.

First Amendment law is thus an anomaly for originalists. And this anomaly points to a possibility: If—and I understand that for most this is an embarrassingly big "if"—methodological consistency were the practice of originalists on this Court, we should expect a shift in this doctrine too.[23]

In the balance of this essay, I will describe an appropriate shift as it applies to the law regulating super PACs. That shift follows, first, from a more principled application of *Buckley*'s rationale, and second, for originalists at least, from a more principled—or we could say, original—application of originalism.

Buckley as Applied to Super PACs

Independent political action committees are committees that spend their money supporting or opposing a candidate without coordinating their spending with that candidate. The Federal Election Campaign Act of 1971 (FECA), as amended in 1976, had limited the size of contributions that any political committees could receive.[24] FECA had also limited the amount that any individual could spend independently of a political campaign to $1,000.[25] That individual limit was challenged in *Buckley*. Applying the First Amendment analysis that the Court had just crafted, the Court struck down the limit on the amount an individual could spend independently of a campaign.

The Court's analysis was straightforward: To uphold the regulation, the Court required that the government demonstrate how its rule would address "corruption" or "the appearance of corruption." "Corruption," as the Court used the term, meant "*quid pro quo* corruption." But if the spending of an individual was actually "independent" of a candidate, then, by definition, that spending would not be part of a *quid pro quo*. Or put differently, if the spending were part of a *quid pro quo*, it would not be "independent." As the Court wrote,

> The absence of prearrangement and coordination of an expenditure with the candidate or his agent . . . alleviates the danger that expenditures will be given as a quid pro quo for improper commitments from the candidate.[26]

For all the *Sturm und Drang* that *Citizens United v. FEC*[27] inspired, its conclusion was a small step from the holding in *Buckley*. The regulation at issue in *Citizens United* limited the power of corporations to spend money independently of a political campaign. The logic of *Buckley* applied directly to that question: If the only justification for limiting political speech was *quid pro quo* corruption, then there could be no justification for its limit, whether by a corporation or an individual, so long as it was independent. Or put differently, whether by an individual or a corporation, independent speech—"by definition," as Justice Kennedy put it—could raise no risk of *quid pro quo* corruption.[28]

Yet neither *Citizens United* nor *Buckley* addressed limitations on *contributions* to independent PACs. That question was first addressed in the DC Circuit. In *SpeechNow v. FEC*, the court, applying *Citizens United*, struck that limit. As the Court reasoned:

> In light of the Court's holding as a matter of law that independent expenditures do not corrupt or create the appearance of quid pro quo corruption, contributions to groups that make only independent expenditures also cannot corrupt or create the appearance of corruption. The Court has effectively held that there is no corrupting "quid" for which a candidate might in exchange offer a corrupt "quo." Given this analysis from *Citizens United*, we must conclude that the government has no anti-corruption interest in limiting contributions to an independent expenditure group such as SpeechNow.[29]

The conclusion of the DC Circuit spread very quickly after its decision. By 2013, five circuits had followed Judge Sentelle and concluded that contributions to independent PACs could not be regulated.[30] And thus freed of any limit on the size of contributions, "super PACs" were born.

Yet the DC Circuit's reasoning is wrong. Obviously wrong—at least once you see it. The error was recognized academically in an important piece written by Professors Al Alschuler, Larry Tribe, Norm Eisen, and Richard Painter.[31] And it was recognized factually in a bizarre motion to dismiss filed by lawyers for New Jersey Senator Robert Menendez.

In 2015, Menendez was indicted for *quid pro quo* corruption. The indictment charged him with offering government favors to a Florida businessman in exchange for a contribution to Menendez's super PACs. Yet that pattern—a *quid pro quo* involving a contribution to a super PAC—was just what the DC Circuit said was not possible, and Menendez's lawyers had the chutzpah to ask the district court to dismiss the indictment.[32] The district court did not dismiss the indictment; the jury instead found there was insufficient evidence of a crime. But in this exchange, the DC Circuit's error was made plain: While an independent expenditure, "by definition," could involve no *quid pro quo*, nothing in the nature or logic or regulation of a PAC requires that a contribution to that committee would, "by definition," also involve no *quid pro quo*.

We can see this point practically: If a PAC coordinates with a candidate, it knows that. The coordination is *by* the committee *with* the candidate. But if a donor to a PAC coordinates with a candidate, the committee has no way to know that. The committee receives a check. It verifies that the donor is qualified to donate. But it has no way to know what interaction the donor has had with the candidate. All the committee has is a check. And plainly, as the indictment in *United States v. Menendez* demonstrates, that check could easily be the *quo* for an illegal *quid*.

Thus, the court's conclusion that "that the government has no anticorruption interest in limiting contributions to an independent expenditure group" is obviously logically incorrect, because obviously, factually, a contribution could involve a *quid pro quo*. And thus, on the reasoning of *Buckley*, which upheld limits on contributions when those contributions created a risk of *quid pro quo* corruption, limits on contributions to independent PACs should also be constitutional. Both involve a risk of *quid pro quo* corruption; depending upon the limits, both should survive *Buckley*'s First Amendment review.

But why should that risk justify a limit on contributions? If the legitimate governmental interest is in avoiding *quid pro quo* corruption, why not prosecute the corruption?

Buckley addresses this question directly. As the Court wrote,

> laws making criminal the giving and taking of bribes deal with only the most blatant and specific attempts of those with money to influence governmental action. And while disclosure requirements serve the many salutary purposes discussed elsewhere in this opinion, Congress was surely entitled to conclude that disclosure was only a partial measure, and that contribution ceilings were a necessary legislative concomitant to deal with the reality or appearance of corruption inherent in a system permitting unlimited financial contributions, even when the identities of the contributors and the amounts of their contributions are fully disclosed.[33]

Thus, applying the analysis of *Buckley* and *Citizens United*, courts should conclude that contributions to independent PACs should be regulable, just as contributions to campaigns are regulable. There is of course no First Amendment obligation that Congress or the states impose limits on contributions to independent PACs. But there is also no First Amendment bar to such regulation, at least under *Buckley*.

Put most directly, embracing the logic of *Citizens United* and *Buckley*, *SpeechNow* is wrong, and super PACs are not constitutionally mandated.

Originalism as Applied to Super PACs

On October 31, 2023, Missouri Senator Josh Hawley (R-MO) did something that surprised many. Hawley introduced into Congress legislation to overturn the Supreme Court's *Citizens United* decision. The "Ending Corporate Influence on Elections Act," S. 3173, would restrict political spending by publicly traded corporations. The bill drew the ire of Senate Majority Leader Mitch McConnell, who has long championed corporate money in American politics.[34] But Hawley defended his bill on the basis of originalism. As he said just after the bill was introduced,

> As an originalist, there is no original meaning giving corporations the right to make political contributions, and it's warping our politics. It is giving them incredible power, and I just think it's a big mistake.[35]

Hawley's bill is not going to become law. But it is important nonetheless, because it signals a critical weakness in the fortress of modern First Amendment law—namely, it signals clearly that a principled originalist could not endorse it.

There are two ways that insight might matter to *Buckley*. First, and most radically, originalism could reject the doctrine that *Buckley* announced and embrace a rule more consistent with the rule at the framing. Second, less radically, it could be used to interpret the doctrine that *Buckley* announced. Consider each in turn.

Radical Originalism

Justice Clarence Thomas has advanced the most fundamental originalist rethinking of First Amendment doctrine. In *McKee v. Cosby*,[36] Thomas called on the Court to revisit *New York Times v. Sullivan*,[37] and to apply an originalist methodology to the question *Sullivan* resolved. *Sullivan*, Thomas insisted, was a "policy-driven decision[] masquerading as constitutional law."[38] Instead of such policymaking, Thomas challenged the Court to determine "the original meaning of the First and Fourteenth Amendments."[39] *Biden v. Knight First Amendment Institute* makes the point most cleanly:

> [R]egulations that might affect speech are valid if they would have been permissible at the time of the founding.[40]

Under this approach, a regulation of contributions to independent PACs would plainly be constitutional. Bracketing whether the regulation of "contributions" would have been considered the regulation of "speech," the original conception of the First Amendment permitted speech regulation if two conditions were satisfied: first, that the regulation was passed by a legislature, and second, that the regulation advanced "the public good."[41] No doubt, a legislature or the public could mistake the "public good" or fail to act according to "general purposes." But as Thomas has argued, no court at the founding would have presumed to question a plausible claim to advance the public good.[42] Neither is there evidence, as Campbell describes, "that the Founders actually supported the judicial protection of retained natural rights, either directly or through a narrow construal of governmental power."[43] Rather, history "shows that they preserved retained natural rights principally through constitutional structure, giving legislators, not judges, nearly complete responsibility for determining their proper scope."[44]

Under this standard, a law limiting contributions to independent-expenditure PACs would plainly advance a public purpose. As James Madison said about the federal republic, the aim of representative democracy was to secure legislatures "dependent on the People alone," where by "the People," he said he meant "not the rich, more than the poor."[45] Unlimited contributions to independent-expenditure PACs defeat that intended dependence—at the state level, by giving non-state residents a voice in the politics of their state,[46] and at both the state and federal level, by giving "the rich, more than the poor" influence over the decisions of representatives. Aiming to secure an appropriate dependence of representatives "on the People alone" would thus have been recognized as a public-regarding reason, plainly permissible under the original meaning of the First Amendment.

Moderate Originalism

So far, Justice Thomas is alone in his radical originalist interpretation of the First Amendment. Yet even under a more moderate First Amendment originalism, independent-expenditure PACs could be regulated.

As I've described, and as many have recognized, originalism is both a theory of meaning and a theory of judicial restraint.[47] As a theory of meaning, originalism asks what the ordinary accepted public meaning of the words of the Constitution was. As a theory of restraint, it embraces the interpretation that minimizes the discretion of judges, to avoid giving judges the power to enforce their own political preferences rather than any preference that could be linked to the Constitution's ratifiers.

Buckley's choice of the term "corruption" to define the scope of the legislature's freedom to regulate political speech creates a judicial-restraint risk.

"Corruption" could have many meanings. The choice of meaning is also a choice about the regulations that would be permitted. The Court's selection of a particular conception of "corruption" would thus directly implicate substantive political values.

Recognizing this fact, a moderate originalism should seek to limit judicial discretion, by using the framing conception of "corruption" to determine the scope of "corruption" within the *Buckley* standard. On this reading, if an influence would have been deemed "corrupt" by the framers, a moderate originalism would allow the regulation of that corruption today.

This was the approach of Justice Scalia in *Michael H. v. Gerald D.*[48] Recognizing the wide range of behavior that might be thought to implicate "due process," Scalia sought to narrow judicial discretion by tying the conception of "due process" to the most "specific level at which a relevant tradition ... can be identified."[49] This was not because such an approach limned the original meaning of "due process." It was instead to limit the freedom of judges—to avoid giving judges the power to "dictate rather than discern" the scope of a legislature's power.

A moderate originalist would apply the same methodology to interpret the term "corruption" within the *Buckley* standard. In the face of the many conceptions of "corruption," a moderate originalist would avoid an approach that was inappropriately "judge-empowering,"[50] and instead link the scope of the "corruption" to the conception of "corruption" used by the Framers. As with "due process" in *Michael H.*, this is not because that is the best or only way to read the term "corruption," but because it is the clearest way to constrain the policy discretion of judges.

So What Did "Corruption" Mean to Our Framers?

The framers of our Constitution were focused intensely on the problem of "corruption."[51] Yet their conception of "corruption" was different from ours. While they certainly understood—and took steps against—individual, or *quid pro quo* corruption, they were much more aggressively focused upon the corruption of institutions, especially the representative institutions they intended to establish. No doubt the Framers were focused upon both individual and institutional corruption, but between the two, they were focused upon institutional corruption more.

This was the conclusion of the uncontroverted evidence submitted in a proceeding in Alaska to test the scope of *Citizens United*.[52] In that case, the trial court asked for testimony about the original understanding of "corruption."[53] Stanford Professor Jack Rakove, one of America's leading scholars of the framing period, testified at length that the historical evidence conclusively established that the Framers were focused on at least three types of corruption: *quid pro quo* corruption, institutional corruption, and societal corruption.[54] Among the three, as Professor Rakove testified, institutional corruption was the most important.

For instance, as Rakove testified, it was common for the Framers to remark upon the "corruption" of the British Parliament. Yet that "corruption" was not evidenced by any bribery engaged in by Members of Parliament. It was instead the consequence of an improper influence of the Crown within Parliament. The House of Commons was to be representative of the People of Britain. But the system of selecting representatives from "rotten" and "pocket" boroughs was viewed by the Framers as "corrupt." It was "corrupt" because those Representatives were effectively dependent on the Crown, not on the people. As "[t]he [royal] government or some local aristocrat or member of the gentry," Professor Rakove explained, would essentially control the electoral outcome, "the improper influence was that the Crown was essentially creating a dependency with those representatives who were in the Parliament."

Professor Rakove's conclusions are confirmed by familiar historical sources. In a study submitted to the US Supreme Court, researchers found that when the Framers spoke of "corruption," they were speaking overwhelmingly of institutional, rather than individual, corruption.[55] This conclusion is confirmed by a focus on structural independence throughout the Constitution's design. The Ineligibility Clause (U.S. Const. art. I § 6.) prevents anyone from serving simultaneously in Congress and the executive branch. This assures that legislators will be dependent on the people, not the President, and therefore "preserv[es] the Legislature as pure as possible, by shutting the door against appointments of its own members to offices, which was one source of its corruption."[56] Similarly, the requirement that legislators live in the state they represent, per George Mason, prohibits "[r]ich men of neighbouring States" from using "means of corruption in some particular district" to "get into the public Councils after having failed in their own State."[57] Avoiding these incentives to institutional, or dependence, corruption was thus the objective of much in the design of the Constitution.

This evidence establishes that if the term "corruption" were interpreted to include the dominant usages at the time of the framing, it would include both *quid pro quo* corruption and dependence corruption. Put differently, if the First Amendment permits the restriction of political speech to address "corruption," and the term "corruption" is given a meaning that is historically sensitive to its usage at the framing, the First Amendment would permit regulations targeting both *quid pro quo* corruption and dependence corruption.

Thus, for an originalist, the *Buckley* rule cannot be defended. Following Justice Thomas's approach, an originalist should interpret the First Amendment as the framers would have. Regulations of super PACs would plainly be permitted under that standard. Or following Justice Scalia's approach in *Michael H.*, an originalist should interpret *Buckley*'s "corruption" according to the conception of corruption dominant at the framing. Institutional corruption was indeed the framers' primary focus. Legislation that addresses institutional corruption—such as limits on super PACs—should therefore satisfy the *Buckley* standard.

Conclusion

Contrary to the universal view among lower courts, neither *Buckley* nor *Citizens United* bans the regulation of contributions to independent political action committees. *SpeechNow* was an obvious misapplication of the *Buckley* standard. It is embarrassing to the legal profession that that misapplication has governed campaigns in America now for fourteen years.

But the more fundamental question for this Supreme Court is whether the principles of originalism, or what I've called "original originalism," will force a more general reform of the rules governing the regulation of campaign finance. There is no democratic sanction for the most extreme view advanced about campaign finance regulation—that by "Congress shall make no law . . . abridging the freedom of speech," we, the people, meant to ban any regulation of campaign finance. Recognizing this truth, a consistent originalist would thus need to determine just how committed she will remain to the modern rule.

Non-originalists, of course, are free to remain committed to the *Buckley* framework. But even here, we should recognize just how mistaken *Buckley* was about the consequences of its own rule. *Buckley* was motivated by the empirical belief that by eliminating regulation of campaign spending, and by restricting the regulation of contributions to campaigns, it would enhance political discourse and increase competition among the parties and within democracy generally. Those empirical beliefs have proven false. Incumbents today are more protected than they were in 1976; the rise of super PACs has meant that outsiders have less ability to compete today than they did in 1976. If *Buckley* was—as Justice Thomas claimed *NYT v. Sullivan* was—a "policy-driven decision[] masquerading as constitutional law," we should recognize how flawed its policy was. That recognition at the very least should induce a retreat from the judicialization of campaign finance regulation, thus leaving to legislatures a much wider range of freedom than the current regime does.

PART VI

The Effect of Campaign Finance

On Political Institutions

12

Buckley v. Valeo

Doctrinal Difficulties and Institutional Failure

Samuel Issacharoff

Beginning in 1976, the United States embarked upon an experiment in having decisional constitutional law serve as the primary regulator of the funding of political parties, candidates, and campaigns. With *Buckley v. Valeo*,[1] the US Supreme Court displaced nascent regulatory efforts by Congress in the post-Watergate period with a regime based on First Amendment principles of free expression. In the intervening fifty years, that constitutional framework has commanded the field, with even scattered congressional reforms circumscribed by the conflicting doctrinal commands.

After a half century under *Buckley*, we may propose that the regulatory regime has never achieved doctrinal coherence and has never provided an institutionally viable regulatory environment. Much more significant, however, is that *Buckley* ushered in a period of campaign finance that has largely taken the control of political money from the hands of visible actors such as parties and candidates and delivered it to a shadow world of single-issue advocates, well-heeled individuals, and other actors substantially removed from the problems of actually governing a democratic polity.

Buckley was a judicial response to the 1974 reforms under the Federal Elections Campaign Act (FECA), the attempt to control the post-Nixon horror over campaign donations as large as (gulp!) $100,000. This was coupled with the typical reformer's distrust of money altogether. FECA set the amount of federal funding at two-thirds of what George McGovern spent in 1972 in the least successful presidential campaign in American history. Unsurprisingly, most candidates willing to endure the rigors of modern campaigning do not seek to reproduce any feature of the McGovern campaign, including its limited resources.

Whereas FECA attempted an integrated regulatory response of limiting contributions and campaign spending, coupled with federal funding of presidential campaigns, *Buckley* read the Constitution to permit only a truncated system of restrictions on contributions and free rein for spending whatever money was in the possession of candidates or parties. For the Court, there is a "fundamental constitutional difference between money spent to advertise one's views independently of the candidate's campaign and money contributed to the candidate to be spent on his campaign."[2] Divorced from the reality of providing resources to parties and candidates, this was not so much half a regulatory system as an incoherent one which no policymaker had ever advocated and no regulator had ever enacted. To unleash expenditures but constrict contributions does not so much eliminate the centrality of money as guarantee an unyielding focus on how to obtain it. The result prompted what Pam Karlan and I long ago dubbed the "hydraulic effect," in which the press for money to fuel mounting campaign expenditures pushed electoral activity heavily into the unregulated domain of political actors outside the ambit of federal law.[3]

The destabilizing doctrine surgically divided the FECA reform package between the domains of contributions and expenditures. The Court showed itself willing to uphold almost any limit on contributions, with only a handful of local rules being struck down for overly starving political actors of their ability to communicate their message. By contrast, and increasingly over time, the Court viewed any restriction on expenditures as an affront to the expressive role of speech. *Buckley* then granted a mild regulatory dispensation for efforts to combat corruption, the appearance of corruption, and even fleetingly the perception of the appearance of corruption, an especially nebulous concept upon which to ground constitutional law.[4]

There is a sad logic when constitutional law controls important societal institutions. *Bakke* once held out the claim that racial considerations in school admissions could only be justified by an interest in promoting diversity.[5] Over the ensuing fifty years, the ill-defined concept of "diversity" went from being almost unknown in educational policy to an ever-present factor of university life, now roiling campuses in its "DEI" incarnation. In similar fashion, the equally imprecise concept of "corruption" has come to command the repeated reform efforts in order to evade otherwise withering First Amendment scrutiny.

An incident in a Vermont case in 2006 showed the excruciating confines of *Buckley*. Vermont passed a state law limiting candidate expenditures and setting contribution limits of only $200. In Chief Justice Roberts's first year on the Court, the state was challenged over how its restrictive regime fit within the *Buckley* framework. Dutifully, the State responded that it had an interest in combating corruption. Chief Justice Roberts, bringing to oral argument the tradition of asking why the emperor had no clothes, asked the State's counsel if Vermont had, in its 200-plus-year history, ever prosecuted anyone for political corruption or had documented any case of political corruption. Vermont is a rural, largely ethnically homogeneous population made up largely of long-term residents—not exactly Chicago or New York. Vermont's inability to adduce even a modicum of experience with corruption resulted, in *Randall v. Sorrell*,[6] not only in its expenditure limitations being struck down but ignominiously losing its contribution limits as well.

Probing the history of actual corruption in Vermont fairly exploded the *Buckley* myth that the invocation of corruption or the fear of its appearance could somehow talismanically ward off the penetrating reach of the First Amendment. Invoking the risk of corruption poorly framed the necessity of money to fuel democratic politics. Survey evidence reveals that the best predictor of what leads voters to detect the appearance of corruption is the fact that their candidate of choice lost—much like losing sporting fans believe that the referee must have been on the take.[7] *Buckley* naively thought that the answer to how money should work in politics could be resolved as a matter of First Amendment doctrine, not as a coherent understanding of how a democracy functions.

The argument that follows is that the core doctrinal divide between contributions and expenditures never cohered, and that the corruption escape portal could not survive even the most rudimentary demand for empirical proof. After half a century, the result is a system more dominated than ever by the power of money, and much less organized around the defining institutions of democratic life, elections, and functioning political institutions. More fundamentally, the use of First Amendment doctrine has led to a disregard of the institutional forms of thought which healthy democratic politics need to operate. I will conclude with a brief contrast to a recent opinion of the

German Constitutional Court to show an alternative jurisprudential approach organized around principles of democratic governance rather than freedom of expression.

Money, Inescapably

Most of our critical campaign finance jurisprudence starts from the premise that money in politics is evil. The source of that view is readily apparent. Democracy increasingly assumes as its touchstone the equality of citizens, most readily summed up as one person, one vote. Yet the introduction of private money in a system with conspicuous inequalities of wealth must stand in tension with the cardinal principle of citizen equality. At the same time, inescapably, politics requires money at each level from election administration to partisan mobilization.

Many countries have tried to address this through a highly regulatory system of public financing. For reasons beyond the scope of the current exposition, public underwriting of political parties and candidates has never taken hold in the United States. So, the money must come from private hands, hence the inescapable prospect of improper influence, and influence that destabilizes the equal-citizenship premise of modern understandings of democracy.

The core difficulty is that, if private money is truly evil, then it should be banned. What followed from *Buckley* was a regulatory system based on private money raised awkwardly in limited increments, but matched by limitless expenditures. So long as expenditures were uncapped, there was permanent pressure to expand the pool of available funds. Here the logic of *Buckley* revealed a second regulatory failure: only part of the financial ecosystem was regulated. Under FECA, what was termed "hard money" was subject to controls, with hard money being defined centrally as direct contributions to candidates and parties, while "soft money" referred to political funds that were raised outside the strictures of FECA. This left broad domains outside the FECA restrictions, so long as they could not be attributed to activities coordinated with either candidates or parties. Among the most central domains outside the reach of FECA were state political parties and campaigns, and institutions granted "political committee" status by various provisions of the Internal Revenue Code, but outside the definition of regulated entities for federal campaign laws. The ensuing "hydraulic effect," the search for the next-level unregulated pool, witnessed all actors in the system reaching for ways of leveraging financial power just beyond the reach of FECA.

Our current campaign finance regime therefore offers, as Senator Romney once said, the "worst of both worlds."[8] From *Buckley* forward, the demand for money in campaigns has steadily increased, as Figure 12.1 below from Open Secrets data shows, and the rise has been fairly linear since at least 1998, long before the much-derided 2010 landmark *Citizens United*[9] decision.[10]

Given the constricted pathways for fundraising under FECA, the question is how to fuel the perceived need for campaign funding. In the 1990s, the Democrats and Republicans began channeling national funding through state parties by transferring money raised at the state level up to the federal level and thereby making non-federal funds clean federal dollars.[11] This was the world of trips on Air Force One or nights in the Lincoln Bedroom or golf outings with congressional leaders that raised funds outside the formal restrictions of FECA. The nominal recipients were state political parties, and the money passed through cutouts to reach the national campaigns. Down to the 15% rate that state parties typically charged their national counterparts, the practice shockingly resembled that of money laundering.[12]

While this practice was largely banned by the 2002 Bipartisan Campaign Reform Act (BCRA),[13] which the Supreme Court upheld in

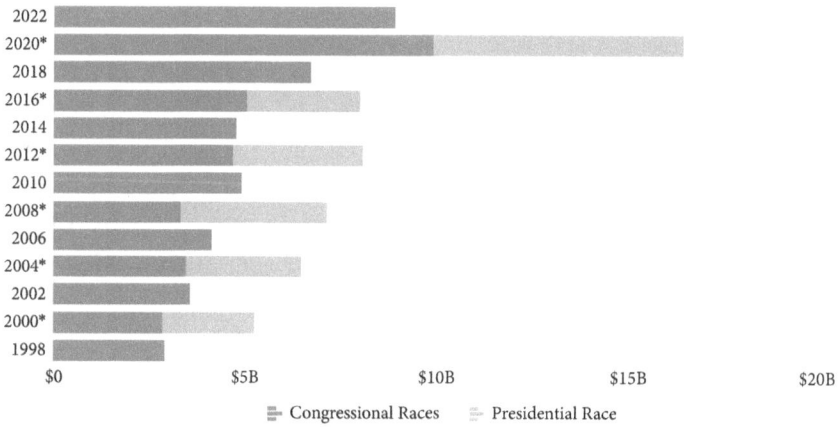

Figure 12.1 Congressional and Presidential Races as a Proportion of Total Electoral Expenditures, 1998–2020.

Source: OpenSecrets.org

McConnell v. FEC,[14] the demand for money remained unabated; just the pathways were altered. After BCRA, the current of money was simply redirected—this time away from the parties altogether and to decentralized sources for independent expenditures.[15] BCRA starved political parties of soft-money funding and prompted the modern era of what Heather Gerken and Joseph Fishkin term "shadow parties" to operate as the real sources of both contributions and expenditures, but outside the reach of regulatory oversight.[16]

Data maintained by OpenSecrets reveals that the ensuing independent expenditures essentially emerged on the national scene with BCRA and increased steadily, finally exploding in the 2010s:[17]

Increasingly, large amounts of funding have been splintered across progressively less accountable sources. While there is great certainty among campaign finance reformers on the perfidy of *Citizens United*, both the doctrine and the facts are more complicated. *Citizens United* involved what should be the core of First Amendment speech concerns: a political message attacking a candidate for president. But because the independent expenditure had some corporate backing, this was deemed by the FEC to be a corporate contribution. The Court, following the logic of *Buckley*, found that speech by independent actors was protected so long as it was not coordinated with the regulated entities, candidates and parties. However, the fact that corporate money was at stake made the case the bête noire of those who see money as necessarily corrupting.

As mentioned, the data show that the overall costs of elections have risen fairly linearly since at least 1998, long before *Citizens United*.[18] As Figure 12.2 below shows, there is no obvious jump in election costs from before to after *Citizens United*. Independent expenditures began their rise beginning with BCRA and that trended up starting with the Obama campaign decision to forgo federal matching funds in 2008 and then following *Citizens United*, (Figure 12.2), with the ruling arguably playing a causal role in that increase.[19]

Nonetheless, there is relatively little appetite for political contributions by publicly traded corporations, and corporations played no apparent role in the rise of independent expenditures after *Citizens United*.[20] Rather, wealthy individuals, nonprofits, and 527 groups have been the primary drivers of rising independent expenditures. From 2010 to the beginning of 2020, individuals gave $2.96 billion in independent expenditures, compared with only $539 million given by corporations.[21] In 2018, corporations contributed only 5% of the funding for super PACs,[22] and in states where *Citizens United* struck down regulations on independent expenditures by corporations, corporate expenditures increased only nominally at most after the ruling.[23] Apart from family corporations and some older extractive industry firms,[24] corporations tend to give through PACs they themselves coordinate,[25] a small and increasingly irrelevant portion of the money in politics.[26] Given the amount of money that corporations theoretically could get from the government relative to the amount they donate, one study provocatively asked: Why is there so little money in US politics?[27] Indeed, corporations strikingly "didn't take full advantage of their new political powers" under *Citizens United*.[28]

Instead, the ten biggest individual donors went from accounting for 1% of total election funding in 2008 to *7%* in 2018.[29] While donations by small donors have been increasing markedly, independent expenditures by the wealthiest individuals have increased faster.[30] Small donors outspent the largest donors in 2010, but in the 2022 midterm the 100 biggest donors gave 60% *more* than all small donors.[31] One study found that twelve individual donors accounted for $1 of every $13 spent or contributed toward federal elections from 2009 to 2020.[32] And of independent expenditures by individuals from 2010 to the beginning of 2020, 47% came from a mere *twenty-five* donors, and 77% came from the top 500 donors.[33]

Evidently, wealthy individuals and other independent operatives have found super PACs a sufficient equivalent to political parties.[34] In retrospect, BCRA appears to have forcibly habituated donors and candidates to living at one

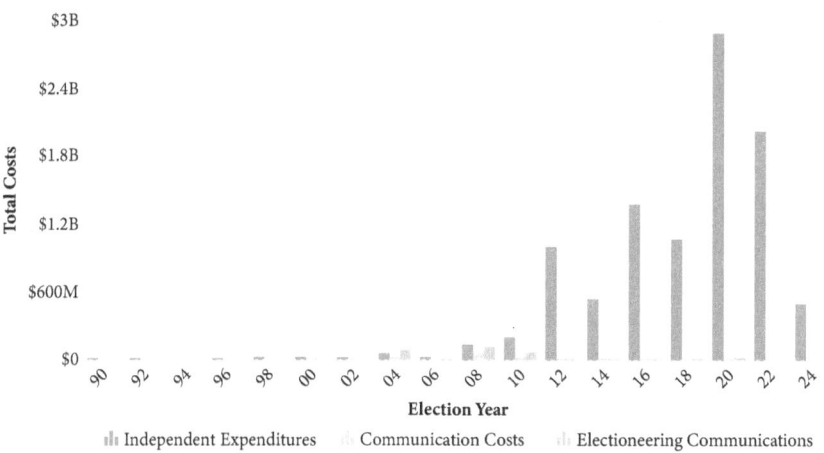

Figure 12.2 Total Cost of Independent Electoral Expenditures, 1990–2024.
Source: OpenSecrets.org

remove from formal political campaigns as the habitat for largesse. While campaigns cannot formally coordinate with super PACs, in 2012 officials from the Obama and Romney campaigns—and Mitt Romney himself—began speaking at super-PAC events, which is permissible as long as they did not directly ask for money.[35] Now, headlines abound about massive donor events for wealthy individuals that feature political candidates. Most recently, an event at Radio City Music Hall with President Biden, former presidents Obama and Clinton, and numerous celebrities raked in $26 million.[36] Just one week later, then-former President Trump spoke at a fundraiser in Florida that raised a record $50.5 million and reportedly featured ticket prices as high as $814,000.[37] By one estimate, total outside spending exceeds candidate-controlled spending by a factor of three to one.[38]

Hydraulics indeed.

The Role of Political Parties

The hydraulic argument illustrates two of the principal failings of the *Buckley* regime: the inability to control the flow of money, and the redirection of funds to unaccountable and unregulated actors beyond the reach of FECA. Indeed, the search for alternative funding arrangements after BCRA prepared the organizational terrain for the explosion of outside money that began following the decision of the Obama campaign in 2008 to forgo federal funding in favor of private fundraising.

What the hydraulic argument anticipated was the regulatory failure of the *Buckley* approach of expressive spending and corrupting contributions. On the other hand, what the hydraulics of donation does not quite reach, and a key to the deeper methodological shortcomings of *Buckley*, is the institutional question of how exactly does democratic politics work. Hydraulics addresses the needs and motivations of political actors and donors, but does not touch upon the normatively optimal institutional form of politics, independent of the source of its financing. The lack of institutional focus is even more pronounced in the First Amendment jurisprudence that organizes democratic politics as just another manifestation of freedom of expression. The doctrinal weakness is revealed in two cases that arose from a 1986 Colorado election but were not decided until 1996 and 2001, long after the contested election had come and gone and all actors in the drama had left politics, with the winner having been seated and then retired (itself an indictment of using constitutional litigation to regulate politics).

In *Colorado Republican I*[39] and *Colorado Republican II*,[40] the Court confronted the efforts of the Colorado Republican Party to use its funds to attack the Democratic nominee for the Senate—in the first case, before a Republican candidate had even been selected. Seemingly, a political party using its resources to oppose the candidate of the other major party should be the highpoint of political expression and mobilization in a democracy. Parties marking the boundaries that distinguish each other during elections is what informs the voters and allows citizens to make retrospective judgments about their elected officials. While the definition of "democracy" may be nuanced and contested, at its core must lie that ability of voters to dislodge incumbents based on the information generated in electoral battle.[41]

Under *Buckley*, however, the sole issue was whether the expenditures of a political party in support of its own candidate should be characterized as an effort to circumvent contribution limits to candidates, and thereby open the prospect of the party corrupting its candidates through its expenditures. Under the conditions of *Colorado Republican I*, in which there was no Republican candidate yet chosen, the Court sustained a factually bound challenge (as applied rather than on its face) to restricting party expenditures. The *Colorado Republican I* Court held narrowly that limits to independent party expenditures were unconstitutional, giving parties the same rights as anyone else to use of private funds for expression.[42] The *Colorado Republican I* Court declined to reach the question of whether coordinated party expenditures were unconstitutional, finding that the only factual issue presented was in regard to an independent expenditure.[43]

However, in *Colorado Republican II*, the Court rejected a facial challenge that would have allowed parties to freely spend their resources in support of their candidates. A split court upheld limits to coordinated party expenditures on the grounds that such expenditures constitute a de-facto contribution,[44] deeming that FECA requires "a functional, not formal, definition of 'contribution.'"[45] The case squarely presented conflicting visions of politics in which "parties are organized for the purpose of electing candidates" and the money-dominated view in which parties are primarily "instruments of some contributors whose object is not to support the party's message or to elect party candidates across the board. . . ."[46] Parties are thus conduits for those who want "to support any candidate who will be obligated to the contributors," in circumvention of statutory contribution limits.[47] For the Court's majority, "[p]arties thus perform functions more complex than simply electing candidates; whether they like it or not, they act as agents for spending on behalf of those who seek to produce obligated shareholders."[48]

For the most part, the *Colorado Republican* cases are now treated as just another example of the doctrinal instability of *Buckley*. For decades, a wing of the Court centered on Justices Thomas and Scalia rejected the premise that contributions could be regulated on any basis other than the form of *quid pro quo* corruption associated with bribery. The liberal wing of the Court, initially led by Justices Brennan, Marshall, and Stevens, refused to accept that money was speech and argued for the permissibility of regulation of all campaign finance, subject only to review for its rationality. Neither pole of the Court could command a majority, and in a series of divided opinions, *Buckley* was kept alive by stasis, with more votes to reject it than uphold it, but the division kept in place the status quo.

But these opinions reveal the Court's lack of interest in how democracy works. On a surface level, looked at from two decades later, the Court's venture into organizational analysis seems hopelessly naive. The idea that candidates would be beholden if funds were donated through a party but would not be so beholden if a nominally independent (and uncapped) contribution were made to the "X Candidate Victory Fund" is preposterous. Examined from the basis of money that necessarily corrupts, the Court found that a political party was to be treated as just another electoral actor, no different in kind from any other supplicant seeking to curry favor with an actual or potential officeholder.[49] Further, the Court held that where a party acts in concert with its candidates, its expenditures may be treated as de facto contributions from the party to the candidate, no different from the contributions of any other private actor, and subject to the same restrictions to avoid the risk of a pass-through to the candidate.[50]

It is not simply a matter of the constitutional line-drawing not working in reality. In treating contributions by parties to candidates as no different from contributions by any other private actor,[51] the *Colorado Republican I* and *Colorado Republican II* majorities ignored a second feature of politics: parties, as institutional actors, have organizational aims of their own—a critical insight from V. O. Key on the struggle for control among the competing constituencies of the party.[52] A party is not simply another electoral actor seeking favor with an actual or potential officeholder. To the contrary, a well-functioning political system wants the candidates beholden to the party, so that elections will present voters with meaningful choices and there will be the prospect of coherence in office that allows for smart policy aims.[53] Once in office, parties overcome the collective-action problems that would overwhelm the ability of leaderless representatives pursuing disparate agendas. As well expressed by political scientist Seth Masket:

> [A] partyless legislature is a collective action nightmare. Having to cobble together a winning coalition on every bill one cares about is nearly impossible, ensuring that incumbents will fail to enact much of the agenda on which they ran for office and will fail to deliver redistributive benefits to their district.[54]

In concurrence in *Colorado Republican I*, Justice Kennedy added, "It makes no sense . . . to ask, as FECA does, whether a party's spending is made 'in cooperation, consultation, or concert with' its candidate."[55] Of course, there likely was and should have been coordination, with a measure of constitutional protection offered to the party.[56]

It is hard to disentangle *Colorado Republican I* and *II* from the emergence of political parties as the driving money engines of the 1990s—the same impulse that gave rise to BCRA. But as parties have further weakened and as the composition of the Court has changed, it is hard to imagine that the world of outsider-dominated funding is not ripe for revisiting. A potential vehicle has emerged in the courts, currently awaiting en banc review in the Sixth Circuit.[57] *National Republican Senatorial Committee v. FEC* presents both narrow questions about whether a party may assist with campaign infrastructure in promoting its candidates and the broader question about whether parties must have autonomy from restriction in pursuing their expressive aim of organizing democratic politics. It is hard to see how this broader question does not return to the Supreme Court, either through this case or another.

Funding Through the Prism of Democracy

The most straightforward critique of *Buckley* is that it has neither yielded doctrinal stability nor constrained the flow of money into politics. But the *Colorado Republican* cases point to another, more lasting harm. The campaign finance laws have contributed to the withering of political parties as the central organs of democratic politics. Viewed exclusively through constitutional terms, the parties are fairly defenseless. The Constitution originally allowed no scope for political parties, and only the Twelfth Amendment, with its recognition of Presidents and Vice Presidents running together, backhandedly gives parties an organizational role in politics.[58] When it comes to money to fund their organization, parties can claim only weak associational rights that doctrinally lag the freedom-of-expression protections offered to individuals.

Parties emerge no different from any individual actor in the political arena, and weaker than self-funded candidates whose access to private resources do not trigger any form of regulatory constraint. This means that if parties are seen as potential conduits for evasion of limits on the corrupting influence of money, they are subject to the same restrictions as private citizens as a matter of constitutional oversight.

Embedded in First Amendment jurisprudence is a secondary strain that looks to the role of expressive freedoms as being necessary to democratic self-governance, apart from establishing individual rights against the state. Under this view, the purpose of freedom of expression—even false statements, as in the *New York Times Co. v. Sullivan*[59] line of cases—is to provide the citizenry with the ability to challenge the political status quo.[60] This is the subject of extraordinary academic inquiry, oftentimes uniting scholars on the right and the left.[61] The instrumental account of the First Amendment as aimed at giving space for the types of engagements that promote democracy might caution against a reflexive application of the corruption rationale to political parties, as opposed to ordinary actors that come and go in democratic politics.

What if a party was seen instead as not just another individual actor in the political arena? While parties must collect funds to survive, they operate on a bigger platform, with multiple and conflicting constituencies to satisfy. Like the scale of the national republic identified by Madison in the *Federalist Papers* (No. 10), parties are less prone to immediate capture by narrow factional interest. Well-functioning parties must ensure the electability of their candidates across a broad variety of voters and interests.[62] A party's environmental policies might reflect support from extractive industries, or its opposition to charter schools might reflect support from teachers' unions. But even leaving aside the question whether the financial support is cause or effect of these policy positions, the immediate positions on oil exploration or educational offerings must be integrated into a broader platform capable of engaging voters in multiple constituencies and providing a coherent basis for legislative enactments by the party's elected representatives.

No doubt the campaign finance cases play only a partial role in the weakness of contemporary political parties, not just in the United States but across the democratic world. Successful parties were rooted organically in mass civic organizations and could serve as the bridge between the citizenry and the state. For the parties of the social-democratic left, including the Democratic party in the United States, this meant a strong connection to the labor movement and to unions. For the moderate right, the base tended to be the churches for the Christian Democratic organizations, and the local associations of entrepreneurs for the Republicans in the United States as well as for the Tories in Britain and the Gaullists in France. The historic erosion of these organizational foundations of mass democracy left the parties and democratic politics unmoored, to borrow the term from a book of mine.

In addition, legal reforms gradually removed some of the internal glue that held parties together, even if not always benightedly.[63] Parties offered patronage to their backers and promoted their best operatives to office through their control of the process of selecting and backing candidates. Civil service reforms, no doubt well motivated, had the consequence of taking away some of the cohesion of party politics, as Justice Scalia noted in his dissent from the patronage cases.[64] In the United States, the reforms went further to promote primaries to nominate candidates, with no special role for the party hierarchy to determine even who their flagbearers should be.

But it is on the money front that the parties have suffered the most. Parties play the long game, meaning that they have to balance interests among many constituencies and have to deliver across a program of governance. Incremental amounts of money are less likely to push the party toward extremes than money in the hands of a single candidate or controlled by a single-issue outside actor. A party-centered finance system serves as a mediating entity between candidates and the voters that pushes positions back toward the median voter realm where electoral success usually lies.

Instead, FECA and BCRA, and especially the case law flowing from *Buckley*, have largely limited the ability of parties to channel a campaign's funds between donors and its candidate. The result has been to push the funding of politics outside the regulated domain and weaken the only entity that has both the power and the incentive structure required to coordinate the distribution of campaign funds.

The result has been an institutional shift toward the extremes, because "as donors become more ideologically extreme, they tend to prefer giving directly to candidates ... that reflect their ideological preferences."[65] Political scientists La Raja and Schaffner observe that "[w]hen the pragmatic party organization has a restricted role in elections, the opportunities expand for more ideological elements to support party candidates. As candidates rely increasingly on the purists for their campaigns, the collective party becomes more ideological and distinctive."[66]

In turn, the party organization loses not only power but also relevance, with political "leadership lack[ing] the disciplinary power over their members that they once held" because the "financial support for candidates has now shifted . . . to outside organizations, such as super PACs and their formidable war chests."[67] These outside influences on voting behavior also open the door for "free agent successors" to challenge and ultimately replace party crusaders, which in turn "fragment[s] the party's voting cohesion."[68] Thus, La Raja and Schaffner find that when states place "few[er] restrictions" on party campaign financing, there is "less polarization of parties."[69]

Unbridled Parties

If the central concern in party funding is not a general concern for First Amendment liberties but rather the unique role of political parties in mediating democratic politics, a different approach to campaign finance is in order. In a recent book, *Democracy Unmoored*,[70] I address the implications of a system that has no effective constraints on money-raising except as to parties and candidates. I suggest that the aims of democracy would be better served by doing what is necessary to rechannel the direction of politics away from unaccountable private entities and back to political parties. When Elon Musk announced he would make tens of millions of dollars available monthly to the reelection efforts of President Trump, he effectively took over a significant portion of presidential politics with no ultimate accountability to the voters. The donor class did not come to controlling campaigns as the most desired option but rather in response to the impossibility of donating to parties.

To address this by-product, I suggest that there be no contribution limits to parties at all. The idea is to recognize the distinct role that parties play in combating extremism and bringing coherence to governance. Since money given to parties is less corrupting, the constitutional rationale for avoiding corruption does not apply so readily when the entity under regulation has the proven capacity to recenter the pull of money as such. Such a proposal would do nothing to mollify the concern that money is inherently evil and corrosive of the equality commitment of democracy. But it would address the reality of a broken funding system that *disadvantages* parties relative to the independent and uncoordinated actors that currently dominate our political ecosystem.

This argument is more compelling as a matter of policy than of constitutional law. So long as *Buckley* controls, and so long as the risk of corruption remains the sole consideration for constitutional scrutiny of contribution limits, the argument requires a doctrinal stretch. Unfortunately, our law of democracy remains wedded to formal rights categories that do not well address the question of how democratic politics should operate.

An Alternative Constitutional Framework

The *Buckley* framework is a decided outlier among constitutional democracies. To my knowledge, no other democracy has a system based on private funding of political campaigns that allows unlimited expenditures, restricted private contributions to parties and candidates, and unlimited uncoordinated spending by outside entities. Some democracies may approximate such a system as a result of a de facto breakdown of legal oversight, but none has enshrined this curious cocktail as a matter of constitutional law.

A worthy comparison is provided by Germany's postwar constitution, which is organized around the central principle of enshrining democracy and preventing the resurgence of Nazism or other threats to core democratic values. While the American Constitution is silent on the role of political parties in a democracy, Article 21 of the German Constitution places parties front and center in the organization of democratic politics, and it commands that "parties participate in the formation of the political will of the people."[71] While parties in turn receive state funding, their "internal organi[z]ation must conform to democratic principles," according to the Basic Law of the Constitution.[72]

In 2023, the German Constitutional Court considered a challenge to the Bundestag's having voted an increase in the level of state funding for political parties. Though German constitutional law has long recognized the centrality of funding for parties to function,[73] voting on the funding of parties was in effect voting to pay itself, a clear moral hazard. The Constitutional Court arbitrated this dilemma by looking to the prerequisites for parties to function properly in a democracy. It found in the Constitution's Basic Law a limit on state financing of political parties "determined by what is necessary to maintain the functional capabilities of the political parties and to fulfil their constitutional mandate, but which cannot be obtained by the parties' own means."[74] That role in turn is defined by the role of parties in organizing and integrating the citizenry into democratic governance. Thus, the Court held: "In order for political parties to fulfill their ascribed role as mediators between the state and society, the people must have a sufficient amount of trust in the independence of parties from state influence. This trust is impaired when political parties could make unlimited use of state funds to cover their financial needs."[75]

What is significant is that the German court saw the question as one of enhancing democracy, not simply of formally explicating constitutional doctrine. The constitutional jurisprudence of the US Supreme Court lags far behind on this score.

13

Campaign Finance and Political Polarization

Richard H. Pildes

Judicial decisions and legal scholarship on campaign finance focus principally on issues such as corruption and the constitutionally forbidden value of political equality. This scholarship is often conceptual and normative, with reformers advocating more expansive interpretations of "corruption" or taking issue with the Supreme Court's refusal to permit anti-distortion and undue-influence concerns to justify regulatory constraints.

But campaign finance law and policy also affect the functioning of American government and the political culture more generally. And a central challenge American democracy currently faces, along with other Western democracies, is demonstrating that it can once again deliver effectively on the issues citizens care most urgently about.[1] When democratic governments fail to do so, that can prompt anger, division, distrust, and even longing for strongman figures who purport to be able to cut through this dysfunction. In an era of hyperpolarized political parties, effective governance is particularly difficult in the United States, given bicameralism and an independently elected President.[2] Government has been divided 70% of the time since 1968, and even during unified government most major legislation has required bipartisan support.[3] Extreme polarization is thus a particular threat to the ability of the political system to deliver.

While much has been written about various other potential factors in the rise of polarization,[4] campaign finance has received minimal attention, particularly in the legal literature.[5] This is surprising, because one of the most robust findings in the empirical literature on campaign finance is that donors are

Richard H. Pildes, *Campaign Finance and Political Polarization*. In: *Money, Politics, and the First Amendment*.
Edited by: Lee C. Bollinger and Geoffrey R. Stone, Oxford University Press. © Oxford University Press (2026).
DOI: 10.1093/9780197821947.003.0014

much more ideologically extreme than other citizens. Nor has the emergence of small-donor financing, in the last several election cycles, changed this pattern. Indeed, more extreme candidates and officeholders are the ones most dependent on small-donor financing. And small donors, unlike large donors, respond to viral moments of outrage, which encourages extremist rhetoric and tactics to mobilize attention and turn on the flow of small dollars.

Part I of this chapter focuses first on the relationship between individual donors and political polarization. In recent years, we have learned much more about the motivations and ideological preferences of individual donors. Part II then argues that recognizing the relationship between individual donors and polarization has implications for the appropriate direction of political reform. After fifty years or so of attempting to constrain the system of privately financed elections, there is broad recognition that that effort has failed. The alternative approach is public financing, but the particular form of public financing matters. Reforms that would provide public financing to match the contributions of small donors, currently a preferred approach in parts of the reform community, are appealing because they enhance political equality and encourage participation. But they would also enhance the polarizing tendencies of campaign finance. If we want to minimize corruption and advance political equality without further fueling the dangerous tendencies toward polarization and extremism, traditional forms of public financing best satisfy that range of goals.

I

Individual Donors

As noted above, one of the most robust findings in empirical work on campaign finance is that individual donors are much more ideologically polarized than non-donors. This finding is consistent with the more general point that the more actively involved in politics people are, the more partisan they are.[6]

Figure 13.1 below makes the point dramatically: the distribution of individual donors is bimodal, with most donors located toward either the very liberal or very conservative side of the ideological spectrum, and few coming from the ideological center. This contrasts sharply with the ideological profile of non-donors, who are distributed more broadly across the ideological spectrum:[7]

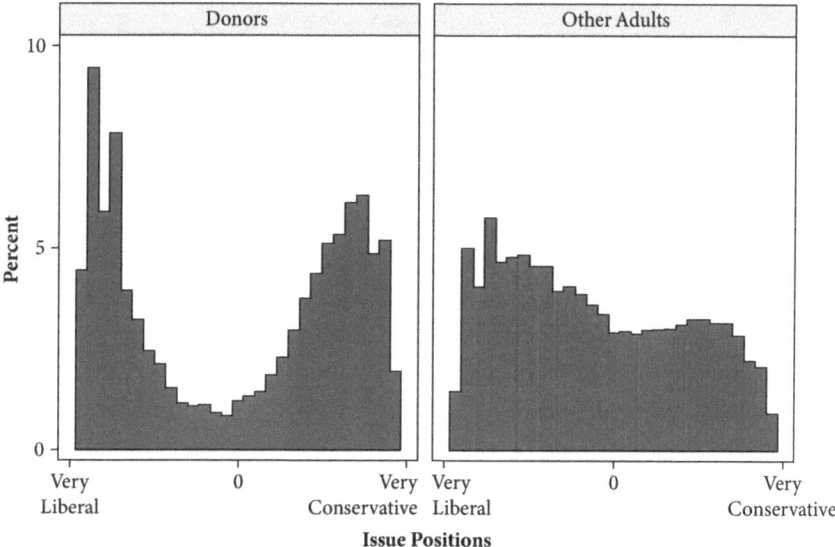

Figure 13.1 Ideological distribution of individual campaign donors as compared to other adults.

Source: La Raja & Schaffner, Campaign Finance and Political Polarization.

In one of the largest surveys of campaign donors, the results showed "extremely large differences" in ideology between donors and even non-donor partisans of the same party.[8] These differences vary across issues. Republican donors, for example, are much more conservative on economic issues than other Republicans; on issues like tax rates on millionaires, provision of health insurance, or enacting programs to support those with lower incomes, Republican donors are consistently more conservative than Republican voters. On social issues, Republican donors and non-donors are more closely aligned. On the Democratic side, donors are substantially more liberal on social issues, such as capital punishment and abortion, than other Democrats, while their views on economic issues are more similar. Both Republican and Democratic donors are more cosmopolitan or "pro-globalism" than the parties' other supporters. Thus, donors push Republicans further to the right on economic issues and Democrats further to the left on social issues than the parties' other supporters prefer. Perhaps as a result, both representatives and senators take positions more extreme than those of their median constituents and even of their median partisan supporters.[9]

Another study found that donors have more ideologically extreme preferences than not only general-election but even primary voters, a finding all the more noteworthy given the perception that primary voters are particularly ideological.[10] And similarly, another major study found that donors are more ideological even than "active partisans," defined as "voters who identify with a political party and engage in political activities in addition to simply voting."[11] In a particularly striking finding, it turns out that the preferences of donors are also more ideologically extreme than those of affluent non-donors; in other words, donors are wealthier than non-donors, but their different policy preferences are not merely a reflection of their greater resources.[12]

Of the various sources of campaign funding and spending, individual donors are among the most ideological. Political parties seek to maximize partisan advantage; they fund competitive candidates regardless of ideology. Traditional political action committees (PACs) which contribute to candidates, such as business PACs, often represent access-seeking donors rather than ideological ones. The Supreme Court's *McConnell v. FEC* decision, for example, noted that more than half of the fifty largest corporate soft-money donors to the political parties in 2000 gave to both parties, a clear sign that access, not ideology, motivated those donations.[13]

Moreover, campaigns have become more dependent on individual donors in recent years.[14] Thus, candidates have greater incentives to move to the extremes to attract these donors. In addition, the nationalization of elections and fundraising has meant that more individual donations to House and Senate candidates now come from outside their district or state than in earlier years. From 1998 to 2022, the average percentage of in-district money for House candidates fell from 37% to 26%.[15] Similarly, the percentage of donations that even came from within a candidate's state was 81% in 1998, but had dropped to 62% by 2022.[16] For the Senate, out-of-state donations traditionally had been proportionally higher than for the House, but there, too, the role of out-of-state money has grown substantially. In 2000 around 62% of donations were in-state, while in 2020 that had declined to 33%.[17]

Ideological views particularly motivate money from outside a district or state, because those donations reflect national ideological concerns rather than local issues specific to a district or even state.[18] In 2020, for example, more than 99% of the contributions to New York Representative Alexandria Ocasio-Cortez came from outside her district, as did 92% for Florida Representative Matt Gaetz.[19] Studies show that out-of-district donors are more ideologically extreme than a legislator's in-district constituents and more extreme than in-district donors.[20] Moreover, these outside donations are reflected in the policy positions legislators take, at least in certain contexts. Representatives in safe districts, for example, take positions closer to the preferences of their more extreme out-of-district ideological donors than to the preferences of their in-district constituents.[21] Conversely, members in competitive districts tend to take positions closer to their constituents' preferences rather than to the more ideologically extreme positions of their out-of-district donors. Because around 85–90% of House seats are safe ones these days, this effect of nationalized donations is highly significant. Greater dependence on individual donors, and on out-of-district donors, increases the incentives legislators face to respond to the ideological poles rather than the center.

Donors are not just more ideologically extreme, but unrepresentative of the general electorate in many other dimensions. Perhaps not surprisingly, they are older, more educated, more male (although women are increasingly donating),[22] and wealthier than non-donors. Younger voters and racial minorities are particularly under-represented. While the median age in the country is thirty-eight, the median age of donors is fifty-nine, and when weighted by the size of donation, the median donor age is sixty-six; the age of a donor also correlates significantly with the age of the candidates to whom they give.[23]

Some empiricists go so far as to conclude that the emergence of the partisan educational divide between college-educated and non-college voters has been driven in part by the role of out-of-state, high-education Democratic-primary donors. On economic policy these voters support redistributive policies, while the non-college voters who were formerly Democrats instead favor pre-distribution policies (such as protectionist trade policies, pro-union industrial policies, a federal jobs guarantee, and higher minimum wages).[24] As college-educated voters and donors pushed the Democratic party toward redistributive policy instead, these non-college voters increasingly became Republicans. (It should be noted that the same educational divide appears in most Western democracies.)

Small Donors

Recent elections have seen an explosion in small-donor (under $200) contributions to federal elections. In 2016, small donors contributed $1 billion to federal elections; in 2020, that rose to more than $4 billion. The rise in small-donor financing, which the Internet enables, has been heralded as a way to "reclaim" our republic,[25] a development which would not only "significantly enhance the quality of democracy in the United States"[26] but also "restore citizens to their rightful pre-eminent place in our democracy."[27]

The rise of small donors has indeed increased participation in the campaign-finance system. But the rise of small donors does not diminish the relationship between donors and polarization. In a series of articles, I have chronicled that small donors are *at least* as ideologically extreme, compared to the general electorate, as larger donors—and they raise further concerns about the rise of political extremism.[28] In the most comprehensive study of small donors to presidential elections, which focused on the 2008 and 2012 elections, the authors found that "donors differ from voters in being older, more affluent, better educated, more partisan, and more ideological."[29] More recent studies confirm this.[30] Like large donors, small donors are also geographically concentrated in unrepresentative ways; they cluster in the Northeast, on the coasts, and in other large metropolitan areas such as Atlanta, Dallas-Fort Worth, Chicago, and Minneapolis.[31] In most of the Midwest and the South, contributions are rare.

In addition, small donors particularly help fuel the extremes of the parties because candidates closer to the poles of the ideological spectrum are the most dependent on small donors.[32] The ten House members in the 177th Congress (2021–2023) who received the highest share of their funds from small donors included Marjorie Taylor Greene, Alexandria Ocasio-Cortez, Katie Porter, Jim Jordan, Dan Crenshaw, and Matt Gaetz, along with party leaders. In 2016, Donald Trump became the most successful candidate ever in raising money from small donors, whether measured in total dollars raised or as a percentage of his overall fundraising. Nearly 70% of individual contributions to his campaign, and 58% of the campaign's total dollars raised, came from small donors.

Small donors also play a role in the internal fragmenting of the political parties, which makes effective governing even more difficult.[33] Among the twenty Republicans who voted repeatedly against Rep. Kevin McCarthy's speakership, for example, nine raised more than half their money for the 2022 elections from small donors.[34] Political strategists note that candidates who can rely on small donations are not as subject to the influence of their political party and party leaders. As a top aide to two former speakers put it, "these obstructionists raise all the money online, creating a very destructive cycle."[35] Small donors are not the only funding source that erodes the party discipline often necessary for Congress to function effectively; super PACs can do so as well.[36] But small donors amplify the reasons parties find it difficult to unify today.

Moreover, small donors are highly responsive to viral moments of outrage. Within seven hours of being convicted of thirty-four felony counts in the New York courts, Donald Trump raised nearly $35 million in small donations, which doubled the campaign's single-day fundraising record.[37] When Representative Marjorie Taylor Greene was stripped of any committee assignments shortly after she was first elected, she immediately raised a stunning $3.2 million in the first quarter of 2021, with an average donation of $32. When Rep. Ilhan Omar was sharply criticized, including by her own party leaders, for raising antisemitic caricatures about politicians' support for Israel, she quickly received $832,000 in the first quarter of 2019, making her one of the top fundraisers that quarter among House Democrats.[38] Back in the early days of small donations, when Representative Joe Wilson defied decorum by shouting "You lie!" at President Obama during the State of the Union, he quickly raised nearly $3 million, most of it in small donations.[39]

The hunt for small donations also drives some of the extremist rhetoric and tactics in our political culture.[40] Just as we have learned that the fight for attention on the Internet and social media drives a culture of divisiveness and outrage, candidates have discovered that the spigot of Internet-fueled small donations gets turned on by extreme, attention-seeking behavior. This should come as no surprise; the same was true in the days of direct-mail campaigns,[41] and social media simply amplifies by orders of magnitude the dynamics of direct-mail fundraising. Members of Congress now comment explicitly about this. Republican Senator Thom Tillis, for example, recently said that attention-grabbing has "become part of a business model for people here. . . . They're doing it for the purposes of exposure and money."[42] Similarly, Democratic Senator Michael F. Bennet has observed of online fundraising: "The more extreme you are, the more rewarded you are."[43]

Small donors are also unrepresentative of the general electorate. They are more highly educated, whiter, older, and more likely to be married and to have higher incomes. On these measures, they are more representative of the general electorate than are larger donors, but still unrepresentative.

II

The fact that individual donors, large and small, fuel the ideological extremes in our politics and are unrepresentative in other ways as well should have implications for how we think about campaign finance reform. Many reformers, for example, long for a future in which the Supreme Court overrules *Buckley v. Valeo*[44] and permits legislatures to cap election spending. But even were that day to arrive, money would still matter. Candidates and officeholders—and hence our politics—would still be hostage to an individual donor base far more ideologically polarized and extreme than the general public. Politicians would still have incentives to skew policy away from the preferences of most citizens, and hyperpolarization would still make it difficult in our bicameral, separated-powers system for the political branches to generate policies to address our most pressing problems.

Rather than continue to try to modify the current system of privately financed elections, the major current reform proposal has shifted to a form of public financing: a small-donor matching program. As proposed in the Democrats' comprehensive voting-reform legislation which passed the House in March 2019, known as the "For the People Act of 2019," the government would provide $6 in matching funds for the first $200 of contributions to a House candidate, up to a fixed maximum. This is modeled on a New York City program that provides eight-to-one matches on donations up to $250 for citywide candidates. Such programs are justified as enhancing political equality and potentially encouraging greater participation in funding campaigns.

But given what we know about individual donors, tying public financing to their preferences will only further fuel the flames of polarization and extremism. (I would also caution about drawing inferences from local government elections to how small-donor matching funds for national elections would work.) This problem is magnified all the more with small donors. Moreover, the hunt for small donors has already inflamed the political culture, because more extreme appeals have turned on the flow of small donations.

I have suggested that, if Congress were to adopt a small-donor matching program, the program should be limited to in-district small donors.[45] Recently the Brennan Center, which has been a major proponent of national small-donor matching legislation, has shifted gears and accepted this modification to its proposal, in order to blunt the polarizing effects of national small donors.[46] As the Brennan Center now agrees, an in-district limitation will "steer[] more candidates to fundraise among their own constituents rather than rely on a more polarized donor base."[47] Moreover, it acknowledges, "[t]he sort of inflammatory fundraising strategies that critics tend to worry the most about depend on having a nationwide donor base."[48]

An in-district limitation would diminish some of the most polarizing aspects of individual donations, though in-district donors would still be more polarized than the electorate. Such a limitation would also bolster the ties between representatives and their constituents. But federal public subsidies limited to matching only in-district donations would raise First Amendment issues. The Supreme Court has never directly addressed whether jurisdictions can ban out-of-jurisdiction campaign donations, though the few lower courts to address the issue have tended to find such bans unconstitutional.[49] Assuming such outright bans are unconstitutional, the issue of limiting public subsidies to in-district donations still raises distinct questions.

The government has more latitude when exercising its spending powers than when exercising its coercive powers. Speech restrictions are more suspect than speech subsidies. When spending money to fund public programs, Congress has significant discretion to define the scope of the program it wants to fund.[50] Generally, the Court will uphold government subsidy programs that facilitate speech, particularly if they do not discriminate based on viewpoint.

In *Buckley v. Valeo* itself, the Court applied minimal scrutiny in upholding the presidential public-financing system, even though that system disadvantaged independent candidates by providing no funds to candidates who did not run in the primaries and disadvantaged smaller parties by not providing funds during the campaign to a party's candidate unless that party had received 5% of the vote in the prior election.[51] Nonetheless, the Court said: "Without any doubt, a range of formulations would sufficiently protect the public fisc and not foster factionalism, and would also recognize the public interest in the fluidity of our political affairs...."[52]

If Congress's primary justification for limiting matching funds to in-district donors were that outside donors were more ideologically polarizing than in-district donors, that limitation might trigger significant First Amendment issues. But if Congress's primary justification were that such limits foster the constituent-representative relationship that is the basis of using districted elections in the first place, such a limitation would stand a better chance of passing constitutional muster.

One of the major purposes behind the federal statutory requirement that members of Congress be elected from single-member districts—rather than elected at-large or through a system of proportional representation—is that districted elections give constituents a particular representative who is supposed to be distinctly responsive to their interests. Limiting public matching funds to in-district donors, while still permitting outside contributions, is consistent with this fundamental purpose of districted elections and with the nature of representative government in the United States.

The Supreme Court has never decided whether "political theory" justifications of this sort are permissible for public subsidies of political speech. In upholding the federal ban on foreign contributions to American political campaigns, however, the DC Circuit accepted a version of such a rationale.[53] That court recognized that the interest in American self-governance justified such a ban. Limiting matching funds to in-district donors could be justified on an analogous "political theory" grounds, one grounded on the type of political representation districted elections are designed to create.

Even if limiting matching funds to in-district donors would be constitutional, I am skeptical that Congress would adopt such a limitation. Small donations (like large ones) are heavily concentrated geographically. An in-district limitation would dramatically constrain the scope of a matching program. Moreover, if Congress adopts a small-donor matching program, it will be because Democrats push it through; yet Democratic donations are particularly concentrated on the coasts and in major metropolitan areas.

Campaign vouchers are another proposed direction for reform. Seattle has been running an experiment with vouchers since 2017. Registered voters receive four $25 vouchers through the mail, which they can donate to local government candidates who agree to lower contribution limits and a spending cap. These vouchers can be donated by mail, online, or in-person to a campaign worker. About 80% of candidates opt into the system.

Vouchers are designed to promote political equality and participation, among other goals. They have been used in only four election cycles thus far, and the different contexts of these cycles (some involve open-seat mayoral contests, some only city-council races) make empirical generalizations difficult. In 2017 and 2019, only about 2–5% of vouchers were used; with an open-seat mayoral context in 2021, the usage rate rose to 7.6%, but in 2023 that rate fell back down again.[54] At the peak of voucher use, in 2021, nearly 10% of eligible voters contributed either cash or vouchers, a much higher contribution rate than in most local government elections.

Even with higher participation levels, the critical question for present purposes is whether voucher users are representative of the general electorate. The two most recent studies conclude they are not, though these studies reach different conclusions about other aspects of voucher users. One study finds that those who donate through vouchers are the same groups overrepresented among cash donors.[55] Participation basically reflects the propensity of different voters to donate before the voucher system was adopted. That is true with respect to "race, income, past political participation, age, and partisanship."[56] In other words, this study concludes that the voucher program does not appear to change the mix of donors along any of these dimensions (perhaps because candidates appeal for vouchers to voters already known to be highly engaged).

In contrast, another major study is more enthusiastic about the effects.[57] It finds that voucher users are *more* representative of eligible voters than cash donors, though still not fully representative. Along lines of race, age, and class, voucher users are more broadly representative than cash donors. Nonetheless, this study concludes that white, older, and more affluent residents disproportionately use vouchers. Political reformers should not assume that most citizens are as politically engaged as the reformers themselves, or would be if given the appropriate opportunities. Vouchers do not yet appear to be the answer to a campaign finance regime that would reflect the political preferences of eligible voters. Seattle's experiment also has not been successfully exported elsewhere thus far; voters in Austin, Texas, and Albuquerque, New Mexico, rejected ballot measures when given the chance to adopt vouchers.[58]

III

One means of reducing the polarizing effects of individual donors, while retaining our system of privately financed elections, is to encourage more money to flow through the political parties, rather than to individual candidates or outside groups. Parties aggregate the broadest array of interests; they fund a range of competitive candidates of diverse ideological orientation; because they seek to maximize partisan advantage, they fund competitive challengers as well as incumbents; they are heavily regulated and hence more transparent than other groups; and they are accountable to voters for their actions. Strong parties can also make it easier to reach tough legislative deals; when party leaders can press rank-and-file members to act as a team, that provides protection for all of them to make difficult policy choices. Even if donors are highly ideological, the parties will use donor money in alignment with the parties' broader interests.

For these reasons, I and several others have supported policy and doctrinal changes that would strengthen the role of the political parties in the campaign finance system.[59] The academic Task Force on Institutional Reforms to Combat Extremism (of which I'm a member) makes a similar recommendation.[60] As an initial matter, the amount individuals can contribute to parties can be raised. The amount that the 1974 campaign finance law permitted individuals to contribute to parties has not kept up with inflation; in today's dollars, that amount would now be about $130,000, whereas the current cap is just over $41,000.[61] Current law also caps the amount of money parties may spend in coordination with their candidates; we might instead permit parties to engage in higher levels of coordinated spending with their candidates, or not limit coordinated spending at all. Many important democratic values are better served by candidates and officeholders being more dependent on their party organizations than on outside spenders. In addition, under current law only the candidates, not the parties, benefit from the "lowest unit rate" charge for campaign advertising on broadcast and cable. Policy reform could extend to parties the same benefit on the same terms.

To be sure, some state parties have been captured in recent years by their more extremist factions. But in states where that has happened, funding has dropped. Moreover, our current financing rules have weakened state parties, which makes them both more irrelevant and easier to capture. The stronger and more relevant parties become, the more likely they are to attract more representative participation.

Still, those concerned about corruption might worry that officeholders would be beholden to large donors, even if that money were funneled through the parties. And even if more money flows through the parties, candidates would still likely remain significantly dependent on individual donors and their unrepresentative policy preferences.

But America's campaign finance regulatory regime is more candidate- than party-centered. If that remains the case, an alternative means of pursuing political equality and the avoidance of corruption, while reducing the tendency of election financing to fuel polarization, is to embrace traditional forms of public financing, akin to the way elections are financed in most other major democracies.[62] Rather than tying public funds to the preferences of individual donors, more traditional public financing relies on an ideologically neutral source of funds: the general treasury. Around fourteen states and another twelve or so local governments use some form of public financing. In what are known as "clean money" systems, candidates must raise a small threshold amount of money from individual donors; this threshold is low and designed mainly to weed out non-credible candidates. After that, candidates receive one or more grants of public funds over the course of the campaign. Some of the longest experiences with these systems come from Arizona, Connecticut, and Maine; these systems have been found to increase the competitiveness of elections, increase the pool and diversity of candidates, and reduce the burdens of fundraising.[63] Most of these systems apply to the primaries as well as the general election.

To be sure, there are interrelated practical and doctrinal challenges that an effective system of public financing must overcome. If these systems are voluntary, they can impose conditions on candidates who opt in, such as limits on how much they can still raise, if at all, from individual or other donors. But as long as *Buckley* remains the law, these systems cannot impose constraints on how much can be spent by self-funding candidates, outside groups, and, perhaps, political parties. Thus, public-financing schemes must provide enough funding, and in timely-enough fashion, to be attractive enough for candidates to accept limits on private financing and to enable candidates to be competitive in light of the other sources of election spending. In addition, these systems must be designed to keep up with the changing costs of campaigns over time. The inability of the public-financing scheme for presidential elections (established in 1974) to do so is what led to the functional collapse of that system.[64]

But one of the Court's most troubling, though less widely recognized, campaign finance decisions has made it more difficult for traditional public-financing systems to do that. *Arizona Free Enterprise Club's Freedom Club PAC v. Bennett*[65] (*AFE*) involved the triggering formula Arizona voters had adopted as part of a voter-initiated public-financing scheme. Under it, candidates who accepted public funds received an initial allotment. They were then granted additional matching funds when (for general elections) the amount of money a privately financed candidate received in contributions, combined with the expenditures of independent groups made in support of the private candidate (or in opposition to the publicly financed candidate), exceeded the initial public allotment. Self-funded spending by a privately financed candidate also counted for these purposes.

During a general election, a dollar that a privately financed candidate spent over the amount of the initial public subsidy triggered roughly one dollar in additional state funding for his or her publicly financed opponent, up to three times the initial public subsidy. In the same way, if the initial public subsidy was exceeded through additional spending by independent groups, that also triggered the public matching funds, up to the same point. The purpose of this system was to enable public financing to reflect the actual cost of specific campaigns.

But in a 5–4 decision, the Court held that these matching funds violated the First Amendment. In the Court's view, they substantially burdened the First Amendment rights of privately financed candidates by triggering greater funding for publicly financed candidates based on the private candidate's spending (and that of their independent supporters). In a powerful and persuasive dissent, Justice Kagan argued that this subsidy system fostered more speech, not less, and that the Court had never held that a viewpoint-neutral subsidy for some speech burdened the speech rights of others.

AFE thus makes it more difficult to tailor public financing to the costs of specific races. The decision also creates a challenge for limiting any public funds-matching program to in-district contributors, as discussed above. Relying on *AFE*, challengers would argue that this limitation substantially burdens the speech rights of out-of-district donors. But that limitation would not seem to constitute the kind of "substantial burden" on speech that was central to the Court's decision in the *AFE* case. The "trigger formula" at issue there substantially burdened speech, in the Court's view, because it could deter candidates from raising or spending campaign funds, given that doing so could trigger the flow of more public funds to their opponents. That formula also punished "responsive speech," in the Court's view. Neither of those factors is present in a public matching-funds program. The funds provided to a participating candidate have nothing to do with how much any opposing candidate raises or spends.

Despite *AFE*, there are also still ways of trying to make more traditional forms of public financing work. Public-financing grants could be based on the average amount spent in the most recent competitive race or races for the relevant office, with an adjustment upward each election cycle based on the average rate of increase in campaign spending over recent years. Publicly financed candidates might also be left free to raise additional private funds as a safety valve against races suddenly becoming much more expensive; with large-enough public grants, however, there would be diminishing marginal utility (and hence potential influence) to these private funds in most elections. Public-financing advocates might also hope that a future Court would overrule *AFE*, which is easier to imagine than the Court overruling *Buckley*, given how much more deeply embedded *Buckley* is in the Court's First Amendment jurisprudence.[66]

The political support for traditional public financing is as much an issue as the practical mechanics for a workable system. Whether significant public support exists for any form of public financing is an open question. In addition, reformers at the national level have become more interested in small-donor matching programs, perhaps because of the difficulties *AFE* created in designing effective traditional public financing. Traditional forms of public financing have, for now, taken a back seat. But as polarization has become a more difficult problem and we learn more about the extent to which individual donors, large and small, reflect the ideological poles and not the broader center in our politics, attention might return to building upon the model most states have traditionally used.

Conclusion

Extreme polarization of the parties in Congress has made delivering effective government on major issues far more difficult. Because citizens take many of their cues from political figures, particularly high-profile figures, this polarization has also contributed to a broader political culture that is increasingly toxic and emotionally polarized, in which citizens despise supporters of the opposite party more than they like their own party.[67] As we have learned more about individual donors, who have become a more significant element in election finance, we have learned that large and small donors reflect the ideological poles in our politics, not the broader center, and are unrepresentative in other ways.

Campaign finance reform must be thought about more broadly than just the conventional focus on political equality, corruption, and participation. The institutional framework within which democratic politics takes place must also aim at empowering a government capable of delivering on the issues citizens care most centrally about.[68] Indeed, this is the central challenge democratic governments currently face. In my view, public financing that matches small donations will only make effective government more difficult. It would dramatically escalate the extremist rhetoric already central to the hunt for small donations; it would further incentivize candidates and officeholders to seek viral moments, through stoking outrage and attention, that turn on the flow of small donors; and it would significantly enhance the prospects of those figures who rely most heavily on small donations, who disproportionately tend to come from the poles of each party.

To be sure, our campaign finance regime is only one element that contributes to the extreme polarization of our era. In other work, I have suggested a number of other institutional design reforms that could also help combat polarization.[69] Moreover, institutional design reform is not a silver bullet that could magically dissolve polarization. But institutional design shapes the incentives to which candidates and officeholders respond; even if reforms can only influence polarization at the margins, those margins can matter for how effectively the political process functions.

Even if one takes issue with any of those claims, there is no doubt that small donors, like other donors, reflect the ideological poles of the electorate. Why would we want a system of public financing that enhances the incentives toward polarization? A small-donor matching program that limits the match to in-district contributors diminishes some of these issues and is a step in the right direction. But more traditional forms of public financing advance political equality without throwing more fuel on the already raging fires of polarization. Even if political will might be lacking at the moment, traditional public financing should be part of the reform conversation.

14

Party Campaign Finance
From FECA To Modern Hyperpartisanship

Michael S. Kang

Introduction

Political parties were largely an afterthought in the original conception of the Federal Election Campaign Act during the 1970s. Since then, political parties—and their relationship to partisanship and campaign financing—have become increasingly relevant in the current super-PAC era. Today, some scholars and activists view political parties as vehicles for moderating polarization and hyperpartisanship and propose deregulating party campaign finance as a result to strengthen parties vis-à-vis outside groups and individual donors.

I challenge that view here. Although campaign finance laws have contributed to modern polarization and hyperpartisanship, I argue that further deregulation would simply enable highly polarized and ideological donors to capture party campaign finance, to a greater degree beyond what they have already, and drive the parties even farther apart.

The Evolution of Party Campaign Finance

Parties from the 18th century into the 1960s flourished in what Walter Dean Burnham described as a "militarist" era of highly elaborated party organizations, bolstered by patronage, deep party loyalties, and firm control over candidate nominations.[1] Party bosses typically selected candidates for party nominations and then boosted them into office by directing grassroots organizations to foster voter loyalty and mobilize voters to the polls on Election Day.

As a result, for most of the 20th century, candidates earned their nominations by rising hierarchically through the party, winning favor with party leaders, and then relying on their party organization to turn out the party faithful on Election Day. During this era, election campaigning was party-centered and labor-intensive, reliant on the standing party networks and infrastructure built for controlling elections before mass-media advertising in politics.[2] Party campaign finance was important, but secondary at best to these traditional party functions.

The passage of the comprehensive amendments to the Federal Election Campaign Act (FECA) in 1974, which initiated the basic architecture of modern campaign-finance law, occurred just when political parties had entered a low point in their political relevance.[3] Television and radio advertising destabilized political parties by the 1960s. Candidates became less reliant on party organizations to mobilize winning majorities on their behalf and increasingly able to reach voters directly through mass media advertising.[4] Through mass media liketelevision, candidates could, and needed to, cultivate a campaign presence through which voters could personally identify and support specific candidates beyond general party loyalty and party mobilization. By the 1960s, voters were less defined by their partisanship than voters of the earlier era, and more likely to vote based on the qualities of an individual candidate rather than faithful partisanship. Television enabled candidates to reach millions more voters directly and win their votes without the elaborate infrastructure that parties had long used to control elections. Candidates therefore no longer depended on grassroots mobilization to attract voters; indeed, candidates with television appeal gained competitive advantages as television became more important.

Parties, responding to these incentives, eventually adopted direct primary elections to decide party nominations, ushered in by McGovern–Fraser and parallel reforms on the Republican side. During the 1970s, both major parties moved decisively away from boss-centered politics toward nominations decided by direct primary elections that shifted the focus from parties to candidates.[5] Candidates' personal popularity and television appeal became far more important than personal favors and affiliations with party bosses and their organizations. Direct primaries required candidates to win the support of voters through direct campaigning for the party nomination rather than currying favor with party bosses.

Political parties of this time, the 1960s and 1970s, were still constructed for an earlier era, building local party loyalties and mobilizing voters at a grassroots. But mass communications, and specifically television advertising, had become more important and required a great deal of campaign money to purchase it. As the Supreme Court would later observe in *Buckley v. Valeo*, "The increasing importance of the communications media and sophisticated mass-mailing and polling operations to effective campaigning make the raising of large sums of money an ever more essential ingredient of an effective candidacy."[6] Candidates quickly shifted from relying on party organizations for campaign outreach to reaching voters directly through candidate-organized financing and candidate-centered advertising appeals. These dynamics conspired to ensure, at least relative to the earlier era, that "[t]he party organization and the party in government were almost entirely stripped of any significant voice in the decision."[7]

The timing of FECA's passage and comprehensive amendment during the early 1970s both aligned with, and helps explain the seeming irrelevancy of political parties in federal campaign finance law at this time. While modern federal campaign finance law was being created, candidate-financed advertising and voter outreach superseded party-funded operations.[8] The traditional role of parties had seemingly passed: Political scientists lamented "the ruins of the traditional partisan regime."[9] Martin Wattenberg's book *The Decline of American Political Parties*[10] described it as follows: "[T]he two major parties [were] no longer as central as they once were in tying people's everyday concerns to their choice in the political system."[11] As I've argued elsewhere for redistricting and election administration, the comprehensive regulation of federal campaign finance unfolded at a historically low point for partisanship during the Cold War.[12] Electoral politics moved from the party-centered era of the early 20th century to a new era of candidate-centered campaigns and elections.

Under these conditions, political parties may have seemed incidental to campaign finance lawmaking relative to the prominent center stage of candidate-focused fundraising. As one political scientist put it, parties at the time "seemed so irrelevant or unpopular that candidates often avoided using the party label in campaigns while party organizations seemed almost absent in elections."[13] As a result, "[r]egulating parties appeared as an afterthought" in congressional deliberations over the FECA amendments of 1974, and the far greater attention to the regulation of candidate committees and PACs "revealed the marginalized position of American political parties."[14] According to Raymond La Raja's account of the legislative history, a late version of the FECA amendment bill lumped political parties with nonparty political committees with exactly the same $5,000 contribution limit on donations applicable to any PAC.[15] Only a last-minute amendment from Republicans, who benefited more from party campaign finance, lifted the contribution limit for party committees to $10,000.[16]

In short, modern campaign finance law began during a period when parties and partisanship were less salient and important than they had been in American politics (and less important than they would become again). Modern campaigning shifted toward broadcast advertising that was both expensive and aimed at a broad, heterogeneous audience. Candidates needed to raise money to pay for their own broadcast advertising and use their advertising to win over the general electorate in the face of waning partisan loyalties among voters.

Parties never fully regained their dominance from the pre-FECA era, though they enjoyed a resurgence during the 1980s and 1990s. The major parties gradually adapted to television politics and the new importance of campaign finance. As political scientists put it, parties pivoted from their command-and-control militarist roots to a new model of parties in service to candidates.[17] With the growing importance of television and campaign financing to pay for it, parties invested in the provision of services to support their candidates in the television age. They developed resources and expertise in, among other things, recruiting competitive candidates, advising and running mass media campaigns, and, perhaps most importantly, raising campaign finance money to pay for it all.

The parties then benefited immensely during the 1990s from loosening of federal campaign finance restrictions on what was called "soft money." The FEC liberalized rules limiting the national party committees' fundraising and spending outside of FECA regulations for purposes other than election advocacy. Parties were permitted to raise soft money outside FECA contribution limits provided those monies were spent on party-building activities or issue advocacy.[18] Party-building activities including voter registration, get-out-the-vote mobilization, and organizational development that did not sponsor express campaign advocacy. Despite these limitations on soft money's use, money is fungible: soft money raised and spent on party building activities nonetheless freed up hard money for use on campaign advertising. Issue advocacy constituted campaign ads that stopped short of express advocacy, by the terms of *Buckley*,[19] but served much the same function as express campaign advertising by praising and criticizing candidates before voters over broadcast media during the campaign season. Still, by refraining from words of express advocacy, issue advocacy fell outside campaign finance regulations on fundraising, such as contribution limits and source restrictions.

As a consequence, parties enjoyed a substantial legal advantage in fundraising that they exploited very aggressively on behalf of their candidates during the 1990s into the early 2000s. Parties were able to raise uncapped amounts of soft money in support of their candidates.[20] Issue advocacy, funded by unrestricted soft money, quickly had exploded in importance. Candidates themselves could not engage in soft-money fundraising and thus came to rely on the national parties for this valuable source of additional support. By the end of the 1990s, the national parties dedicated a substantial portion of their fundraising efforts on soft money. For the 2002 cycle, the major party committees combined to raise roughly half a billion dollars in soft money, which accounted for almost half their total fundraising.[21] Soft money enabled parties to regain at least some of the relevance they lost.

Congress, though, responded to soft money explosion by enacting the Bipartisan Campaign Reform Act of 2002 (BCRA).[22] BCRA prohibited the national party committees for raising and spending soft money, while raising the hard money contribution limits. BCRA therefore eliminated the legal advantage of parties from the previous decade. However, BCRA did nothing to prohibit nonconnected political committees, unaffiliated with parties and candidates, from spending and raising soft money in the parties' place. As a consequence, after BCRA, insiders created 527 organizations: tax-exempt entities named for their origin in Section 527 of the Internal Revenue Code. These 527 organizations were formally unconnected to any party or candidates, and did not formally coordinate with them.[23] They then legally raised and spent soft money through these new organizations on the same sort of issue advocacy previously produced by the parties.

BCRA thus changed, but did not end, soft money. Parties were replaced in their role by 527 organizations. Issue advocacy continued, funded often by many of the same wealthy donors, but parties no longer controlled soft money campaign finance as they had. The national parties no longer could feed soft money to state and local parties for party-building and grassroots activities, which shrunk dramatically in BCRA's aftermath. Candidates still needed soft-money support and shifted their focus from their parties to this larger ecosystem of outside groups. This campaign finance ecosystem would evolve further away from the national parties after *Citizens United v. FEC*[24] to include super PACs and other outside groups, as the next section describes.[25]

Ironically, though, the increasing importance of outside groups relative to the national party committees has occurred at a time of increasing partisanship.

In previous work, I describe this dramatic increase in partisanship among voters and politicians as "hyperpartisanship."[26] Democrats and Republicans are more ideologically cohesive and hostile to each other than they have been in a century. Partisan loyalty is strong and more predictive of voting behavior than it has been since the 19th century. Even as party organizations are relatively weak, partisanship as an influence on voters is historically powerful.[27] It is this contemporary mismatch of highly polarized party politics, fueled by campaign finance and outside groups, that motivates new calls for party campaign finance reform.

The Rise of the Wealthy Donor and Hyperpartisanship

Even as soft money enabled the national parties to rebound during the 1990s from their earlier nadir, the party soft-money era might be best remembered as introducing the preeminence of billionaire megadonors and their ideological influence on the American political landscape. Of course, there always has been wealthy sponsors funding campaigning in American politics dating back to the Founding, but in modern politics, federal campaign finance law placed firm limits on both individual and aggregate contributions to parties, PACs, and candidates that capped the potential influence of major donors. *Buckley v. Valeo* and subsequent court decisions upheld these limits in the interest of restricting *quid pro quo* corruption.[28]

In the 1990s, soft money opened up national politics to the potential of unrestricted fundraising. Federal campaign finance law and the FEC limited the uses of party soft money, but the absence of contribution limits for soft money meant that an individual donor could donate as much as they wished. Although the parties benefited from soft money as an initial matter during the 1990s, BCRA subsequently closed off national party involvement and began a progression of unrestricted money away from parties and to outside groups. As I explain above, nonconnected 527 groups quickly replaced party nonfederal accounts in soft money campaign finance and increasingly shifted power to wealthy donors and outside groups informally allied with, but formally independent of the national parties.

Soft money and these 527 groups were soon superseded in turn by super PACs after *Citizens United v. FEC*.[29] Super PACs also were formally independent of parties and candidates. Just like nonconnected 527 groups, legally they were prohibited from coordinating with parties and candidates and limited to independent expenditures as the condition of operating outside of contribution limits. However, super PACs could engage in express advocacy, as opposed to mere issue advocacy, and following *Citizens United* they could raise money from corporate sources as well as wealthy individuals, both of which grew further in importance.[30] Wealthy individual donors could donate unlimited amounts of money to super PACs, which thus provided an unfettered outlet for billionaires to channel their wealth into politics and influence electoral races. After *Citizens United*, super PACs almost immediately became a critical component of national politics and campaign finance, essential for leveraging the wealth of top donors beyond the reach of federal campaign-contribution limits.[31]

As the Roberts Court rolled back campaign finance restrictions, political money shifted to super PACs, and other similar campaign finance vehicles. In practical terms, the deregulation of independent expenditures meant an increase in importance and quantity of independent expenditures by outside groups, almost completely free of restriction, and at the margin, away from contributions to candidates and parties that alone remain subject to the full array of federal campaign finance regulation. Candidates and their political parties, not super PACs, appear on the ballot and are electorally accountable for their actions. Candidates and parties should be the best spokespeople (or at least have the best incentives to enlist the best spokespeople) for their candidacies. If money flows away from candidates and parties to outside groups, it flows away from those who would best speak for themselves and those whose views are most relevant to voters.

Of course, ultrawealthy individuals had been constitutionally permitted to spend unlimited amounts on their own independent advocacy since *Buckley v. Valeo*, and even earlier, but until the evolution of soft money through super PACs, very few did. It made a crucial difference that, beginning with the soft-money era, political professionals organized campaign finance vehicles to solicit and spend campaign money in a sophisticated, efficient way that donors could trust and support with a minimum of complication. Those infrastructures adapted smoothly from the evolution from party soft money to nonconnected 527s to super PACs. What is more, the culture of campaign finance evolved over the period through *Citizens United*. As one commentator put it at the time, there was a "huge shift in cultural norms and assumptions on the part of donors and money brokers.... There's a sense now that you might as well try anything."[32]

The increasing influence of individual donors is consequential because wealthy donors who spend the most money on campaign finance and fund outside groups are motivated by ideology and partisanship. Individual donors at the high end are highly polarized and highly driven in their campaign spending by their more extreme ideological beliefs. Empirical work on this donor class has established that they are overwhelmingly more likely to be ideologically extreme by American standards and likewise focus their spending on candidates, challengers, and incumbents who are similarly extreme.[33] Individual contributors donate large amounts of campaign finance money because they not only have the financial resources, but they have the fervent personal interest and desire to advance their particular political preferences in an increasingly partisan and intense political context.[34]

Individual donors are so firmly committed to their ideological principles that they donate generously and overwhelmingly to only one party. From 2016 to 2020, just 1% of federal campaign finance money came from individuals who split their giving more or less evenly between the major parties.[35] Over the same time, donors who gave exclusively to one party contributed roughly 85% of federal campaign finance money.[36] These partisan commitments are greatest for so-called superelite donors in the top 1% donated in campaign finance.[37] In other words, individual donors at the top of the scale today are ideologically extreme and highly concerned with advancing one party over the other in the hyperpartisan fight. Nor is the picture terribly different if we shift from ultrawealthy donors to so-called small donors who give in smaller amounts. With technological innovation, it has become easier for individuals to contribute to campaigns in smaller increments, and easier for campaigns to solicit contributions from individuals through the Internet and other means.[38] However, small donors do not appear to be less ideological or partisan than ultrawealthy donors.[39] Individual contributors, whether billionaires or not, typically are motivated to donate because they hold strong ideological and partisan views consistent with today's hyperpartisanship.

In this important sense, hyperpartisanship increasingly drives modern campaign finance. It provides the motivation for individual donors to invest their personal money in politics. In an earlier age of less intense partisanship and more moderate politics, individuals faced a less polarized choice between the major parties and therefore less reason to invest heavily in one party against the other. Today, the major parties are so polarized and ideologically cohesive that they invite full-fledged commitment by the ideologically extreme members of the ultrawealthy with the money to actively shape national politics. And this happened in time with the relaxation of legal restrictions on the magnitude of spending we now see during the super-PAC era.[40] Campaign finance today is therefore both a symptom and a cause of hyperpartisanship. Hyperpartisanship drives a great deal of campaign finance activity, but campaign finance also, by empowering more extreme individual donors and extreme candidates, helps drive hyperpartisanship.

Party Campaign Finance Reform and Its Prospects

By virtually every measure, American politics are more polarized today along party and ideological lines than in many decades. In Congress, Republicans and Democrats are more sharply differentiated and internally homogeneous than they have been since the 19th century.[41] This polarization has occurred in both houses of Congress and mirrors similar trends at the state level and among executive officers throughout American politics. Citizens as voters increasingly vote for one party over the other up and down the ballot, election after election. Ticket splitting, once commonplace, has decreased dramatically, and very few voters report party switching even in presidential elections.[42] Voter animosity against members of the opposing party has risen so sharply that roughly a third of Democratic and Republican voters feel that the opposing party is "so misguided that [it] threaten[s] the nation's well-being," with roughly half of partisans from both sides reporting they feel fearful of the other side.[43]

Modern campaign finance is at least partly responsible for today's hyperpartisan polarized politics. Although partisan polarization began building long ago for many deeply rooted reasons, campaign finance law has accelerated the ongoing process of polarization even further. Deregulation of campaign finance permitted wealthy donors to donate more money and greater influence over the electoral process. Wealthy donors now can assert their financial wherewithal not only through direct contributions, which were always permitted subject to limitation, but also through powerful super PACs and 501(c) organizations almost entirely free from legal restrictions. Because wealthy donors tend to be ideologically extreme and motivated in their campaign finance activity by their ideological and partisan preferences, their greatly expanded capacity to fund their favored candidates has enpowered wealthy donors with far greater influence to push the parties toward increasingly polarized ends.

Some critics of hyperpartisanship and polarization now propose a surprising but simple new reform approach: deregulation of party campaign finance.[44] Deregulation empowered activist donors by freeing up their financing and control of outside groups like super PACs and 501(c) organizations. If fundraising restrictions on the major parties likewise were relaxed, then parties might acquire new financial capacity to resist the influence of these donors and their outside groups. Deregulation of the major parties then might restore balance to the system by revitalizing the parties as a counterweight against donors and their outside groups. Parties, with their electoral incentives to satisfy the median voter, might use these resources to encourage their candidates to adopt a more moderate party line closer to what should be their parties' majoritarian aspirations.

Richard Pildes, for example, contends that party leaders tend to be ideological middlemen with internalized incentives to broaden the electoral appeal of their parties and broker effective governance across party lines.[45] Across a landscape of fragmented, polarized party politics, "party leaders can play this role only if they have the tools and leverage to bring along their caucuses in the direction that [they] believe best positions the party as a whole."[46] Drawing from political science and other advocates of campaign finance deregulation like Ray La Raja, he suggests further deregulation of party-related campaign finance by removing restrictions from coordination between party spending and candidates and significantly raising contribution limits on party committees.[47] He claims that parties donate twice as much to centrist candidates than to ideological extreme ones and thus are "a force for moderation compared to individual contributions," which are ideologically motivated and highly polarized.[48]

The critical question, though, is whether deregulation of party campaign finance will enable the major parties to serve as a counterweight to outside groups, as Pildes, La Raja, and others predict, or whether the influx of new money from the donor class will further co-opt the parties. Any notion that such deregulation will boost the formal party leadership's influence assumes that deregulation allows the formal party committees to collect and spend more campaign finance money. The questions are where that new money comes from and whether increased contributions from those sources affects how the parties subsequently behave. It would be one thing if we could assume the parties will receive new money from new sources indifferent to its use and thus allow the parties to deploy it freely as the parties wish. But this assumption would violate the overarching premise in the first place that campaign finance contributors, whether parties or individuals, care about how the money is used and thoughtfully deploy their money to achieve their strategic aims. If we assume that under deregulation the parties will strategically use new campaign finance money to gain greater leverage over their presidential candidates and achieve certain ideological ends, we ought also to expect, one step further back, that the original sources of the parties' new money also will gain greater leverage over the parties.

Most proposed deregulation of party fundraising effectively encourages the major parties to rely even more heavily on their wealthiest donors for financial support. The primary intention of most forms of deregulation is to facilitate very large, even uncapped contributions from these few individuals who can afford large donations for political causes well beyond the means of most Americans.[49] For instance, deregulation that authorizes political parties to operate their own super PACs or raise soft money again would enable the parties to collect campaign money in larger chunks from very wealthy donors. So too would higher contribution limits for party-related vehicles, or the elimination of the aggregate limit on total contributions to the national parties. The so-called Cromnibus of 2014, as a concrete example, increased the maximum an individual donor may give to each national party's committees to an aggregate of more than $1.5 million over an election cycle.[50] As a consequence, the only individuals meaningfully affected by most proposed forms of party deregulation are the same mega-donors who already have fueled polarization through their campaign financing.[51] Apart from a few spending-side exceptions, proposals for party deregulation largely would encourage parties to depend even more on their wealthiest donors than they currently do.

The hope that deregulated party fundraising reduces partisan polarization rests on a faith that, when it comes to new opportunities under deregulation, the party leadership will successfully resist the additional influence of these wealthy donors. This faith has not been realized so far, at least since *Citizens United*. If anything, party leadership has become more ideologically extreme by historical standards as campaign finance plays an increasing role in leadership selection. The literature is now ambivalent on whether party leadership are actually ideological middlemen as some contend or, instead, are more extreme than their party median.[52] Because individual donors are so ideologically motivated and highly polarized, party officeholders who are themselves ideologically extreme enjoy increasing advantages in fundraising and therefore exercise growing leverage because of their financial resources.[53] Eric Heberlig and his co authors contend that this fundraising advantage actually imparts an edge to ideologues when it comes to party leadership selection, particularly as the emphasis on fundraising increases.[54] Ideologues in party leadership have incentives not only to broaden the party's mainstream appeal, which does not seem the current priority of the Republican party,[55] but are also charged with realizing the median preferences of polarized, increasingly cohesive caucuses as a matter of conditional party government.[56] In this alternative telling, party polarization may have increased not because party leadership is weak right now, but because the party leadership represents ideologically cohesive, historically extreme caucuses and reflects the strength of those polarized preferences.[57] This dynamic is exacerbated by divided government, which makes party accountability even more difficult for independent voters to sort out.[58] As a result, deregulation of party fundraising does not appear likely to result in de-polarization.[59]

To the degree that campaign finance deregulation channels money to state and local parties, the prognosis might be even worse for polarization. Today's state parties, at least on the Republican side, appear no less extreme than what we see at the national level. Many Republican state parties are either captured by MAGA activists, or wracked with division between MAGA activists and establishment Republicans.[60] The *New York Times* summarized early in the 2024 presidential election year that "[s]tate Republican parties in roughly half of the most important battleground state are awash in various degrees of dysfunction, debt, and disarray."[61] In Michigan, for example, Trump loyalist Kristina Karamo won election as state party chair but was removed by the state committee after eleven months of infighting, litigation, and alleged mismanagement.[62] The Nebraska Republican Party, captured by MAGA forces, endorsed primary challengers against all its congressional incumbents, in what must be a historical first.[63] It is hard to imagine at the moment that devolving more campaign finance money to state and local parties, at least on the Republican side, would produce greater centrism. As a former political director of Republican Voters Against Trump argued, "The evidence is overwhelming that local parties across the country, in blue and red states, are radicalized and support extremely far outside the mainstream positions."[64] Strengthening state parties in this direction, certainly on the Republican side, would not reduce partisan polarization or encourage ideological moderation.[65]

As a consequence, the deregulation of party campaign finance threatens to accelerate the distributional and ideological lurch in American campaign finance toward the concentrated interests of the very wealthy. Any deregulation of party fundraising today would occur in a campaign finance system that has already been thoroughly deregulated, when fundraising and spending have already skyrocketed, and when the influence of wealthy donors is unprecedented since *Buckley v. Valeo*. Further deregulation would occur at a time when this donor class appears to becoming more assertive in their control of their money for ideological, as opposed to straightforwardly partisan purposes.[66]

It is difficult to overstate the surging influence of very wealthy donors in this rapidly evolving system already skewed so far in favor of their interests. Martin Gilens and Larry Bartels, among others, have compellingly documented the extent to which the political system is almost singularly responsive to the stratified preferences of the richest Americans over their fellow citizens of ordinary means.[67] Gilens and Benjamin Page summarized that "economic elites and organized interest groups ... play a substantial part in affecting public policy, but the general public has little or no independent influence."[68] These findings make it difficult not to believe the political system already is tilting precipitously toward the preferences of the wealthy. Whatever the role of campaign finance law in setting political responsiveness, the additional removal of restrictions on party fundraising may just accelerate the effects of super PACs and other forms of deregulation in multiplying the political capacity of the very rich and their polarizing tendencies.

Conclusion

Parties traditionally have played a centralizing function in American politics and have done so earlier in campaign finance history. However, in today's hyperpartisan environment, de-regulating party fundraising would simply increase the influence of individual donors with highly ideological and polarized views. As a result, deregulating party fundraising should be expected to achieve little to mitigate, and perhaps would only exacerbate, hyperpartisanship and polarization by making those donors even more important in party campaign finance.

I conclude by offering the possibility of a compromise middle path for advocates of campaign finance deregulation. A middle path for party reformers may be to deregulate party *spending* without deregulating party *fundraising*. In previous work, I've argued that any moderating reform of party campaign finance should aim to centralize party politics in the party leadership, but without increasing the sway of major contributors and policy-demanding activists in the same process.[69] Federal law, for instance, comprehensively regulates party fundraising through source restrictions, contribution limits, and disclosure requirements that restrict how parties receive campaign money, from whom, and in what amounts. Federal law likewise regulates party campaign spending in a variety of ways. It restricts how and when money can be spent, to whom it can be given and in what amounts, and what and how often spending must be disclosed. These are two related but separate components of campaign finance regulation. Deregulation of party spending does not necessarily require deregulation of party fundraising.

The advantage in deregulating party spending, by contrast from party fundraising, is that it frees parties to do more with their money without at the same time opening the door to more money from policy-demanding donors. As donors are legally free to inject more money into politics, their influence increases, and since *Citizens United* there has been dramatic deregulation of campaign finance, almost entirely on this fundraising side of party politics. *Randall v. Sorrell* struck down low contribution limits.[70] *Citizens United* and *Speechnow.org* opened the door to super PACs without contribution limits.[71] *McCutcheon v. FEC* struck down the aggregate contribution limit on individuals.[72] The deregulation of campaign finance likely has encouraged polarized party politics because it allows ideologically extreme contributors greater political influence through more and more opportunities to spend. However, new deregulation of the parties need not follow the same path of loosening fundraising rather than, or in addition to, the party spending side.

One example is raising the federal limits on coordinated party expenditures.[73] Although party committees are free to engage in independent expenditures without legal limit, federal law still caps the amount that they may spend on expenditures in formal coordination with their candidates. Raising limits on coordinated party expenditures might increase the national parties' leverage over party politics without significantly expanding the power of major contributors. Parties would be able to make greater use of their money to support candidates. Because they would have more resources to deploy on behalf of candidates, parties would potentially have more influence over candidates who hope to benefit from party coordinated spending and perhaps, at the margin, deflect candidate loyalties from their biggest donors instead to the party and its leadership. However, raising limits on coordinated expenditures would not increase contributors' ability to funnel more money into party politics. Although the enhanced usefulness of party money might encourage donors to give more money to the parties, the applicable contribution limits on individual contributions to the party, as well as ancillary restrictions on earmarking, would remain in place.

Indeed, federal courts may beat reformers to the punch on coordinated party expenditures. Under *Buckley v. Valeo*, coordinated expenditures were deemed equivalent to contributions to candidates.[74] Contributions to candidates could be constitutionally restricted because they raised a compelling government concern about *quid pro quo* exchanges between donor and candidate. The Court reasoned, sensibly, that even in the absence of a formal contribution to the candidate, a campaign spender could simply spend the money on her own as the candidate would have spent it. Provided that the spender and candidate could communicate, or "coordinate," in the campaign finance parlance, the two could replicate the political result of transferring the money to the candidate and therefore raise the same *quid pro quo* risk as a contribution. As a consequence, the Court held that such coordinated expenditures could be regulated and limited just like contributions. In *FEC v. Colorado Republican Federal Campaign Committee*, the Court held that coordinated expenditures could be so limited even if made by a political party committee on behalf of its candidates.[75]

This longstanding rule is now under attack. In *National Republican Senatorial Committee v. FEC*, the Republican Party is challenging the constitutionality of restrictions on party coordinated expenditures before the Sixth Circuit.[76] Republicans argue that both the law and politics surrounding party campaign finance have changed sufficiently since *Colorado Republican* to justify its revisitation. They contend that Congress has opened up other avenues for funding party committees that call into question any narrow tailoring of the current restrictions on party-coordinated expenditures, all while the Roberts Court has tightened restrictions on the government's discretion to limit campaign finance. But more notably for my purposes, the Republicans prominently cite scholarship by Pildes and La Raja, among others, claiming that these changes in campaign finance have "increased political polarization and fragmentation, such that even those sympathetic to campaign-finance restrictions in general have criticized the [party] limits as 'exceptionally harmful' to the Nation."[77]

In any event, the policy justification for limits on coordinated party expenditures is not obviously compelling. The rationale for limiting coordinated expenditures is grounded in general campaign finance theory about coordinated expenditures. Coordination of expenditures with the candidate threatens circumvention of applicable contribution limits on donations directly to the candidate and therefore raises a corruption risk. But any corruption worry in the usual sense, however plausible between an individual donor and candidate, is attenuated when postulated between a party and its candidate. Candidates are the party flagbearers who define what the party stands for and execute the party's agenda, such that it is hard to conceive what it would mean for a party itself to "corrupt" its candidates through coordinated expenditures. Indeed, the motivation for deregulation would be to increase the party's leverage over its candidates, not to corrupt them in any pernicious sense. Consistent with party reformers' intentions, corruption through party-coordinated expenditures might be to coax candidates toward the party line and ideally counteract the other polarizing influences of high-level federal campaign finance.

A focus on party spending is more promising and more cautious than the wholesale embrace of deregulation of party campaign finance sometimes proposed. If increasing limits on coordinated expenditures is the most obvious suggestion, there are others.[78] Deregulating party campaign finance, without attending to the risk of further fortifying this big-money -donor influence, may only worsen hyperpolarization, despite the best of reform intention. But measures that expand the reach of parties while resisting an increased role for contributors have a better chance of strengthening parties while minimizing the risk of worsening polarization.

15

Plutocratic Democracy, Elon Musk, and the Limits of Campaign Finance Reform

Farris Peale and Guy-Uriel E. Charles

Introduction

In 1974, Congress amended the Federal Election Campaign Act (FECA) and enacted a comprehensive regime designed to address the pathologies of big money in democratic politics.[1] The Act had many goals. One target was political corruption—a concern gripping Washington as it weathered the crisis of the Watergate scandal.[2] Political campaigns had long been magnets for corruption, from the Gilded Age to the first decade of the 20th century to the 1970s.[3] Private donations to political campaigns and expenditures on behalf of political campaigns lined the pockets of corrupt politicians and delivered public-policy benefits for corporations.

Another concern was the sheer cost of campaigns. The 1972 presidential election set spending records, and Democrats, unable to attract the big-money donors that "dominated" Nixon's campaign, were outspent two-to-one in the general election and summarily shellacked at the polls.[4]

In down-ballot races, the increasing expense of campaigns also proved an obstacle to potential candidates, determining who could run for office and who could win. In short, as Professor Joel Fleishman stated soon after the 1974 amendments were passed, the amendments aimed to "(1) diminish[] the deterrence of candidates from running for office, (2) diminish[] candidates' differential advantage arising from disparate access to wealth; and (3) diminish[]

contribution-based, post-election influence on policy or in the obtaining of appointments to office."[5]

In furtherance of these goals, Congress regulated the "supply side" and the "demand side" of campaign financing. Supply-side regulations limited the money flowing into campaign coffers. They were designed to ensure that public policy was primarily responsive to voters' needs and not to the interests of a wealthy donor class. Perhaps the quintessential supply-side regulation is Congress's cap on political contributions. These contribution limits aimed to control money at its source, limiting the hauls that campaigns could quickly pull in from a small class of donors and preventing any particular donors from purchasing outsized influence. Along with contribution limits, Congress regulated supply by limiting candidates' personal spending. The amendments also mandated an extensive disclosure regime to expose the candidates' funding sources.

Demand-side regulation addressed the need or appetite for money. It did so by regulating the cost of political campaigns. Perhaps the quintessential demand-side regulation is Congress's limit on political expenditures. And so, in 1974, Congress not only limited campaign contributions but also placed a cap on the amount of money federal candidates and national parties could spend on campaigns and the amount of money that individuals and institutions could independently spend on political campaigns.[6] Those "demand-side" provisions were essential to the regulatory scheme that FECA imagined, as Congress had long recognized the incoherence of regulating only supply without also regulating demand. For example, as early as 1911, Congress amended the Federal Corrupt Practices Act to impose a spending cap on federal congressional elections.[7]

Contrary to the comprehensive and institutional approach that Congress and the reformers adopted in FECA 1974, in *Buckley v. Valeo*[8] the Court focused primarily on one of the Act's goals: preventing corruption.[9] The Court in *Buckley* announced a regulatory framework that still channels campaign finance regulation today. Doctrinally, campaign finance contributions are permissible, but any regulation characterized as an expenditure limitation will be struck down.[10]

Conceptually, the Court removed one half of FECA 1974's two-part framework: Congress could regulate the supply of money but not the demand for money. The result is that the Court created a system that no regulator would have designed. As Professor Samuel Issacharoff put it: "No rational regulatory system would seek to limit how money is supplied to political campaigns, then leave unchecked the demand for that same money by leaving spending uncapped."[11] The Court created the worst possible world by limiting the supply of money but constructing unlimited demand. Because of that artificial scarcity, campaign donations became more valuable than ever.

Since *Buckley*, the campaign finance reform discourse has largely oscillated over the meaning of corruption. This focus on corruption has created three problems for reformers. First, *Buckley* and the cases that followed have boxed reformers into addressing the problem of money in politics as a supply-side problem. Focusing on what reformers believe they could do within the jurisprudential framework constructed by the Court, the campaign finance reform agenda has been largely limited to tinkering with contribution limits and other restrictions that will restrict the flow of money into the system. The most that reformers could hope for is a restoration of the pre-*Buckley* world, a return to the holistic regulatory approach of FECA's 1974 amendments.

Second, *Buckley* has taken away our ability to articulate a more comprehensive and holistic approach to money in politics. As one of us put it, "to be taken seriously in this doctrinal debate, all of our discourse must be articulated within the corruption framework, which causes us to ignore other concerns that ought to be of interest when considering a system of campaign financing."[12] There have been bouts of reformist enthusiasm and some legislation that has been enacted since *Buckley*, such as the Bipartisan Campaign Reform Act of 2002.[13] Still, the current energy for addressing the issue appears all but absent. Consequently, few new ideas have been generated in the intervening decades regarding what should be done about money in politics. After fifty years of running in these same circles, the campaign finance reform movement seems exhausted, even though money's influence on politics has not correspondingly waned. If anything, money's impact on our politics is more acute today than it was when Congress promulgated and amended FECA.

Third, and most concerningly, corruption—however broadly defined—cannot fully capture the challenge that money poses to democratic politics. Back in 1974, Congress primarily worried that campaign money would corrupt politicians and distort public policy in favor of the rich by making elected officials dependent on donors and ensuring that only those with ties to monied interests could take office in the first place. With those problems in mind, it made sense to think of the problem of political money as a problem primarily of campaign financing: politicians need money to finance their campaigns, and campaign financing also creates perverse systemic effects. The issue for Congress was devising a holistic mechanism to address those perverse effects.

Into the third decade of the 21st century, while some of the same corruption and distortion concerns are present, the fundamental problem is different. Rich people and corporations have long been valuable to candidates for political office. Their political contributions or expenditures have served as universal passports granting them access to politicians and the halls of political power. The problem is *not* corruption or distortion as they manifested in 1974.

Instead, the problem is self-government and representation. A small group of ultra-wealthy elites—individuals, not corporations—appear to be increasingly indispensable to the functioning of public governance. Beyond their political contributions and expenditures, these new oligarchs are demonstrating that they are capable of providing the infrastructure necessary to elect candidates to office and keep them there. For example, they can effectively operate a candidate's get-out-the-vote (GOTV) efforts. Such operations are commonly associated with political parties in a well-functioning representative system; these new oligarchs, however, can fund and manage critical GOTV efforts at least as effectively as the national political parties. Additionally, they own and have the financial resources to purchase critical information systems, indispensable conduits for communicating with voters. Further, they possess crucial expertise and know-how that are deeply valuable to the state. Relatedly, their companies and private economic enterprises are vital to the government's ability to meet its essential public-policy goals.

As their reward, these oligarchs are not asking for access or influence; they already have access and influence because of their wealth. They are not requesting rent-seeking public-policy benefits; those are already part of the package. Instead, they seek free rein over the government. They want to govern, though they were never formally elected.

We are calling this arguably new development "plutocratic democracy." We have governors that we did not elect. We have a facade of a republic, but it is the plutocrats who are pulling the strings. The formal mechanisms of representative democracy—namely elections—are insufficient. They are supplemented by an informal, though no less consequential, structure.

Plutocratic democracy is not operating in the shadows—it is unfolding openly and with the full knowledge of the public. Indeed, it may be the case that politicians and political candidates can enhance their credibility with the electorate when the politicians are aligned with the oligarchs. Some voters—perhaps a significant number—might be willing to take some politicians more seriously because the plutocrats are vouching for them. The politicians and the plutocrats openly acknowledge their alliance and are relatively forthright about their objectives. After all, these plutocrats are widely hailed as the brilliant titans of technology, finance, and industry.

To come to terms with the rise of plutocratic democracy, one must attend to the fertile ground that nourishes it: political polarization and economic stratification. We have a political system that cannot solve our pressing problems but can create immense wealth for a small number of people. Scholars of law and democracy have brilliantly cataloged the stark economic divide and partisan polarization as a problem for campaign finance.[14] However, the literature has categorized the problem as either equality or corruption. We break out of that template here and emphasize a new and different threat: the core idea of self-government itself and the formal conception of representation.

Plutocratic democracy presents a fundamental and tricky challenge to the reform agenda. Reformers will have to develop novel and creative solutions to address the democratic breakdowns that we currently face, as distinct from the different set of problems that blighted an earlier era. Any such reforms can and must include both the supply side and the demand side of the equation, looking beyond the contribution-and-expenditure framework within which the doctrine has left little room to maneuver.

But it also seems trite to think of plutocratic democracy simply as a campaign finance problem. Although oligarchs may make campaign donations and involve themselves in political campaigns, the issue is not limited to campaign spending or contributions. Indeed, defining plutocratic democracy as only or primarily a campaign finance problem would be a category mistake. Campaign finance problems are generally defined by a transfer of money from a source to the politician, resulting in *quid pro quo* corruption or distortion, or at least the purchase of favor or influence. By contrast, today's democratic plutocrats want to govern. Because they control, capture, or create institutional mechanisms that are helpful, if not essential, to getting elected and succeeding in office, they have leverage. Put differently, *Buckley* is just one part of a larger structural democratic problem.[15] It is not just money that is now indispensable to political campaigns. The plutocrats, the services they provide, the technologies that they develop, and their technical know-how are becoming vital to the political aspirations of our political candidates, to elected officials, and perhaps more broadly to the people themselves.

This chapter articulates the rise of plutocratic democracy. It also emphasizes the mismatch between that problem and the current thinking about money in politics—which remains largely stuck in a narrow band of supply-side campaign finance conversations that date back to the 1970s. Part I provides a quick overview of the current regulatory and jurisprudential framework—emphasizing how doctrine, regulation, and reform efforts remain captured by a narrow slice of the money-in-politics problem. Part II uses Elon Musk as the poster child for the nascent plutocratic electors. Musk was indispensable to the reelection of Donald Trump, but not merely because of the money he gave to the Trump campaign. Musk did far more, deploying the social-media platform he owns to support Trump's election while also operating Trump's turnout infrastructure in battleground states. Part III links the rise of plutocratic electors to the problems that our democracy currently faces—emphasizing economic inequality as an outgrowth of political polarization. Finally, Part IV offers a set of exploratory proposals. It first contemplates more modest and achievable demand-side reforms, then suggests that plutocracy may be best addressed by looking beyond campaign finance solutions—and altogether rethinking the category of "campaign finance reform."

Supply-Side Regulation After *Buckley*

For the past fifty years, both courts and commentators have engaged in a fairly familiar dance regarding campaign finance regulations. The fundamental question, asked again and again, is whether big-money campaign contributions and expenditures impair our political system. FECA 1974 embraced one side of that debate and enacted an expansive set of campaign-finance reforms targeted at the contributions and expenditures that some believed were wreaking democratic havoc.[16] The statute "established the Federal Election Commission to enforce a variety of new regulations, including optional public financing for presidential campaigns, full disclosure of all campaign contributions and expenditures, rigid contribution and expenditure limits for all federal campaigns, and restrictions on contributions from personal wealth."[17]

Early on, David Bazelon, Chief Judge of the DC Circuit, offered one helpful framing of the core debate.[18] In his partial concurrence in the court's en banc *Buckley* opinion, he remarked that campaign finance regulation "involved the agonizing process of weighing competing values of the most fundamental importance in a democratic society."[19] On his view, the statute was "designed to effectuate the one person one vote principle."[20] In other words, an animating goal of FECA was to prevent the corrupting and distorting influence of wealthy donors that eroded the value of equal participation by equal citizens. But that principle had to be weighed against "first amendment guarantees for candidates and voters."[21]

Indeed, one fundamental difficulty is that money, in the American political system, is essential to facilitating self-government. To reach voters—and to provide them with relevant political information and encourage them to vote—you need to spend a lot of money.[22] But that same money can dangerously undermine self-government. Thus, the Supreme Court's decision in *Buckley* could be characterized as simply arbitrating between these two presumably equally valid considerations. Addressing the constitutionality of expenditure limits, the Court observed that "a primary effect of" campaign expenditures "is to restrict the quantity of campaign speech by individuals, groups, and candidates."[23] On this view, striking down the expenditure limits was the tribute that had to be paid to the centrality of money in enabling self-government.

On the other side of the ledger, upholding contribution limits is the requisite genuflection to the reality that large contributors are more important and valuable to elected officials and candidates than the average voter, who can contribute only her ballot. Acknowledging that reality, the Court noted that the cost of running an "effective campaign makes the raising of large sums of money an ever more essential ingredient of an effective candidacy."[24] But raising large sums undermines "the integrity of our system of representative government."[25] There are no free lunches. Money can also undermine self-government.

In the five decades since *Buckley*, the cases repeatedly relitigated the same basic interest-weighing that marked *Buckley*—and nearly all campaign finance cases framed the relevant questions in much the same terms by which FECA was originally understood. For example, in 1978, in *First National Bank of Boston v. Bellotti*,[26] the Court applied the strict-scrutiny framework that *Buckley* commanded. At issue in *Bellotti* was state law prohibiting corporations from spending money to support or oppose ballot propositions, unless, *inter alia*, the proposition materially affected their business.[27] The Court recognized that the government possessed compelling interests in "[p]reserving the integrity of the electoral process, preventing corruption, and sustain[ing] the active, alert responsibility of the individual citizen in a democracy."[28] But the Court found there to be too little evidence that the particular corporate expenditures before it in fact implicated those interests.[29]

In 1990 in *Austin v. Michigan Chamber of Commerce*,[30] the Court addressed the constitutionality of a state law prohibiting corporations from making independent expenditures from their general treasuries. The Court clarified that the state's justification for campaign finance reform did not need to relate solely to *quid pro quo* corruption, and articulated the bounds of the second compelling interest potentially at stake in campaign finance cases: "[T]he corrosive and distorting effects of immense aggregations of wealth that are accumulated with the help of the corporate form and that have little or no correlation to the public's support for the corporation's political ideas."[31] The Court then upheld Michigan's limits on corporate independent expenditure because they aimed to address this distortion problem.[32]

At the beginning of the 21st century, after Congress had passed the only major campaign finance litigation to follow FECA—the Bipartisan Campaign Reform Act of 2002—the Court initially upheld "in the main" the statute's "two principal, complementary features: the control of soft money and the regulation of electioneering communications."[33] Much of the Court's analysis centered on how broadly or narrowly various provisions of the statute were drawn to fit the array of related corruption, distortion, and transparency interests that the Court had previously found to be sufficiently compelling when weighed against competing First Amendment interests.[34]

Finally, in 2010 in *Citizens United v. Federal Election Commission*,[35] the Court partially departed from the logic it had used in prior cases. It rescinded its endorsement of the *Austin* distortion rationale and, in embracing a more searching version of its First Amendment strict-scrutiny analysis, limited the possible justifications for campaign finance regulations.[36] Now, only the narrowest form of *quid pro quo* corruption could support restrictions on campaign money cognized as campaign speech.[37] However, even in working what seemed a dramatic shift in the law, the Court continued to operate within the same basic framework. The question remained whether supply-side and demand-side restrictions could be justified by a set of FECA-era corruption concerns. The Court simply reconsidered how broadly to frame and how heavily to weight those concerns.

In the years after 2010, much of the scholarship has understandably focused on critiquing *Citizens United* or finding ways to work around the decision.[38] And a substantial portion of that scholarship focused on the corruption interest.[39] But even as *Citizens United*'s role as primary villain has steadily petered out, the same core conversation has continued, extending a version of the debate that has been ongoing for decades. Advocates and scholars struggle against the bounds of the doctrinal limitations while trying to find a path toward the same sorts of FECA-style reforms that have long been on the table: contribution limits, expenditure limits, disclosure rules, and the like. And because only spending limits—and only spending limits conceivably justified by the *quid pro quo* corruption interest—seem legally viable, the energy around money in politics is often channeled into discussions about corruption.[40] Several scholars have continued to offer significant contributions[41], but even insightful observations operate within a narrow doctrinal framework.

This is not to say that there have been no creative reform efforts. For example, we have seen innovative reforms in public financing. Some localities have adopted voucher-based programs, allowing average voters to donate to campaigns, on a theory that they might counterbalance the influence of the wealthy.[42] Some of those programs have survived legal challenges, at least thus far.[43] However, these public-financing programs still attack the supply side of the campaign finance equation, focusing on how money enters the political scene instead of how it is used after it has arrived. The rationale of public-financing reform efforts also parallels the equation that FECA's authors used back in the 1970s: Candidates respond to their donors, so the more money a particular group gives, the more responsive candidates will be to that group. It is that logic that justifies putting more money into the hands of average voters.[44]

In short, campaign finance might be changing, but it is changing slowly. And our national discussion around money's impact on politics continues to adhere to a fifty-year-old set of first principles. This, then, is the world we know. Proponents and opponents of campaign finance reform may repackage their respective positions using different terminology—different state justifications versus different burdens on speech and associations—but the territory remains the same. Too much money unduly limits the voters' political agency, but money is also necessary to enable voters to exercise their political agency. So we flitter between efforts to stem the flow of money and efforts to turn on the spigot.

The New Democratic Plutocrats

The classic campaign finance equation was developed in a different era. It may no longer represent how money and politics are interconnected, nor capture how powerful and wealthy interests interfere with the democratic process. Indeed, it appears we are entering a different era—an era of what we call "plutocratic democracy." In this brave new world, it is no longer clear that the problems of monied influence on democracy are confined to money's role in financing political campaigns. Instead, there is a deeper challenge to our notions of self-government and representation. Plutocratic democracy—our willingness to be functionally governed by unelected plutocrats—is related to our dysfunctional political system paired with profound economic stratification.

The Old and New Trump Administration

To make the shape of "plutocratic democracy" concrete, consider the old and the new Trump Administration. As many political scientists before us have persuasively articulated, President Trump ran his 2016 election as a populist but delivered plutocracy.[45] He framed his campaign and his goals in that way. A certain breed of populist (and nationalist) impulse motivated many voters to turn toward him in 2016 and to return to the fold in 2024.[46] His campaign's financing, in some respects, reflected that populism. In his first run, he was largely self-financed in the primary and contributed his own money to his general election accounts.[47] He relied less on super PACs, and in the general he ultimately raised half as much money as Hillary Clinton did.[48] Trump was, of course, a candidate connected to the business world. But the success of his 2016 campaign did not turn wholly on the willingness of wealthy donors to back him, and he was not obviously more reliant on monied interests than were Hillary Clinton, Barack Obama, Mitt Romney, or John McCain.[49]

Nonetheless, although Trump sold (and continues to sell) populism, upon taking office he delivered more as a plutocrat on economic issues.[50] Trump's agenda benefited the wealthy and rewarded the corporations, and some have claimed that economic inequality increased significantly in his first term.[51] In some of his first moves in office, he set out to repeal the Affordable Care Act and passed a set of massive corporate tax cuts.[52]

Trump's first campaign made concrete what political-science data had long suggested: The impact of campaign financing on our politics is not as simple as discussions of campaign finance reform often suggest. Political scientists have long debated whether higher fundraising simply signals which candidates already have a better chance of winning or whether higher fundraising in fact advantages candidates.[53] The relationship between money, political outcomes, and public policy is complicated.

How money influences our politics is also continuously evolving. Indeed, much like his 2016 campaign, Trump's 2024 campaign—and the role of Elon Musk in that campaign—suggests one novel and potentially troubling form of money in politics today. Musk is not an ordinary big-money donor who gave money to a campaign in the hopes of favorable regulation, an ambassadorship, or some other reward that proximity to power might bring. Instead, Musk wielded two unique kinds of influence.

First, two years before the 2024 election, Musk purchased Twitter (later X), a primary hub of political media and political discussion.[54] By the 2024 election, Musk, in a sense, owned the modern "town square" (or at least one of them). Through his private ownership of a public forum, he could and did change the messages that users received. While other platforms attempted to stay away from politics (and avoid the problems that beset their leaders in the wake of the 2016 and 2020 elections), X dove into the fray headlong. Musk unblocked accounts that had been previously removed, and President Trump himself eventually reengaged with the platform.[55] During the campaign, Musk used his own account—the most-followed on the platform—to deliver an array of political messages in favor of Trump and a broader conservative agenda.[56] And some have argued that Musk altered the platform's algorithm to ensure that users received more information supportive of President Trump.[57]

Second, Musk became deeply involved with President Trump's campaign. He did not merely act as a surrogate and spokesperson, but ran the campaign's ground game using $175 million in money streamed through his independent super PAC, America PAC.[58] Musk, and not Republican operatives, dictated the campaign's strategy in battleground states.[59] He decided that the campaign would focus on so-called low-propensity and often rural voters in key areas of battleground states.[60] And he decided how they would do so, designing a unique canvassing GOTV operation. Musk deployed many traditional methods long used by campaigns—but rarely used by super PACs—including knocking on 11 million doors.[61]

But Musk also went far beyond ordinary canvassing efforts—for example, by paying canvassers.[62] And while not all his methods have been entirely sanctioned, the FEC appears to have recently endorsed the idea that super PACs *can* engage in ground-game operations.[63] Given how costly and difficult ground operations are to run, Musk's super PAC looks like a blueprint and not an outlier.

In effect, Musk and plutocrats like him have begun to fill many of the roles that political parties have traditionally performed. It was Musk and not the RNC who decided key strategy in battleground states in the lead-up to the election. It was Musk and not Republican operatives who operationalized the GOTV apparatus necessary to get Trump voters out to the polls. And it was Musk and other conservative social-media megastars like him who constructed much of the messaging surrounding the Trump campaign. A presidential campaign might once have been understood as the outgrowth of a party's broader campaign operation. But in a media and information environment where parties can wield less influence—and private plutocrats can wield far more—there is substantial potential for plutocrats to replace party structures.

Of course, some could argue that there is nothing new about Musk. He paid big bucks, like many other donors, to get the public policies that are favorable to his business interests. And he did so because he saw the lines drawn in the sand. Democrats in California shut down his Tesla plants in 2020 during the pandemic, interfering with his revenue stream.[64] Big-government Democrats and their administrative state interfered with his companies repeatedly—perhaps most recently when the liberal media came after SpaceX for harming nesting birds in the blast radius of his rockets.[65] And after the Biden Administration failed to invite Tesla to a roundtable on electric vehicles, Musk took the snub personally, understanding it as a sign that Biden's plans for an electric-vehicle future would not reward his company and would instead focus on union-based manufacturers.[66] Given this backdrop, investing heavily in a Trump victory perhaps made sense as a business strategy. And indeed, back in 2017, Musk also reportedly had a "bromance" with Trump, a relationship that seemed clearly strategic.[67] Viewed this way, there is nothing new here.

Musk may have been partially driven by the financial incentives that presidential proximity begets. But the sort of control he sought has only a limited relationship with the success of his companies. In many respects, his companies' successful entanglement with the government was already a given, with Pentagon contracts for Starlink and NASA contracts for SpaceX rolling in.[68] His current efforts seem not primarily motivated by money (not something he particularly needs more of) and appear instead to connect to broader attempts to control the levers of political speech, the mechanisms of political competition via campaigns, and the national policy agenda of the elected administration. Put differently, Musk was maxing out on political access and even public-policy benefits.

But there was something that Musk did not have: governance. Musk was not shy about describing those governance-oriented goals, including by inventing the meme-like Department of Government Efficiency.[69] He didn't merely wheedle his way into the Trump cabinet but invented an entirely new approach to small-governance libertarianism—an approach that he hoped to oversee. In the days after Trump's victory, Musk also promptly found himself on calls with world leaders, including President Zelensky.[70] He met with the Iranian Ambassador to the United Nations.[71] And he became, at least preliminarily, involved in the coming Administration's crafting of its foreign policy.

This more fundamental shaping of an incoming political administration looks not like corruption or distortion—the traditional means by which we worry that billionaires will damage our democracy. Instead, this partial capture of unelected political power differs in scale—and, perhaps, in kind. In this system, it is not merely that wealthy people are capable of having their voices heard and their preferences served by elected officials. Instead, a small subset of unelected wealthy individuals can participate in governance, crafting and implementing a political vision of their own creation.

It is too soon to say, but Musk may be a prototype of a novel brand of mid-21st-century plutocratic democratic politics. These uniquely wealthy individuals could run crucial aspects of campaign operations—a role also previously enacted by Charles Koch and his Americans for Prosperity network.[72] These democratic plutocrats may also engage more directly in governance. Far beyond lobbying or seeking government contracts, they would have a direct say in policy, literally sitting in on calls with world leaders and running executive agencies of their own creation.

These plutocrats might also control the informational environment. Consider: Perhaps the biggest impact of X was not on the campaign alone. Instead, X has changed how millions of people receive information and thus altered the underlying informational landscape far beyond the particular conflicts that transpire during the peak months of a presidential campaign. And X is not the only such platform. Indeed, plutocrats have previously constructed media empires that advanced ideology and transformed national politics. Think of Fox News and the Murdoch empire. Critically, these activities are taking place in plain sight. Indeed, one might even argue that Trump campaigned on the promise that Musk would play a significant role in a second Trump Administration if Trump emerged as the electorate's choice. The combination of these activities undermines the idea of representation that is at the heart of our political system.

Plutocracy in a Hyperpolarized, Hyperstratified Democracy

To contextualize plutocratic democracy, we must understand it against a shift in our background politics. Our partisan politics have become hyperpolarized. Our economic system has become hyperstratified. And these twin phenomena have fueled one another. The collision of these two forces has also upended the practice of American politics, undoing the background assumptions against which FECA was passed and around which *Buckley*-era debates were framed.[73] Given these changes, money can now influence politics in ways that were neither readily considered nor obviously possible fifty, twenty, or even ten years ago. Supply-side campaign finance reforms no longer fit this evolving picture— and our traditional focus on campaign finance fails to comprehend the coming harm.

To understand the depth of the background political transformation, briefly consider the world that preceded FECA and *Buckley*. In the mid-20th century, between roughly 1950 and 1970, the two political parties were near mirrors of one another, and the "trend" was "of the two parties" moving "towards the center."[74] The parties only weakly disagreed on policy; between the New Deal and the rise of Reaganomics, there was relative economic consensus,[75] and views on the most divisive of cultural and social issues, such as abortion, did not yet clearly align with either of the parties.[76] Liberal voters, therefore, were more willing to vote for Republicans and conservative voters more willing to vote for Democrats.[77] That political stability also corresponded with relative economic equality—at least amongst the white Americans who made up the major share of the voting population. Between the mid-1940s and mid-1970s, the income distribution was relatively flat, with the top 1% of earners holding about 10% of national income, and the bottom 90% holding around 68% of income.[78]

Fast-forward to the present and the picture looks entirely different. Economic inequality has grown dramatically. To stick with one admittedly reductive metric, income inequality grew about 20% between 1980 and 2016.[79] At the same time, polarization has taken off. Beginning in the 1980s and 1990s, voters' partisan identities began to resolidify.[80] Rising polarization soon followed as the parties moved further and further away from the center and from one another.[81] One party—the Republican party—also polarized more quickly, a phenomenon political scientists term "asymmetric polarization."[82] The parties also eventually became more *affectively* polarized, meaning that they have pulled apart along our most fundamental social cleavages—making polarization not merely political but also sociocultural.[83]

It is no accident that polarization and economic inequality have risen simultaneously. Extremist politics and economic stratification have long been linked. Political scientists Jacob Hacker and Paul Pierson have traced this dynamic's recent history. On their telling, the affective polarization of the Republican party combined with "[r]unaway inequality" to "rema[ke] American politics."[84] A class of disproportionately conservative and hyper-wealthy donors fueled the parties' rapid shift to the right.[85]

At the same time, as Donald Trump did in 2016, Republicans steadily learned to wield the language of populism—and a rising sense of economic satisfaction—to promote their agenda.[86] Their policies largely benefited the wealthy, further ensconcing the political and economic power of a small donor class.[87] And the cycle only continued. Polarization fueled greater reliance on a narrow class of donors, and those donors encouraged rapid polarization, exploiting and solidifying systemic inegalitarianism along the way.[88] As a result, we have now entered an era of polarized plutocracy.

Looking to the future, these fundamental changes to our politics have changed and will continue to change the ways that political money operates. Analysts have begun to chart some contours of these changes. Professor Michael Kang, for example, has noted a feedback loop between political dysfunction and the economics that enable hyper-rich donors to fund campaigns.[89] And he has pointed out how party-based and ideology-based donations have become more important, while individual candidates' campaigns have diminished in importance.[90]

FECA-era politics, though, mainly imagined individual campaigns as the vector for donations and for spending, because partisan ideology did not so firmly sort people into indivisible camps. As Kang recounts, the campaign finance structures developed out of that era's framework are ill-fitting and incompletely regulate the existing donation ecosystem.[91] These more modest regulatory disconnects are part of the picture, and they can and should be addressed. As Kang has emphasized, a return to a focus on spending, or the demand side of the equation, is likely necessary.

But it is not merely that campaign finance tools poorly match current problems. As Elon Musk's example suggests, there also appear to be more extreme transformations afoot. And addressing this new role for political money is, in some sense, existential. A system of government, if it is to be legitimate, must facilitate the ability of the people to govern themselves. It must also be capable of solving fundamental problems. Increasingly, however, our system is failing at both tasks. Our system benefits the rich and powerful at the expense of the average citizen and those who are not well-off. Our political system is also increasingly unable to solve some of our most pressing problems. These include truly difficult issues such as climate change, but also such basic issues as housing and transportation that we expect a healthy political system to address.

There are many reasons for these failures—and many are not squarely related to the problems of the campaign finance regime. For instance, our political structure is far too decentralized to address the numerous collective-action problems that currently beset us. Nevertheless, political money does have a clear role to play. It is still through money—and the various forms of influence and control that it might purchase—that a wealthy class of individuals and corporations are able to enact policies that reinforce our unequal system, while electing increasingly extreme candidates who deliver on their plutocratic ideals.

However, as we have tried to show, focusing on the influence that money can buy is myopic. Plutocratic democrats are looking for more than influence. They would like to take the reins of government to enact the vision of the good that they believe is in the best interest of society.

Beyond Campaign Finance

Confronting this challenge to representation and self-governance will be difficult. There are no easy solutions. Outdated regulatory schemes, born of a more economically equal and politically cooperative era, are a poor fit for present politics. No narrow set of supply-side campaign finance reforms will address democratic plutocracy or the more fundamental democratic dysfunction that underlies plutocracy's rise. Given these limitations on extant campaign finance thinking, some have suggested that "chasing after effective campaign finance reforms is futile."[92] There is something to be said for that point. But we are not there yet.

Instead, we propose two ways of rethinking "campaign finance." First, and more modestly, we suggest a new and more creative focus on the underconsidered "demand side" of the campaign finance equation. While the doctrine may preclude the return of expenditure limits, there may be other viable ways to limit and channel the flow of money once it has entered the political arena. Second, and more boldly, consistent with Professor Tabatha Abu El-Haj, we advocate a shift away from thinking about money in politics as solely or primarily a "campaign finance" problem. Instead, addressing the shift to plutocratic democracy requires thinking about control of political money as part of a broader package of reforms addressed at the root problems of polarization and economic inegalitarianism.

Begin with the demand-side reforms. As described above, given doctrinal restrictions on expenditure limits, the campaign finance literature has focused relatively little energy on the demand side of the equation. But while raw caps on campaign spending are unlikely to prove viable in any near legal future, there are other ways in which we might channel or redirect political spending. Those efforts may not directly prevent political expenditures by wealthy people (or even by plutocrats themselves). But channeling money differently could help to mitigate the background polarization and inequality that generates rising plutocracy.

We propose one such possibility: changing coordination and spending rules to empower party organizations to control political money. Ironically, while our politics have become more partisan and more polarized, the political parties have become weaker as institutions.[93] Party leadership could once control candidate selection and resist the demands of their most extreme members. Wielding dollars—and the value of the party's megaphone in a more limited media environment—the party's organizational leadership could carefully administer the partisan message.[94]

Not so anymore. Factions within the parties can muster attention and support—in part by using new media, and in part by looking to individual activist donors. In doing so, they can capture the party's message, energy, and policy. As political scientists have recounted, the asymmetric polarization of the Republican party is partly explained by that precise phenomenon. Fifteen years ago, Tea Party activists generated media attention, built grassroots organizations, and constructed a base of activist donors, then used those advantages to fracture and capture Republican-party institutions.[95] The Republican elite proved disorganized, and the party ultimately lacked powerful levers to rein in this rising faction, and soon mainstream Republican politics was displaced by the more assertedly populist-plutocratic brand that Trump embodies.[96] If hyperpolarization is partly attributable to the breakdown of party structure, then reversing the polarization cycle might be achieved, in part, by reinvigorating party institutions.[97] Strengthening parties again will prove difficult, and it will require providing parties with organizational sources of power. Exerting control over money is one obvious way in which the parties could get their power and their groove back.

As it stands, party organizations wield relatively little control over the inflow or outflow of money to candidates. The most recent presidential election exemplified this dynamic. On the Democratic side, the DNC raised about $540 million across the whole of 2024.[98] By comparison, Vice President Harris's presidential campaign raised more than $1 billion in just three months.[99] In turn, it was her presidential campaign that shared millions of that massive haul with downballot candidates.[100] Similarly, while the DSCC raised just above $270 million in the 2024 cycle,[101] by early fall the most competitive Democratic Senate candidates were raking in as much or more cash on their own—for example, $31 million in a single quarter in Ohio.[102] Similar numbers appear on the Republican side. For instance, the RNC raised just under $400 million in the 2024 cycle,[103] about the same amount that the Trump campaign raised.[104]

It is not merely, though, that the parties are unable to raise enough, or even that donors don't want to give to party organizations. Anti-coordination rules are the true obstacle. FECA limits parties' coordinated donations to candidates but allows candidates to donate in an unlimited fashion to parties.[105] Thus, parties cannot directly fund, or directly control, even the campaigns of candidates formally selected and nominated by that party.[106]

Another obstacle is the rise of super PACs, which tend to weaken party fundraising control—although not for the reasons that might seem most obvious. Party anti-coordination rules also mean that neither candidates nor parties can coordinate with super PACs, creating a wall of ostensible independence.[107] In practice, that independence erodes whatever control the party might have wielded over the expenditure of money that the PAC raises. Neither parties, nor even their candidates, can wholly influence the spending. As a result, the ability to shape perceptions of the party and of its candidates is more severely limited.

Restrictions on party fundraising and party coordination are creatures of statute, created by FECA and BCRA. The doctrine likely does not preclude changes to these rules. To the contrary, the Court has permitted Congress to make policy choices about party expenditures, perhaps most notably by upholding limits on party expenditures to Congressional campaigns in *FEC v. Colorado Republican Federal Campaign Committee*.[108] And there is little reason to suspect that this conservative Court would be inclined to try to preserve party coordination limits or restrict party spending. Thus, it is merely Congress, and not the Constitution, that stands in the way of party reinvigoration—and, potentially, the creation of a new partner in the fight against ever-rising polarization. Party reinvigoration breaks with the campaign finance mold that FECA and *Buckley* left us. Such creative reforms, which focus on the demand-side of the equation, should be part of the picture.

And yet party reinvigoration and the reform of coordination rules— these are reforms centered on campaign finance. But we must not continue to think about plutocratic democracy primarily as a problem of campaign finance. That framing no longer captures the issue of political money and the role it plays. In a political environment that is both hyperpolarized and hyperstratified, money is constantly influencing politics, because politics is ever-present, not contained to any particular candidate or any particular election cycle. Moreover, the problem of plutocratic democracy is not a problem of money alone. Certainly, wealth may facilitate plutocratic control. But wealthy individuals exert power not through dollars donated, but through the capture and deployment of institutions. In exchange, they obtain not merely influence over tax policy that benefits the rich, nor do they merely gain in ways that benefit their business interests. Instead, they seek to remake the government in their image—effectively becoming puppeteers.

Ultimately, it is not a "campaign finance reform" that will truly prevent a capture of our political system by Silicon Valley magnates like Elon Musk. Instead, it is a change to our underlying economic order. It is the capture of a message of populism—one that exploits genuine economic anxieties—that allows candidates who deliver plutocracy to ascend to office. It is also economic inequality and economic deregulation that allow plutocrats to wield control in the first place. We embrace systems that enable single individuals to amass wealth dramatically and rapidly. And we impose no regulations on crucial institutional mechanisms—such as speech platforms like X—to prevent their capture by monied interests.

In this brief space, we have not sketched a full program for a rethinking of political money. But we issue an invitation to others, for this is a project that we intend to begin. Money in politics can no longer be thought about only in terms of the transactions that occur surrounding campaigns. Nor can political money be understood in isolation from the other forces at work in our politics, siloed to its own isolated category of technocratic reforms.

Conclusion

As we have shown throughout this chapter, our system is no longer plagued by a "campaign finance" problem. Instead, representative democracy may best be described as a plutocratic democracy. Politicians appear to be increasingly dependent on a cast of newly ascendant plutocrats, and look to this subset of wealthy private citizens not merely for funding but for the tools and structures of governance. This relationship is a departure from the classic campaign finance equation: Politicians need donors' money, and they are thus more responsive to the wealthy and even act corruptly to curry favor with the donor class. In a plutocratic democracy, there is a more fundamental outsourcing of electoral politics, as plutocrats fill the roles traditionally occupied by expert political consultants or trained bureaucrats. We have illustrated one manifestation of plutocratic democracy in Elon Musk. Musk is not an outlier, but a flashing red light warning us of what could lie ahead. His model may be the future.

Plutocratic democracy is not the product merely of flaws in the campaign finance system, nor can it be addressed solely by remedying flaws in that system. Instead, plutocratic democracy forms one piece of a broader democratic crisis caused by an interdependent cycle of hyperpolarization and wealth inequality. Addressing the problems now posed by money in politics, then, requires addressing these more fundamental disjunctures. We have proposed some avenues forward. But this chapter is an invitation, not a prescription. It is time to face a new era of money in politics—one defined not by corruption or distortion but by self-government and representation.

PART VII

The Relationship Between Campaign Finance and the State of American Democracy

16

A Political Question?

Partisan Gerrymandering, Campaign Finance Regulation, and the Supreme Court

David A. Strauss

Citizens of a democracy can participate in different ways in elections for public office. They can vote for the candidates they favor, of course. They can try to persuade their fellow citizens to vote for those candidates. Or they can spend money to try to make their efforts at persuasion, or the efforts of others, more effective. Campaign finance laws regulate that kind of spending, but there are strict constitutional limits on what those laws may do. In particular, if a regulation is designed to limit the influence of the people who are doing the spending, that regulation is, in most circumstances, unconstitutional.

There is a paradox, though. Voting, surely, is the most basic form of democratic participation. But some laws that deliberately reduce the influence of citizens' votes will not be declared unconstitutional. Specifically, partisan gerrymanders affect how influential a citizen's vote is. They do so not by accident but by deliberate design. Yet partisan gerrymanders, the Supreme Court has told us, present a "political question." That means that courts will not consider a claim that a partisan gerrymander violates the US Constitution.

This disparity—strict constitutional limits on regulation that try to limit the influence of election-related spending; no limits on gerrymandering that deliberately reduce the influence of actual votes—is hard to justify. It is true that campaign finance regulation can, in various ways, endanger the proper functioning of democratic politics—that is one of the reasons for the long-standing judicial skepticism of campaign finance regulation. But partisan gerrymandering overtly warps democratic government, and partisan gerrymandering is now placidly accepted.

Gerrymandering and campaign finance regulation do not present the same issues, of course, but they are not different enough to justify such a stark difference in the way they are treated. Both partisan gerrymandering and unrestrained spending on politics threaten central democratic values. In both cases, it is very difficult to know how to deal with the threat, as a practical matter, without potentially making matters worse. But the Supreme Court has reacted in directly opposite ways to these similar questions. Legislatures cannot be trusted at all when they try to limit the influence of spending on politics. But legislatures have carte blanche to engage in partisan gerrymandering.

There is, or should be, room for an approach that recognizes the complexity of the issues in both areas and that brings the two subjects more into alignment: disallowing gerrymanders that are particularly inconsistent with the values of democratic government, and allowing regulation of campaign finance when it promotes those values. Having said that, it is unlikely that there is a ready-made solution that can be taken off the shelf and immediately adopted. So it might be best to do something that is, perhaps contrary to appearances, common in constitutional law: to allow the courts' role in both areas to evolve, over time, with trial-and-error experimentation in order to get a better understanding of the harms and benefits of different constitutional regimes. That approach would not be risk-free, of course; it could open the door to misjudgments and abuses, by both the courts and political actors. But the current state of affairs also presents dangers of abuse and neglects important democratic values, and it is internally inconsistent in a way that suggests we should try to do better.

Voting Versus Spending

In 2016, the North Carolina General Assembly, which was controlled by Republicans, drew new lines for congressional districts in the state. The US Supreme Court described what happened:

> The Republican legislators leading the redistricting effort instructed their mapmaker to use political data to draw a map that would produce a congressional delegation of ten Republicans and three Democrats. As one of the two Republicans chairing the redistricting committee stated, "I think electing

Republicans is better than electing Democrats. So I drew this map to help foster what I think is better for the country." He further explained that the map was drawn with the aim of electing ten Republicans and three Democrats because he did "not believe it [would be] possible to draw a map with 11 Republicans and 2 Democrats."[1]

Democrats objected that, as recently as 2012, Democratic congressional candidates had gotten more votes statewide than Republicans. So the lopsided gerrymander in favor of Republicans seemed inconsistent with basic democratic principles. But the General Assembly adopted the gerrymander, and, unsurprisingly, Republicans won ten of North Carolina's thirteen seats in Congress in the next election.[2]

In *Rucho v. Common Cause*,[3] some Democratic voters from North Carolina asked the Supreme Court to hold that the partisan political gerrymander was unconstitutional. That was the case in which the Court, ruling against those voters, held that political gerrymandering presents a "political question." A "political question," in this sense, is a federal constitutional issue that courts will not resolve one way or the other. They will instead accept whatever resolution another institution provides. In *Rucho*, that meant accepting the North Carolina legislature's gerrymander. So after *Rucho*, as far as federal courts are concerned, a state legislature is free to draw district lines in a way that deliberately reduces the influence of citizens who voted for the opposition party.

Election-related spending is, to say the least, treated differently. The throughline in the Supreme Court's campaign finance cases is that the government may not restrict individuals' spending in support of candidates in order to limit the influence of people who spend more. The government has no legitimate "interest in 'equalizing the relative ability of individuals and groups to influence the outcome of elections.'"[4] In other words: When the government is drawing district lines, it is free to go out of its way to give an advantage to the political party it favors. When the government is regulating spending, it certainly cannot do that, and—the truly stark contrast—it cannot even try to make sure that no one gets an advantage.

The main source of this disparity seems to be the premise that laws limiting campaign-related spending raise First Amendment issues in more or less the same way that restrictions of speech generally do—but that partisan gerrymandering does not raise First Amendment questions, at least not in the same way. That premise misconceives the issues and has led the Court astray, in its treatment of both campaign finance and gerrymandering.

First Amendment Misunderstandings

The Supreme Court's decisions assume, without ever explicitly stating, that regulation of spending related to political campaigns is in a separate constitutional category from the drawing of district lines. Any regulation of campaign-related spending, according to this way of thinking, amounts to a regulation of speech, and the First Amendment imposes strict limits on the government's power to regulate speech. That is especially true of speech on matters related to politics, a domain in which, according to established First Amendment principles, government regulation is especially troubling because it might be used against groups who oppose the people in power.

By contrast, on this account, the drawing of legislative district lines belongs to a category of government actions in which that familiar principle—government actions should be examined carefully by the courts when the government might be targeting political opponents—does not apply. In fact, as far as districting is concerned, that principle—according to the Supreme Court—might even be inverted; maybe targeting opponents is an integral feature of our system. The idea, embraced by the Court in *Rucho*, is that the Constitution reflects a decision to "entrust districting to political entities" and therefore anticipates that political favoritism will play a role in districting decisions.[5] "To hold that legislators cannot take partisan interests into account when drawing district lines" would "essentially countermand" the constitutional allocation of power.[6] That allocation, the Court said, is dictated by the Elections Clause of the Constitution, which gives state legislatures—political entities—the primary responsibility for drawing congressional district lines.[7]

This justification for treating spending and voting differently is deeply mistaken, in several ways. To begin with, campaign finance regulation and partisan gerrymanders are both ways of allocating political power. Campaign finance laws affect people's ability to influence others' votes; gerrymanders affect the influence that votes will have on electoral outcomes. The First Amendment does properly apply to campaign finance laws. But—crucially—because of the connection between election-related spending and elections, the First

Amendment does not, or at least should not, apply to campaign finance laws in the same way that it applies elsewhere. In particular, the courts' hostility to campaign finance laws that try to equalize political influence is not sufficiently justified.

By the same token, partisan gerrymanders also affect First Amendment rights. The facts of *Rucho* demonstrate, vividly, that partisan gerrymanders overtly discriminate against citizens because of their political views—something that would ordinarily be a textbook violation of the First Amendment. It is quite obviously wrong to say, as the Court did in *Rucho*, that those limits on political discrimination do not apply to gerrymanders because the responsibility for districting has been assigned to elected legislatures. Elected legislatures are responsible for all kinds of regulation, and the First Amendment always applies to their actions. No one would say that state legislatures, because they are political entities, are free to do whatever they want to keep political opponents out of power. It would obviously be unconstitutional for a state legislature deliberately to make it more difficult for Democrats to organize or speak or vote, even if the legislature believed—paraphrasing the chair of the North Carolina legislature's redistricting committee—that doing so would "help foster what . . . is better for the country" because having Republicans in office is better than having Democrats in office.[8]

So there is, in principle, no reason to allow state legislatures, however political they are, to accomplish the same thing by drawing district lines. And *Rucho* acknowledged, as courts consistently have, that other constitutional principles—such as the prohibition against racial discrimination—apply to the districting decisions that have been assigned to legislatures.[9] So just as the First Amendment does not fully justify the skepticism of campaign finance laws, the First Amendment should require more skepticism of gerrymanders.

Equality and Campaign Finance Regulation

The First Amendment does not immunize from regulation all spending related to political activity. The government can make it a crime to bribe public officials, obviously, even though that is a way of spending money to bring about a political outcome. More prosaically, political operatives can be taxed on their income in the same way as everyone else, even though political groups could communicate with the electorate at lower cost if they could promise tax-free compensation to their employees

For the most part, whether there is a significant First Amendment issue about a regulation of election-related spending depends on the reason for the regulation: specifically, whether it reflects an effort by the government to limit how influential political speech will be. The point becomes clearer if we leave spending aside and consider just the regulation of acts that are unquestionably "speech." The government can regulate speech because it is too noisy, or too disruptive in some other way; but if the government regulates speech because it is too influential, then there is, to say the least, a First Amendment problem. This is a consistent principle of First Amendment law, most recently stated in decisions dealing with state laws that regulated social-media firms: "[T]he government cannot get its way just by asserting an interest in improving, or better balancing, the marketplace of ideas."[10]

But the regulation of campaign finance is different in ways that the Supreme Court's decisions do not fully recognize. The difference should raise a question about whether that familiar principle—the government may not restrict speech on the ground that it is too influential—should apply to campaign finance regulation in the same way that it applies to other laws that affect speech. Campaign finance regulation is directed at spending that tries to affect how people vote. People who spend more have more influence over the voting behavior of the electorate—not always, but that is a reasonable generalization. And when it comes to voting, equality is an inviolable principle, summarized in the slogan "one person, one vote."

It is not easy to identify any reason, in principle, that people who can spend more in connection with elections should have more influence. A state could not allocate voting rights on the basis of individuals' willingness and ability to pay, even if it wanted to. Even the most modest poll tax, for example, would be unconstitutional.[11] So why can't a state decide that the ability to affect how others vote also should not depend on what an individual, or an entity, is willing to spend? The regulation of campaign finance, like the regulation of voting itself, is a component of a system in which equality is a paramount governing principle; it should follow that campaign finance regulation presents issues different from other regulations of speech. In particular, there is at least a question whether the government should be able to try to promote equality when it regulates campaign-related spending. So, contrary to what the Supreme Court has said, the government does have a legitimate "interest in 'equalizing the relative ability of individuals and groups to influence the outcome of elections,'"[12] because it has a legitimate interest in maintaining the regime of equality in voting, the regime of "one person, one vote."

The Supreme Court has rejected this way of thinking, but it has done so too reflexively. *Buckley v. Valeo*, the foundational modern decision about the constitutionality of campaign finance regulation, explicitly repudiated the idea that campaign finance regulation can be used to promote equality: "[T]he concept that government may restrict the speech of some elements of our society in order to enhance the relative voice of others is wholly foreign to the First Amendment."[13] That famous (or notorious) passage is central to the constitutional law of campaign finance.

But there are some problems with that passage. For one thing, the "concept" of limiting an individual's speech in order to provide equal opportunities to other speakers is not at all "foreign" to a system of free expression. Any number of institutions, conspicuously including courts, provide equal time to representatives of opposing views, and that means "restricting the speech of some . . . in order to enhance the relative voice of others."[14]

When the source of the inequality is a difference in resources, limiting the effect of those differences is even less "foreign to" the values of free expression. No one would seriously suggest that an auction is a good way to allocate the time that advocates can speak in court or that participants in a scientific conference can use to defend their findings—or that candidates for public office can speak in a debate. Campaign finance laws, to the extent that they try to promote equality, reflect the same principle: the ability to affect the outcome of an election should not depend on how much money someone is willing and able to spend.

Principle Versus Practice

Having said that, there is, in fact, a justification for the persistent skepticism about allowing equality to justify campaign finance regulation—not because the underlying principle is unsound but because of problems in implementing that principle. It may be difficult for courts to decide when a regulation actually does promote equality or instead favors one side in a way that should not be allowed. In principle, equality is—contrary to the Court's unreflective statements—a legitimate objective. But figuring out when a limit on spending actually promotes equality presents intertwined, and quite possibly intractable, normative and empirical questions.

Part of the problem is that differences in spending are only one source of inequality. If one candidate has access to more volunteer labor, for example, does a limit on spending—which could prevent a competitor from overcoming that advantage—promote equality? Maybe candidates who are able to attract volunteers should be allowed to take advantage of their ability to do so because, in a democracy, that ability should be rewarded. It is an inequality, but an acceptable form of inequality, like (to give the most obvious example) having policy positions that appeal to more voters. Or maybe not; maybe the ability to attract volunteer labor is no different in principle from the ability to attract large amounts of financial support. If that is true, then a limit on spending might perpetuate an unjustified inequality by favoring contributions of labor over contributions of money. The answer is not obvious.

Similarly, incumbents generally have an advantage over challengers; in fact, probably the most common criticism of limits on election-related spending is that those limits are a way of protecting incumbents, because spending can overcome the advantages of incumbency. But again, this argument, familiar as it is, conceals some complexities. Does the concern about protecting incumbents really justify unlimited spending, so that all restrictions on campaign-related spending are impermissible? Maybe some limits will still leave challengers with the ability to compensate for the advantages of incumbency. But if that is true, it will obviously be very difficult to determine what those limits are and when a regulation is too restrictive.

Then there is the question—parallel to the question about volunteer support—whether the advantages incumbents have are undeserved. It is not clear that that is true, or to what extent it may be true. Again the contrast with gerrymandering is revealing. Gerrymanders, unsurprisingly, routinely protect incumbents. But even critics of gerrymandering sometimes accept incumbent protection as a legitimate basis for drawing district lines, because it is a "'traditional' districting criteri[on]" comparable to "maintaining political subdivisions [and] keeping communities of interest together."[15] To restate the question about the disparity between districting and campaign finance regulation: If the government can deliberately set out to protect incumbents when it draws district lines, why is it such a problem that campaign finance regulation designed to promote equality might, as a byproduct, also protect incumbents?

"Judicially Manageable Standards"

As the "wholly foreign" dictum shows, the Court has treated campaign finance regulations that are designed to promote equality as unacceptable in principle. In fact, they are, in principle, not only acceptable but salutary measures. Equality is not only a permissible objective of regulations related to voting; equality is, in principle, mandatory. The problems come in implementation. The empirical and normative problems of deciding when a measure actually promotes equality, or instead distorts the political process and the system of free expression, might be too severe to allow a court to make that decision.

But partisan gerrymandering presents the same problem. The principle is clear, but implementing the principle is difficult. And in dealing with gerrymandering, the Court did more or less understand that. The first sentence of the dissenting opinion in *Rucho* was: "For the first time ever, this Court refuses to remedy a constitutional violation because it thinks the task beyond judicial capabilities."[16] The majority did not take issue with that characterization; it never tried to show that partisan gerrymandering of the kind North Carolina engaged in was somehow consistent with central constitutional principles. And, of course, it could not have shown that. The North Carolina legislature deliberately denied some voters political influence because it expected that they would vote for Democrats.

In fact, the *Rucho* Court acknowledged that "[e]xcessive partisanship in districting leads to results that reasonably seem unjust" and seemed to accept that "such gerrymandering is 'incompatible with democratic principles.'"[17] But that "does not mean that the solution lies with the federal judiciary"; instead, "partisan gerrymandering claims present political questions beyond the reach of the federal courts."[18] The principal reason that partisan gerrymandering claims present a political question is that there are no "judicially manageable standards" for determining when district lines are drawn in a way that constitutes an unacceptable partisan gerrymander.[19] The lack of judicially manageable standards is, in general, one of the primary reasons for treating a constitutional issue as a "political question" that the courts will not resolve, and that is how *Rucho* viewed constitutional challenges to partisan gerrymanders.

The problem of devising judicially manageable standards is a real one, with respect to both gerrymandering and campaign finance regulation. The Court did not say, in terms, that there was a lack of "judicially manageable standards" to determine when campaign finance regulation genuinely promoted equality, but that is an accurate description of the problem. It is hard for courts to determine when regulations of campaign-related spending actually do promote equality without having unacceptable side effects. But the Court resolved these parallel problems in opposite ways. Because it is difficult to devise judicially manageable standards for distinguishing acceptable from unacceptable gerrymanders, the Court abdicated: It allowed legislatures to do what they wanted. But when it comes to promoting equality by means of campaign finance regulation, the Court's solution has been to say that legislatures may not do anything at all.

One way to deal with this disparity would be to say that constitutional challenges to campaign finance laws also present a political question—that legislatures should have carte blanche in that area as well. But that does not seem like the right resolution. For one thing, it would overturn, wholesale, at least a half-century of precedent. But even apart from that, the *Rucho* Court itself seemed to understand, grudgingly, that partisan gerrymandering should not be a model for other forms of regulation related to politics. The campaign finance analogue to North Carolina's gerrymander would be something like a law that capped spending in support of Democrats but not spending in support of Republicans. No court would uphold such a law—which draws into question the Court's decision in *Rucho* to uphold its gerrymandering counterpart.

The more plausible resolution would be to treat as a political question a challenge to a regulation of election-related spending that could reasonably be seen as promoting equality—or, to put it another way, for the Court just to back away from the "wholly foreign" dictum and give some deference to restrictions on election-related spending that arguably promote equality. Given the problems of determining what kinds of regulations do promote equality—or even what equality would look like—there would be risks of abuses and distortions. But it is hard to see how those risks would be worse than the risks created by the unlimited power to gerrymander that *Rucho* endorses.

Trial-and-Error Evolution

The colloquial way of answering the concern about a lack of judicially manageable standards is: You never know until you try. Judicially manageable standards do not always appear, fully developed, the first time that courts address a question. So it may take some trial-and-error experimentation to identify standards—potentially addressing both campaign finance regulation and gerrymandering—that are judicially manageable and that implement constitutional principles to an acceptable extent.

Constitutional law often develops in just that way. The evolution of federal power under the Interstate Commerce Clause is an example.[20] Beginning especially in the late nineteenth century, Congress relied on the Constitution's Commerce Clause and Necessary and Proper Clause to enact far-reaching laws regulating the economy. Because the national economy had become increasingly integrated, many laws had at least a plausible connection to interstate commerce, even if they applied only to intrastate activity, or even if they applied to conduct that would not normally be described as commercial.

But Congress is not supposed to have a general regulatory power, so the Supreme Court tried to articulate, and enforce, limits on what the Commerce Clause authorized. Some decisions held that the Commerce Clause extended only to commerce and not, for example, to manufacturing. Others said that Congress could not regulate activities that had too remote an effect on interstate commerce, or that had only "indirect" effects on interstate commerce. Or even when there was a relationship to interstate commerce, Congress, the Court decided, could not use that relationship as a pretext when Congress's actual concern was something different.[21]

Over time, it became clear to the Court that these limits could not be applied in a non-arbitrary way. They remained nominally in effect, but for several decades every challenged law satisfied them. So there were, in practice, no limits on the Commerce Clause power (other than those derived from other constitutional provisions). The Court did not use the terminology of "judicially manageable standards," but it had effectively concluded that there were no judicially enforceable limits on Congress's power under the Commerce Clause.[22]

Then, in the 1990s, the Court again began to try to establish enforceable standards.[23] Whether the new standards will prove to be any more manageable than their predecessors is an open question. But the lesson is that whether there are "judicially manageable standards," and what they might be, is not something that has to be decided all at once. The answers to those questions can be worked out over time, taking advantage of experience. In fact, it is hard to see how, in dealing with genuinely complicated problems, things could be otherwise.

There is another lesson as well: There will often be a trade-off between manageability and substantive correctness. The theoretically ideal standard may be something that a court cannot implement, and the standards that a court can easily implement may deviate from the theoretical ideal. "One person, one vote"—a nearly inflexible rule governing the apportionment of representatives in an elected governing body—is an example. Until the 1960s, some state legislatures were massively malapportioned: there were, for example, urban districts that had the same number of representatives as some rural districts, even though the urban districts had many more inhabitants. But the Court initially treated challenges to the constitutionality of malapportionment as political questions.

Part of the reason the Court did so was that it thought there were no judicially manageable standards to govern legislative apportionment. There are many plausible theories of democratic representation besides the "one person, one vote" idea that each member of a state legislature should represent approximately the same number of people. Representatives might represent interests, like farmers or factory workers. Or they might represent political divisions defined by geography; that, of course, is how the US Senate is apportioned. The (genuine) problem of choosing among those approaches to representation was one reason that the courts decided that challenges to malapportionment presented a political question.

By the 1960s, though, the Supreme Court had decided that malapportionment was an unacceptable perversion of basic democratic principles, so that constitutional challenges to malapportionment would no longer be treated as political questions but had to be heard in court. The Court solved the problem of judicially manageable standards by creating a standard that was judicially manageable: districts had to represent nearly equal populations. Dissenters in the cases that established the equal-population rule protested that that standard denied states the power to choose other, reasonable approaches to representation (one of which, inconveniently for the majority, was of course the basis of the Senate). But the Court chose a standard that was judicially manageable, in order to overcome the abuses of malapportionment, at the cost of the constitutional value of allowing states to choose among other forms of representation.

The dissenting opinion in *Rucho* essentially embraced an evolutionary trial-and-error approach. The dissent said that lower courts had identified ways of dealing with partisan gerrymanders. The central issues, the dissent said, were the motivation behind the district lines and the effect of alleged gerrymanders; it is possible to work out reasonably reliable ways of ascertaining both motives and effects, as courts do in other areas. Also, a court could start with an extreme case, like North Carolina's, and develop standards by comparing other cases to it. That is also a way in which constitutional law develops: by identifying a clear example of unconstitutional government action and deciding other cases by comparing them to that core case. To give another familiar example: Racial discrimination against Black people in the Jim Crow South was a core example of a violation of the Equal Protection Clause that provided a paradigm for deciding whether other forms of discrimination—against women or LGBT individuals, for example—is also unconstitutional.

Can the same approach be used when courts review campaign finance regulation that is justified as a means of promoting equality—this time, to determine when that kind of regulation is permissible, as opposed to determining when gerrymandering is impermissible? The answer is not entirely clear, but, at the risk of overusing the catchphrase, you don't know until you try.

There is some low-hanging fruit. The Court could, for example, explicitly decide whether protecting incumbents is or is not a legitimate objective. An answer to that question would help to determine what kinds of campaign finance regulations are permissible. If incumbent protection is actually an acceptable objective—contrary to most current understandings, but consistent with the deference given to gerrymandering—then limits on election-related spending should be treated much more deferentially, because the most clearly legitimate concern about those limits is that they help protect incumbents.

Perhaps more important, if the Court were to say, in terms, that incumbent protection is an acceptable objective, it would have to articulate more clearly its actual objections to equality-based limits on spending. As things stand now, it is hard to avoid the suspicion that opponents of campaign finance regulation, including those on the Court, are not primarily concerned about identifiable abuses. Instead, they just believe, perhaps not fully consciously, that people with more resources are entitled to have more influence over elections. But there is no reason that popularly elected legislatures have to accept that view, inconsistent as it is with central principles of political equality.

More generally, a clear declaration that incumbent protection is not an acceptable objective would give disputes over campaign finance regulations a focus that they do not now have. Instead of a vague (although, in fairness, not wholly unwarranted) sense that regulations of campaign-related spending that try to promote equality can be problematic—the most charitable way to interpret the Supreme Court's "wholly foreign" dictum—there would be a relatively specific question that would be susceptible, at least to a degree, to an empirical inquiry: Do incumbents actually do better when certain kinds of restrictions on campaign-related spending are in effect?

The question whether protecting incumbents is permissible under the Constitution may be difficult to answer; plausible arguments could be made for either conclusion. But there is nothing judicially unmanageable about trying to answer it. In the absence of anything clear in the text of the Constitution, the answer would be based, as answers to difficult constitutional questions routinely are, on history, precedent, and analogies to other constitutional principles—for example, that a central purpose of the First Amendment is to prevent incumbents from insulating themselves.

There are other judicially manageable ways to deal with campaign finance regulation that would not make it off-limits for legislatures to try to promote equality. Just as the *Rucho* dissent suggested that courts could examine the motivations for gerrymanders to determine if they were excessively partisan, it should be possible for a court to examine the motivations of a law limiting campaign-related spending: whether it is a genuine effort to address inequalities in ability to pay or is instead a covert effort to favor certain interests. States have their own campaign finance laws, governing state elections; the experience in those states can be a source of evidence about what kinds of laws produce unacceptable distortions. Variation among jurisdictions can be helpful in determining the effects of different forms of regulation. Or if a particular form of regulation is common, has been in existence for a long time, has generally been accepted in many jurisdictions, and does not have clearly identifiable bad effects, that might be a good reason for courts to leave it alone.

Constitutional, Not Political, Questions

One way to describe judicial review (as *Marbury v. Madison* itself suggests) is that it requires courts to decide when a question is political and when it is constitutional. In concrete terms, that presents at least two central questions. One is whether, and when, elected representatives—the "political" branches of the government—can be trusted to act in a way consistent with constitutional democracy. The other is whether judges, invoking the Constitution, can be trusted to correct the political branches' actions when they do not.

Taken in isolation from each other, the Supreme Court's respective approaches to campaign finance and gerrymandering are at least understandable. It is reasonable to be nervous when the government says it is "restrict[ing] the speech of some . . . in order to enhance the relative voice of others." Gerrymandering is a conundrum because there are many ways to draw district lines that can make claims to acceptable partisan neutrality. But the juxtaposition suggests that the Court does not have a coherent conception of the relationship of its role to the political branches. At least when it comes to these central regulations of campaigns and elections, it does not have a satisfactory way of deciding when questions are political and when they are constitutional.

When Congress or a state legislature tries to reduce inequality in people's influence over elections—particularly inequality attributable not just to happenstance but to factors that should not play a role, like differences in wealth or income—those efforts by political institutions should, other things equal, be welcome. They should not be accepted uncritically, but they should not be rejected reflexively, which is what the Supreme Court has done. There are risks of abuse, as there always are when people in power regulate matters related to expression, but the risks are just that—risks that may or may not be acceptable, depending on their magnitude and on whether the potential gain is worth it. When the elected representatives are doing what they are supposed to do—at least ostensibly, and arguably in fact—the court's job should be to try to find a way to accommodate them, or even to further their efforts.

Political gerrymandering of the kind involved in *Rucho* does not just present a risk of an abuse: It is an outright, unapologetic abuse, and an explicit effort to disadvantage political opposition without even a pretense of justification (other than that they are the opposition). One might be forgiven for thinking that if there is ever a time when courts should intervene, that is it. If they cannot immediately figure out the right way to intervene, they can at least try something and see if it works, rather than preemptively surrendering—especially when the Court is so aggressively concerned about potential abuses in campaign finance regulation. Maybe it will turn out that the paradoxical position in which the Court has left us is the best that it, and we, can do. But at least for now, there is good reason to try to do better. A good place to start would be take a few steps toward limiting the threat that election-related spending poses to democracy.

17
Without *Buckley*, Would American Democracy Really Be All That Different?

Pamela S. Karlan

Counterfactual history can be a risky business.[1] But so, too, can the assumption that a single Supreme Court decision, or even the doctrine that flows directly from it, can explain anything so complex as the troubled state of US democracy today. To be sure, *Buckley v. Valeo*[2] is the foundational case in the modern law of campaign finance. It "established the general framework within which all subsequent regulation and constitutional doctrine have been addressed."[3] First, *Buckley* foregrounded the First Amendment as the pivotal constitutional provision in campaign finance cases: Because money spent on elections facilitates communications to the electorate, restrictions on that spending are treated as restrictions on core political speech subject to searching judicial scrutiny. Thus, even if campaign contributions could be limited, campaign expenditures could not. Second, *Buckley* relegated the commitment to equalizing citizens' influence on the political process that had animated the one-person, one-vote cases to the formal election process. It rejected the proposition that the government has a legitimate interest in leveling the campaign playing field. Third, *Buckley* limited the universe of interests that could justify restrictions on both campaign contributions and election spending to the prevention of corruption and the appearance of corruption. And finally, having limited the set of interests that could legitimately be considered, *Buckley* drew a constitutional distinction between contributions to candidates' campaigns and other forms of political spending. The Court permitted far more

Pamela S. Karlan, *Without* Buckley, *Would American Democracy Really Be All That Different?*. In: *Money, Politics, and the First Amendment*. Edited by: Lee C. Bollinger and Geoffrey R. Stone, Oxford University Press. © Oxford University Press (2026). DOI: 10.1093/9780197821947.003.0018 extensive regulation of the former than of the latter because it believed that only contributions, and not independent expenditures, posed a risk of corruption or the appearance of corruption.

There is a rich literature on how *Buckley* and its progeny have shaped our current political environment—a literature to which I have contributed.[4] Many observers point to *Buckley* and its framework as a major source of the pathologies that afflict us: huge amounts of dark money, the decline of parties and the rise of polarization, and even more broadly, a level of economic inequality incompatible with democracy.[5] But in this chapter, I ask what would have happened had the Supreme Court decided *Buckley* differently. Suppose the Court had upheld the relevant provisions of the Federal Election Campaign Act of 1974 on the theory that limitations on election-related spending, by either candidates or independent actors, were justified, and justified by the government's interest both in preventing corruption and the appearance of corruption and "in equalizing the relative ability of individuals and groups to influence the outcome of elections."[6]

Would our democracy look markedly different today? Or would a number of other developments, roughly coincident with *Buckley* or thereafter, have inflected our politics and the money that flows through it in a similar way even absent *Buckley*'s constraints? A quarter-century after *Buckley*, Sam Issacharoff and I suggested that the campaign finance regime "is only one symptom of a deeper problem that requires addressing more fundamental pieces of our political culture and institutions."[7] The experience of a second quarter-century has borne out that suggestion. Even without *Buckley* and the campaign finance regime it produced, American democracy today would face daunting challenges.

The Hydraulic Effect and the Hollowing Out of the Political Parties

As long as gaining control of the government can benefit various actors, those actors have an incentive to spend cost-efficient resources on elections, either to increase the number of voters who cast ballots for the actors' preferred candidates or to decrease the number of votes that go to candidates the actors oppose. From the outset, the Supreme Court recognized that if actors can't spend money one way—because, for example, federal law prohibits that type of spending—they will spend it another. Thus, in *Buckley* itself, the Court struck down FECA's $1,000 ceiling on any expenditures "relative to a clearly identified candidate,"[8] on the grounds that it would do little to eliminate the dangers of corruption. Actors could easily avoid using express terms about a particular candidate, and "[it] would naively underestimate the ingenuity and resourcefulness of persons and groups desiring to buy influence to believe that they would have much difficulty devising expenditures that skirted the restriction on express advocacy of election or defeat but nevertheless benefited the candidate's campaign."[9]

The generalized form of this insight is the "hydraulic effect":[10] Not only is it impossible to squeeze all the money out of the system, but reforms that channel that money elsewhere may produce an effect akin to "what the Corps of Engineers learned over the years in trying to redirect the Mississippi River. Money, like water, will seek its own level. The price of apparent containment may be uncontrolled flood damage elsewhere."[11]

One central criticism of *Buckley* and its progeny is that these decisions weakened political parties because they pinched off the flow of money to the parties (and from the parties to candidates) while leaving unrestricted the flow of money into and out of other newly minted election-oriented entities, such as political action committees (PACs), independent expenditure committees (super PACs), and 527 organizations.[12] Ideally, parties serve a coordinating function both during election season and afterwards—when they develop and pursue, through the party's elected officials, policy agendas responsive to the interests of broad, enduring coalitions that can hold the parties' candidates accountable in future elections. By contrast, the newer arrivals on the election spending scene are more likely to be focused on a narrow set of issues or to be opaque to voters. They both undermine accountability and produce greater polarization.[13]

That criticism is no doubt true. But there are at least four other developments that also weakened parties and increased polarization, largely independent of the campaign finance regime shaped by *Buckley*.

The first is the changed process for nominating presidential candidates. As late as 1968, the vast majority of delegates to the two parties' national conventions (66% of Republican delegates and 62% of Democratic delegates) were selected through conventions; Hubert Humphrey received the Democratic nomination even though he was not an announced candidate in the primaries, where Eugene McCarthy received the most votes.[14] By 1976, when the Court announced *Buckley*, those ratios had flipped: 68% of Republican delegates and 73% of Democratic delegates were selected through primaries, and the percentages have increased since then. The upshot was a "consequential change in democratic-institutional design" that unintentionally weakened the parties.[15]

Political parties are made up of three elements: the party in government (the elected officials who are party members), the party organization (the party's national and state committees who work for the party organizations), and the party in the electorate (the individual citizens who vote for the party's candidates).[16] The move to primaries reduced the role of party insiders in picking the parties' standard-bearers. It allows voters only weakly connected to (and in states with open primaries, not necessarily even affiliated with) the party to exercise decisive control over the nomination process. Consider the Republicans' experience in 2016, when party insiders tried unsuccessfully to prevent the nomination of Donald Trump.[17] Trump was "an independent free agent who successfully hijacked the party label for his own candidacy."[18] Trump's subsequent victory may have benefited the Republican Party's agenda in a variety of ways (not least in enabling the Party to install a durable majority on the Supreme Court for the foreseeable future), but Trump's insistence on personal fealty has hollowed out the party as an instrument of governance: In 2020, for example, the party did not even adopt a new platform, since its only expressed priority was to reelect Trump.[19]

A second development that has weakened the parties is the significant increase in the number of safe seats in Congress. A number of factors contributed to this increase. To name just a few: Americans have increasingly moved to, and live in, communities that are homogeneous with respect to a number of important characteristics, including political affiliation.[20] Improved redistricting technology has enabled ever more efficient partisan gerrymanders (and the Court's imposition of an equipopulosity requirement mandates redrawing district lines every ten years while also permitting—indeed, sometimes demanding—that district boundaries disregard neutral factors like political subdivision lines).

Perhaps counterintuitively, safe seats can weaken political parties by producing more ideologically extreme legislators who are less likely to follow party leadership.[21] (One salient example: Every one of the eight Republican House members whose votes ousted Kevin McCarthy from the speakership in 2023 came from a safe Republican district.)

A third development that may have weakened parties is the demise of political patronage. Patronage was long thought to contribute to strong parties in two ways. Before elections, it created incentives for individuals to invest time and energy in helping the party to function—for example, by doing get-out-the-vote activity. After a successful campaign, it increased a party's ability to achieve its policy preferences by populating government offices with workers aligned with the party and committed to its success. As Tammany Hall boss George Washington Plunkett once warned, "parties can't hold together if their workers don't get offices when they win."[22] That being said, unrestrained partisan personnel practices also embodied clear drawbacks to the public interest. Thus, the political branches struck a balance, starting in 1883 with the federal Pendleton Act and New York's state civil-service law, that placed a large proportion of government jobs within a civil-service system. At the same time, however, elected officials retained some latitude to take party loyalty into account for some positions.

The Supreme Court decisively shifted that balance. In the same term that the Court decided *Buckley*, it also decided *Elrod v. Burns*,[23] which held that firing lower-level non-civil-service employees because they were "not affiliated with or sponsored by" the party of a newly elected official violated the First and Fourteenth Amendments. The Court then extended this principle to promotion and hiring decisions as well as to government-contracting decisions.[24] The upshot was that parties lost much of their remaining leverage.[25]

Finally, the communications revolution almost certainly weakened the parties. Traditionally, one of the parties' central roles over time had been coordination; they served as a trusted intermediary providing "brand name identification" of candidates' policy preferences.[26] But a fundamental feature of the Internet is that it enables "disintermediation" in which "middlemen of all sorts find themselves increasingly unnecessary."[27] Individual candidates and officeholders now have a suite of mechanisms that enable them to reach the public directly. This enables them "to build a personal brand apart from the party label" and outside of party control.[28]

The Rejection of Equalization as a Permissible Government Purpose and the Shape of Public Policy

Buckley held that only "the prevention of corruption and the appearance of corruption" constitute "sufficiently important" governmental interests to justify regulating election spending.[29] By contrast—and also in contrast with the

Court's decisions in cases involving voting itself—the Court held that the interest in "equalizing the relative ability of individuals and groups to influence the outcome of elections" cannot justify restrictions on election spending: "[T]he concept that government may restrict the speech of some elements of our society in order to enhance the relative voice of others is wholly foreign to the First Amendment."[30]

But by the time of *Buckley*, the Burger Court was already in full retreat from the Warren Court's view that economic inequality posed a threat to democracy. In *Harper v. State Board of Elections*,[31] the Court had struck down Virginia's imposition of a poll tax as a prerequisite for voting in state elections as a violation of the equal-protection clause. Chief Justice Warren's opinion for the Court offered two bases for subjecting the tax to heightened judicial scrutiny. First, the right to vote was "a fundamental matter in a free and democratic society."[32] Thus, any restriction on that right required special justification. Second, the Court declared that "[l]ines drawn on the basis of wealth or property, like those of race, are traditionally disfavored."[33] However, in *San Antonio Independent School District v. Rodriguez*,[34] the Burger Court repudiated the proposition that wealth-based classifications trigger strict scrutiny. Moreover, it did so in the face of Justice Marshall's argument in dissent that education should be treated as a fundamental constitutional right because of the "direct relationship between participation in the electoral process and level of educational attainment."[35]

The Court's indifference to equality-based concerns has also played out in its divergent treatment of corporate and union participants in the political process. In *Austin v. Michigan Chamber of Commerce*,[36] the Court upheld a Michigan statute that prohibited nonmedia corporations from using general treasury funds for independent expenditures in connection with state candidate elections. The Court pointed to how "the unique state-conferred corporate structure" might enable "immense aggregations of wealth" whose injection into the political process threatened "corrosive and distorting effects" because the available funds might have "little or no correlation to the public's support for the corporation's political ideas."[37] The Court, however, overruled *Austin* in *Citizens United v. Federal Election Commission*, holding that "[n]o sufficient governmental interest justifies limits on the political speech of non-profit or for-profit corporations."[38] And the Court rejected the proposition that the government had an interest in "protecting dissenting shareholders from being compelled to fund corporate political speech."[39] That concern, where it existed, could be "corrected by shareholders 'through the procedures of corporate democracy.'"[40]

By contrast, the Court's labor-law decisions have shown far more solicitude for individuals who seek to avoid funding union speech. Nearly half of all union members belong to public-sector unions.[41] In *Knox v. SEIU*,[42] the Roberts Court held that the First Amendment required an opt-in process before those unions could charge bargaining-unit workers who were not union members an assessment to be spent on election-related issues. And in *Janus v. AFSCME*,[43] the Court went even further, holding that it violates the First Amendment to require dissenting employees even to pay their share of a public-sector union's collective-bargaining–related expenses because this could force them to subsidize positions on issues of public concern with which they disagree. The Court utterly ignored (or perhaps silently celebrated) how the rulings in *Knox* and *Janus* can tilt the political playing field regardless of the formal parity between corporations and unions.

As a legal matter, *Citizens United* freed both corporations and unions to spend general treasury funds to influence elections. But unions now face greater barriers to acquiring those funds because they can derive them only through an opt-in process in which they can draw from a far narrower pool than corporations can. In the meantime, corporations remain free to make election expenditures "in aid of electing candidates solely for the reason that these candidates would embrace the regulatory policies that the corporation finds most favorable."[44]

Moreover, even when it came to voting itself, the Court has retreated from its commitment to strict scrutiny. In *Burdick v. Takushi*,[45] the Court rejected the idea that "a law that imposes any burden upon the right to vote must be subject to strict scrutiny."[46] That requirement, the Court declared, would too stringently "tie the hands" of the states, because every election law "will invariably impose some burden upon individual voters."[47] So the Court borrowed the more "flexible" standard it had earlier applied to laws restricting candidates' access to the ballot.[48] Under that standard, only if the burdens on the right to vote are "severe" does the state needs to provide a "compelling" justification."[49] Otherwise, a state's regulatory interests "'are generally sufficient to justify' the restrictions."[50] The Court has yet to hold that any restriction fails this new test. And it has given the green light to restrictive voter-ID laws,[51] gutted the Voting Rights Act's preclearance regime,[52] and adopted a cramped reading of section 2 of the Voting Rights Act.[53] On top of all this, the Roberts Court has held that political gerrymandering claims are nonjusticiable.[54] Overall, "[a] striking feature of the Roberts Court is that, when it comes to the act of voting, the Justices are decidedly less skeptical of government restrictions" than they are when it comes to the act of spending.[55]

Each of the Court's voting-rights and redistricting decisions helped to shape the electorate, which in turn affects who wins elections and thus what policies elected officials pursue. None of the Court's recent decisions makes it easier for less affluent or less well-educated citizens to vote; some have resulted in its becoming more difficult. And "[t]hat less educated people in the United States vote less frequently than highly educated people is among the better-established empirical regularities in political science research."[56] So, too, voting rates in the United States have a high positive correlation with family income; for example, individuals in the lowest income category voted at roughly half the rate of individuals in the highest income category.[57]

As Bruce Cain once observed, "51% of the vote dominates an infinite amount of campaign money."[58] So it may well be that a socioeconomically "imbalanced electorate" would have produced public policies favoring the wealthy even in the absence of the post-*Buckley* campaign finance regime.[59]

The Roadblocks to Public Financing of Elections

There is no doubt that *Buckley* and its progeny made it harder to adopt public-financing regimes that can effectively displace private political spending. Realistically, to displace private political spending, it would not be enough in many races (and certainly not enough in high-stakes races for Congress) simply to persuade *candidates* to forgo private contributions in favor of taking public funding. Public financing would still leave the panoply of independent expenditures untouched. Indeed, actors who now contribute to candidates' campaigns might simply move their funds over to these groups. So the public financing must be set at a level where public money would drown out private funds.

Political spending in the 2020 federal election totaled $14.4 billion.[60] And of course billions more are no doubt spent on state and local elections as well.

If *Buckley* and its progeny had never been decided, would we have public financing today? It's possible to craft an argument to that effect. After all, the 1974 Act itself contained a provision for public financing of presidential campaigns. But it set the level of public funding at an unsustainably low level—"substantially below the $30 million spent in the prior presidential election by George McGovern in one of the worst landslide losses in American history."[61] Beginning in 2000, major-party candidates began to opt out of the primary-election public-financing system, and since Barack Obama's decision to opt out of general-election public financing, no major-party candidate has accepted public financing. The money that can be raised through the private system is simply too attractive. So unless a world without *Buckley* could be a world in which independent expenditures can be shut off entirely, it would have to be a world in which public funding would be quite substantial.

But over the past twenty years, there has been relatively little political appetite for spending money to make elections work better in a host of ways.[62] For example, "[the] current level of spending puts election [administration] at near the bottom of spending for public services, ranking at approximately the same levels as spending by local governments to maintain parking facilities."[63] And "[t]he history of federal injections of money has been short and sporadic."[64] So even absent *Buckley*, it's unclear whether we would see robust public financing of campaigns. The absence of effective public financing may be more a problem of political will than of constitutional impediments.

Conclusion

The Supreme Court's decision in *Buckley v. Valeo* has had all sorts of consequences for American democracy, most of them negative. But as Sam Issacharoff and I suggested at the midpoint between *Buckley* and its fiftieth anniversary, we "should at least recognize the possibility that the current flow of money is a product of problems upstream rather than the cause of all our woes."[65]

Buckley was only a part of a larger set of political choices and choices about politics that have contributed to the current state of American democracy. The Court's decades-long retreat from democracy-reinforcing judicial review and the breakdown of various democratic institutions cannot be laid, certainly not entirely, at the feet of campaign finance decisions. To tease out just a couple of threads in the manner that counterfactual histories often do: Suppose that 537 more voters in Florida had marked their ballots for Al Gore in 2000. Then he, rather than George W. Bush, would have appointed the successor to

Chief Justice Rehnquist, and the Court would almost certainly have decided many of the cases discussed in this chapter differently. We would have a more vigorous Voting Rights Act, which might in turn have changed election outcomes, and thereby changed public policy in ways that would further change our democracy.

The problems with our democracy are not just problems caused by the campaign finance regime. They are the product of larger forces as well—forces that might have existed even if the Supreme Court had upheld the Federal Election Campaign Act of 1974 in its entirety.

18

Campaign Finance and Contemporary Political Dysfunction

Nathaniel Persily

Those who have lost faith in the American political system often blame government dysfunction on the oversized role that money plays in US elections. For much of the first decade of the 21st century, similar to a century earlier, progressives viewed campaign finance reform as a critical step toward addressing corruption and unequal political power. Whether one was concerned about leveling the electoral playing field or reducing the political influence of moneyed interests, campaign finance reform constituted an indispensable part of the reform agenda.

Today, most look back with nostalgia on the political dysfunction of the early 2000s. Preoccupying oneself with the question of whether corporations or rich people have biased the system to their advantage is a luxury one does not have when insurrectionists are at the door and the basics of democracy are being questioned. Corruption of the Tammany Hall or 1990s soft-money variety seems a sweet pill to swallow if the fundamentals of the constitutional system are otherwise guaranteed.

Of course, just because there are "bigger problems" does not mean we should ignore intractable challenges of corruption and political inequality. If reforms and the political and judicial countermobilization against them may have increased the likelihood of (if not caused) the current sorry state of political affairs, then the "story" of campaign finance can serve as a cautionary tale as we consider other political and electoral reforms.

To suggest that money in politics or reform efforts to combat it directly led to the contemporary moment of polarization, populism, and democratic decline, though, fetishizes political reform at the expense of more knotty and long-term sociological phenomena challenging political systems around the world. There are multiple explanations as to how we got here from there, but to say, for example, that McCain-Feingold[1] started pushing dominoes that decades later eventually broke down the doors of the Capitol is a stretch for even the most critical of reform critics.

Nevertheless, campaign finance rules exist as part of the crumbling infrastructure of the political system under stress. Even if those rules might not be a principal cause of any specific present-day catastrophe, perhaps redirecting the flow of money in politics might help stem (or even begin to reverse) the tide that threatens to inundate and capsize the ship of state. In any event, understanding the history of parallel, rather than intersecting, trajectories toward political dysfunction may be useful, if only to isolate long-term from short-term developments and structural from sociological influences.

This chapter attempts to situate the last two decades of campaign finance law and policy alongside (if not within) the larger trends of political dysfunction in the United States. The chapter begins by examining the arguments and counterarguments relating to campaign finance as a cause of political polarization and decline of the party system. It then turns to *Citizens United v. FEC*,[2] a much-misunderstood decision that distracted the campaign finance debate toward the problem of corporate influence, but which led indirectly to the rise of super PACs and the explosion in outside sources of campaign spending. The last section focuses on how changes in the information ecosystem exacerbated the balkanizing impact of changes in the legal regime of campaign finance and further eroded party institutions as uniquely powerful players both in elections and in government.

To be very clear from the outset, this chapter argues that the campaign finance system has played a small, but supporting, role in the drama of political dysfunction and polarization over the last few decades. One cannot lay all the blame for the incremental contribution of campaign finance to contemporary political problems at the feet of either the relevant statutes (such as the Federal Election Campaign Act or the Bipartisan Campaign Reform Act) or the landmark court decisions (such as *Buckley v. Valeo* or *Citizens United v. FEC*). The system we have today is not one anyone has voted for or desired. Even among Supreme Court Justices, a majority has consistently disagreed with the extant First Amendment jurisprudence relating to campaign finance. Because they disagree for different reasons, with some Justices preferring to strike down all limits and others willing to uphold limits on spending and contributions alike, the rickety system of contribution limits to candidates and parties alongside constitutionally protected unlimited independent spending (by corporations and outside groups) remains.

The constitutional-plus-statutory context for campaign finance thereby provides fertile ground for the growth of unaccountable and independent political actors with less of a stake in governance. These candidates and organizations would exist in some form irrespective of the rules regarding political money, but they thrive under a system that privileges outsider status and independence and places stringent financial restrictions on the most accountable actors in the system, namely parties and candidates. The global socioeconomic forces that have sparked populist and extremist movements around the world, alongside a disintermediated information ecosystem, may shoulder much of the blame for the current, sorry state of US politics. However, the campaign finance system has served as an accelerant for this spark, and it has placed the United States in a uniquely difficult position to steer the flow of political money in ways that might counteract the powerful forces pushing in the direction of fragmentation and polarization.

A Theoretical Framework for Thinking About Campaign Finance and Political Polarization

Reformers focus on the unique structural features of American elections to try to address various pathologies in American politics. They do so, understandably, because the sociological roots of political dysfunction will be less amenable to change, particularly in the short term, than the rules governing elections. Tweaking the ways we run primaries, draw district lines, or control the flow of political money might help blunt the larger forces at work that distort electoral outcomes.

Campaign finance reform promises to address several different types of problems. First and foremost, it attempts to control the influence of money and moneyed interests both on elections and on policy. Both of those dimensions—election outcomes and policy—are important. For elections, rich candidates and rich interests might have outsized influence over which candidates decide to compete and which might end up winning (in primaries or general elections). Money, like other political resources, may serve as a filtering mechanism that winnows the candidate pool to those who are either beholden to certain interests or ideologically in line with them. The promise of future funding (or even worse, the threat to fund an opponent) may then affect the behavior of officials once in office.

A second set of impacts related to campaign finance concern the types of interests and institutions that are privileged or disfavored by rules surrounding political money. A ubiquitous critique of campaign finance reforms relates to the so-called hydraulics argument:[3] "Money, like water, will always find an outlet."[4] People who want to spend money on campaigns will inevitably do so, but the law can shape how they do it and to which intermediaries money will flow. If you limit money to candidates, it will flow to parties. If you limit party money, then people will contribute to outside interest groups (PACs, etc.). If you further limit contributions to any or all of these groups, then independent expenditures might increase. And so on. The point here is not that campaign finance reform is ineffective or pointless. Rather, one impact of campaign finance reform is to steer money toward certain actors in the system and away from others.

So, what does this have to do with polarization? Through these three categories of influences—election outcomes, official behavior, and the relative power of different actors in the system—campaign finance rules might shape the tenor of campaigns, the kind of candidates who get elected, and how they behave in office. To the extent our definitions of polarization relate to these phenomena, the amount and flow of money in the system may contribute to or retard polarization.

However, talk of polarization is often sloppy and abstract, and when making the connection to campaign finance, it is important to be very specific about the mechanisms at work and the implied hypotheses.[5] One dimension of polarization concerns the extremism of the candidates who run and are elected. If by polarization we mean the growing ideological distance between the median legislator in, respectively, the Republican and Democratic parties, then campaign finance rules might contribute to polarization by biasing in favor of the nomination and election of extremist candidates. For example, if small donors are more ideological than big donors (a contested proposition, as described later), then campaign finance rules (such as small-donor matching programs or low contribution limits) might contribute to polarization. Similarly, if regulation targets certain entities, such as corporations, that often give to both political parties in order to preserve access, it may diminish the influence of less ideological contributors and (relatively speaking) amplify the voices of contributors on the extremes.

The corporation example also exemplifies how the hydraulic nature of political money may affect the way campaign restrictions favor or disfavor the political actors contributing to polarization. Most directly, the concern for the last twenty years has focused on how the system of campaign contribution limits might move money away from the most accountable actors in the system, namely candidates and parties, and toward less transparent and accountable groups, such as super PACs and 501(c)4 organizations. Parties (usually) have as their primary goal winning elections and gaining majorities in legislatures. Outside groups, all things being equal, may be more inclined to "make a statement" with their money, irrespective of its effect on who wins or loses. Therefore, outside money may be more "polarizing" through its support of "movement candidates," as opposed to those closest to the median voter, let alone those most connected to a party apparatus that will need to govern and make compromises. The relative disadvantage of party organizations *vis a vis* other actors, under this view, breaks the connection between political finance and governing, and it facilitates the election of hardliners who cater more to an independent, and often extreme, base of funders.

To the extent they affect not just who receives and spends money but how they spend it, campaign finance rules can implicate a different dimension of polarization. Beyond candidate success and official behavior, campaign finance rules may favor certain types of spending (e.g., television commercials) as well as certain types of candidate appeals. To the degree that different types of spending lead to different types of messaging strategies, they may affect the tenor of campaigns and exacerbate the rising incivility that is often implicit in various definitions of polarization.

As an example, some campaign finance laws regulate spending on certain modalities of political communication more than others. Title II of the Bipartisan Campaign Reform Act[6] regulated corporate and union treasury spending on "broadcast, cable, or satellite communications," but not Internet-based communications, which at the time of the BCRA's passage had not become a prominent method of campaigning. The choice to regulate one type of technology more than another inevitably channels political spending toward less regulated avenues. If we think, for example, that targeted campaign communications over the Internet might tend to appeal to emotion, engage in exaggeration, and promote division, then a campaign finance system that pushes people toward that form of communication may contribute to polarization. Similarly, if campaign finance disclosures and disclaimers apply to some forms of spending and not others, then we might expect polarizing and uncivil appeals to be more prevalent when spenders do not need to reveal themselves (on the theory that anonymous speech, on average, will lead to less accountability for the tone and truthfulness of the message).[7]

To be clear, though, this point might be less about regulation per se and more about how technological developments in communication interact with campaign finance rules to affect the behavior of all strategists and speakers in the system. As will be discussed later, there seems to be a consensus, for example, that the Internet proved to be a revolutionary tool for raising money, especially from small donors. Candidates with the acumen and resources (and sometimes shamelessness) to exploit new online tools can therefore be favored in a system that facilitates certain types of polarizing appeals and strategies. It is not uncommon for a member of Congress to do something outrageous in the halls of Congress (e.g., interrupt the State of the Union), only to turn it immediately into an online fundraising opportunity.[8] In this way, the campaign finance system shapes incentives to engage in official behavior that will pay rewards through different tactics of campaigning. Moreover, to the extent that elite signals and opinion leadership might foster greater polarization in the mass public, the kind of spending and messages the campaign finance system facilitates could produce a feedback loop in which candidates assist in polarizing voters and then voters tend to support polarizing candidates.

The Uncertain Impact of Campaign Finance on Polarization

There can be no doubt that we are living in an age of heightened polarization (along all dimensions discussed above), and that polarization has reached new heights ever since the passage of certain campaign finance laws, such as the Bipartisan Campaign Reform Act. However, the relative impact of campaign finance on polarization is very hard to disentangle from long-term sociological forces and other features of the election system, and its effect on polarization should not be overstated. In addition, humility is warranted in assessing the relative importance of statutory change, as opposed to statutory-plus-constitutional change, as the Supreme Court's First Amendment decisions have resculpted nearly every federal campaign finance law ever passed.

One of the sources of controversy over the relationship between campaign finance and polarization in Congress concerns the way we measure elite polarization. There is no doubt that, as measured by roll-call voting behavior, the parties in Congress are more internally cohesive and more ideologically distant from each other now than they have been in the last century. In other words, as compared to a period when there were basically two Democratic parties (South and non-South) and a conservative coalition made up of Dixiecrats and Republicans could control the House of Representatives, today the Democrats are more like Democrats and Republicans are more like Republicans, and Democrats and Republicans are more unlike each other.[9]

Even so, the link between campaign finance reform and this particular form of polarization is difficult to isolate. All the longitudinal data on roll-call voting show monotonic trends in the direction of greater polarization since the early 1970s.[10] Given the timing of the increase in polarization, it is theoretically possible that the restrictions on contributions in the Federal Election Campaign Act Amendments of 1974[11] (combined with the Supreme Court's decision in *Buckley v. Valeo*[12] in 1976) may have contributed to rising polarization. Here, the mechanism would probably be the shift during that period toward greater fundraising from individual donors. But the dates do not match up perfectly, and in any event, it would be difficult to connect campaign finance changes, for example, to the realignment of Southern Democrats following the leftward move of the party on civil rights.

The same might be said of the 2002 Bipartisan Campaign Reform Act's[13] effect on roll-call voting patterns. The trend toward greater polarization since 2002 according to this metric is undeniable, but the trajectory of polarization seems about as steep before the passage of the law as it was afterward.[14] BCRA may have pushed this trend along (or maybe made its reversal less likely), but the causal story is difficult to demonstrate from the longitudinal data.

Longitudinal data on roll-call votes in Congress is not the only way to assess the impact of reform on polarization. Heterogeneity between the states provides some natural experiments to assess how different types of rules might affect rates of polarization in state legislatures. Here, Professors Raymond La Raja and Bryan Schaffner, in their masterful book, *Campaign Finance and Political Polarization: When Purists Prevail*, find differences between legislatures. They find substantively significant differences in legislative polarization between states that allow political parties to raise and spend unlimited sums and those that place limits on parties. States without limits on party contributions and expenditures are considerably less ideologically polarized.

The authors hypothesize that the mechanism for this polarization is that individual donors are necessarily more ideological and their giving reflects issue preferences. In contrast, campaign finance rules that allow parties, in effect, to launder donations (from whatever source) and redirect them (without limits) toward competitive candidates lead to less ideological polarization in the legislature as a whole.[15] The outsized financial role that party organizations play in such a system may lead them both to select candidates who are less ideological and, once elected, to insulate them from pressures and financial threats from strident interest groups.

Campaign Finance and Party "Strength"

The argument that rich parties serve as an antidote to polarization has its detractors. The criticism comes from several corners. Some do not see parties as weakened by campaign finance restrictions. Others view the trade-off, in terms of the potential for corruption, as too great to justify exempting parties from limits on their raising and spending money. Still others see strong parties as an engine of polarization, theorizing that they have been captured (financially and otherwise) by extremist donors, so we should not expect them to act in ways to support moderate candidates and officeholders.

To some extent, the differing positions arise from different notions of party "strength." If one measures strength by the cohesiveness of party coalitions, according to roll-call votes or lack of dissent, then the parties in Congress are about as strong as ever.[16] Indeed, under this view, polarization is an indicator of party strength. In contrast, the critics of financial limits on parties measure party strength according to the relative financial influence that parties, as compared to other sources of campaign cash, might have in the ecosystem of funding available to candidates. Even if party members are polarized in their voting patterns, the substance of legislation and the roll-call votes taken might be different, as parties might be able to ward off threats by balkanizing special interests able to elect extremist candidates and influence all candidates once in office.

There is also a sense in which this praise of party organizations as beneficent and depolarizing forces in the campaign finance system represents an outdated assessment of the role parties play. It might be outdated in three respects. First, party organizations can be captured by extremists, such that they become forces of polarization rather than counterbalances to it. The notion that party organizations are inherently most interested in gaining legislative majorities belies the evidence that parties sometimes become handmaidens for the very centrifugal forces that the strong-parties hypothesis suggests they should be counteracting. Either because of the extremism of donors to the parties or because of changes in leadership of the party organization, parties can use their financial clout to attack moderates instead of extremists.

This point about the heterogeneity and evolution of party organizations leads to a second point related to the contingent position of parties in the trend toward polarization. Whatever metric of strength we use for party organizations, there is nothing inherent in a party qua party that will lead it to behave in a way that is either depolarizing, or even electorally relevant. Parties are organizations like all others, after all, and their willingness to behave in certain ways depends on their leadership and the willingness of their members. Some party organizations may exist as mere pass-throughs for wealthy donors attempting to skirt individual contribution limits. (This "conduit corruption" rationale was central to the Court's upholding of party contribution limits in both *FEC v. Colorado Republican Federal Campaign Committee*[17] and *McConnell v. FEC*.[18]) If parties exist only as glorified bank accounts, in which contributors make deposits and candidates withdraw, then they lose much of their power and influence as counterbalances to outside sources of polarization.

Finally, this whole discussion, as well as the discourse in general related to party organizations as leaders in the campaign finance system, may assume an anachronistic definition of party organizations. Party organizations evoke an image of cigar-chomping party bosses in smoke-filled rooms doling out patronage and predetermining who the party's nominees will be. But this Tammany Hall model of parties has not existed for a long time and was especially undermined at the national level by the McGovern-Fraser reforms of the 1970s, which established the modern presidential primary system, among other changes.[19] Few people these days can name the leaders of the RNC and DNC, for example, let alone the leaders of their own state parties. Particularly during presidential election years, when the party organizations might seem most salient, given the debates and conventions, the party organization basically becomes an outgrowth or alter ego of the presidential campaign.

More to the point about contemporary party structure, though, the political party organizations exist as loose confederations of formal and informal institutions, some of which are themselves creatures of laws and court decisions.[20] A loose confederation of PACs, super PACs, 501(c)(4) organizations, data-mining companies, political consultants, and federal, state, and local incarnations of quasi-party entities exist as a network that comprises the modern party.[21] Party leaders themselves establish "independent" organizations outside the framework of the DNC and RNC. In the 2022 congressional elections, for example, the Senate Leadership Fund, a super PAC aligned with Mitch McConnell, as well as its Democratic counterpart, the Senate Majority PAC, aligned with Chuck Schumer, spent hundreds of millions of dollars on competitive Senate races.[22] These types of vehicles for spending are not technically part of the party organization, but elected party leaders either control or heavily influence their spending. There are dozens of similar examples of organizations with close ties to party leaders or other influential insiders, who nevertheless are formally outside the legally defined boundaries of "the party," as such. From the standpoint of the party's ability to force coalition formation or bolster the electoral prospects of moderates in competitive districts, it is unclear why these alter egos of the party (if led by party leaders with incentives to win legislative majorities) should behave differently from the formal party organizations, such as the DNC/RNC or congressional campaign committees.

The aforementioned hypotheses do not settle the question whether parties have changed sufficiently so as to reduce their role as counterweights to polarization. The answer, as with many such questions, is "it depends." The role parties play differs over time and space, and indeed differs between the two major parties. As La Raja and Schaffner demonstrate, it is clear that, in some states, rich parties continue to play the role of a responsible link between elections and governance, promoting candidates according to electability and other non-ideological criteria. However, not only do parties differ between the states, they also differ over time. Consider, for example, the view of John Watson, the former chair of Georgia's Republican party, in his description of the trajectory of his state's party in the last four years: "There has been an emphasis on ideological cleansing instead of electioneering. If those new entrants to the party want to argue the earth is flat and the election is stolen, those are counterproductive to winning elections."[23] Some state parties have been captured by extremists, such that they have become engines of polarization rather than antidotes to it.

One other datum supporting this argument is the changing leadership of the RNC. Lara Trump, the then-former President's daughter-in-law, was appointed cochair of the RNC in 2023. She, along with Michael Watley, the former chair of the North Carolina Republican Party, replaced Ronna McDaniel, who was ejected, for all practical purposes, for being too moderate (in behavior, if not ideology).[24] The elevation of Lara Trump lends support to two of the hypotheses above: (1) that the national party committees, especially in election years, can become alter egos (or in this case, literally close relatives) of the presidential campaigns; and (2) that party leadership is not necessarily chosen for or committed to building a big tent with a guiding principle of electability or legislative control. (Lara Trump resigned as RNC co-chair in 2024, and Michael Whatley resigned in 2025 to run for a North Carolina Senate seat. He was replaced on August 22, 2025, by Joe Gruters, former RNC Treasurer and chair of the Florida Republican Party, who also co-chaired Donald Trump's 2016 campaign in Florida.) Of course, this does not mean that parties have given up on those depolarizing impulses referenced earlier. Rather, their willingness to do so is contingent on all kinds of political and historical factors that influence party leadership and strategy. That the Democratic Party of 2024, with its associated committees, appeared more like a traditional party organization that cared about governance is likely a product of its alignment with President Biden and his style of governing, instead of an inevitability. When a party controls the presidency, the President, for all practical purposes, is the leader of the party.[25]

In the end, arguments about parties, polarization, and campaign finance depend on a set of "all else equal" assumptions that do not hold for the extraordinary conditions of contemporary American politics. The polarization-relevant impact of campaign finance regulations on party organizations depends on the capacity and willingness of party leaders to influence elections with the goal of building legislative majorities, winning in marginal districts, and forming a governing coalition. Nevertheless, one still might be able to argue that well-financed party organizations are, on average, less polarizing than other sources of electoral influence. Even if some parties have been co-opted and also manifest as putatively independent outside organizations, their formal organs are still more likely (even if only slightly so, in some cases) to care about winning elections and building majorities.

Strong forces of balkanization and extremism have emerged throughout the campaign finance system. Campaign finance reform debates should always include considerations of trade-offs and relative harms. Contemporary party organizations may display a surprising lack of willingness to engage in traditional coalition and party-building activities. Nevertheless, the question is always "as compared to what?" Today, this translates into parties as compared to the most extreme and least accountable forces in American politics: organizations, such as certain super PACs and 501(c)(4)s, which exist specifically to provide an independent alternative to the insiders overly focused on governing.

The *Citizens United* Distraction

The Supreme Court's decision in *Citizens United v. FEC*[26] has become a metaphor and rallying cry for all that ails the campaign finance system, if not American politics in general. *Citizens-United*-the-metaphor has become detached from the actual holding in the case, which simply said that corporations and unions enjoy a First Amendment right to spend their treasury funds on express advocacy for the election of candidates.

There can be no doubt that polarization (however measured) has increased in the wake of *Citizens United*. As with the connection of BCRA's soft-money ban to polarization, though, the precise mechanism for the causal argument is a bit difficult to identify. To the extent, however, that *Citizens United* (and more importantly, its progeny) has further accelerated the growth of independent expenditures of all types, it compounds the problems recognized in the earlier sections concerning the transfer of power away from accountable actors in the campaign finance system toward unaccountable actors, in particular the rise of super PACs.

The first step in assessing the specific impact of *Citizens United*'s holding concerning corporate electioneering expenditures on polarization would be to estimate the size of aggregate corporate expenditures in the decision's wake. This turns out to be quite challenging, because it is difficult to follow all types of spending to their original source and to capture the amount of spending that goes undisclosed. However, all who have tried have found surprisingly little corporate independent spending in the immediate wake of *Citizens United*.[27] In the words of a 2017 Committee for Economic Development report, *Citizens United* "was expected to produce a surge in business spending. We found little to support this expectation. In fact, few business corporations or associations have made independent expenditures in recent elections."[28] Corporations have become bigger players in campaigns since that time. But many of the most active corporations in politics remain privately held, serving almost as alter egos of the individuals who control them.

Even for the large corporations historically most active in campaign finance, their giving patterns tended to reflect an "access strategy" rather than an ideological commitment. During the heyday of soft money, many corporations would give large sums of money to both political parties, in order to hedge their bets so they could have influence regardless of who might be elected. This pattern, in fact, was highlighted in the original litigation challenging BCRA, which culminated in *McConnell v. FEC*, to demonstrate the corruption danger from corporate money. But corruption in the traditional, material sense is, in some ways, the opposite of ideology: It reflects the strategy to use campaign money to gain particularized goods as opposed to advancing a coherent political platform.

Just because the expected avalanche of corporate expenditures might not have emerged after *Citizens United* does not mean the case had little impact on the campaign finance system. In addition to the holding on corporate and union expenditures, the Court (in dicta) narrowed critical precedent regarding the meaning of corruption for First Amendment analysis of campaign finance restrictions, making it more difficult for the state to justify restrictions aimed at combating anything short of quasi-bribery. The tenor of the opinion, if not the actual holding, seemed to lead to a more consequential decision by the DC Circuit in *SpeechNOW.org v. FEC*.[29] That decision gave birth to "Independent Expenditure Committees," now known as super PACS. The court reasoned that no anti-corruption interest could justify restricting groups of individuals from pooling their money to engage in independent electioneering expenditures.

SpeechNOW did not involve corporate spending, so to blame its result solely on *Citizens United* ignores other cases pushing in the same direction. In many respects, *SpeechNOW* is more of a classic *Buckley*[30] case, in that the determinative question concerns the independence of the group of *individuals* seeking to make expenditures. In fact, from the standpoint of its adjudication of expenditure restrictions, the only real difference between *SpeechNOW* and *Buckley v. Valeo* is that *Buckley* involved one person, while *SpeechNOW* involved a group of people seeking to do the same thing (make unlimited independent expenditures). *SpeechNOW* follows in the line of lower-court cases, such as *EMILY's List v. FEC*,[31] in which the DC Circuit held that certain nonprofits could establish accounts to raise unlimited contributions and make unlimited expenditures. Insofar as *SpeechNOW* grew out of *Citizens United*, it was more of a continuation of a vibe shift, in which the signal from the Supreme Court was one of deep skepticism regarding any regulation of expenditures.

Regardless of their origin story, super PACs have been transformative to the campaign finance system. In the 2020 election, super PACs spent over two billion dollars, which represented more than half of total outside spending.[32] As illustrated in Figure 18.1 and reprinted with permission from a new book by Diana Dwyre & Robin Kolodny,[33] super PACs have been growing in dominance ever since *SpeechNOW* as a preferred vehicle for outside spending. By the 2020 election, the share of outside spending represented by super PACs nearly mirrored the share enjoyed by soft-money party spending before Congress banned it. As discussed earlier, some of this super-PAC spending might come from the alter egos of parties and candidates, although very few appear to be primarily funded by businesses or labor unions.[34] But the bottom line is that aggregations of individual outside money have become a dominant force in the campaign finance ecosystem and have far surpassed the traditional categories of party spending. For those worried about the polarizing impact of the shift in political spending from formal party organizations to independent, often ideologically driven super PACs, this trend should be a focus of concern.

Campaign Finance, Polarization, and the Changing Media Environment

The story told to this point is one of legal change facilitating the development of outside sources of financial power in the campaign finance system with possible knock-on effects for polarization in Congress and state legislatures. This polarization manifests in the election of more politically extreme legislators and more extreme behavior once in office. To the extent party institutions no longer have as robust financial tools and institutional capability to sanction or rein in extremist politicians (or protect moderates from primary challengers sponsored by well-financed extremists), politicians are freer today than previously to engage in norm-breaking behavior. Not only can extremists rely on independent sources of funding, but the technological environment both rewards extremist appeals and facilitates the development of these independent donor relationships. Social media and other digital tools for fundraising exacerbate

CAMPAIGN FINANCE AND POLITICAL DYSFUNCTION 307

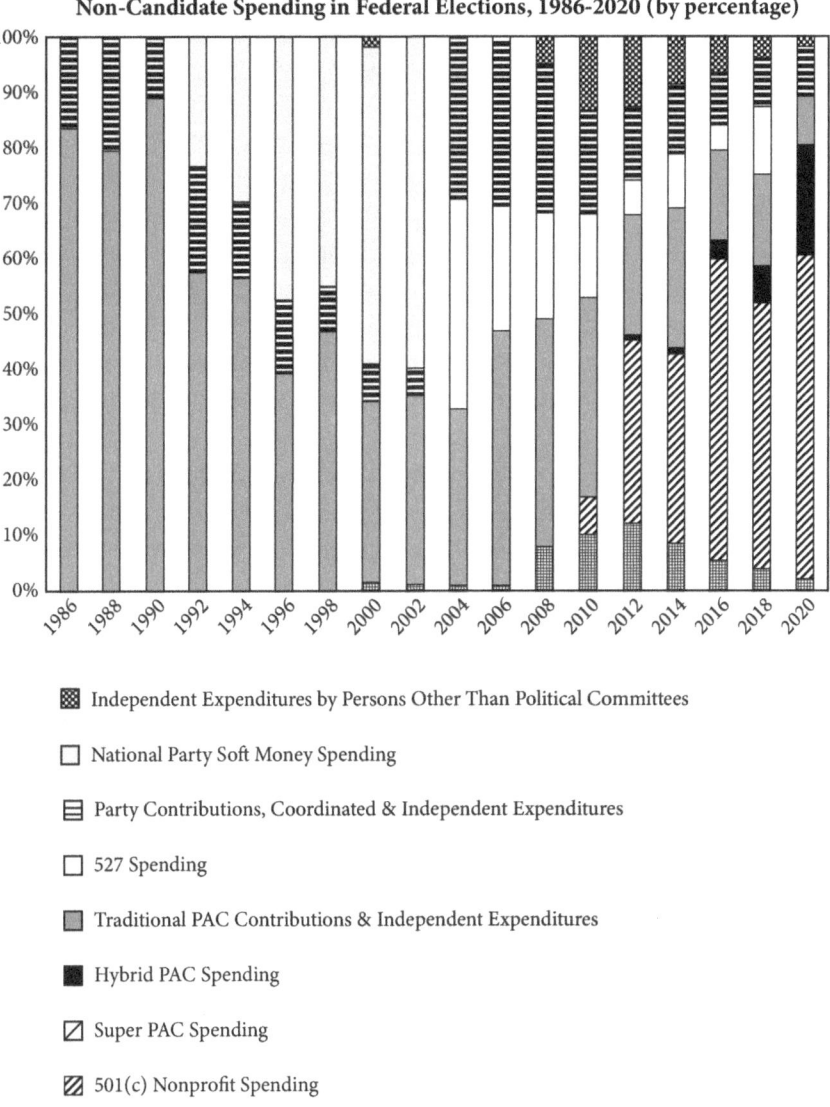

Figure 18.1 Non-Candidate Spending in Federal Elections, 1986–2020

the polarizing influences of the legal push toward independence, as well as amplify the electoral impact of individual donors over institutional actors.[35]

The role of online platforms, social-media algorithms, and digital communication technologies in general in exacerbating polarization is a well-researched topic.[36] In particular, the digital ecosystem is blamed for radicalizing users as well as pushing people into hermetically sealed information echo chambers in which they lose exposure to crosscutting or moderating content.[37] Considerable debate rages regarding the degree to which platform users are really that different from those off-platform, but there can be no doubt that, as with all other Internet-related pathologies, some subset of users fall into digital rabbit holes or get pushed to extremes by content they seek out or encounter. Whatever one might say about the larger causal claims related to digital technology and polarization, the key feature of social media is that it is, in fact, social: that is, legacy intermediaries, such as broadcast networks, newspaper editors, or political parties no longer stand in the way of politicians or other influencers seeking to communicate directly with voters with whatever incendiary rhetoric is most likely to capture attention. Moreover, the value of the targeted advertising that these platforms offer and depend upon comes from their ability to find amenable consumers and to deliver to them personalized content that will likely spur purchases or, in the case of political advertising, votes or contributions.

The Internet remains the Wild West when it comes to campaign finance regulation.[38] Certain disclosure and disclaimer obligations apply to online expenditures by both candidates and parties, but much political spending online is both unregulated and unregulatable. The ability of Russian nationals to purchase over $100,000 in Facebook ads in the 2016 elections tells you all you need to know about the insight that enforcement authorities might have into what is actually happening online.[39] Indeed, even the category of "paid communications" becomes blurred with "organic content" as paid influencers hawk for candidates in a high-tech version of political product placement.[40]

As with digital communication generally, online advertising or campaigning is both a blessing and a curse. Social-media ads are much cheaper than television ads, so they allow a greater number of candidates (e.g., cash-strapped challengers competing against well-financed incumbents) to run effective campaigns.[41] For all the hyperventilating about microtargeted advertising, moreover, these new capacities allow campaigns to communicate most effectively with the voters they consider movable or able to be mobilized. Although the data mining available today may be taking advertising (or if you prefer, psychological manipulation) to new levels, microtargeting is certainly not a new phenomenon; it has existed for generations, usually in the form of direct mail and other forms of personalized communications. The amenability of online ads to rigorous and repeated A/B testing, in which multiple versions of ads can be easily tested to see which has the desired effect, may distinguish them from early efforts, as will the use of AI once political consultants perfect its application to their work. But it should be noted that the use of online campaign fundraising strategies was seen as a brilliant move of the Howard Dean, Barack Obama, and even Bernie Sanders campaigns before they were decried after Donald Trump used similar tactics in 2016.[42] The use of digital tools both to raise money and to target voters has empowered candidates across the political spectrum.

The online campaign environment is tailor-made to exploit the decline of mediating institutions, such as political parties, between candidates and voters. It exacerbates the balkanization we already observe growing from the perverse legal incentives in the system. It does so by *democratizing* the system of campaign contributions, particularly through strategies well-designed to mobilize small-dollar donations. The system facilitates polarization by rewarding antics, rhetoric, and position-taking that are most likely to persuade contributors to give for ideological or tribalist reasons. An early example comes from South Carolina Representative Joe Wilson, when he interrupted President Barack Obama's State of the Union speech by screaming "You lie!" He raised over $2.7 million dollars in the wake of that incident.[43] The trend continues to this day. Representative Matt Gaetz's most successful fundraising days in recent memory, for instance, occurred just after he led a group of eight conservative members to oust Kevin McCarthy from his perch as Speaker of the House.[44]

Of course, not all online donors give money because they have been whipped into a froth by extremist appeals. All politicians, even those deeply embedded in the establishment, as well as the parties themselves, now use digital campaign tools to raise money. But as with the rise of super PACs and other dynamics noted earlier, the technological environment provides yet another avenue for candidates of all stripes (including those on the extremes who may have had a more difficult time raising money in the "legacy" media environment) to raise the funds necessary to launch an effective campaign.

As a matter of first principles, it is important to recognize that only a small percentage of Americans give any money to campaigns. The data differ whether one looks at actual FEC records[45] or survey results, which suggest the number might be as high as 12%.[46] But the number of small donors (those who give less than $200 in a federal election campaign) has grown dramatically—both in absolute terms and as a share of total donors—over the last two decades since the advent of Internet fundraising. Laurent Bouton, Julia Cage, Edgard

Dewitte, and Vincent Pons estimate that the number of donors giving less than $200 in federal campaigns grew from 50,000 in 2006 to nearly 12 million in 2020, while the number of donors giving more than $200 has grown from 1.3 million to 8.2 million over that same period.[47] FEC records suggest that, over the same period, the number of donations in excess of $2,000 grew from 221,385 to 1,688,000.[48]

An active debate exists as to whether small donors are much more ideological than big donors (especially if one distinguishes the two groups at the $200 level, which is only relevant because contributors' names are disclosed above that level).[49] In truth, most individual donors, at whatever level, give money for ideological reasons,[50] and the donor class, as a whole, is more ideologically extreme than those who do not give money to campaigns.[51] That said, it would appear that small-dollar donations account for a larger share of fundraising for some candidates on the political extremes. Of congressional candidates in 2020 who received more than $5 million in total individual contributions, the following candidates received most of it from small donors: Alexandria Ocasio-Cortez (79.53%), Duncan D. Hunter (67.45%), Jim Jordan (66.19%), Matt Gaetz (65.09%), Adam Schiff (58.96%), Ilhan Omar (57.74%), Nancy Pelosi (56.55%), Devin Nunes (52.64%), Katie Porter (52.01%), and Dan Crenshaw (50.00%).[52]

Whatever the ideological differences between small and large individual donors, it seems safe to say that individual contributors are more ideological than other actors in the campaign finance system. Unsurprisingly, they are more ideological in their giving than corporations, which, as noted above, sometimes give to both parties and are more likely to pursue a strategy of bet-hedging and ensuring access.[53] They are also more ideological than traditional PACs, according to studies of state legislative behavior.[54] And, as Schaffner and La Raja show, they are more ideological than parties when parties are able to give money without limits.

As compared to other types of settings and appeals, online fundraising strategies are directed to individuals, not associations. Associations, traditional PACs, corporations, and unions still give or spend a lot of money, of course. Fundraising events and other opportunities for access have not diminished their willingness to be involved with campaigns. But the Internet has unlocked the stored-up potential donations of the average person. As such, it has moved the system of campaign finance in a decidedly more democratic, egalitarian, and polarizing direction.[55]

It should not come as a surprise, then, that a populist campaign finance system, which privileges the voice and influence of individuals, has grown in parallel with populist politics. The legal rules might not have caused the populist political surge, but they certainly have not retarded it. Moreover, they hamstring government efforts to reverse the tide, should policy makers decide to replace the crumbling infrastructure of campaign finance with something less focused on individual contributions and spending. Perhaps the most radical solution would be to enhance the electoral influence of political parties and candidates with direct public funding to them. But doing so would be politically unpopular ("welfare for politicians," or "taxpayer-funded campaigns") in the United States, even if that form of funding is quite typical in other democracies that place party organizations at the center. Direct and substantial funding of parties and candidates would not eliminate the role and influence of outside spending, but it might dilute them. It could help diminish politicians' incentives to strategize for dollars from the masses and could shore up party organizations with money untied to particular interests.

Conclusion

Scholars have offered numerous theories as to why polarization has increased to the heights it reached in 2025.[56] There are sociological explanations, such as rising income inequality, immigration, demographic change, and geographic sorting. There are political explanations such as the narrow margins for control in Congress, teamsmanship among legislative caucuses, and the influence of particular leaders. Then there are institutional or structural explanations, such as those focused on gerrymandering, primary-election rules, the changing media environment, and as discussed here, the rules and dynamics related to campaign finance.

Anyone offering a US-specific explanation, though, should be humbled and perplexed by rates of rising polarization around the world.[57] The center may be holding for the moment in Europe, for example, but the parties on the extremes across the continent are getting stronger with each new election. The unique structural features of the American electoral system—such as districting, party primaries, the Electoral College, and our strange grab bag of campaign finance rules—are not present in those other systems experiencing parallel increases in polarization.

Different systems manage polarization in different ways, though. Parliamentary systems with proportional representation, multiple parties, and coalition governments channel extremism into individual parties. Sometimes (and increasingly these days) those parties gain majorities in parliaments, but often they only grow and remain troublesome from the fringe, providing an outlet for disaffected voters.

In the United States, one way we have managed polarization in the past is through strong party institutions. The parties have historically been ideologically weak, providing big tents for adherents to disparate and often conflicting ideologies. However, the parties remained institutionally strong; individual politicians or fringe interest groups would have great difficulty in removing parties as the primary way of organizing elections and governance. While there have always been extremists in American politics, and some, like Senator Joe McCarthy, could attain significant positions of power, the parties themselves retained their relevance and formidable institutional position.

The changes in the campaign finance system and the media ecosystem, described here, have undermined parties' ability to manage rising polarization. To reemphasize, they are not the primary causes of our political dysfunction, and one could not realistically suggest that blame for the extraordinary events we are witnessing—from the January 6 insurrection to the rise of protofascism—can be laid at the doorstep of campaign reform. Moreover, it is unclear whether these trends can be reversed through legal change. Overturning BCRA or even *Citizens United*, for example, would do little to counteract movements that are now well entrenched and represented inside and outside government. For the foreseeable future, we need to put faith in the electorate and our leaders to steer us away from the most dystopic scenarios that our rates of rising polarization place in the nation's path. That faith is difficult to muster, since the electorate and our leaders are the forces that put us on this trajectory in the first place.

PART VIII

A Comparative Approach to Campaign Finance

19

Leveling The Playing Field
Insights from Comparative Constitutional Law

Mark Tushnet

Buckley v. Valeo ruled out as "foreign" to the US Constitution the possibility that legislatures could adopt campaign finance regulations to level the playing field, to use the metaphor common among regulation proponents. It only allowed regulations sufficiently justified as efforts to prevent corruption. As Ann Southworth's work shows, though, regulation's proponents continued to be motivated by the desire to level the playing field.[1]

Buckley's combination of holdings produced a shadow discourse. Proponents of regulation cast about for ways of recharacterizing attempts to equalize spending as efforts to reduce corruption. So, for example, proponents of regulation say that corruption occurs when legislators don't do the public's business. The Court's increasingly strict definition of corruption has almost entirely eliminated the possibility that it will find plausible such metaphoric uses of the term.

The shadow discourse in which "corruption" stands in for "equalization" has meant that US campaign finance reform hasn't developed a robust account of what leveling the playing field would actually look like—though to my surprise it turns out to be quite difficult to find such a robust account anywhere. I believe that working out what it would mean to level the playing field is actually quite complicated. When fully developed, the account fits uneasily with standard understandings of US free-expression law and constitutional culture. Unhindered by *Buckley*, perhaps campaign finance rules could have contributed to changing those understandings, though my own skepticism about that possibility is quite high.

The core intuition behind the idea of a level playing field, I believe, is the view that voters should choose policies and candidates on the basis of the "merits" of the policies and candidates. A playing field is not level, on this view, if proponents of one policy or candidate dominate the information environment in which voters make their choices. Here, one tension with US political culture arises. That culture does have within it a sense that the merits of a proposed policy have something to do with whether the policy, if implemented, would advance the public good, and a sense that the merits of a candidate have something to do with the candidate's character. Competing with those senses, though, are alternatives—that there is no objective public good independent of the choices made through interest-group politics, and that candidates' character is less important than their ability to get things done.

A decent account of leveling the playing field requires that we accept rough-and-ready judgments by legislatures, electoral-management bodies, and courts about when the field is level "enough." Such judgments lack the precision often sought in US constitutional doctrine. The account also requires either that we accept legislative restrictions on expressive uses by individuals of their personal wealth (including restrictions on political endorsements by celebrities and news organs) or that we develop a political culture in which individuals, news organs, and celebrities believe that they should voluntarily limit their interventions in politics.

The first question the account would have to address is: What exactly is the playing field? The answer turns out to be that there are two or three playing fields. The one with the strongest normative basis is the playing field for development of public policy. The others are electoral playing fields involving major and minor parties. Leveling the playing field for policy development is administratively difficult, which is one place where the rough-and-ready judgments I've mentioned would have to be made. For obvious political-economy reasons, leveling the electoral playing field is likely to entrench major parties and marginalize minor ones—for example (in a common version), by allocating resources to the parties in proportion to the votes they received in the most recent election. And looming over all this, but perhaps most importantly in connection with the policy-development playing field, is the effect of private resources, most notably wealth but also celebrity, in affecting voter choice.

After describing in some greater detail the ways in which a political playing field might be thought of as level, this chapter identifies two features that any system of leveling the playing field would have to have. It then turns to experience with campaign finance systems in Colombia and to a lesser extent Germany, where constitutional courts have treated leveling the playing field, or equalization, as a permissible aim. With that experience in hand, the chapter concludes by returning to the United States, this time to see what features of US and foreign political cultures might account for the differences in receptivity to leveling the playing field as a rationale for campaign finance regulation.

The bottom line is that designing a sensible system of equalization might require—and certainly is made easier by—some principles and institutions that don't feature prominently in US constitutional law. Further, the normative case for equalization has weaknesses, particularly with respect to minority—but not crazy—views about public policy. Taken in combination, these conclusions suggest that leveling the playing field might not be worth devoting much time and effort to (a conclusion that of course requires comparison with other proposals for political reform).

What Is to Be Leveled?

The playing field we are interested in is spending on political campaigns. Spending comes from two sources. The first is political parties. The second is a residual category usually described as independent or third-party spending (where "third-party" does not refer to a political party fielding candidates seeking office).

A level playing field is one in which spending—*on what* is something to be examined in a moment—is roughly equal in some sense. The core intuition is easily stated, though working its implications out in detail is quite complex. In a jurisdiction like the United States as a whole, where there are roughly equal numbers of voters for Democratic and Republican candidates, national Democratic and Republican candidates should spend roughly the same amount of money.

But some questions arise immediately. What about jurisdictions like California and Mississippi, where one major party predominates? Do we level the playing field in California so that Republican and Democratic candidates spend roughly the same amount (basically, limiting spending by Democrats) and similarly in Mississippi (limiting Republican spending)? Or is the idea of leveling the electoral playing field applicable in the United States solely in connection with presidential campaigns?

What about minor parties? Do we not worry about how much they spend because it's going to be trivial relative to spending by the major parties? That is, do we set caps on election spending so high that they level the playing field for major parties and are unachievable by minor parties? As I will argue, this question becomes particularly tricky when we try to develop a system that combines public funding of electoral campaigns with the ability of parties to raise money on their own and with the ability of individuals to contribute their own resources to such campaigns independent of the parties.

Rough equality in spending can be achieved in two ways. We can let political parties and third-party groups accumulate whatever they can, then limit (roughly equally) what they can spend. Or we can give them roughly equal funds and tell them that they can use only those funds. Public funding of political parties is well known. Though there have been proposals for public funding by individual actors,[2] direct public funding is, as far as I know, quite unusual. More commonly, though still rare, individuals are given tax advantages such as deductions for their political expenditures. Where tax rates are progressive, deductions matter more to the better-off, so this version of achieving rough equality is either self-defeating or severely self-limiting.[3] And, of course, we can combine the two methods of achieving equality by limiting spending *and* providing funding, either directly or indirectly.

Under any system, though, we have to know why we want rough equality in spending. Republicans think that Democrats have very bad ideas about public policy; Democrats return the favor. Why should either party think that the other side should be able to disseminate its policy proposals to roughly the same extent as it does? The usual answer is something like this: First, the quite different policies favored by Democrats and Republicans fall within a rather broad range of proposals that have a decent chance of promoting the public good if enacted. (It seems to be thought that this contrasts with the policies promoted by minor parties; for me, this is a serious flaw in the argument for leveling the electoral playing field.) Second, voter choice among candidates or policies is affected to some extent by the sheer amount of information they receive about candidates or policies. Voter choice is "distorted" if voters receive more information about a candidate or policy than they "should," compared to the information they receive about other candidates or policy alternatives.

How do we know how much information voters should receive? We should keep in mind that the measure is always going to be a comparison between information they receive about one candidate or policy and information they receive about alternatives, though my exposition won't always direct attention to the inquiry's comparative nature. There are two core possibilities here. The first attends to the merits; the second treats the idea of "the merits" as vacuous.

Under the first approach, a voter's choice is distorted to the extent that the voter makes her decision based on something other than the merits. Here "the merits" refers to something like "actually advancing the public good" or "good character." The idea of "the merits" can't be too strong, though. It can't mean "actually advances the public good, as determined by some process other than elections." The main alternative here would appear to be judgments by experts in the field. To allow such experts to determine what ideas are meritorious, though, is to abandon our commitment to democratic self-governance.

How then can we build "the merits" into the design for equalization? Consider three candidates for a legislative seat. Two of them are serious, in the sense that they say that, once elected, they will attempt to advance policies that have a reasonable chance of advancing the public good—and, importantly, their claims about good public policy are reasonable as assessed by some significant number of policy experts. The third candidate isn't serious in that sense.

Serious candidates, it might be thought, should be able to publicize their ideas to a roughly equal extent, but unserious ones can be disregarded. Note, though, that there are real problems associated with the idea of seriousness. Consider Green Party candidates several decades ago (the first prominent Green Party was Germany's, which was founded in 1980 but gained substantial political power only in the 1990s). They weren't serious because there was no chance that their programs for addressing the risks associated with climate change would be adopted in the short run. Or consider the Pirate Party a decade ago, challenging the existing system of regulating intellectual property—unserious then, but now, with the risks associated with artificial intelligence a matter of current policy deliberation, perhaps more serious than the major parties.

A more general version is that social processes limit what experts regard as reasonable disagreement: vaccine denialism, no; climate-change denialism, probably not; rejection of nuclear-power generation, probably all right. These examples and those of minor parties "before their time" suggest that the criterion of seriousness should be replaced or at least supplemented by an objective criterion: Are the policies and candidates within some reasonably wide range of policies (and party platforms) that can reasonably be thought of as having some reasonable chance of advancing the public good (perhaps within some specified time period) if adopted? If so, there should be rough equality in spending, subject perhaps to some sort of threshold showing of public support.

Another feature is worth mentioning, in part because it plays a significant role in this chapter's larger argument. The objective approach might have some institutional implications. My repeated use of "reasonable" in describing the proposed criterion suggests that we might want to get experts to weigh in, even if, as noted earlier, we don't give them a dispositive role. To do so, we might want some sort of specialized body—a version of an electoral-management body—to assess a candidate's or policy's seriousness.

An alternative to the objective criterion is pluralist. Every candidate or policy that has "enough" support is on the playing field and should be allowed to disseminate roughly the same amount of information. We can see this as a subheading for the more general proposition that public policy should result from aggregating the views extant in the society—interest-group pluralism, as a shorthand. One way of understanding the US hostility to equalization policies is that US political culture is committed to pluralism across a wide range of matters, whereas other constitutional cultures are more comfortable with the idea that there are objective measures for determining whether a proposal is likely to advance the public good—an "objective order of values," as the German Constitutional Court put it, indicating greater deference to expert judgments about what promotes the public good.

Some Features of Leveling the Playing Field

Who is on the playing field? How level does it have to be? And who gets to give the answers to those questions? In what follows, I frame these questions in terms of a system of public financing of elections, though the considerations are the same with respect to systems regulating campaign expenditures. If spending is capped (at rough equality, with some range open for differences between spending by one or the other side), we have to aggregate all the relevant sources of spending: public financing, individual contributions to parties, subsidies for such contributions through the tax system, and, importantly, direct spending by individuals supporting their favored policies or candidates (this last including something like the monetary value of celebrity and news-organ endorsements).

Independent or Third-Party Spending

My discussion so far has focused on the electoral playing field. As a matter of fundamental principle, though, that playing field is secondary. We have candidate elections as our way of choosing among public policies. The more fundamental playing field, therefore, is the *policy* playing field. Perhaps any policy position that has sufficient support according to some metric is on the field. As Alexander Meiklejohn put it, "The basic need of free discussion ... [is] that everything worth saying shall be said."[4] In another of his formulations, free expression protects the "equality of status in the field of ideas."[5] Efforts to level the playing field for policy positions occur most prominently in connection with independent or third-party expenditures, made by groups or individuals who urge voters to vote for candidates or parties that take a policy position the spender favors. They can also occur in connection with direct legislation such as referendums and initiatives.

Meiklejohn asserted that what mattered was that a position was "worth saying." How can we identify such positions? According to the US Supreme Court, basic principles of free expression as understood here preclude legislatures from placing any limits on truly independent expenditures. One reason might be that lawmakers can't identify positions that *aren't* worth saying. Consider how interest-group pluralists envision the policymaking process. For them, good public policy is nothing more than the aggregation of the policy views prevalent in the society, and lawmaking rules determine how those views are to be aggregated. They believe that any idea that anyone wants to express is, for that reason alone, worth expressing.

Pluralism, particularly interest-group pluralism, plays a role in every modern liberal democracy. Some democracies, though, supplement it or subordinate it to the objective view that public policy should reflect some vision of the public good. That view suggests that the ideas "worth saying" are those (and only those) that would promote the public good if implemented. Canada and the United Kingdom hold that reasonable limits on independent expenditures are consistent with free expression if the regulations satisfy tests of proportionality used pervasively in those constitutional systems. As I argue later, applying a proportionality test makes sense only if one believes that there are some standards for determining that a proposed public policy actually advances the public good—that it is consistent with what German constitutional jurisprudence calls an objective order of values.

Candidate Elections

Candidate elections present a different set of questions. We could say that the players on the field are every party that satisfies the applicable rules about ballot access: If a party gets enough signatures for its candidates to appear on the ballot, it's on the field for purposes of campaign finance. Notably, party programs are aggregates of policy positions, so treating parties as the players is a decent proxy for diverse policy positions. Decent, though of course not perfect: It's possible, maybe even likely, that a policy position with a fair amount of support won't appear in the platforms of enough parties to be commensurate with its actual support. And even when a policy position appears in party platforms, it might not have a priority reflecting its support.

If that's how parties get on the playing field, though, we almost certainly don't want to level the playing field in the sense of providing equal amounts of funds to each party (or imposing the same limits on funding for every party). Maybe the Democratic and Republican parties should get roughly the same amount of funding so that they can compete on roughly equal terms, but it would be crazy to say that the Socialist Workers Party should get that amount as well—or to say that spending by the major parties should be no greater than spending by the Socialist Workers Party so that the latter can compete on a level playing field.

We have to be cautious here, though. Minor parties have historically played an important role in policy development through their effects on the platforms of the major parties. Here it helps to distinguish between having access to "leveling" funding and the amount of such funding. We might initially be tempted to impose some sort of threshold for access to funding—only "serious" parties, for example.

Consider joke candidates or parties. Count Binface has run in several campaigns in Great Britain, receiving about one percent of the vote each time. Count Binface is in "real life" a comedian, but his ability to get on the ballot reflects some degree of dissatisfaction with the current structure of party competition—and the existence of such dissatisfaction is a fact about politics that voters should have access to.

A related example is the fringe single-issue party, the best example of which is New York's The Rent Is Too Damn High Party. Its leader's participation in candidate debates, where he answered almost every question with a tirade about how the rent was too damn high, pretty clearly pushed more serious candidates to acknowledge the issue's importance.

Seemingly eccentric parties sometimes become important in national politics. The Pirate Party started in Sweden as a movement to encourage piracy of intellectual property and to oppose expansive legislative definitions of such property. Pirate Parties have proliferated and become important players in the multiparty politics of several nations, including Iceland and the Czech Republic, as well as the European Parliament.

These examples suggest the hazards of excluding some parties at the threshold. At the same time, of course, it would be ridiculous to say that Count Binface should compete on a level playing field with the representative of the Green Party sitting next to him.

We can approach the question of the level of funding from both the top and the bottom. Consider a simple system with two or three major parties and a handful of smaller ones. We wouldn't think the playing field was level if each party received funding (or was limited in its expenditures) in proportion to the votes it received in the immediately preceding election; that's actually a formula for freezing the distribution of seats. (Or almost a formula. Tectonic shifts in popular sentiment might actually lead to the party with 60% of the seats in the immediately preceding legislature, and so 60% of the funding, losing by a substantial amount.)[6] Not surprisingly, of course, major parties are attracted to such a system: Give us some amount for each vote we got in the last election and we will divvy up political power between ourselves, put up with minor adjustments that occur as our vote shares fluctuate within relatively narrow ranges, and—importantly—we'll basically make it impossible for minor parties to grow enough to threaten us. As a matter of good design, we'd want the leading parties to get a little less funding (or be allowed to spend a little less) than their proportionate share of the prior vote.

The funding formula will get more complicated with serious third parties like the Greens on the field. The formula should take into account the normative proposition that such parties—though perhaps not Count Binface—should have some chance at expanding their share of the vote, or at least should be guaranteed a place on the playing field so that they can influence the platforms of the major parties. The funding formula should therefore give such parties some increment in funding. Indeed, there's a decent case to be made that even if the major parties are left on their own—that is, that they must raise all the money they are allowed to spend—minor parties should receive a public subsidy in recognition of their indirect effects on major parties.

The Problem of (Truly) Independent Expenditures

Suppose we impose caps on spending by major parties. The electoral playing field can be tilted by direct spending by a billionaire urging voters to choose the billionaire's preferred candidate. To keep the playing field level, we could either count independent spending against the caps or directly limit independent spending. Both approaches are in tension with common ideas in the US law of free expression. The former approach means that the message the party or candidate wants to send will be affected by the message the billionaire wants to send. The latter means that an inarticulate billionaire will be limited in hiring people to get her message out to the extent she wants.

Endorsements by news organs and celebrities can also tilt the playing field. I'm confident that experts in campaign finance have developed techniques for estimating the monetary value of such endorsements—for example, by calculating how much less they have to spend on paid advertising in the wake of each endorsement. Again, monetized endorsements could be counted against the caps, with the difficulties already mentioned.

The extent to which truly independent spending and endorsements by celebrities and news organs occur are in part cultural phenomena. My sense is that celebrity endorsements are rare outside the United States and are a relatively recent phenomenon here. News-organ endorsements, on the other hand, have a long history. One can imagine, though, that the transformation of the partisan press into a more professional one might lead to increasing reluctance to endorse candidates (or to the reduction in the monetized value of such endorsements). As before, if US political culture was unburdened by *Buckley*'s ban on limiting campaign spending, we might see changes in the culture of independent contributions induced by spending limits.

It should be clear by now that a decent system of leveling the playing field will incorporate a slew of messy discretionary judgments. That might be enough to make us skeptical about the possibility of developing such a system. There's more to be said, though, about the possible institutional mechanisms for making those judgments.

Regulatory Institutions

What institutions could be used to make threshold determinations (if they are to be made), determinations about level of funding (which will have to be made), and the many other determinations that a decent system of leveling the playing field would require? For all practical purposes, there are two possibilities: (1) legislatures subject to review by a constitutional court, and (2) electoral-management bodies.

Legislatures are unpromising candidates. A sensible "leveling" system will take funds away from the leading party or parties. The latter are going to be quite uncomfortable with regulations aimed at leveling the playing field—and, as the leading parties, they are likely to be in a position to play the spoiler in getting "leveling" regulations adopted, or to ensure that the regulations actually adopted have a tilt despite being advertised as leveling. Constitutional review using a proportionality test might do something to rein in blatant self-interest, but such review seems unlikely to be completely effective in eliminating a tilted playing field.[7] However, constitutional review guided by some objective standards of public policy might do a decent job of giving the legislature some breathing room without allowing it to make the status quo invulnerable in practice to challenge by political outsiders.

If that's so, focusing on the use of proportionality tests would be misleading. This chapter is not the place to explore in detail the reasons for the different approaches—more categorical in the United States, more flexible elsewhere. I suggest that the difference between these approaches reflects differences in deep structures of the underlying constitutional culture not specific to campaign spending or free expression. A crude summary is that the US approach reflects (a) a more complex and decentralized system of governance here than in Canada and the United Kingdom, which the US Supreme Court can regulate better through categorical rules than with a balancing approach, and (b) a political culture more suspicious of the exercise of legislative power by self-interested politicians and the parties with which they are affiliated, in contrast to the more trusting political culture (at least until recently) in Canada and the United Kingdom.

Electoral-management bodies are also promising. *Arkansas Educational Television Commission v. Forbes* provides a useful analogy.[8] There, the US Supreme Court held that the First Amendment did not prevent the state's public-television system from excluding some candidates from debates it sponsored—what I've called a threshold determination. One way to understand *Forbes* is in institutional terms unattended to by the Supreme Court.[9] The public-television system combines ordinary political features with some degree of professionalism. The former characteristic means that the state action requirement is satisfied and the requirement that the system's actions comport with the First Amendment is triggered. The latter characteristic suggests that fears of "purely partisan" and overtly political decision-making might be smaller than would be the case if the legislature was making the decision.

Well-designed electoral-management systems have a similar combination of political responsibility and accountability to professional norms.[10] Many modern constitutional systems use electoral-management bodies, but not, in general, the United States, where such bodies appear almost exclusively as nonpartisan districting commissions in a handful of states.

Leveling the Playing Field in Colombia

With these considerations in mind, I turn to a description of how the Colombian constitutional system deals with campaign finance regulations designed to level the playing field. There are too many differences between the US political system and political systems in other nations for experience elsewhere with regulations aimed at leveling the playing field to translate directly into lessons for the United States. For example, how you level the playing field depends in part on whether you're dealing with a system with two major parties and a handful of minor parties none of which has any real chance of gaining office, or one with numerous parties and a tradition of coalition governments—or, which might come down to almost the same thing, whether your electoral system awards office to the winners of a plurality in a district (the so-called first-past-the-post system) or distributes offices in proportion to parties' vote shares. The robustness of a nation's federalism might matter as well. And campaign finance systems are both complex and diverse; it's probably true that there aren't even any central tendencies discernible in the complete set of regulations of campaign spending. Examining experience elsewhere might, though, at least provoke thought.

In sketching its understanding of "leveling the playing field," the Colombian Constitutional Court was led—haltingly and incompletely, to be sure—to a set of propositions about the existence of a public interest independent of the aggregation of private interests. In a 2005 decision dealing with financing presidential campaigns, the Colombian Constitutional Court stated: "[T]he term 'equal opportunities in electoral campaigning' (taken from the English concept of 'leveling the playing field' or the German term *Chancengleichheit* [equal opportunity]) ... became a founding element of regulations related to democratic fairness for political campaigning in almost all western democracies after World War II."[11]

According to the Court, "the duty of Congress is to guarantee that the presidential election is defined by ideas and not by the weight of power." Its specific concern was the power associated with incumbency, but the formulation covers power associated with money, as later passages in the opinion made clear. The Court continued, "[P]ublic financing of political campaigns seeks to ensure financial balance among candidates ... since it guarantees equal conditions for the confrontation of ideas in a setting where candidates should be more concerned with expressing their views than with finding resources for the campaigns."[12] An earlier decision described how the National Election Commission was to allocate public financing: 10% would be distributed equally among parties and movements, 50% would be distributed to them depending on the number of seats they obtained in elected bodies, 30% was reserved for certain particular kinds of expenses of parties and movements, and 10% was given to organizations dedicated to women, young people, indigenous groups, Afro-Colombian groups, the disabled, and unions.[13]

Regulation was required "to prevent distortions in the voters' will." The Court upheld limits on spending by candidates. The system it found constitutionally permissible required that no more than 20% of the spending limit could come from private sources (including, apparently, independent spending), and provided that an individual could contribute no more than 2% of the limit to the candidate's party, the latter justified as an anticorruption measure. The overall system was justified because it "decreas[ed] resource inequalities among parties, movements, or groups and thus favor[ed] electoral equality"—that is, because it leveled the playing field.[14]

The connection between leveling the playing field and acknowledging competition about ideas is explicit here. The reference to German jurisprudence is instructive as well. The Constitutional Court linked the idea of equal opportunity to a constitutional provision stating that "[p]olitical parties shall participate in the formation of the political will of the people."[15] German jurisprudence likewise associates that idea with another provision stating that legislators are "representatives of the whole people, not bound by orders or instructions and responsible only to their conscience."[16] This provision might be taken as adopting the Burkean idea of representation. In the background is the legacy of the Nazi era, which in this context has been taken to point out the dangers of a state-led "formation of the political will." The German Basic Law recognizes, though, that "the state" is a creature of the political parties that compose the government. Given these considerations, the Burkean idea of legislators' voting their individual consciences fits comfortably with the idea that there is some public good independent of individual will.

These thoughts are reinforced by the reference to "the whole people." This can be taken as an indication that interest-group pluralism is disfavored. German constitutional law does indeed at least sometimes demonstrate hostility to laws that seem explicable primarily as promoting the narrow interests of some group. Germany's Constitutional Court struck down, as interfering with a constitutional right to choose an occupation, a Bavarian statute allowing new pharmacies to open only if the applicant showed that their operation wouldn't harm existing pharmacies. It invoked the same provision to invalidate a national consumer-protection statute prohibiting the sale of chocolate-covered puffed-rice candy that assertedly could be confused with pure chocolate candies.[17]

Interest-group pluralism almost certainly cannot be banished completely from modern legislation, but these and related decisions suggest that German constitutional jurisprudence operates with the sense that there is some public interest independent of the aggregation of private interests. That sense is bolstered by one of the most famous phrases in German constitutional law: that the Basic Law embodies "an objective order of values." Written in the context of a case involving an asserted conflict between constitutional rights of individuals, that phrase resonates more broadly.

Finally, Colombia uses an electoral-management body to administer its equalization regulations. The National Election Commission has nine members chosen by parliament. Members are civil servants who must be lawyers with at least ten years' experience.[18]

Leveling the Playing Field in the United States

Experience elsewhere helps us see more clearly some of the issues that an abstract analysis identifies. Among those issues are the following: First, in working out a system of leveling the playing field, it probably helps if your political culture gives a prominent place to ideas about objectively desirable public policy—if it has a sense that, in addition to promoting whatever people happen to prefer (a characteristic of interest-group pluralism), policy should advance an objectively determinable public good. Second, it probably helps to have a constitutional jurisprudence that allows constitutional courts to evaluate legislative decisions about how to level the playing field by using a flexible balancing test. And third, it probably helps to have an electoral-management body staffed by politically neutral bureaucrats with some expertise in political science and law.

It's immediately apparent that none of these desiderata seem to be available in the United States. Interest-group pluralism rather strongly dominates our policymaking system, even though ideas about the public good haven't disappeared. Lobbying produces interest-group legislation, for example. Perhaps bipartisan legislation, like the McCain-Feingold campaign finance law itself, can be understood as aimed at the public good, but some laws passed with support from both parties involve logrolling and similar legislative tactics that often are driven by interest groups.

US constitutional doctrine contains elements of flexible balancing doctrines, but for the past two or three generations those elements have been subordinated to more categorical and hard-edged doctrines. And, as noted earlier, there are few electoral-management bodies in the United States.[19]

Campaign finance regulations to level the playing field would sit awkwardly within the overall political/legal culture of the United States. This isn't a justification for *Buckley*'s disparagement of equalization as a permissible regulatory goal, though. In introducing this section, I repeatedly used the words "probably helps" deliberately. Nothing in the US political/legal culture forecloses equalization on the grounds asserted—or, put another way, *Buckley* chose one of the many available ways to address equalization. US constitutional doctrine has the resources available to assess equalization systems through flexible balancing, for example. In the absence of electoral-management bodies, the US courts could work out a combination of Thayerian deference and Ely-like skepticism to evaluate legislative choices of thresholds and levels.

I'll conclude with some thoughts from an outsider who claims no expertise in political strategy but has reflected on the history of good-government reforms in the United States, of which leveling the playing field is one. A century ago, the Progressive movement supported a package of what its adherents believed were good-government reforms. The package included direct legislation to get around machine-dominated legislatures, judicial recall to overcome what they regarded as capture by vested interests, transfer of lawmaking authority from generalist legislatures subject to excessive interest-group pressure to administrative agencies that would be guided by expertise, efficiency-directed reforms in city government, and quite a bit more. And, notably, Progressives were reasonably explicit in rejecting interest-group pluralism in favor of a vision of policy as promoting an objective public good.

Today, in contrast, there seem to me to be a number of discrete good-government–oriented organizations each with its own specific hobbyhorse rather than something fairly described as a movement for general good-government reforms. "End *Citizens United*" is about as targeted as one can get. Other organizations promote nonpartisan districting commissions. Still others defend administrative-agency expertise against conservative attacks. This siloing might be a product of increasing recognition that specialized expertise is important in crafting good-government reforms, as well as processes of differentiation made familiar by scholars of nonprofit organizations.

Siloing has its costs, though. A system for leveling the playing field might be improved if it included some proposals for administering substantive rules about thresholds and levels by an electoral-management body. Political support for leveling proposals might be enhanced were they to be combined with proposals for electoral-management bodies that could do districting as well as administer campaign finance rules. In short, leveling the playing field might be more politically achievable were it part of a movement for general good-government reform.

That presupposes, though, that leveling the playing field is good policy. The complexities of working out a system of equalization of campaign spending might be taken to suggest, as I think is probably true, that the game isn't worth the candle. The intuition that Democrats and Republicans should be constrained to roughly the same amount isn't right, at least for those who, like me, think that the range of policies that get serious consideration should be expanded quite dramatically.

Closing Statement

Lee C. Bollinger and Geoffrey R. Stone

We would like to close this volume with some fundamental observations about how to think about the First Amendment in the context of campaign finance reforms and about the state of American democracy.

Anyone who has focused deeply on the First Amendment, and on how we should think about it in the context of American democracy, knows that the ideal of an open and free marketplace of ideas will be profoundly affected by the underlying conditions in the society—the distribution of wealth, the levels of education of citizens, the differential status of citizens, the technologies of communication open to speakers and the press, and a host of other factors that shape how, in fact, people can speak and hear, discuss and debate, and ultimately make decisions about the future of the nation and the broader world. A perennial issue for the First Amendment, accordingly, is how we should interpret it to take account of these basic realities.

As one should expect of a common-law approach to freedom of speech and press over the course of a century and more, the jurisprudence we inherit today is very complex, even at times internally inconsistent. And so it is on this fundamental question about the First Amendment and inequalities of access and participation in public discussion of public issues.

There are, of course, legions of decisions that articulate forcefully, and very often beautifully, the barriers that the First Amendment places against government—or state—censorship. The people, we say, must be free to discuss and debate the issues of the moment without fearing the interventions of the State, which can never be trusted as an arbiter of free ideas.

But there are also decisions that recognize and respond to the risks of private power of censorship or monopolization of public opinion, such that the government may or even must step in to provide correction and counterbalance.

Perhaps even the First Amendment itself must be a sword on behalf of equalization of expressive opportunities. One example is in the public-forum doctrine, which originated in the 1930s. Public streets and parks, the Court held, cannot be removed from citizens who wish to use them to express their views. There is a First Amendment right of citizens to command the availability of these spaces for speech purposes, despite the inconveniences that may bring to others. We sometimes call this doctrine the "poor person's printing press," making the point that ordinary citizens should have the means to bring attention to their ideas. But the very notion of a free and democratic society suggests the principle of "one person, one vote," and that individuals should have a reasonably equal opportunity to help shape public discourse.

As noted in our introductory comments, perhaps the most eloquent articulation of the rights of citizens to be free of the dominance of private wealth and power over public discourse and the public forum in a free and fair democracy, and of the essential role of the government in securing that right, was the area of broadcast regulation and the decisions of the Supreme Court upholding that regime, principally the seminal decision in *Red Lion Broadcasting Co. v. FCC*, 395 U.S. 367 (1969). There, the Court spoke of how the "people as a whole retain their interest in free speech by radio [and television] and their collective right to have the medium function consistently with the ends and purposes of the First Amendment," and how it "is the right of the public to receive suitable access to social, political, esthetic, moral and other ideas and experiences," and, finally, how there "is no sanctuary in the First Amendment for unlimited private censorship operating in a medium not open to all."

Now, whether the *Red Lion* approach is sui generis to the characteristics of the broadcast medium or whether it is more generally relevant whenever private concentrations of wealth and power interfere with the fair and equal functioning of the marketplace of ideas, no matter how the monopolization arises, is a very complex issue, as illustrated by the essays in this volume. The critical point, however, is this: The idea that the First Amendment should be open to remedial actions by the State to protect the quality and character of public discussion of public issues is not unknown to our constitutional traditions. It is within the bounds of experience and reasonable debate.

Over the span of a half-century, from the Court's first entrance into the realm of regulating money in elections in *Buckley v. Valeo*, 424 U.S. 1 (1976), to today, our world has changed in profound ways. The differential distribution of wealth in our society, with *much* higher concentrations at the upper end of the scale, has been magnified beyond historical experience. The spending by individuals, organizations, corporations, and candidates in elections has grown exponentially. The citizenry has become more polarized in their political views, as we are reminded every day. The sources of the spending in elections tends on average to be from the extremes of the political spectrum. And traditional institutions such as political parties and professional journalism have withered. It is not unreasonable to look at all these trends, along with others, and feel alarmed at the trajectory of American democracy. The plain and simple fact is that the expenditure of huge amounts of money in the electoral process can have two very negative effects on democracy. It can seriously distort the central principle of "one person, one vote," and it can lead elected officials to shape their conduct and decision-making to benefit, not "the people," but their huge donors. These are serious threats to the very principle of a free and open democracy as envisioned by the Framers.

Many see Western liberal democracy, a comparatively recent invention in the broad scope of human history, as fragile and on the edge of failing. There are myriad potential causes of concern that can be identified as contributing to this state of affairs. Several of the most significant have been ones we have focused on in our projects: the role of new technologies of communication, especially the Internet and social media, in isolating citizens in their own viewpoints and nurturing their anger toward opposing views; and the rise of single issues that divide the country into fiercely opposed political camps, such as the right to abortion and the Republican Party campaign over many decades to reshape the Supreme Court to overturn *Roe v. Wade*, 410 U.S. 113 (1973). But the one we focus on here—the corrosive effects of money in our political system—is most definitely in the top category of potential causes.

There is a profound irony to be faced in the area we take up here. When scholars and practitioners debate the demise of democracy, they point first to the failure of government to address the needs and concerns of society. Deliberative dysfunction is a key culprit, it is often said. Yet, in the area of remedial actions to address the perceived unfairness in elections, we have multiple examples over the last fifty years of strong bipartisan legislation to cope with public concerns. It is the Supreme Court, our least democratic institution, that has stepped in to render ineffectual our legislative chambers. This is not to say that there are not legitimate reasons for courts to be concerned about legislative regulation of the electoral process. Courts should, indeed, be skeptical of such efforts because they may often be designed not to enhance but to undermine democracy. At the same time, though, courts should recognize that the absence of such regulation can also have a devastating effect on the core aspirations of a well-functioning and fair democracy. The Court's early decisions in this regard sought thoughtfully to strike an appropriate balance in guarding against these competing dangers. In its more recent decisions, though, the Court has largely prohibited even quite sensible and legitimate efforts to preserve the fundamental values of our democracy.

It will be worth considering, over the next fifty years, what the consequences of that choice have been.

Other Books by Bollinger & Stone

Eternally Vigilant: Free Speech in the Modern Era, 2001.
The Free Speech Century, 2018.
National Security, Leaks and Freedom of the Press: The Pentagon Papers Fifty Years On, 2021.
Social Media, Freedom of Speech, and the Future of Our Democracy, 2022.
A Legacy of Discrimination: The Essential Constitutionality of Affirmative Action, 2023.
Roe v. Dobbs: The Past, Present, and Future of a Constitutional Right to Abortion, 2024.
Academic Freedom in the Era of Trump, forthcoming 2026.

Notes

CHAPTER 1

1. *See, e.g.*, Archibald Cox, *Foreword: Freedom of Expression in the Burger Court*, 94 HARV. L. REV. 1, 58 (1980) ("The majority . . . sought to chart a constitutional distinction between the ceilings upon expenditures, which were held to violate the First Amendment, and the ceilings upon contributions, which were sustained. This is plainly the most difficult and important aspect of the case"). *Accord* David Schultz, *Revisiting* Buckley v. Valeo: *Eviscerating the Line Between Candidate Contributions and Independent Expenditures*, 14 J.L. & POL. 33, 69 (1998) (criticizing the distinction but noting that it was usually "decisive" in campaign finance cases).
2. *See, e.g.*, Kenneth J. Levit, *Campaign Finance Reform and the Return of* Buckley v. Valeo, 103 YALE L.J. 469, 473 (1991) (noting that the contribution–expenditure distinction "spawned a money chase that requires constant fundraising and a continual dependence on wealthy donors").
3. *See, e.g.*, David K. Neidert, Comment, *Campaign Reform: Fifteen Years After* Buckley, 17 J. CONTEMP. L. 289, 295 (1991).
4. *See, e.g.*, Harold Leventhal, *Courts and Political Thickets*, 77 COLUM. L. REV. 345, 358–359 (1977); Willys Schneider, Comment, Buckley v. Valeo: *The Supreme Court and Federal Campaign Reform*, 76 Colum. L. Rev. 852, 860, 868 (1976) (describing the distinction as "not easily acceptable on close analysis," a "conceptual weakness," and "irrational[]"); Arthur N. Eisenberg, Buckley, *Rupert Murdoch, and the Pursuit of Equality in the Conduct of Elections*, 1996 Ann. Surv. Am. L. 451, 457 (the distinction was "the weakest facet of the Court's opinion").
5. 424 U.S. 1, 235 (1976) (Burger, C.J., concurring in part, dissenting in part); *id.* at 290 (Blackmun, J., concurring in part, dissenting in part).
6. *Id.* at 257 (White, J., concurring in part, dissenting in part).
7. *See, e.g., id.* at 286 (Marshall, J., concurring in part, dissenting in part) (finding that the statutory limit on a candidate's use of personal or family funds should be treated as a contribution limit rather than, as the majority held, an expenditure limit).
8. Peter M. Shane, *Commentary: Back to the Future of the American State: Overruling* Buckley v. Valeo *and Other Madisonian Steps*, 57 U. PITT. L. REV. 443, 449 (1996).
9. *Id.*

10. *See, e.g.*, Ronald Dworkin, *The Curse of American Politics*, N.Y. Rev. Bks. (Oct. 17, 1996), https://www.nybooks.com/articles/1996/10/17/the-curse-of-american-politics/; *see also* Burt Neuborne, *Buckley's Analytical Flaws*, 6 J.L. & Pol'y 111, 115 (1997); Schultz, *supra* note 1, at 36; James Coleman, *The Slow, Just, Unfinished Demise of the* Buckley *Compromise*, 30 Harv. J.L. & Pub. Pol'y 427, 428 (2006).
11. Neuborne, *supra* note 10, at 116. For rare supportive academic treatments, see Eugene Volokh, *Why* Buckley v. Valeo *Is Basically Right*, 34 Ariz. St. L.J. 1095 (2002); Daniel Lowenstein, *A Patternless Mosaic: Campaign Finance and the First Amendment After* Austin, 21 Cap. Univ. L. Rev. 381, 388–402 (1992).
12. *Buckley v. Valeo*, 424 U.S. 1, 23 (1976).
13. *Id.* at 19.
14. *Id.* at 44–45.
15. *Id.* at 21.
16. *Id.* at 20–21.
17. *Id.*
18. *Cal. Med. Ass'n v. Fed. Election Comm'n*, 453 U.S. 182, 195 (1981) (plurality opinion).
19. *Buckley*, 424 U.S. at 21.
20. *Id.* at 29.
21. *Id.* at 23–35.
22. *Id.* at 27–28.
23. *Id.* at 47.
24. *Id.* at 48–49.
25. *Id.* at 29, 64.
26. Justice Stevens took office after *Buckley* was argued and did not participate in its consideration or decision.
27. Pub L. 92-225, § 201, 86 Stat. 8 (codified at 52 U.S.C. § 50,101 (2018)). The current codified definition is essentially the same—"any gift, subscription, loan, advance, or deposit of money or anything of value made by any person for the purpose of influencing any election for federal office," 52 U.S.C. § 30,101(8)(A)(i).
28. 86 Stat. at 9. The current codified definition is essentially the same—"any purchase, payment, distribution, loan, advance, or gift of money or anything of value, made by any person for the purpose of influencing any election for Federal office." 52 U.S.C. § 30,101(9)(A)(i).
29. *Buckley*, 424 U.S. at 52.
30. *Id.* at 287 (Marshall, J., concurring in part and dissenting in part).
31. *Id.* at 289.
32. *Id.* at 46–47.
33. *Colo. Republican Fed. Campaign Comm. v. Fed. Election Comm'n* (*Colorado Republican I*), 518 U.S. 604 (1996).

34. *Fed. Election Comm'n v. Colo. Republican Fed. Campaign Comm.* (*Colorado Republican II*), 533 U.S. 431 (2001).
35. *Colorado Republican I*, 518 U.S. at 619–623 (plurality opinion); *id.* at 631 (Thomas, J., concurring in part and dissenting in part).
36. *See id.* at 608, 612 (plurality opinion).
37. *Colorado Republican II*, 533 U.S. at 445.
38. *Id.* at 458. *See also id.* at 464 ("Coordinated expenditures of money donated to a party are tailor-made to undermine contribution limits").
39. *Fed. Election Comm'n v. Christian Coal.*, 52 F. Supp. 2d 45, 92 (D.D.C. 1999).
40. *Id.*
41. *See* Pub. L. 107–155, § 211, 116 Stat. 81, 92 (codified at 52 U.S.C. § 30,101(17(b))(2018)).
42. *Id.* at § 214(c), 116 Stat. at 95.
43. 11 C.F.R. 109.21 (2024). Additional factors in determining whether a communication is coordinated or independent is whether the candidate's campaign and the spender contract with or employ a common vendor of campaign communication services or whether the spender was an employee or contractor of the candidate's campaign within 120 days before the expenditure.
44. *See, e.g.*, FEC, ADVISORY OPINION 2011-12 (MAJORITY PAC, HOUSE MAJORITY PAC) (2011), https://www.fec.gov/files/legal/aos/2011-12/AO-2011-12.pdf.
45. *See, e.g.*, FEC, ADVISORY OPINION 2024-01 (TEXAS MAJORITY PAC) (2024), https://www.fec.gov/files/legal/aos/2024-01/2024-01.pdf.
46. *See, e.g.*, Isaac Arnsdorf & Jack Dawsey, *Trump Team Gambles on New Ground Game Capitalizing on Loosened Rules*, WASH. POST (Aug. 3, 2024), https://www.washingtonpost.com/politics/2024/08/03/trump-allies-ground-game/; Jessica Piper, *Super PACs Keep Testing the Limits of Campaign Finance Law*, POLITICO (Apr. 8, 2024), https://www.politico.com/news/2024/04/08/super-pac-fec-limits-00150672.
47. *See, e.g.*, Gabriel Foy-Sutherland & Saurav Ghosh, *Coordination in Plain Sight: The Breadth and Uses of "Redboxing" in Congressional Elections*, 23 ELECTION L.J. 149 (2024).
48. *See, e.g.*, Theodore Schleifer, *Who Are the Biggest Donors to Trump and Harris*, N.Y. TIMES (Sept. 1, 2024), https://www.nytimes.com/2024/09/01/us/elections/democratic-republican-political-donors.html?searchResultPosition=1; Clara Ence Morse, Luis Melgar & Maeve Reston, *Meet the Megadonors Pumping Millions into the 2024 Campaign*, WASH. POST (Aug. 26, 2024), https://www.washingtonpost.com/elections/interactive/2024/biggest-campaign-donors-election-2024/.
49. 556 U.S. 868 (2009).

50. *Id.* at 882. *See also id.* at 872, 873, 884–889 (referring to the campaign spending as contributions).
51. 454 U.S. 290 (1981).
52. 554 U.S. 728 (2008).
53. 454 U.S. at 296.
54. *Id.* at 299.
55. 554 U.S. at 740.
56. 540 U.S. 93, 138–142 (2003).
57. *Id.* at 134–138.
58. 451 U.S. 182 (1981).
59. *Id.* at 202.
60. *Id.* at 202–203.
61. 459 U.S. 197 (1982).
62. 470 U.S. 480 (1985).
63. *Id.* at 497.
64. *Id.* at 501.
65. 479 U.S. 238, 253 (1986).
66. *Id.* at 251–252 (quoting *Buckley*, 424 U.S. at 39).
67. *Id.* at 259–260.
68. 494 U.S. 652, 657 (1990).
69. 528 U.S. 377 (2000).
70. *Id.* at 387–388.
71. *Id.* at 387.
72. *Id.* at 391.
73. *Id.* at 395
74. *Colorado Republican II*, 533 U.S. 431, 440–441 (2001) (citing *Shrink* for the proposition that "limits on political expenditures deserve closer scrutiny than restrictions on political contributions").
75. 539 U.S. 146, 161–162 (2003).
76. 540 U.S. 93, 134 (2003).
77. *Beaumont*, 539 U.S. at 161–162.
78. 548 U.S. 230 (2006).
79. *Id.* at 246–247.
80. *Id.* at 248–263.
81. *Id.* at 284–290 (Souter, J., dissenting).
82. 589 U.S. 1 (2019).
83. *Id.* at 4–6.
84. 572 U.S. 185 (2014) (plurality opinion).
85. *Id.* at 218–223.
86. *Id.* at 223–224.
87. 596 U.S. 289 (2022).
88. *Id.* at 314 (Kagan, J., dissenting).
89. *Id.* at 302–305 (majority opinion).

90. *Id.* at 311.
91. 558 U.S. 310, 345, 356–359 (2010).
92. *Arizona Free Enterprise Club's Freedom Club PAC v. Bennett*, 564 U.S. 721, 734–751 (2011).
93. *Buckley*, 424 U.S. 1, 244 (1976).
94. *Id.* at 253.
95. *Id.* at 265.
96. *Id.* at 261.
97. *Fed. Election Comm'n v. NCPAC*, 470 U.S. 480, 521 (1985) (Marshall, J., dissenting).
98. *See, e.g., Davis v. Fed. Election Comm'n*, 554 U.S. 724, 750–752 (2008) (Stevens, J., concurring in part and dissenting in part); *Randall v. Sorrell*, 548 U.S. 230, 273–281 (2006) (Stevens, J., dissenting).
99. *See, e.g., Nixon v. Shrink Mo. Gov't PAC*, 528 U.S. 377, 405 (2000) (Breyer, J., concurring).
100. *See, e.g., Randall*, 548 U.S. at 281–284 (Souter, J., dissenting).
101. *Colorado Republican I*, 518 U.S. 604, 635–644 (1996).
102. 528 U.S. at 410–420.
103. 533 U.S. 431, 465–466 (2001).
104. 548 U.S. at 266–267.
105. 533 U.S. at 465–466.
106. *Shrink Missouri*, 528 U.S. at 410.
107. 548 U.S. at 265.
108. *Id.* at 228 (quoting *Shrink Missouri*, 528 U.S. at 412).
109. *McCutcheon v. Fed. Election Comm'n*, 572 U.S. 185, 228–232 (2014) (Thomas, J., concurring).
110. *Shrink Missouri*, 528 U.S. at 406.
111. *Id.* at 408.
112. *Id.* at 409.
113. *See Landell v. Sorrell*, 382 F.3d 91, 106–137 (2d Cir. 2004).
114. Justice Alito joined Justice Breyer's plurality except for the discussion of *Buckley* and *stare decisis*. *See Randall v. Sorrell*, 548 U.S. 230, 263–264 (2006) (Alito, J., concurring in part and concurring in the judgment).
115. *McCutcheon*, 572 U.S. at 199.
116. *Id.*
117. 596 U.S. at 305.
118. *NCPAC*, 470 U.S. at 520.
119. *See, e.g.,* Shane, *supra* note 8, at 450.
120. *See, e.g.,* Andrew Duehren & Theodore Schleifer, *Donors Quietly Push Harris to Drop Tax on Ultrawealthy*, N.Y. TIMES (Aug. 29, 2024), https://www.nytimes.com/2024/08/29/us/politics/donors-harris-tax-ultrawealthy.html; Josh Dawsey & Maxine Joselow, *What Trump Promised Oil CEOs as He Asked Them to Steer $1 Billion to His Campaign*, WASH. POST (May 9,

2024), https://www.washingtonpost.com/politics/2024/05/09/trump-oil-industry-campaign-money/.
121. *See, e.g.,* Volokh, *supra* note 11, at 1102.
122. *See* Ralph K. Winter, *The History and Theory of* Buckley v. Valeo, 6 J.L. & POL'Y 93, 105 (1997); Lowenstein, *supra* note 11, at 401 (noting that "contribution limits address the conflict-of-interest problem more directly"); *cf.* Bradley A. Smith, *Super PACs and the Role of "Coordination" in Campaign Finance Law*, 49 WILLAMETTE L. REV. 603, 613, 620 (2013) (noting that "[t]he Court upheld limits on contributions because the process of contributing opened the possibility for explicit exchange bordering on bribery" and that "there are reasons for treating contributions and expenditures differently").
123. In this chapter, I take no position on what should count as a threat to political integrity that would justify restrictions on campaign contributions and expenditures. Accepting the Court's current view that the only constitutionally acceptable justification is the prevention of *quid pro quo* corruption and its appearance, it would still be better to have a uniform standard of review for contributions and expenditures that takes into account the nature of the regulation's burden on expression and association and the nature of the corruption danger addressed.
124. *See, e.g.,* ROBERT C. POST, CITIZENS DIVIDED: CAMPAIGN FINANCE REFORM AND THE CONSTITUTION 56 (2014). *Accord* JOHN SAMPLES, THE FALLACY OF CAMPAIGN FINANCE REFORM 65 (2006); Joel M. Gora, Buckley v. Valeo: *A Landmark of Political Freedom*, 33 Akron L. Rev. 7, 23 (1999) (stating that *Buckley* bears "the hallmark of judicial compromise"); Dworkin, *supra* note 10; Miriam Galston, Buckley 2.0: *Would the* Buckley *Court Overturn* Citizens United*?*, 22 U. Pa. J. Const'l L. 687, 690 (2020) (discussing how the Buckley Court was "striking a balance between the free speech claims of individuals and groups, on the one hand, with societal interests, especially the integrity of elections in a representative democracy, on the other").
125. *See, e.g.,* Coleman, *supra* note 10, at 427.
126. Neuborne, *supra* note 10, at 118.
127. *See Fed. Election Comm'n v. Wis. Right to Life, Inc.,* 551 U.S. 449 (2007); *Davis v. Fed Election Comm'n,* 554 U.S. 728 (2008); *Citizens United v. Fed. Election Comm'n,* 558 U.S. 310 (2010); *Ariz. Free Enter. Club's Freedom Club PAC v. Bennett,* 564 U.S. 721 (2011); *McCutcheon v. Fed. Election Comm'n,* 572 U.S. 185 (2014); *Thompson v. Hebdon,* 589 U.S. 1 (2019); *Fed. Election Comm'n v. Cruz,* 596 U.S. 289 (2022).
128. It is less clear whether prevention of the *appearance* of corruption would be a compelling interest.
129. The Supreme Court sustained the federal ban on corporate campaign contributions in *FEC v. Beaumont,* 539 U.S. 146 (2003). Part of Beaumont's reasoning turned on the idea—later repudiated in *Citizens United*—that

corporate money raises a special danger of corruption. *See id.* at 155. But the Court also relied on Buckley's lower standard of review of contribution restrictions and the prevention of circumvention on individual contribution limits. *See id.* at 155, 160–161. Lower courts have continued to invoke the lower standard of review and the anticircumvention justification in sustaining federal and state corporate contribution bans. *See* Richard Briffault, *The Surprising Survival—So Far—of the Corporate Contribution Ban*, 3 U. CHI. BUS. L. REV. 397 (2024).

130. *Nat'l Republican Sen. Comm. v. Fed. Election Comm'n*, 117 F.4th 389 (6th Cir. 2024) (en banc).
131. In 2022, twenty-seven states currently set limits on PAC-to-PAC transfers. *See Campaign Finance Regulation: State Comparisons*, NAT'L CONF. STATE LEGISLATURES, https://www.ncsl.org/elections-and-campaigns/campaign-finance-regulation-state-comparisons (last updated Oct. 24, 2022).
132. *See, e.g., Republican Party of N.M. v. Torrez*, 687 F. Supp. 3d 1095, 1129–1130 (D.N.M. 2023) (invalidating state law limiting party-committee-to-party-committee contributions); *Thompson v. Hebdon*, 7 F.4th 811, 823 (9th Cir. 2011) (invalidating state law limiting donations to political committees); *Free & Fair Election Fund v. Mo. Ethics Comm'n*, 903 F.3d 759 (8th Cir. 2018) (invalidating state constitutional amendment prohibiting PAC-to-PAC transfers).
133. *See Campaign Finance Regulation: State Comparisons, supra* note 131.
134. *See, e.g.,* Ann Southworth, *The Consequences of* Citizens United: *What Do the Lawyers Say?*, 93 CHI.-KENT L. REV. 525, 538–539 (2018); Anthony J. Gaughan, *The Futility of Contribution Limits in the Age of Super PACs*, 60 DRAKE L. REV. 755 (2012).
135. *See* John J. Martin, *Danger Signs in State and Local Campaign Finance*, 74 ALA. L. REV. 415, 446–447 (2022).
136. Raymond J. La Raja, *Why Super PACs: How the American Party System Outgrew the Campaign Finance System*, 10 FORUM 91, 101 (2012).
137. *See* Martin, *supra* note 136, at 447–448.
138. *See* Thomas Stratmann & Francisco J. Aparicio-Castillo, *Competition Policy for Elections: Do Campaign Contribution Limits Matter?*, 127 PUB. CHOICE 177 (2006).
139. *See* Thomas Stratmann, *Contribution Limits and the Effectiveness of Campaign Spending*, 129 PUB. CHOICE 461, 472 (2006).
140. *See* Thomas Stratmann, *Do Low Contribution Limits Insulate Incumbents from Competition?*, 9 ELEC. L.J. 125, 135–139 (2010).
141. *See* Eric Dunaway & Felix Munoz-Garcia, *Campaign Contributions and Policy Convergence*, 184 PUB. CHOICE 429 (2020).
142. *See* Patrick Flavin, *Campaign Finance Laws, Policy Outcomes, and Political Equality in the American States*, 68 POL. SCI. Q. 77 (2015).

143. *See* Michael J. Barber, *Ideological Donors, Contribution Limits, and the Polarization of American Legislatures*, 78 J. Pol. 296 (2016).

CHAPTER 2

1. 424 U.S 1 (1976).
2. *See id.* at 26–28.
3. *Id.* at 49–50.
4. *Id.* at 55–58.
5. *Id.* at 48.
6. *Id.* at 48–49 (quoting *New York Times v. Sullivan*, 376 U.S. 254, 266, 269 (1964)).
7. 494 U.S. 652 (1990).
8. *Nixon v. Shrink Miss. Gov't PAC*, 528 U.S. 377, 402 (2000).
9. 572 U.S. 185 (2014).
10. *Id.* at 236–237 (emphasis added).
11. 395 U.S. 367 (1969).
12. 412 U.S. 94, 123 (1973) (emphasis added) (citations omitted).
13. 424 U.S. at 47.
14. 424 U.S. at 28.
15. 540 U.S. 93, 143 (2003) (quoting *Nixon v. Shrink Miss. Gov't PAC*, 528 U.S. 377, 389 (2000)).
16. 424 U.S. at 27.
17. 540 U.S. at 144 (quoting *Nixon*, 528 U.S. at 390).
18. *SpeechNow.org v. FEC*, 599 F.3d 686 (D.C. Cir. 2010).
19. 558 U.S. 310 (2010).
20. 548 U.S. 230 (2006).

CHAPTER 3

1. *See* 424 U.S. 1 (1976). For a discussion of the crisis facing American democracy, see Erwin Chemerinsky, No Democracy Lasts Forever: How the Constitution Threatens the United States 3–6 (2024).
2. *See* Richard L. Hasen, Plutocrats United: Campaign Money, the Supreme Court, and the Distortion of American Politics (2016).
3. *Bellotti v. First Nat'l Bank of Boston*, 435 U.S. 785, 787 n.26 (1978); *Ariz. Free Enter. Club's Freedom Club PAC v. Bennett*, 564 U.S. 721, 776 (2011) (Kagan, J., dissenting).
4. *McCutcheon v. Fed. Election Comm'n*, 572 U.S. 185, 206 (2014).
5. *See* Zephyr Teachout, *The Anti-Corruption Principle*, 94 Cornell L. Rev. 341, 387–397 (2009).
6. *Bellotti*, 435 U.S. at 788 n.26.
7. *Ariz. Free Enter.*, 564 U.S. at 776.

8. Maggie Koerth, *How Money Affects Elections*, FiveThirtyEight (Sept. 10, 2018), https://fivethirtyeight.com/features/money-and-elections-a-complicated-love-story/.
9. *See* Note, *Drowning Out Democracy*, 137 Harv. L. Rev. 2386, 2392 (2024).
10. Andy Cerda & Andrew Daniller, *7 Facts About Americans' Views of Money in Politics*, Pew Rsch. Ctr. (Oct. 23, 2023), https://www.pewresearch.org/short-reads/2023/10/23/7-facts-about-americans-views-of-money-in-politics/.
11. *Id.*
12. *See Austin v. Mich. Chamber of Com.*, 494 U.S. 652 (1990); *McConnell v. Fed. Elec. Comm'n*, 540 U.S. 93 (2003).
13. *Citizens United v. Fed. Elec. Comm'n*, 558 U.S. 310 (2010); *Ariz. Free Enter.*, 564 U.S. 721 (2011).
14. *Austin*, 494 U.S. at 660.
15. *See* Deborah Hellman, *Money Talks but It Isn't Speech*, 95 Minn. L. Rev. 953, 955 (2011) (arguing that spending money need not be protected by the First Amendment but observing that "[m]oney is clearly important to speaking. Without money, how would one publish a newspaper, buy a television advertisement, or pay campaign workers? Sometimes giving money is also . . . expressive of one's support for a . . . candidate").
16. *Buckley*, 424 U.S. at 66.
17. *Id.* at 67.
18. *Id.* at 68. This is the one area where we are largely in agreement with the Court, in that it generally has upheld disclosure requirements for election campaigns, including in *Buckley v. Valeo*.
19. *United States v. O'Brien*, 391 U.S. 367, 376–377 (1968).
20. 519 F.2d 821, 841 (1975).
21. 391 U.S. 367, 376–377 (1968).
22. 424 U.S. 1 (1976). For an excellent description of the background of the case, *see* Richard L. Hasen, *The Nine Lives of* Buckley v. Valeo, *in* First Amendment Stories (Richard Garnett & Andrew Koppelman eds., 2011).
23. *Buckley*, 405 U.S. at 14.
24. *Id.* at 16.
25. *Id.* at 19.
26. J. Skelly Wright, *Politics and the Constitution: Is Money Speech?*, 85 Yale L.J. 1001, 1019 (1976).
27. *Nixon v. Shrink Mo. Gov't PAC*, 528 U.S. 377, 398 (2000) (Stevens, J., concurring).
28. *See San Antonio Ind. Sch. Dist. v. Rodriguez*, 411 U.S. 1 (1973).
29. *United States v. Playboy Ent. Grp., Inc.*, 529 U.S. 803, 816 (2000) ("When the Government restricts speech, the Government bears the burden of proving the constitutionality of its actions").
30. *Buckley*, 405 U.S. at 19–21.

31. *Id.* at 26.
32. *Id.* at 26–27.
33. *Citizens United v. Fed. Election Comm'n*, 558 U.S. 310, 356, 360–362 (2010).
34. *See* Samuel Issacharoff, *On Political Corruption*, 124 HARV. L. REV. 118, 120 (2010) (describing *Buckley*'s distinction between contributions and expenditures as incoherent).
35. *See, e.g.*, Lillian R. BeVier, *Money and Politics: A Perspective on the First Amendment and Campaign Finance Reform*, 73 CALIF. L. REV. 1045 (1985).
36. *Citizens United*, 558 U.S. at 458 (Stevens, J., concurring in part and dissenting in part).
37. *Colo. Republican Fed. Campaign Comm. v. Fed. Election Comm'n.*, 518 U.S. 604, 640–641 (1996) (Thomas, J., concurring in the judgment and dissenting in part).
38. 435 U.S. 765 (1978).
39. *Id.* at 776–777.
40. *See* Daniel Lowenstein, *Campaign Spending and Ballot Propositions: Recent Experience, Public Choice Theory and the First Amendment*, 29 UCLA L. REV. 505 (1982).
41. 539 U.S. 146, 161 n.8 (2003) (citations omitted).
42. *Cf., e.g.*, David A. Strauss, *Persuasion, Autonomy, and Freedom of Expression*, 91 COLUM. L. REV. 334 (1991) (discussing autonomy as a value that justifies freedom of expression); Jack M. Balkin, *Digital Speech and Democratic Culture: A Theory of Freedom of Expression for the Information Society*, 79 N.Y.U. L. REV. 1 (2004) (advocating a theory of free speech organized around encouraging a beneficial democratic culture).
43. *Citizens United*, 558 U.S. at 394 (2010) (Stevens, J., dissenting).
44. Mark Tushnet, *An Essay on Rights*, 62 TEX. L. REV. 1363, 1387 (1984) (footnotes omitted).
45. *See, e.g.*, Marlene Arnold Nicholson, Buckley v. Valeo: *The Constitutionality of the Federal Election Campaign Act Amendments of 1974*, 1977 WIS. L. REV. 323, 336.
46. *See, e.g.*, Edward B. Foley, *Equal-Dollars-Per-Voter: A Constitutional Principle of Campaign Finance*, 94 COLUM. L. REV. 1204 (1994); Jamin Raskin & John Bonifaz, *Equal Protection and the Wealth Primary*, 11 YALE L. & POL'Y. REV. 273 (1993).
47. 494 U.S. 652 (1990).
48. *Austin*, 494 U.S. at 660 (citations omitted) (quoting Justice Kennedy's dissent at 705).
49. 540 U.S. 93 (2003).
50. 558 U.S. 310 (2010).

51. *Id.* at 354 (citations omitted) (first quoting McConnell, 540 U.S. at 257–258; then quoting *United States v. Cong. of Indus. Orgs.*, 335 U.S. 106, 144 (1948)).
52. *Id.* at 394.
53. Georgia Lyon, *How Does the* Citizens United *Decision Still Affect Us in 2022?*, CAMPAIGN LEGAL CTR. (Jan. 21, 2022), https://campaignlegal.org/update/how-does-citizens-united-decision-still-affect-us-2022.
54. Richard L. Hasen, *The Decade of* Citizens United, SLATE (Dec. 19, 2019), https://slate.com/news-and-politics/2019/12/citizens-united-devastating-impact-american-politics.html.
55. 564 U.S. 721 (2011).
56. *Id.* at 763 (Kagan, J., dissenting).
57. *Citizens United*, 558 U.S. at 425–426 (Stevens, J., concurring in part and dissenting in part).
58. *Id.* at 388–389 (Scalia, J., concurring).
59. *See* Eugene Volokh, *Why* Buckley v. Valeo *Is Basically Right*, 34 ARIZ. ST. L.J. 1095, 1101 (2003) ("Well, of course money isn't speech. But so what? The question is not whether money is speech, but whether the First Amendment *protects your right to speak using your money*").
60. *Texas v. Johnson*, 491 U.S. 397 (1989).
61. *United States v. O'Brien*, 391 U.S. 367 (1968); *Spence v. Washington*, 418 U.S. 405 (1974).

CHAPTER 4

1. *Citizens United v. Fed. Election Comm'n*, 558 U.S. 310 (2010).
2. Shane Goldmacher & Maggie Haberman, *Kamala Harris Has Raised $1 Billion Since Entering 2024 Presidential Race*, N.Y. TIMES (Oct. 9, 2024), https://www.nytimes.com/2024/10/09/us/politics/harris-billion-dollar-fundraising.html.
3. Alex Leeds Matthews et al., *Follow the Money: How Much Have the 2024 Presidential Candidates Raised?*, CNN (Oct. 25, 2024), https://www.cnn.com/politics/elections/presidential-candidates-money-raised-dg.
4. 377 U.S. 533 (1964).
5. This phenomenon reached its apogee in Elon Musk's scheme to give away $1 million a day to selected voters in "swing" states willing to sign a petition favoring "free speech" and "the right to bear arms." See Ellen Ioanes, *Elon Musk Says He's Giving Away $1 Million a Day to Voters. Is That Legal?*, VOX (Nov. 4, 2024), https://www.vox.com/politics/378912/musk-trump-voting-contest-million-dollars-swing-state-lottery-pennsylvania.
6. *Reynolds v. Sims*, 377 U.S. at 562.
7. *See*, e.g., Simon Ostrovsky & Yegor Troyanovsky, *How Russia Is Using Artificial Intelligence to Interfere in Elections*, PBS NEWS HOUR (Sept. 4, 2024), https://www.pbs.org/newshour/show/how-russia-is-using-artificial-

intelligence-to-interfere-in-elections; Julian E. Barnes et al., *U.S. Announces Plan to Counter Russian Influence Ahead of 2024 Election*, N.Y. TIMES (Sept. 4, 2024), https://www.nytimes.com/2024/09/04/us/politics/russia-election-influence.html.
8. 163 U.S. 537 (1896).
9. 347 U.S. 483 (1954).
10. So-called superprecedents are cases that have become so entrenched in our constitutional law that they are especially difficult—maybe even impossible—to overrule. *See* MICHAEL J. GERHARDT, THE POWER OF PRECEDENT (2008); Gerhardt, *Super Precedent*, 90 MINN. L. REV. 1204 (2006); but see, e.g., Randy E. Barnett, *It's a Bird, It's a Plane, No, It's Super Precedent: A Response to Farber and Gerhardt*, 90 MINN. L. REV. 1232 (2006). Interestingly, even before *Citizens United* was decided, one scholar argued that its predecessor case, *Buckley v. Valeo*, 424 U.S. 1 (1976), should not have "superprecedent" status. See Allison R. Hayward, *The Per Curiam Opinion of Steel*: Buckley v. Valeo *as Superprecedent? Clues from Wisconsin and Vermont*, 2006 CATO SUP. CT. REV. 195. Then-Professor, now Justice Amy Coney Barrett expressed skepticism about the existence of superprecedent in her article *Precedent and Jurisprudential Disagreement*, 91 TEX. L. REV. 1710, 1735 (2013). The cases normally cited for this special status, she wrote, are no more precedential than cases that rest on rules that are sufficiently well accepted that litigants choose not to challenge them. *Id.*
11. *See* U.S. CONST. Art. I, sec. 4, cl. 1. The Court cited this clause in *Buckley*. 424 U.S. at 13 & n. 16.
12. WILLIAM H. REHNQUIST, ALL THE LAWS BUT ONE (2000). The book catalogs the ways in which Presidents and the Court have balanced rights such as those in the First Amendment and habeas corpus during wartime. The author notes that President Lincoln not only suspended the privilege of the writ of habeas corpus, initially without Congress's approval, but also limited freedom of speech and the press during the Civil War, and arguably kept political criminals out of the civil courts to which they were entitled. My point here is not to endorse any of those actions; it is just to note that the task of balancing constitutional rights against one another is one we have lived with for a long time.
13. U.S. CONST. Art. IV, sec. 4.
14. That is, the conduct prohibited by 18 U.S.C. § 201–203. Notably, Section 203 makes it a crime for a member of Congress or an officer or judge of the United States to "demand[], seek[], receive[], accept[], or agree[] to receive or accept any compensation for any representational services" at a time when the person is in office. Section 216 provides that the punishment is imprisonment for not more than a year, but that it increases to a maximum of five years if the conduct is willful.

15. *Burroughs v. United States*, 290 U.S. 534 (1934) (upholding certain financial disclosure and reporting requirements for PACs under the Federal Corrupt Practices Act amendment); *United States v. Auto Workers*, 352 U.S. 567 (1957) (finding constitutional a law prohibiting corporations and labor organizations from making contributions or expenditures in federal elections); *Wesberry v. Sanders*, 376 U.S. 1 (1964) (holding that one person's vote in a congressional election must be worth as much as another person's vote); *Rosario v. Rockefeller*, 410 U.S. 752 (1973) (finding that preservation of the integrity of the electoral process is a legitimate and valid state goal).
16. 424 U.S. 1 (1976).
17. 424 U.S. at 14.
18. *Id.* at 15 (rejecting the argument that the giving and spending of money are best characterized as conduct, not speech, and thus concluding that the decision in *United States v. O'Brien*, 391 U.S. 367 (1968), about the act of burning a draft card, was not applicable to the law at issue in *Buckley*).
19. *Id.* at 18.
20. *Id.* at 17.
21. *Minn. Star & Trib. Co. v. Minn. Comm'r of Revenue*, 460 U.S. 575 (1983).
22. *Id.* at 581, 589 & n.12.
23. 424 U.S. at 19; *Citizens United*, 558 U.S. at 339.
24. 424 U.S. at 262–263.
25. *Id.* at 29.
26. *Id.* at 20–21.
27. *Id.* at 39 (emphasis added).
28. *Id.* (internal quotation marks omitted).
29. 424 U.S. at 44.
30. *Id.* at 46.
31. *Id.* at 48–49.
32. *Id.*
33. *See id.* at 60 (citing Act of June 25, 1910, c. 392, 36 Stat. 822). The 1910 law required political committees (a defined term) to disclose the names of all persons who contributed $100 or more to a campaign for Congress; recipients of expenditures of $10 or more also had to identify themselves. The Federal Corrupt Practices Act of 1925, upheld by the Supreme Court in *Burroughs v. United States*, 290 U.S. 534 (1934), broadened these disclosure requirements.
34. 424 U.S. at 64 (citing cases).
35. *Id.*
36. *Id.* (internal quotation marks omitted).
37. *Id.* at 67–68.
38. Pub. L. No. 107-155, 116 Stat. 81 (Mar. 27, 2002).
39. 540 U.S. 93 (2003).
40. 494 U.S. 652 (1990).
41. *Id.* at 660.

42. In support, the Court cited *Comms. Workers v. Beck*, 487 U.S. 735, 745 (1988), and *Abood v. Detroit Bd. of Ed.*, 431 U.S. 209 (1977) (holding that compelling nonmember employees to contribute to union's political activities infringes employees' First Amendment rights).
43. *Austin*, 494 U.S. at 665–666.
44. *Citizens United*, 558 U.S. at 322.
45. 558 U.S. at 322–326.
46. *Id.* at 326–327.
47. *Id.* at 327–329.
48. *Id.* at 330–332. The Court's path to that conclusion was a bit convoluted. It began by confirming that *Citizens United* had preserved an as-applied challenge to BCRA. That challenge, the Court then said, "assumed a premise—the permissibility of restricting corporate political speech—that is itself in doubt." *Id.* at 331. This supported a facial attack on the statute—that is, an attack based on the proposition that there are absolutely no permissible applications of the law. With that done, the coast was clear to reach the merits.
49. *Id.* at 337–339.
50. *Id.* at 339.
51. *Id.* at 340 (internal quotation marks deleted).
52. *Id.* at 341.
53. 558 U.S. at 348.
54. *Id.* at 357.
55. *Id.* at 361–362.
56. *Id.* at 361.
57. *Id.* at 364.
58. *Id.*
59. *Id.* at 365. One wonders how the Court knew this, or how a party in a future case might be able to contest that apparently empirical proposition.
60. *Id.* at 362. That holding is more interesting than the Court may have realized. Under international law, a corporation is deemed to have the citizenship of its place of incorporation, not of some or all of its shareholders. See Case Concerning Barcelona Traction, Light and Power Co., Ltd. (Belg. v. Spain), Judgment, 1970 I.C.J. 1 (Feb. 5). A Delaware corporation whose shareholders were all from Germany would "count" as a domestic company. And in many instances, piercing the corporate veil would be a much more complex undertaking than this example illustrates. The example of Enron is a particularly sobering one. See Adam Hayes, *What Was Enron? What Happened and Who Was Responsible?*, INVESTOPEDIA, https://www.investopedia.com/terms/e/enron.asp (last visited Oct. 21, 2024).
61. 558 U.S. at 366 (citing 2 U.S.C. § 441d(d)(2)).
62. *Id.* (citing 2 U.S.C. § 434(f)(1), (2)).
63. *Id.*
64. *Id.* (internal quotation marks omitted).

65. *Id.* at 367 (internal quotation marks omitted).
66. *Id.* at 400.
67. *Id.* at 409.
68. *Id.*
69. *Id.* at 413.
70. *Id.* at 426–429.
71. *See generally* HERBERT HOVENKAMP, ENTERPRISE AND AMERICAN LAW 1836–1937 (1991).
72. 558 U.S. at 479.
73. *Id.* at 480 (Thomas, J., concurring in part and dissenting in part).
74. *Id.* at 481.
75. 594 U.S. 595 (2021).
76. 594 U.S. at 608.
77. *Id.* at 612.
78. *Id.* at 613.
79. 596 U.S. 61 (2022).
80. *Id.* at 69.
81. *Id.* at 73.
82. *Id.* at 73–74.
83. 18 U.S.C. § 201.
84. 41 U.S.C. § 8702.
85. *See, e.g., Overnite Transp. Co. v. NLRB*, 104 F.3d 109, 112–113 (7th Cir. 1997).
86. 567 U.S. 709 (2012).
87. *Id.* at 718, 729–730 (no general exception to the First Amendment for false statements).
88. *See* 35 U.S.C. § 100; *see also Thaler v. Vidal*, 43 F.4th 1207 (Fed. Cir. 2022).
89. Alvarez, 567 U.S. at 721.
90. *See, e.g., Burwell v. Hobby Lobby Stores, Inc.*, 573 U.S. 682 (2014).
91. *Janus v. American Fed. of State, County, and Mun. Employees, Council 31*, 585 U.S. 878 (2018).
92. *Id.* at 893.
93. *Id.* at 930.
94. 487 U.S. 735 (1988).
95. Press Release, Federal Election Commission, *Statistical Summary of 18-Month Campaign Activity of the 2023–2024 Election Cycle* (Sept. 25, 2024), https://www.fec.gov/updates/statistical-summary-of-18-month-campaign-activity-of-the-2023-2024-election-cycle/.

CHAPTER 5

1. 403 U.S. 713 (1971).
2. *United States v. Nat'l Comm. for Impeachment*, 469 F.2d 1135, 1142 (2d Cir. 1972).

3. 366 F. Supp. 1041 (D.D.C. 1973).
4. 424 U.S. 1, 19 (1976).
5. *Id.* at 48–49 (citing *New York Times Co. v. Sullivan*, 376 U.S. 254 (1964)).
6. Charles W. Logan, Jr., "Getting Beyond Scarcity: A New Paradigm for Assessing the Constitutionality of Broadcast Regulation," 85 CAL. L. REV. 1687, 1694 (1997).
7. *In Re Complaint of Syracuse Peace Council Against Television Station WTVH Syracuse, New York*, 2 F.C.C. Rcd. 5043, 5052 (1987).
8. ROBERT CORN-REVERE, THE MIND OF THE CENSOR AND THE EYE OF THE BEHOLDER 181–182 (2021).
9. *Id.* at 49.
10. *Citizens United v. Fed. Election Comm'n*, 558 U.S. 310, 340 (2010).

CHAPTER 6

1. *See* Abhay P. Aneja, Jacob M. Grumbach & Abby W. Wood, *Financial Inclusion in Politics*, 97 N.Y.U. L. REV. 566, 566 (2022).
2. *Id.*
3. *Buckley v. Valeo*, 424 U.S. 1, 14–23 (1976). Buckley and its progeny have not gone without scholarly challenge, of course. *See, e.g.*, Richard Briffault, *On Dejudicializing American Campaign Finance Law*, 27 GA. ST. U. L. REV. 887, 898–900 (2011).
4. Michael S. Kang, *The End of Campaign Finance Law as We Knew It*, 98 VA. L. REV. 1, 34–35 (2013).
5. Nick Noel et al., *The Economic Impact of Closing the Racial Wealth Gap*, MCKINSEY & CO. (Aug. 13, 2019), https://www.mckinsey.com/industries/public-sector/our-insights/the-economic-impact-of-closing-the-racial-wealth-gap [https://perma.cc/VYZ8-P5NU].
6. Aneja et al., *supra* note 2, at 588.
7. Jacob M. Grumbach & Alexander Sahn, *Race and Representation in Campaign Finance*, 114 AM. POL. SCI. REV. 206, 214 (2020).
8. Hans J. G. Hassell, *Party Control of Party Primaries: Party Influence in Nominations for the US Senate*, 78 J. POL. 75, 81 (2016); HANS J. G. HASSELL, THE PARTY'S PRIMARY: CONTROL OF CONGRESSIONAL NOMINATIONS 31 (2017).
9. This is an ongoing debate. *See generally* Katherine Tate, BLACK FACES IN THE MIRROR: AFRICAN AMERICANS AND THEIR REPRESENTATIVES IN THE U.S. CONGRESS (2003).
10. *See* NICHOLAS O. STEPHANOPOULOS, ALIGNING ELECTION LAW (2024).
11. Aneja et al., *supra* note 2, at 602.
12. *Id.* at 590.
13. *Id.* at 600 (citing *Buckley v. Valeo*, 424 U.S. 1, 17–18 (1976)).
14. *See, e.g.*, *Citizens United v. FEC*, 558 U.S. 310 (2010); *McCutcheon v. FEC*, 572 U.S. 185 (2014).

15. *See, e.g., FEC v. Akins,* 524 U.S. 11, 21 (1998) ("There is no reason to doubt their claim that the information would help them (and others to whom they would communicate it) to evaluate candidates for public office. . . .").
16. Adam Bonica, *Mapping the Ideological Marketplace*, 58 AM. J. POL. SCI. 367, 367 (2014).
17. *See* Arthur Lupia, *Shortcuts Versus Encyclopedias: Information and Voting Behavior in California Insurance Reform Elections*, 88 A.M. POL. SCI. REV. 63, 72 (1994).
18. *See* Abby K. Wood, *Voters Use Campaign Finance Transparency and Compliance Information*, 45 POL. BEHAV. 1553, 1554 (2023).
19. *See* Abby K. Wood & Christian R. Grose, *Campaign Finance Transparency Affects Legislators' Election Outcomes and Behavior*, 66 AM. J. POL. SCI. 516, 528 (2021).
20. The Court also has recognized an *enforcement* benefit and *anticorruption* benefit to campaign finance disclosure. However, recently in *Americans for Prosperity Foundation v. Bonta*, 141 S. Ct. 2373 (2021), the Court struck down a non-campaign-related financial-transparency regulation for which the state only claimed an enforcement benefit. *Id.* at 1–2.
21. *See generally* Abby K. Wood, *Learning from Campaign Finance Information*, 70 EMORY L. J. 1091 (2021).
22. Anna Massoglia, *Outside Spending on 2024 Elections Shatters Records, Fueled by Billion-Dollar "Dark Money" Infusion*, OPENSECRETS (Nov. 5, 2024), https://www.opensecrets.org/news/2024/11/outside-spending-on-2024-elections-shatters-records-fueled-by-billion-dollar-dark-money-infusion [https://perma.cc/VGA6-QMRM].
23. *Outside Spending*, OPENSECRETS, https://www.opensecrets.org/outside-spending?type=A&filter= [https://perma.cc/ZN5M-VJCE] (last visited Nov. 19, 2024).
24. This math is: 435 US Congress seats, 33 US Senate seats, and 1 Presidential seat, and 56/469 = 11.9%. *Races in Which Outside Spending Exceeds Candidate 2024 Election Cycle*, OPENSECRETS, https://www.opensecrets.org/outside-spending/outvscand [https://perma.cc/II7SU-GYT4] (last visited Nov. 19, 2024).
25. *See* Consolidated Appropriations Act, Pub. L. No. 114-113, § 707, 129 Stat. 3029–3030 (2015); *see also* Roberta S. Karmel, *Little Power Struggles Everywhere: Attacks on the Administrative State at the Securities and Exchange Commission*, 72 ADMIN. L. REV. 207, 255 (2020).
26. *See* Further Consolidated Appropriations Act, Pub. L. No. 118-47, § 633, 138 Stat. 460 (2024).
27. Nonregulated entities can naturally opt to disclose their donors, but they rarely do.
28. *See* Stan Oklobdzija, *Public Positions, Private Giving: Dark Money and Political Donors in the Digital Age*, 6 RSCH. & POL. 1, 6 (2019).

29. Shomik Jain & Abby K. Wood, *Facebook Political Ads and Accountability: Outside Groups Are Most Negative, Especially When Hiding Donors*, 18 PROC. INT. AAAI CONF. WEB & SOC. MEDIA 717, 722 (2024).
30. The remedy for disinformation is "counterspeech." *See United States v. Alvarez*, 567 U.S. 709, 709, 726; Abby K. Wood & Ann M. Ravel, *Fool Me Once: Regulating "Fake News" and Other Online Advertising*, 91 S. CAL. L. REV. 1223, 1238 (2018).
31. Christopher S. Elmendorf & Abby K. Wood, *Elite Political Ignorance: Law, Data, and the Representation of (Mis)Perceived Electorates*, 52 U.C. DAVIS L. REV. 571, 606–608 (2018).
32. Filipe N. Ribeiro et al., *On Microtargeting Socially Divisive Ads: A Case Study of Russia-Linked Ad Campaigns on Facebook*, ACM CONF. FAIRNESS, ACCOUNTABILITY & TRANSPARENCY 140, 141 (2019); Abby K. Wood, *Facilitating Accountability for Online Political Advertisements*, 16 OHIO ST. TECH. L.J. 520, 525.
33. *See Alvarez*, 567 U.S. at 726.
34. I have raised the importance of disclosing targets in various venues, including in my role as a campaign finance regulator, and resistance has been strong, particularly among candidates and former candidates, who have argued that it is a key part of campaign strategy.
35. Shan Jiang & Christo Wilson, *Linguistic Signals Under Misinformation and Fact-Checking: Evidence from User Comments on Social Media*, 2 PROC. ACM HUM.-COMPUT. INTERACTION 1, 12 (2018).
36. *Partnership by Race, Ethnicity and Education*, PEW RSCH. CTR. (Apr. 9, 2024), https://www.pewresearch.org/politics/2024/04/09/partisanship-by-race-ethnicity-and-education/ [https://perma.cc/3XFQ-DZMC].
37. *See* Figure 6.2 for an example of policy preferences differing by race. Elmendorf and Spencer (2015) also show that, within congressional districts, large racial differences in opinion may exist. Christopher S. Elmendorf & Douglas M. Spencer, *Administering Section 2 of the Voting Rights Act After* Shelby County, 115 COLUM. L. REV. 2143, 2210 (2015).
38. Spencer Overton, *State Power to Regulate Social Media Companies to Prevent Voter Suppression*, 53 U.C. DAVIS L. REV. 1793, 1793 (2020).
39. S. Rep. No. 116-XX, at 35 (2020); Roger Vann, *Why We're Targeting the Hardest to Reach Voters*, STAN. SOCIAL INNOVATION REV. (Sept. 11, 2023), https://ssir.org/articles/entry/why_were_targeting_the_hardest_to_reach_voters [https://perma.cc/4U2P-RSTS].
40. *Voting Rights and Election Administration: Combatting Misinformation in the 2020 Election: Hearing Before the Subcommittee on Elections of the Committee on House Administration*, 116th Cong. 26 (2020); *see also* Deen Freelon et al., *Black Trolls Matter: Racial and Ideological Asymmetries in Social Media Disinformation*, 40 SOC. SCI. COMP. REV. 560 (2020).

41. Professor Atiba Ellis reminds us that disinformation tactics are reminiscent of Jim Crow–era attempts "to disenfranchise people of color, going back to voter intimidation and suppression efforts after the Civil Rights Act of 1866." Christine Fernando, *Election Disinformation Campaigns Targeted Voters of Color in 2020. Experts Expect 2024 to Be Worse*, ASSOC. PRESS (Jul. 28, 2023), https://apnews.com/article/elections-voting-misinformation-race-immigration-712a5c5a9b72c1668b8c9b1eb6e0038a [https://perma.cc/GDK8-394E].
42. *Id.*
43. *Id.*
44. *Id.*
45. Aneja et al., *supra* note 2, at 609.
46. *See, e.g.*, Robert Yablon, *Voting, Spending, and the Right to Participate*, 111 Nw. U. L. REV. 655, 691–692 (2017); Yasmin Dawood, *Democracy Divided: Campaign Finance Regulation and the Right to Vote*, 89 N.Y.U. L. REV. 17, 25 (2014).
47. *Harper v. Va. State Bd. of Elections*, 383 US 663, 669 (1966).
48. *Bullock v. Carter*, 405 U.S. 134, 149 (1972).
49. *Reynolds v. Sims*, 377 U.S. 533, 557–558 (1964).
50. *White v. Regester*, 412 U.S. 755, 769 (1973).
51. Aneja et al., *supra* note 2, at 609 (quoting *White*, 412 U.S. at 721, 734).
52. *See generally* Christopher W. Schmidt, *On Doctrinal Confusion: The Case of the State Action Doctrine*, 2016 B.Y.U. L. REV. 575, 575 (describing the state action doctrine as a "notoriously murky field of constitutional law").
53. *Terry v. Adams*, 345 U.S. 461, 481 (1953).
54. *See supra* note 3, at 610; *see also* Jamin Raskin & John Bonifaz, *Equal Protection and the Wealth Primary*, 11 YALE L. & POL'Y REV. 273, 278 (1993); Cass R. Sunstein, *Political Equality and Unintended Consequences*, 94 COLUM. L. REV. 1390, 1399 (1994).
55. *Burton v. Wilmington Parking Auth.*, 365 U.S. 715, 725 (1961) ("By its inaction, the Authority, and through it the State, has not only made itself a party to the refusal of service, but has elected to place its power, property and prestige behind the admitted discrimination"); *cf. Flagg Bros., Inc. v. Brooks*, 436 U.S. 149, 164 (1978) (noting that "a State's mere acquiescence in a private action" does not suffice to establish state action).
56. *See* Aneja et al., *supra* note 2, at 616.
57. *Thornburg v. Gingles*, 478 U.S. 30 (1986).
58. S. Rep. No. 97-417, at 28–29.
59. Michael J. Malbin, Peter W. Brusoe & Brendan Glavin, *Small Donors, Big Democracy: New York City's Matching Funds as a Model for the Nation and States*, 11 ELECTION L.J. 3, 3 (2012); Brian J. McCabe & Jennifer A. Heerwig, *Diversifying the Donor Pool: How Did Seattle's Democracy Voucher Program*

Reshape Participation in Municipal Campaign Finance?, 18 ELECTION L.J. 323, 332–333 (2019).

60. ELISABETH GENN, MICHAEL J. MALBIN, SUNDEEP IYER & BRENDAN GLAVIN, DONOR DIVERSITY THROUGH PUBLIC MATCHING FUNDS 4–5 (2012), https://www.brennancenter.org/sites/default/files/2019-08/Report_DonorDiversity-public-matching-funds.PDF [https://perma.cc/TJ7B-M49N]; *see also* Malbin et al., *supra* note 59, at 8.

61. Kenneth R. Mayer, *Public Election Funding: An Assessment of What We Would Like to Know*, 11 F. 365, 370–371 (2013).

62. Malbin et al., *supra* note 59, at 3; *see also* McCabe & Heerwig, *supra* note 63, at 323; Jennifer A. Heerwig & Brian McCabe, BUILDING A MORE DIVERSE DONOR COALITION: AN ANALYSIS OF THE SEATTLE DEMOCRACY VOUCHER PROGRAM IN THE 2019 ELECTION CYCLE 9 (2020), https://georgetown.app.box.com/s/r2skgxfnc230ukkb3dfqgm4576phzabd [https://perma.cc/KX7T-59Q6].

63. For more on public financing as a judicial remedy, *see* Aneja et al., supra note 2, at 627–629.

64. *See generally* Christopher S. Elmendorf & Abby K. Wood, *Elite Political Ignorance: Law, Data, and the Representation of (Mis)Perceived Electorates*, 52 U.C. DAVIS L. REV. 571 (2018).

65. Genevieve Lakier, *The Limits of Antidiscrimination Law in the Digital Public Sphere*, in SOCIAL MEDIA, FREEDOM OF SPEECH, AND THE FUTURE OF OUR DEMOCRACY (Lee C. Bollinger & Geoffrey R. Stone eds., 2022).

66. *See* Wood, *supra* note 36, at 553–554; Wood, *supra* note 21, at 1142.

67. *See, e.g., Thompson v. Hebdon*, 140 S. Ct. 348 (2019); *Randall v. Sorrell*, 548 U.S. 230 (2006).

68. Examples include the United Kingdom, France, and Sweden, among others. *Are There Provisions for Direct Public Funding to Political Parties?*, INT. IDEA, https://www.idea.int/data-tools/data/question?question_id=9212&database_theme=302 [https://perma.cc/N7T7-TGHB] (last accessed Nov. 20, 2024). Our first-past-the-post system may add a wrinkle here, but it's unlikely to be insurmountable.

CHAPTER 7

1. *See* Democracy Is Strengthened by Casting Light on Spending in Elections (DISCLOSE) Act of 2023, S. 512, 118th Cong. (2023).

2. Keith Newell, *With Deadlocked Vote on Dark Money, DISCLOSE Act Fails to Clear Senate*, OpenSecrets (Sept. 22, 2022), https://www.opensecrets.org/news/2022/09/with-deadlocked-vote-on-dark-money-disclose-act-fails-to-clear-senate.

3. *See* Chuck Marr et al., *The 2017 Trump Tax Law Was Skewed to the Rich, Expensive, and Failed to Deliver on Its Promises*, CTR. ON BUDGET & POL'Y PRIORITIES (June 13, 2024), https://www.cbpp.org/

research/federal-tax/the-2017-trump-tax-law-was-skewed-to-the-rich-expensive-and-failed-to-deliver.
4. Ian W. H. Parry & Simon Black, *Still Not Getting Energy Prices Right: A Global and Country Update of Fossil Fuel Subsidies* 22 (IMF Working Paper No. WP2021/236, 2021).
5. *See* Adav Noti et al., *Why the FEC Is Ineffective*, CAMPAIGN LEGAL CTR. (Aug. 8, 2022), https://campaignlegal.org/update/why-fec-ineffective.
6. *E.g.*, DANIEL CARPENTER & DAVID A. MOSS, PREVENTING REGULATORY CAPTURE: SPECIAL INTEREST INFLUENCE AND HOW TO LIMIT IT (2013).
7. SHELDON WHITEHOUSE WITH JENNIFER MUELLER, THE SCHEME: HOW THE RIGHT WING USED DARK MONEY TO CAPTURE THE SUPREME COURT (2022).
8. *See, e.g.*, Daniel I. Weiner & Tim Lau, *Citizens United Explained*, BRENNAN CTR. FOR JUST. (Dec. 12, 2019), https://www.brennancenter.org/our-work/research-reports/citizens-united-explained; Michael Beckel, *Dark Money Illuminated: The Top 15 Dark Money Groups in the Post-*Citizens United *Era*, ISSUE ONE (Sept. 11, 2018), https://issueone.org/articles/dark-money-illuminated-the-top-15-dark-money-groups-in-the-post-citizens-united-era/; Georgia Lyon, *How Does the Citizens United Decision Still Affect Us in 2024?*, CAMPAIGN LEGAL CTR. (Jan. 17, 2024), https://campaignlegal.org/update/how-does-citizens-united-decision-still-affect-us-2024.
9. Anna Massoglia, *"Dark Money" Groups. Have Poured Billions into Federal Elections Since the Supreme Court's 2010* Citizens United *Decision*, OPENSECRETS (Jan. 24, 2023), https://www.opensecrets.org/news/2023/01/dark-money-groups-have-poured-billions-into-federal-elections-since-the-supreme-courts-2010-citizens-united-decision/.
10. *E.g.*, Sharon Zhang, *Since "Citizens United," Billionaires Are Spending Nearly $1B More on Elections*, TRUTHOUT (Jan. 26, 2022), https://truthout.org/articles/since-citizens-united-billionaires-are-spending-nearly-1b-more-on-elections/; AMS. FOR TAX FAIRNESS, *Billionaires Are Spending 39 Times More on Federal Elections Since Citizens United Supreme Court Decision in 2010* (Jan. 21, 2022), https://americansfortaxfairness.org/billionaires-spending-39-times-federal-elections-since-citizens-united-supreme-court-decision-2010/.
11. *See Citizens United v. Fed. Election Comm'n*, 558 U.S. 310, 394–433 (2010) (Stevens, J., concurring in part and dissenting in part).
12. Sheldon Whitehouse, *Knights-Errant: The Roberts Court and Erroneous Fact-Finding*, 84 OHIO ST. L.J. 837 (2024).
13. *See, e.g., Citizens United*, 558 U.S. at 400 (Stevens, J., concurring in part and dissenting in part); *McConnell v. Fed. Election Comm'n*, 540 U.S. 93, 132–333 (2003); S. Rep. No. 105-167 (1998).
14. *See Citizens United*, 558 U.S. at 360–361 (majority opinion).

15. *See, e.g.*, Trevor Potter, *The Failed Promise of Unlimited "Independent" Spending in Elections*, ABA Hum. Rts. Mag. (June 25, 2020), https://www.americanbar.org/groups/crsj/publications/human_rights_magazine_home/voting-in-2020/the-failed-promise-of-unlimited-independent-spending/; Saurav Ghosh, *Voters Need to Know What "Redboxing" Is and How It Undermines Democracy*, Campaign Legal Ctr. (May 13, 2022), https://campaignlegal.org/update/voters-need-know-what-redboxing-and-how-it-undermines-democracy; Matea Gold, *It's Bold, but Legal: How Campaigns and Their Super PAC Backers Work Together*, Wash. Post (July 6, 2015), https://www.washingtonpost.com/politics/here-are-the-secret-ways-super-pacs-and-campaigns-can-work-together/2015/07/06/bda78210-1539-11e5-89f3-61410da94eb1_story.html; Thomas B. Edsall, Opinion, *After Citizens United, a Vicious Cycle of Corruption*, N.Y. Times (Dec. 6, 2018), https://www.nytimes.com/2018/12/06/opinion/citizens-united-corruption-pacs.html.

16. *See Citizens United*, 558 U.S. at 370–371.

17. Brief of US Senators Sheldon Whitehouse and John McCain as Amici Curiae in Support of Respondents at 6, *Am. Tradition P'ship, Inc. v. Bullock*, 567 U.S. 516 (2012) (No. 11-1179), 2012 WL 1829058.

18. *See, e.g.*, *Top Supporters of Federalist Society for Law and Public Policy Studies*, Conservative Transparency, http://conservativetransparency.org/top/?recipient=842&yr=&yr1=&yr2=&submit= (finding that through 2014, based on IRS Form 990 data and other sources, the Koch-controlled Claude R. Lambe Charitable Foundation (now defunct) gave the Federalist Society at least $1,956,500, and the Charles Koch Foundation gave at least $1,405,000); *AFP Leads the Way in Grassroots Efforts to Confirm Next Supreme Court Justice*, Ams.for Prosperity (July 26, 2018), https://americansforprosperity.org/blog/afp-leads-the-way-in-grassroots-efforts-to-confirm-next-supreme-court-justice/; *Testimony of Lisa Graves Before the United States Senate Committee on the Judiciary Subcommittee on Federal Courts, Oversight, Agency Action and Federal Rights, "What's Wrong with the Supreme Court: The Big-Money Assault on Our Judiciary"* (Mar. 10, 2021), https://www.judiciary.senate.gov/imo/media/doc/Final_CMD_Lisa%20Graves_Written%20Testimony%20for%20March%2010%202021%20Subcommittee%20Hearing1.pdf.

19. *See, e.g.*, Sheldon Whitehouse, *How Citizens United Altered the Climate Debate* (July 25, 2014), https://www.whitehouse.senate.gov/news/speeches/how-citizens-united-altered-the-climate-debate/; *Congress Climate History*, Ctr. for Climate & Energy Sols., https://www.c2es.org/content/congress-climate-history/ (last visited Oct. 14, 2024).

20. *See* Amber Phillips, *Congress's Long History of Doing Nothing on Climate Change, In 6 Acts*, Wash. Post (Dec. 1, 2015), https://www.

washingtonpost.com/news/the-fix/wp/2015/12/01/congresss-long-history-of-inaction-on-climate-change-in-6-parts/.
21. *See Citizens United*, 558 U.S. at 370–371 ("[D]isclosure permits citizens and shareholders to react to the speech of corporate entities in a proper way. This transparency enables the electorate to make informed decisions and give proper weight to different speakers and messages").
22. *See Ams. for Prosperity Found. v. Bonta*, 594 U.S. 595, 618 (2021).
23. *E.g.*, VA. CODE ANN. § 59.1–69 (West 2024) (illustrating the Virginia scheme for fictitious-name use); *Business FAQs: Fictitious Names*, VA. STATE CORP. COMM'N, https://www.scc.virginia.gov/pages/Fictitious-Names (last visited October 14, 2024); Concord Fund, *Fictitious Name Certificate: Judicial Crisis Network*, COMMONWEALTH OF VA. STATE CORP. COMM'N (Feb. 7, 2020) https://www.documentcloud.org/documents/6893513-Concord-Fund-Ficticious-Name-JCN.html.
24. Sheldon Whitehouse, *A Flood of Judicial Lobbying: Amicus Influence and Funding Transparency*, 131 Yale L.J.F. 141, 147–148 (2021).
25. *E.g.*, Scott Shane, *These Are the Ads Russia Bought on Facebook in 2016*, N.Y. TIMES (Nov. 1, 2017), https://www.nytimes.com/2017/11/01/us/politics/russia-2016-election-facebook.html; Harper Neidig, *Franken Blasts Facebook for Accepting Rubles for U.S. Election Ads*, THE HILL (Oct. 31, 2017), https://thehill.com/policy/technology/358102-franken-blasts-facebook-for-accepting-rubles-for-us-election-ads/.
26. *See* Supreme Court Ethics, Recusal, and Transparency Act of 2023, S. 359, 118th Cong. (2023).
27. *See, e.g.*, Joshua Kaplan, Justin Elliott & Alex Mierjeski, *Clarence Thomas and the Billionaire*, PROPUBLICA (Apr. 6, 2023), https://www.propublica.org/article/clarence-thomas-scotus-undisclosed-luxury-travel-gifts-crow (last updated Apr. 7, 2023); Justin Elliott, Joshua Kaplan & Alex Mierjeski, *Justice Samuel Alito Took Luxury Fishing Vacation with GOP Billionaire Who Later Had Cases Before the Court*, PROPUBLICA (June 20, 2023), https://www.propublica.org/article/samuel-alito-luxury-fishing-trip-paul-singer-scotus-supreme-court; Joshua Kaplan, Justin Elliott & Alex Mierjeski, *Clarence Thomas Secretly Participated in Koch Network Donor Events*, PROPUBLICA (Sept. 22, 2023), https://www.propublica.org/article/clarence-thomas-secretly-attended-koch-brothers-donor-events-scotus; Brett Murphy & Alex Mierjeski, *Clarence Thomas' 38 Vacations: The Other Billionaires Who Have Treated the Supreme Court Justice to Luxury Travel*, PROPUBLICA (Aug. 10, 2023), https://www.propublica.org/article/clarence-thomas-other-billionaires-sokol-huizenga-novelly-supreme-court.
28. *See* Supreme Court Biennial Appointments and Term Limits Act of 2023, S. 3096, 118th Cong. (2023).
29. *See* Whitehouse, *supra* note 12, at 886–891.

30. *See, e.g.*, JANE MAYER, DARK MONEY: THE HIDDEN HISTORY OF THE BILLIONAIRES BEHIND THE RISE OF THE RADICAL RIGHT (2016) (documenting the vast network of dark-money groups funded by the Koch family and a small group of like-minded wealthy individuals to influence academic institutions, think tanks, courts, statehouses, Congress, and the presidency); Andrew Perez, Andy Kroll & Justin Elliott, *How a Secretive Billionaire Handed His Fortune to the Architect of the Right-Wing Takeover of the Courts*, PROPUBLICA (Aug. 22, 2022), https://www.propublica.org/article/dark-money-leonard-leo-barre-seid.

CHAPTER 8

1. NEW HAMPSHIRE DEPARTMENT OF JUSTICE, PRESS RELEASE, *Steven Kramer Charged with Voter Suppression over AI-Generated President Biden Robocalls* (2024), https://www.doj.nh.gov/news-and-media/steven-kramer-charged-voter-suppression-over-ai-generated-president-biden-robocalls.
2. Martin Pengelly & Rachel Leingang, *Democrats Sound Alarm over AI Call to Voters Mimicking Biden*, THE GUARDIAN (Jan. 22, 2024), https://www.theguardian.com/us-news/2024/jan/22/biden-fake-robocalls-new-hampshire.
3. Alex Seitz-Wald, *A New Orleans Magician Says Democratic Operative Paid Him to Make the Fake Biden Robocall*, NBC NEWS (Feb. 23, 2024), https://www.nbcnews.com/politics/2024-election/biden-robocall-new-hampshire-strategist-rcna139760.
4. *Id.*
5. *Id.*
6. PRESS RELEASE, *supra* note 2.
7. FED. COMMC'NS COMM'N, PRESS RELEASE, *FCC Proposes $6 Million Fine for Deepfake Robocalls Around NH Primary* (May 23, 2024), https://www.fcc.gov/document/fcc-proposes-6-million-fine-deepfake-robocalls-around-nh-primary.
8. Ken Bensinger, *Elon Musk Shares Manipulated Harris Video, in Seeming Violation of X's Policies*, N.Y. TIMES, July 27, 2024, https://www.nytimes.com/2024/07/27/us/politics/elon-musk-kamala-harris-deepfake.html.
9. Steve Contorno & Donnie O'Sullivan, *DeSantis Campaign Posts Fake Images of Trump Hugging Fauci on Social Media Video*, CNN, June 8, 2023, https://www.cnn.com/2023/06/08/politics/desantis-campaign-video-fake-ai-image/index.html.
10. Carl Campanile, *Attack Ad Uses AI-Generated Voices of Nikki Haley and Tim Scott to Claim They're "Too Woke,"* Sept. 10, 2023, N.Y. POST, https://nypost.com/2023/09/10/attack-ad-uses-ai-generated-voices-of-nikki-haley-and-tim-scott-to-claim-theyre-too-woke/.

11. Aleks Phillips, *Deepfake Video Shows Elizabeth Warren Saying Republicans Shouldn't Vote*, NEWSWEEK, Feb. 27, 2023, https://www.newsweek.com/elizabeth-warren-msnbc-republicans-vote-deep-fake-video-1784117.
12. Whitney Downard, *Braun Hits McCormick with Negative, Digitally-Altered Ad in Governor's Race*, INDIANA CAPITAL CHRON., Sept. 30, 2024, https://indianacapitalchronicle.com/2024/09/30/braun-hits-mccormick-with-negative-digitally-altered-ad-in-governors-race/.
13. David Brooks, *The Fight for the Soul of A.I.*, N.Y. TIMES, Nov. 23, 2023, https://www.nytimes.com/2023/11/23/opinion/sam-altman-openai.html.
14. Gary D. Robertson, *North Carolina Judges Strike Down State's Voter ID Law*, ASSOCIATED PRESS, Sept. 17, 2021, https://apnews.com/article/north-carolina-25c1633fd815ae57ca6c703a45c9d636.
15. BRENNAN CTR. FOR JUST., VOTING LAWS ROUNDUP (Dec. 2021), https://www.brennancenter.org/our-work/research-reports/voting-laws-roundup-december-2021.
16. Molly Weisner, *Trust in Government Hits Fresh Lows Ahead of US Presidential Election*, FEDERAL TIMES, June 10, 2024, https://www.federaltimes.com/management/career/2024/06/10/trust-in-government-hits-fresh-lows-ahead-of-us-presidential-election/.
17. FEDERAL ELECTION COMMISSION, "Commission Updates Regulations to Address Technological Advances," Feb. 20, 2024, https://www.fec.gov/updates/commission-updates-regulations-to-address-technological-advances/.
18. Allison Carter, *Where Americans Get Their News: New Data from Pew Research*, PR DAILY, Nov. 16, 2023, https://www.prdaily.com/where-americans-get-their-news-new-data-from-pew-research/.
19. Kerry Flynn, *How Gen Z Gets Its News*, AXIOS, Feb. 16, 2024, http://www.axios.com/2024/02/16/tiktok-news-gen-z-social-media.
20. Dan Eggen, *Post-Watergate Campaign Finance Reforms Undercut by Changes*, WASH. POST, June 16, 2012, https://www.washingtonpost.com/politics/post-watergate-campaign-finance-limits-undercut-by-changes/2012/06/16/gJQAinRrhV_story.html.
21. Bob Woodward & Carl Bernstein, *Nixon Debated Paying Blackmail, Clemency*, WASH. POST, May 1, 1974, https://www.washingtonpost.com/wp-srv/national/longterm/watergate/articles/050174-2.htm.
22. P.L. 93-443.
23. *Buckley v. Valeo*, 424 U.S. 1, 19 (1976).
24. *Id.* at 29, 51.
25. *Id.* at 48.
26. *McConnell v. Federal Election Commission*, 540 U.S. 93 (2003).
27. P.L. 107-155.
28. *McConnell*, 540 U.S. at 126-129.

29. Amy Howe, *Sandra Day O'Connor, First Woman on the Supreme Court, Dies at 93*, SCOTUSBLOG, Dec. 21, 2023, https://www.scotusblog.com/2023/12/sandra-day-oconnor-first-woman-on-the-supreme-court-dies-at-93/.
30. *McConnell*, 540 U.S. at 136–137 (internal citations omitted).
31. *Id.* at 143, 150.
32. *Id.*
33. David Gans, *Roberts at 10*: *Campaign Finance and Voting Rights*, CONST. ACCOUNTABILITY CTR., Nov. 14, 2014, https://www.theusconstitution.org/think_tank/chapter-2-campaign-finance-and-voting-rights-easier-to-donate-harder-to-vote/.
34. Monica Youn, *Citizens United*: *The Aftermath*, BRENNAN CTR. JUST., June 8, 2010, https://www.brennancenter.org/our-work/research-reports/citizens-united-aftermath-issue-brief-american-constitutional-society.
35. *See id.*
36. *See* Order in Pending Case *Citizens United v. Federal Election Commission*, 558 U.S. 310 (2010), https://www.fec.gov/resources/legal-resources/litigation/citizens_united_sc_08_order_rearg.pdf.
37. 558 U.S. at 365–366.
38. *Id.* at 359.
39. *McConnell*, 540 U.S. at 143.
40. *Citizens United*, 558 U.S. at 360; *see also* Youn, *supra* note 35.
41. *Citizens United*, 558 U.S. at 357.
42. *Id.* at 447, 448 (Stevens, J., dissenting).
43. Anna Massoglia, *"Dark Money" Groups Have Poured Billions into Federal Elections Since the Supreme Court's 2010* Citizens United *Decision*, OPENSECRETS, Jan. 24. 2023, https://www.opensecrets.org/news/2023/01/dark-money-groups-have-poured-billions-into-federal-elections-since-the-supreme-courts-2010-citizens-united-decision.
44. FED. ELECTORAL COMM'N, CONTRIBUTION LIMITS 2013–2014, https://www.fec.gov/help-candidates-and-committees/candidate-taking-receipts/archived-contribution-limits; UNITED STATES CENSUS BUREAU, INCOME AND POVERTY IN THE UNITED STATES: 2014, https://www.census.gov/library/publications/2015/demo/p60-252.html.
45. Jesse Wegman, *McCutcheon: Another Blow to Democracy*, N.Y. TIMES, Apr. 2, 2014, https://archive.nytimes.com/takingnote.blogs.nytimes.com/2014/04/02/mccutcheon-another-blow-to-democracy/; Michael Beckel, *Supreme Court Mulls Axing Campaign Donation Limits in "McCutcheon" Case*, CTR. FOR RESPONSIVE POL., Oct. 8, 2013, https://publicintegrity.org/politics/supreme-court-mulls-axing-campaign-donation-limits-in-mccutcheon-case/.
46. *McCutcheon v. Federal Election Commission*, 572 U.S. 185, 192, 207 (2014).
47. *Id.* at 208 (internal citations omitted).
48. *Id.* at 192.

49. *Buckley*, 424 U.S. at 67.
50. *Id.*
51. *Id.* at 68.
52. *Citizens United*, 558 U.S. at 371.
53. *Id.* at 370 (internal citations omitted).
54. *Id.* at 367 (quoting *McConnell*, 540 U.S. at 197), 371.
55. *McCutcheon*, 572 U.S. at 223–224.
56. *Doe v. Reed*, 561 U.S. 186, 228 (2010) (Scalia, J., concurring).
57. END CITIZENS UNITED, ET AL., *For the People Act Support and Messaging: Research Findings Prepared for End Citizens United*, Feb. 2021, https://ecuactionfund.org/wp-content/uploads/2021/03/ECU-LAV-AF-HR1-F02.26.pdf.
58. *See generally* JANE MAYER, DARK MONEY: THE HIDDEN HISTORY OF THE BILLIONAIRES BEHIND THE RISE OF THE RADICAL RIGHT (2016).
59. Danielle Kurtzleben, *How Politics Is Shaping Language: "Dark Money" Added to Dictionary*, NPR, May 27, 2015, https://www.npr.org/sections/itsallpolitics/2015/05/27/410019723/how-politics-is-shaping-language-dark-money-added-to-dictionary.
60. Anna Massoglia, *Record Contributions from Dark Money Groups and Shell Companies Flooded 2022 Midterm Elections*, OPENSECRETS, June 23, 2023, https://www.opensecrets.org/news/2023/06/record-contributions-dark-money-groups-shell-companies-flooded-midterm-elections-2022.
61. Massoglia, *"Dark Money" Groups.*Click here to enter text.
62. H.R. 5175 (111th Cong.); Senate Roll Call Vote Number 240, Sept. 23, 2010 (111th Cong.).
63. H.R. 1 (116th Cong); H.R. 1 (117th Cong.); H.R. 5746 (117th Cong.).
64. April Rubin, *Former Ohio Legislator Found Guilty of Racketeering in $60 Million Scheme*, N.Y. TIMES, Mar. 9, 2023, https://www.nytimes.com/2023/03/09/us/politics/ohio-householder-borges-bribery.html.
65. Andrew J. Tobias, *FirstEnergy Document Trove Reveals Dark Money's Extensive Influence over Ohio's Politics. Here's How It Works*, CLEVELAND.COM, Apr. 28, 2024, https://www.cleveland.com/news/2024/04/firstenergy-document-trove-reveals-dark-moneys-extensive-influence-over-ohio-politics-heres-how-it-works.html; Tyler Buchanan, *FirstEnergy Money Flowed to Ohio Politicians Who Supported Householder-Backed HB6*, OHIO CAPITAL J., July 21, 2020, https://ohiocapitaljournal.com/2020/07/21/firstenergy-money-flowed-to-ohio-politicians-who-supported-householder-backed-hb6/.
66. Julie Bykowicz, *Supreme Court's "Dark Money" Rulings Anchor Defense in Ohio Political Corruption Trial*, WALL ST. J., Mar. 7, 2023, https://www.wsj.com/articles/supreme-courts-dark-money-rulings-anchor-defense-in-ohio-corruption-trial-dof2f045.

67. Georgia Lyon, *Secret Money Puts Our Health and Safety at Risk*, CAMPAIGN LEGAL CTR., July 23, 2020, https://campaignlegal.org/update/secret-money-puts-our-health-and-safety-risk.
68. *For the People*: *Our American Democracy*: *Hearing Before the U.S. House Committee on House Administration* (testimony of Peter Earle) (116th Cong.), https://docs.house.gov/meetings/HA/HA00/20190214/108899/HHRG-116-HA00-Wstate-EarleP-20190214.pdf.
69. *See id.*
70. *See id.*
71. Ali Swenson & Kelvin Chan, *Election Disinformation Takes a Big Leap with AI Being Used to Deceive Worldwide*, ASSOCIATED PRESS, March 14, 2024, https://apnews.com/article/artificial-intelligence-elections-disinformation-chatgpt-bc283e7426402f0b4baa7df280a4c3fd.
72. Zeve Sanderson et al., *Misunderstood Mechanics*: *How AI, TikTok, and the Liar's Dividend Might Affect the 2024 Elections*, BROOKINGS (2024), https://www.brookings.edu/articles/misunderstood-mechanics-how-ai-tiktok-and-the-liars-dividend-might-affect-the-2024-elections/.
73. Cybersecurity and Infrastructure Security Agency, *Risk in Focus*: *Generative A.I. and the 2024 Election Cycle* (2024), https://www.cisa.gov/sites/default/files/2024-05/Consolidated_Risk_in_Focus_Gen_AI_ElectionsV2_508c.pdf.
74. *AI and the Future of Our Elections*: *Hearing Before the U.S. Senate Committee on Rules and Administration* (118th Cong.).
75. *Id.*
76. Pranshu Verma & Cat Zakrewski, *AI Deepfakes Threaten to Upend Global Elections. No One Can Stop Them*, WASH. POST, Apr. 23, 2024, https://www.washingtonpost.com/technology/2024/04/23/ai-deepfake-election-2024-us-india; Morgan Meaker, *Slovakia's Election Deepfakes Show AI Is a Danger to Democracy*, WIRED, Oct. 3, 2023, https://www.wired.com/story/slovakias-election-deepfakes-show-ai-is-a-danger-to-democracy; Jack Nicas & Lucía Cholakian Herrera, *Is Argentina the First A.I. Election?*, N.Y. TIMES, Nov. 15, 2023, https://www.nytimes.com/2023/11/15/world/americas/argentina-election-ai-milei-massa.html.
77. OFF. DIR. NAT'L INTEL., ASSESSING RUSSIAN ACTIVITIES AND INTENTIONS IN RECENT US ELECTIONS, Jan. 6, 2017, https://www.dni.gov/files/documents/ICA_2017_01.pdf.
78. *Report of the U.S. Senate Select Committee on Intelligence on Russian Active Measures Campaigns and Interference in the 2016 U.S. Election, Volume 2*: *Russia's Use of Social Media* (116th Cong.).
79. *Joint Statement from the Departments of Justice and Homeland Security Assessing the Impact of Foreign Interference During the 2022 U.S. Mid-Term Election*, DEP'T OF JUST., Dec. 18, 2023, https://www.justice.gov/opa/pr/joint-statement-departments-justice-and-homeland-security-assessing-

impact-foreign-0; *Joint Statement from Elections Infrastructure Government Coordinating Council & the Election Infrastructure Sector Coordinating Executive Committees*, Nov. 12, 2020, https://www.cisa.gov/news-events/news/joint-statement-elections-infrastructure-government-coordinating-council-election.

80. *Director Wray's Remarks at the Intelligence and National Security Alliance Leadership Breakfast, Press Release*, FED. BUREAU OF INVESTIGATION, Feb. 29, 2024, https://www.fbi.gov/news/speeches/director-wray-s-remarks-at-the-intelligence-and-national-security-alliance-leadership-breakfast.

81. Eric Tucker, *FBI Warns That Foreign Adversaries Could Use AI to Spread Disinformation About US Elections*, ASSOCIATED PRESS (May 9, 2024), https://apnews.com/article/fbi-ai-russia-china-election-security-7200abc0215e822c84f032605bed41b9#; Josh Margolin & Sasha Pezenik, *DHS Warns of Threats to Election Posed by Artificial Intelligence*, ABC NEWS (May 20, 2024), https://abcnews.go.com/Politics/dhs-warns-threats-election-posedai/story?id=110367438.

82. Josh A. Goldstein & Andrew Lohn, *Deepfakes, Elections, and Shrinking the Liar's Dividend*, BRENNAN CTR. FOR JUST., Jan. 23, 2024, https://www.brennancenter.org/our-work/research-reports/deepfakes-elections-and-shrinking-liars-dividend.

83. *See* Massoglia, *supra* note 61.

84. Karl Evers-Hillstrom, *More Money, Less Transparency: A Decade Under* Citizens United, OPENSECRETS, Jan. 14, 2020, https://www.opensecrets.org/news/reports/a-decade-under-citizens-united?year=2023.

85. *Did Money Win?*, OPENSECRETS (last visited June 22, 2024), https://www.opensecrets.org/elections-overview/winning-vs-spending.

86. *See* Andy Cerda & Andrew Daniller, *Seven Facts About Americans' Views of Money in Politics*, PEW RESEARCH CTR., Oct. 23, 2023, https://www.pewresearch.org/short-reads/2023/10/23/7-facts-about-americans-views-of-money-in-politics; PEW RESEARCH CTR., *Americans' Top Policy Priority for 2024: Strengthening the Economy*, Feb. 29, 2024, https://www.pewresearch.org/politics/2024/02/29/americans-top-policy-priority-for-2024-strengthening-the-economy/.

87. TRACKER: STATE LEGISLATION ON DEEPFAKES IN ELECTIONS, PUBLIC CITIZEN (last visited August 6, 2024), https://www.citizen.org/article/tracker-legislation-on-deepfakes-in-elections/.

88. *Id.*

89. Michelle Chapman, *AI That Alters Voice and Imagery in Political Ads Will Require Disclosure on Google and YouTube*, ASSOCIATED PRESS, Sept. 7, 2023, https://apnews.com/article/google-ai-ads-political-policy-fake-792cbae3e651d31028ae2c64f65f112c; Katie Paul, *Meta Bars Political Advertisers from Using Generative AI Ads Tools*, REUTERS, Nov. 7, 2023, https://www.reuters.com/technology/meta-bar-political-advertisers-using-

generative-ai-ads-tools-2023-11-06/; Asa Fitch, *OpenAI Bans Use of AI Tools for Campaigning, Voter Suppression*, WALL ST. J., Jan. 15, 2024, https://www.wsj.com/tech/ai/openai-bans-use-of-ai-tools-for-campaigning-voter-suppression-2308fb98.
90. Minn. Stat §, 609.771; Tex. Election Code Ann. § 255.004.
91. *Dollars and Sense: How Undisclosed Money and Post-McCutcheon Campaign Finance Will Affect 2014 and Beyond*, Hearing before the US Senate Committee on Rules and Administration, 113 Cong. (2014) (Testimony of Justice John Paul Stevens).

CHAPTER 9

1. 424 U.S. 1 (1976) (per curiam).
2. *See* Deborah Hellman, *Defining Corruption and Constitutionalizing Democracy*, 111 Mich. L. Rev. 1385 (2013) (arguing that by defining "corruption" in the context of campaign finance cases, the Supreme Court implicitly defines its vision of good government as well and pointing out the tension between the Court's inability to define proper electoral functioning in cases of alleged partisan gerrymandering and its zeal to define corruption in campaign finance cases).
3. *Buckley*, 424 U.S. at 25–27.
4. 494 U.S. 652 (1990), overruled by *Citizens United v. FEC*, 558 U.S. 310 (2010).
5. *Austin*, 494 U.S. at 660.
6. 540 U.S. 93 (2003).
7. *Id.* at 153 (finding that "[j]ust as troubling to a functioning democracy as classic quid pro quo corruption is the danger that officeholders will decide issues not on the merits or the desires of their constituencies, but according to the wishes of those who have made large financial contributions valued by the officeholder").
8. 558 U.S. 310 (2010).
9. *Id.* at 357.
10. *Id.* at 360.
11. *See Davis v. FEC*, 554 U.S. 724, 740–741 (2008) (concluding that "reliance on personal funds reduces the threat of corruption" when corruption is understood as a *quid pro quo* exchange).
12. *Citizens United*, 558 U.S. at 360.
13. *Marbury v. Madison*, 5 U.S. (1 Cranch) 137, 177 (1803).
14. *See, e.g., Lochner v. New York*, 198 U.S. 45, 75 (1905) (Holmes, J., dissenting) (in which Justice Holmes makes a similar point regarding the fact that the Constitution does not embrace any particular economic theory).
15. Some scholars argue that there is a constitutional conception of corruption that can be gleaned from the constitutional text as a whole. See, e.g., Zephyr Teachout, *The Anti-Corruption Principle*, 94 Cornell L. Rev. 341

(2009) (arguing for a structural anti-corruption principle embedded within the Constitution that is akin to the principles of federalism and separation of powers).
16. *New York State Rifle & Pistol Ass'n v. Bruen*, 507 U.S. 1, 17 (2022) (rejecting the approach to analyzing whether laws violate constitutionally protected rights by assessing whether regulation protects an "important interest" and instead requiring that "the government . . . demonstrate that the regulation is consistent with this Nation's historical tradition of firearm regulation").
17. *See* Hellman, *supra* note 3 at 1391–1396 (explaining that corruption is a derivative concept and depends for its meaning on a view about healthy functioning of the particular institution that is arguably corrupted).
18. *Id.* at 1399–1400 (describing one possible conception of corruption, "Corruption as the Distortion of Influence").
19. Justice Kennedy, concurring in the judgment in part and dissenting in part in *McConnell v. FEC*, asserts that such responsiveness to donors is part of a well-functioning democratic system. *See McConnell*, 540 U.S. at 297 (asserting that "[i]t is well understood that a substantial and legitimate reason, if not the only reason, to cast a vote for, or to make a contribution to, one candidate over another is that the candidate will respond by producing those political outcomes the supporter favors").
20. *See* 558 U.S. 310, 361 (2010).
21. *Id.* at 360.
22. *Id.* at 362.
23. 579 U.S. 550 (2016).
24. While McDonnell was charged under statutes prohibiting Honest Services Fraud and extortion, the Court interpreted these statutes to require an exchange of value for an "official act" as understood under the federal bribery statute. *See id.* at 574.
25. *Id.* at 562.
26. McDonnell, 579 U.S. at 574 (holding that "[s]etting up a meeting, talking to another official, or organizing an event (or agreeing to do so)—without more—does not fit that definition of 'official act'").
27. *See id.* at 567–568, 571–572.
28. *See generally* Deborah Hellman, *A Theory of Bribery*, 38 Cardozo L. Rev. 1947 (developing an account of bribery that is capable of distinguishing bribery from payment and that accords with the federal bribery statutes and existing case law).
29. The Supreme Court's conception of what is an official act in *McDonnell* may be in tension with its recent broader understanding of "official" actions of the President. See *Trump v. United States*, 144 S. Ct. 2312, 2339–2340 (2024) (in which the Court includes within the "outer perimeter of" a President's "official responsibilities" things like "most of a President's public communications" which include communications that are not exercises of official

power). The definition of "official act" was also at issue in the prosecution of Senator Robert Menendez, who argued a sort of "heads I win, tails you lose" position that either his actions were not exercises of governmental power and thus not official acts under *McDonnell* or else they were exercises of official power and therefore nearly always immune from liability under the immunity provided by the "Speech and Debate" clause of the Constitution. See Senator Robert Menendez's Memorandum of Law in Support of His First Motion to Dismiss at 13–16, *United States v. Menendez*, No. 23-cr-490 (S.D.N.Y. Jan. 10, 2024).

30. *See, e.g.*, Brief of Amici Curiae Law Professors in Support of Petitioner at 15, *McDonnell v. United States*, 579 U.S. 550 (2016) (No. 15-474), 2015 WL 7252897 (arguing that "[t]he law cannot suggest that 'ingratiation and access . . . are not corruption' (and indeed are protected by the First Amendment), while providing prosecutors with nearly unfettered ability to criminalize the routine behavior of government officials who cater to their supporters in exactly this manner").

31. The Court assessing whether an interest is compelling when applying strict scrutiny would clearly not be deferring to legislative judgments about whether the campaign finance law at issue is justified. Nonetheless, when a Court sets out to determine whether an interest is compelling, it must make an assessment about its importance. That judgment relates to facts in the world, and so other laws enacted by legislatures that prohibit such conduct may be relevant to the Court in reaching its own independent judgment about whether prohibiting certain conduct is, in fact, compelling.

32. This conduct would be unlikely to fall within the prohibitions of other anti-corruption statutes—although that conclusion is not certain—including 18 U.S.C. § 1951 (Hobbs Act), 18 U.S.C. § 1346 (Honest Services Fraud) or 18 U.S.C. § 666 (Federal Programs Bribery). Since *McDonnell*, courts have held *McDonnell*'s definition of "official act" to limit the *quo* necessary for conviction under the Hobbs Act. See *United States v. Silver*, 864 F.3d 102, 116–117 (2d Cir. 2017); see also *Dimora v. United States*, 973 F.3d 496, 504 (6th Cir. 2020). Honest Services Fraud is limited to "bribes and kickbacks," *Skilling v. United States*, 561 U.S. 358, 368 (2010). While it is not certain that courts will apply the *McDonnell* definition of "official acts" when applying this statute, it is also not certain that they will not. *See* Silver, 864 F.3d at 124 (overturning both Hobbs Act and Honest Services Fraud jury instructions as overly broad after *McDonnell*); but see *United States v. Ma*, 2021 WL 5860893 *1, *2 (9th Cir. 2021) (finding sufficient evidence to convict the defendant of honest services fraud when he repeatedly received gifts from a particular sender and acted to the sender's benefit, and the sender referred to the defendant as an "ally in law enforcement," even though there was no explicit agreement made regarding any specific official act). Finally, in the recent Supreme Court case addressing Federal Programs Bribery, the Court used the "official acts"

language from 18 U.S.C. § 201, even though 18 U.S.C. § 666(a)(1)(B) does not actually include such language. See *Snyder v. United States*, 144 S. Ct. 1947, 1954–1955 (2024). That inclusion provides some support for the view that the Court would likely require the same "official act" under 18 U.S.C. § 666(a)(1)(B) that it did in *McDonnell*.
33. *McDonnell*, 579 U.S. at 574–575.
34. See 18 U.S.C. § 597 (criminalizing the offering or accepting of any expenditure to any person to vote or not vote for or against any candidate); Voting Rights Act of 1965, 52 U.S.C. § 10307(e)(1) (prohibiting anyone from voting twice in federal elections).
35. *See Baker v. Carr*, 369 U.S. 186, 237 (1962); *Wesberry v. Sanders*, 376 U.S. 1, 7–8 (1964).
36. *Buckley*, 424 U.S. at 45, 48–49 (rejecting other state interests such as equalizing the ability of citizens to affect electoral outcomes or limiting the influence of money as not sufficiently compelling to justify restrictions on speech).
37. Since *McDonnell*, some states have enacted gift prohibitions barring public officials such as legislators from receiving gifts (see, e.g., Vt. Stat. Ann. tit. 3, § 1203g (2021)), while others have either raised the permissible financial threshold (see Kan. Stat. Ann. § 46-237a (2018)) or lowered it (*see* Okla. St. tit. 74, ch. 62, App. I, Rule 5.8, 5.11 (2014) (amended in 2017)). Some states have also redefined their gift definitions in state constitutions (see, e.g., Ark. Const. art. 19, § 30(b)(2)(A)(ii) (amended in 2017)), executive orders (see Ga. Exec. Order No. 04.01.21.57 § 2 (2021)), or statutes (see Mont. Code Ann. § 2-2-102(3) (2023)). However, since *McDonnell*, no state has modified its definition of bribery to forbid an exchange of value for access.
38. *McDonnell*, 579 U.S. at 568–569, 574, relies on canons of interpretation, including *noscitur a sociis* or "a word is known by the company it keeps," to conclude that the meaning of "official act" in the federal bribery statute excludes merely "[s]etting up a meeting, talking to another official, or organizing an event (or agreeing to do so)."
39. *Id.* at 577.
40. The so-called "criminalization of politics" is a related concern. *See, e.g.*, George D. Brown, *McDonnell and the Criminalization of Politics*, 5 Va. J. Crim. L. 1, 4 (2017) (explaining the essence of the critique as follows: "The major role in prosecuting state and local corruption has been assumed by the federal government, and is discharged by United States attorneys" who "have at their disposal a broad array of broadly worded statutes" which together "raises such dangers as traps for the unwary, partisan prosecutions brought by politically motivated prosecutors, and threats to federalist values").
41. 144 S. Ct. 1947, 1951, 1956 (2024), (finding that Section 666 of Title 18 which "makes it a crime for state and local officials to 'corruptly' solicit, accept, or agree to accept 'anything of value from any person, intending to be influenced or rewarded' for an official act" prohibits only bribery and does

not prohibit the acceptance of a gratuity, in part because "[i]nterpreting § 666 as a gratuities statute would significantly infringe on bedrock federalism principles").
42. *Id.* at 1971–1972 (Jackson, J., dissenting) (arguing that the "the majority's pages of citations to state and local gratuities laws . . . thus belie its ranking so-called 'federalism' interests merely '[f]ifth' on its list of reasons for construing § 666 as a bribery-only statute" and asserting that "the majority itself harbors the belief it repeatedly ascribes to Congress: that regulation of gratuities is better left to state, local, and tribal governments, rather than the Federal Government").
43. By contrast, Jennifer Ahearn argues for revision of federal law in order to "appropriately define which acts it should be a crime for a government official to sell." See Jennifer Ahearn, *A Way Forward for Congress on Bribery After McDonnell*, 121 Dickinson L. Rev. 1013, 1016 (2017) (arguing that Congress should draw on language from federal conflict-of-interest laws in revising federal bribery law).
44. For example, in *McDonnell*, the Court also defends its holding on the grounds that "where a more limited interpretation of 'official act' is supported by both text and precedent, we decline to 'construe the statute in a manner that leaves its outer boundaries ambiguous. . . .'" *McDonnell*, 579 U.S. at 576–577.
45. Daniel Richman sees concerns about selective prosecution as underlying several of the Court's decisions narrowing the reach of federal anti-corruption statutes. *See* Daniel C. Richman, *Navigating Between "Politics as Usual" and Sacks of Cash*, 133 Yale L. J. Forum 564, 565 (2023) (arguing that "the Court is driven by a concern that statutory interpretations criminalizing 'normal' political activity would not lead to even-handed prosecutions of all such political actors but run the risk of partisan targeting").

CHAPTER 10

1. Hughes Mearns, *Antigonish*, Poets.org, https://poets.org/poem/antigonish-i-met-man-who-wasnt-there (last visited Nov. 18, 2024).
2. *FEC v. Wis. Right to Life, Inc.*, 551 U.S. 449, 478–479 (2007).
3. *McCutcheon v. FEC*, 572 U.S. 185, 206 (2014) (plurality opinion) (emphasis added). This is an exaggeration because informing voters is a rationale for campaign finance disclosure laws, *see, e.g., Buckley v. Valeo*, 424 U.S. 1, 66–67 (1976) (per curiam), maintaining public confidence in the judiciary is a rationale for limits on fundraising by judicial candidates, *see, e.g., Williams-Yulee v. Fla. Bar*, 575 U.S. 433, 444–446 (2015), preserving the American political community is a rationale for barring contributions by foreign citizens, *see, e.g., Bluman v. FEC*, 800 F. Supp. 2d 281, 287–288 (D.C. Cir. 2011), and promoting merit-based public administration is another rationale for pay-to-play laws, *see, e.g., Wagner v. FEC*, 793 F.3d 1, 8–10 (D.C. Cir. 2015) (en banc).

4. In earlier cases, the Court sometimes acknowledged evidence of *quid pro quo* corruption. *See, e.g., Nixon v. Shrink Mo. Gov't PAC*, 528 U.S. 377, 393–394 (2000); *Buckley*, 424 U.S. at 27.
5. 540 U.S. 93 (2003).
6. *Id.* at 149.
7. *McConnell v. FEC*, 251 F. Supp. 2d 176, 395 (D.D.C. 2003) (opinion of Henderson, J.), *aff'd in part and rev'd in part*, 540 U.S. 93 (2003) (emphasis omitted).
8. *See McConnell*, 540 U.S. at 143–145.
9. *Id.* at 152; *see also McCutcheon v. FEC*, 572 U.S. 185, 244 (2014) (Breyer, J., dissenting) (flagging the Court's "rejection of the broader definition of corruption, upon which *McConnell*'s holding depends").
10. 558 U.S. 310 (2010).
11. *Id.* at 360 (internal quotation marks omitted).
12. *Id.* at 357.
13. *Id.*
14. *Id.* at 361 (italics omitted).
15. 596 U.S. 289 (2022).
16. *Id.* at 307 (italics omitted).
17. *Id.*
18. *Id.* at 313.
19. *See, e.g., McCutcheon v. FEC*, 572 U.S. 185, 209 n.7 (2014) (plurality opinion) ("The Government presents no evidence concerning the circumvention of base limits from the 30 States with base limits but no aggregate limits."); *Randall v. Sorrell*, 548 U.S. 230, 261 (2006) (plurality opinion) ("The record contains no indication that . . . corruption (or its appearance) in Vermont is significantly more serious a matter than elsewhere.").
20. For good descriptions of this literature, see Stephen Ansolabehere et al., *Why Is There So Little Money in U.S. Politics?*, 17 J. ECON. PERSPS. 105 (2003); Douglas D. Roscoe & Shannon Jenkins, *A Meta-Analysis of Campaign Contributions' Impact on Roll Call Voting*, 86 SOC. SCI. Q. 52 (2005); Thomas Stratmann, *Some Talk: Money in Politics. A (Partial) Review of the Literature*, 124 PUB. CHOICE 135 (2005).
21. Ansolabehere et al., *supra* note 21, at 116.
22. *Id.*
23. *Id.*
24. Jeffrey Milyo, *Corporate Influence and Political Corruption: Lessons from Stock Market Reactions to Political Events*, 19 INDEP. REV. 19, 31 (2014).
25. Eleanor Neff Powell & Justin Grimmer, *Money in Exile: Campaign Contributions and Committee Access*, 78 J. POL. 974, 976 (2016).
26. *Id.*; *see also, e.g.*, Anthony Fowler et al., *Quid Pro Quo? Corporate Returns to Campaign Contributions*, 82 J. POL. 844, 854 (2020) ("Taking both our findings as well as those in the literature at face value, corporate campaign

contributions may be cause for concern in (only) a limited number of circumstances"); Christopher Robertson et al., *The Appearance and the Reality of Quid Pro Quo Corruption: An Empirical Investigation*, 8 J. LEGAL ANALYSIS 375, 392 (2016) ("[T]he consensus in the field of political science remains skeptical that political spending does produce results that are anything like a *quid pro quo* exchange.").

27. *See* Roscoe & Jenkins, *supra* note 21, at 57.
28. *See* Stratmann, *supra* note 21, at 146.
29. *See, e.g.*, Ansolabehere et al., *supra* note 21, at 114 (discussing this "simultaneity" problem).
30. *See* Christopher Witko, *Campaign Contributions, Access, and Government Contracting*, 21 J. PUB. ADMIN. RSCH. & THEORY 761, 770 (2011).
31. *See id.* at 774.
32. *See id.*
33. *See id.* at 775.
34. *See* Mihály Fazekas et al., *Agency Independence, Campaign Contributions, and Favoritism in US Federal Government Contracting*, 33 J. PUB. ADMIN. RSCH. & THEORY 262, 266 (2022).
35. *See id.* at 271.
36. *See id.*
37. *See* Piet Eichholtz & Oana Floroiu, *Corporate Political Contributions and the Allocation of U.S. Federal Procurements*, 65 J. FIN. 687 (2017).
38. *See* Daniel Bromberg, *Can Vendors Buy Influence? The Relationship Between Campaign Contributions and Government Contracts*, 37 INT'L J. PUB. ADMIN. 556, 562, 564 (2014).
39. *See* Jonathan Brogaard et al., *Political Influence and Government Investment: Evidence from Contract-Level Data* 13, 16 (Aug. 2016).
40. *See* Jeffrey R. Brown & Jiekun Huang, *All the President's Friends: Political Access and Firm Value*, 138 J. FIN. ECON. 415, 427–428 (2020).
41. *See* Michael J. Hogan et al., *Campaign Contributions, Post-War Reconstruction Contracts, and State Crime*, 27 DEVIANT BEHAV. 269, 283 (2006).
42. *See* Michael J. Hogan et al., *Campaign Contributions, Lobbying, and Post-Katrina Contracts*, 34 DISASTERS 593, 600 (2010).
43. *See* Brogaard et al., *supra* note 40, at 20.
44. *See id.* at 22.
45. *See* Fazekas, *supra* note 35, at 272–275.
46. *See supra* note 41 and accompanying text.
47. *See* Brown & Huang, *supra* note 41, at 419–420.
48. *See* Ahmed Tahoun, *The Role of Stock Ownership by US Members of Congress on the Market for Political Favors*, 111 J. FIN. ECON. 86, 95–96 (2014).
49. *See id.* at 100–102.
50. *See* Carl Dahlström et al., *Partisan Procurement: Contracting with the United States Federal Government, 2003-2015*, 65 AM. J. POL. SCI. 652, 660–661

(2021); Fazekas, *supra* note 35, at 272–275; George A. Krause & Matthew Zarit, *Selling Out? Contingent Politicization and Contracting Risk in U.S. Federal Procurements, 2001–2016*, 2 J. POL. INST. & POL. ECON. 509, 525–528 (2021).
51. *See* Dahlström et al., *supra* note 51, at 660–661; Fazekas, *supra* note 35, at 275; Krause & Zarit, *supra* note 51, at 525–528.
52. *See* Brogaard et al., *supra* note 40, at 17–18.
53. *See* Arturo Romero Yáñez & Neel U. Sukhatme, *Judges for Sale: The Effect of Campaign Contributions on State Criminal Courts* 16 (Apr. 6, 2023).
54. *See id.*
55. *See id.* at 20.
56. *See id.* at 21.
57. *See* Paulo Arvate et al., *Campaign Donation and Government Contracts in Brazilian States* (Sao Paolo Sch. Econ. Working Paper 336, Dec. 6, 2013).
58. *See* Saad Gulzar et al., *Do Campaign Contribution Limits Curb the Influence of Money in Politics?*, 66 AM. J. POL. SCI. 932 (2022).
59. *See* Ana Grdović Gnip, *All You Need Is* Political *Love? Assessing the Effects of Partisan Favouritism in Croatia's Public Procurement*, 75 EUR. J. POL. ECON. 102170 (2022).
60. *See* Vitezslav Titl & Benny Geys, *Political Donations and the Allocation of Public Procurement Contracts*, 111 EUR. ECON. REV. 443 (2019).
61. *See* Audinga Baltrunaite, *Political Contributions and Public Procurement: Evidence from Lithuania*, 18 J. EUR. ECON. ASS'N 541 (2020).
62. *See id.* at 557.
63. *See id.* at 543.
64. *See id.* at 569–572.
65. *See id.* at 544.
66. *See Nixon v. Shrink Mo. Gov't PAC*, 528 U.S. 377, 394–395 (2000).
67. *FEC v. Cruz*, 596 U.S. 289, 309 (2022) (italics omitted).
68. *Id.* (internal quotation marks omitted).
69. *See, e.g.*, Brogaard et al., *supra* note 40, at 14–15; Brown & Huang, *supra* note 40, at 427–428; Eichholtz & Floroiu, *supra* note 38, at 18; Fazekas, *supra* note 35, at 269–270; Witko, *supra* note 31, at 771; Yáñez & Sukhatme, *supra* note 54, at 15–16.
70. *See* Brogaard et al., *supra* note 40, at 13–14.
71. *See* Yáñez & Sukhatme, *supra* note 54, at 20.
72. *See id.* at 21.
73. *See* Baltrunaite, *supra* note 62, at 557.
74. Oral Argument at 40, *Gill v. Whitford*, 585 U.S. 48 (2018) (No. 16-1161).
75. *See Wagner v. FEC*, 793 F.3d 1, 11–12 (D.C. Cir. 2015) (en banc).
76. FINAL RPT. OF SELECT COMM. ON PRESIDENTIAL CAMPAIGN ACTIVITIES, S. REP. NO. 93-981, at 1210 & n.85 (1974) (separate views of Sen. Weicker) (italics omitted).

77. *Wagner*, 793 F.3d at 15 n.17.
78. *United States v. Williams*, 529 F. Supp. 1085, 1091 (E.D.N.Y. 1981).
79. *See id.* at 1090.
80. Ciara Torres-Spelliscy, *Safeguarding Markets from Pernicious Pay to Play: A Model Explaining Why the SEC Regulates Money in Politics*, 12 CONN. PUB. INT. L.J. 361, 385 (2013) (internal quotation marks omitted).
81. *See id.* at 384.
82. *See Wagner*, 793 F.3d at 16–17.
83. *Id.* at 16.
84. *Id.* at 15.
85. *Id.* (internal quotation marks omitted).
86. *See* Marty Schladen, *Analysis: Bribery Scandal Shows How Ohio Politics Is Polluted with Dark Money*, OHIO CAPITAL J., Mar. 15, 2023, https://ohiocapitaljournal.com/2023/03/15/analysis-bribery-scandal-showed-how-ohio-politics-is-polluted-with-dark-money/.
87. *See 70 Current and Former NYCHA Employees Charged with Bribery and Extortion Offenses*, U.S. DEP'T OF JUSTICE (Feb. 6, 2024), https://www.justice.gov/usao-sdny/pr/70-current-and-former-nycha-employees-charged-bribery-and-extortion-offenses.
88. *See, e.g., Wagner*, 793 F.3d at 17 & n.17 (providing "an impressive, if dismaying, account of pay-to-play contracting scandals").
89. *See* CONG. RSCH. SERV., PRIVATE BILLS: PROCEDURE IN THE HOUSE 1 (2024).
90. *See, e.g.*, Michael Hadani et al., *The More You Give, The More You Get? The Impact of Corporate Political Activity on the Value of Government Contracts*, 122 BUS. & SOC'Y REV. 421, 431 (2017) ("distinguish[ing] between diffused or concentrated public policy benefits, and diffused or concentrated public policy costs").
91. *See, e.g.*, Richard A. Hasen, *Why Isn't Congress More Corrupt? A Preliminary Inquiry*, 84 FORDHAM L. REV. 429, 438 (2015) ("An individual U.S. representative [typically] has very little leverage to offer something of use to many people looking for a special interest deal.").
92. Any personal *policy* views, that is. Legislators might have—*should* have—personal *ethical* views preventing them from steering government contracts to particular parties.
93. *See, e.g.*, Roland Zullo, *Public-Private Contracting and Political Reciprocity*, 59 POL. RSCH. Q. 273, 273 (2006) ("[C]ampaign contributions are [more likely] to positively affect political decision-making . . . when the issue is non-partisan and non-ideological . . . when the public is indifferent, divided, or ignorant; and . . . when the position advocated by an interest group is unopposed by any other interest groups.").
94. *Citizens United v. FEC*, 558 U.S. 310, 360 (2010) (internal quotation marks omitted).
95. *Id.* at 357 (italics omitted).

96. Roscoe & Jenkins, *supra* note 21, at 52.
97. *Id.* at 53 (internal quotation marks omitted).
98. *See A Snapshot of Government-Wide Contracting for FY 2022*, U.S. GOV'T ACCOUNTABILITY OFFICE (Aug. 15, 2023), https://www.gao.gov/blog/snapshot-government-wide-contracting-fy-2022.
99. *See* Baltrunaite, *supra* note 62, at 542, 549 n.15.
100. *FEC v. Wis. Right to Life, Inc.*, 551 U.S. 449, 478–479 (2007).
101. *See* 52 U.S.C. § 30119 (2018).
102. *See Blount v. SEC*, 61 F.3d 938, 939–940 (D.C. Cir. 1995).
103. *See N.Y. Republican State Comm. v. SEC*, 927 F.3d 499, 501–503 (D.C. Cir. 2019).
104. *See Ognibene v. Parkes*, 671 F.3d 174, 179–180 (2d Cir. 2011) (describing New York City's "doing business" limits).
105. *See generally* KARL J. SANDSTROM & MICHAEL T. LIBURDI, OVERVIEW OF STATE PAY-TO-PLAY STATUTES (May 5, 2010) (describing pay-to-play laws in all states that have enacted them).
106. *See N.Y. Republican State Comm.*, 927 F.3d at 512 (upholding the SEC's rule for placement agents for pension fund investments); *Wagner v. FEC*, 793 F.3d 1, 34 (D.C. Cir. 2015) (en banc) (upholding the federal law banning contractors from making campaign contributions); *Blount*, 61 F.3d at 949 (upholding the MSRB's rule for brokers and dealers of municipal securities).
107. *See, e.g.*, *Ognibene*, 671 F.3d at 197 (upholding New York City's "doing business" limits); *Green Party of Conn. v. Garfield*, 616 F.3d 189, 213 (2d Cir. 2010) (mostly upholding Connecticut's pay-to-play law); *In re* Earle Asphalt Co., 950 A.2d 918, 927 (N.J. Super. Ct. App. Div. 2008) (upholding New Jersey's pay-to-play law).
108. *See, e.g.*, *Dallman v. Ritter*, 225 P.3d 610, 640 (Colo. 2010) (striking down Colorado's pay-to-play law).
109. *See* Baltrunaite, *supra* note 62, at 543.
110. Jon B. Jordan, *The Regulation of "Pay-to-Play" and the Influence of Political Contributions in the Municipal Securities Industry*, 1999 COLUM. BUS. L. REV. 489, 578.
111. *See, e.g.*, *Wagner*, 793 F.3d at 34 ("[T]he interests supporting the [federal pay-to-play] statute are ones that the Supreme Court has long approved—indeed, endorsed—as legitimate and important grounds for restricting campaign contributions. . . .").
112. *See, e.g.*, *McCutcheon v. FEC*, 572 U.S. 185, 209 (2014) (plurality opinion) ("[W]e leave the base limits undisturbed.").
113. *See Williams-Yulee v. Fla. Bar*, 575 U.S. 433, 457 (2015).
114. *See* 52 U.S.C. § 30119 (2018).
115. For a similar proposal, see Nathan Leys, Note, *"Masters of War"? The Defense Industry, the Appearance of Corruption, and the Future of Campaign Finance*, 39 YALE L. & POL'Y REV. 655, 701–702 (2021).

116. *See, e.g.*, Renata E. B. Strause & Daniel P. Tokaji, *Between Access and Influence: Building a Record for the Next Court*, 9 DUKE J. CONST. L. & PUB. POL'Y 179, 181 (2014) ("The evidence amassed in support of regulation [is] essential ... in demonstrating that legislation is appropriately tailored").
117. *See* Brogaard et al., *supra* note 40, at 17–18.
118. For a similar proposal, see Melanie D. Reed, *Regulating Political Contributions by State Contractors: The First Amendment and State Pay-to-Play Legislation*, 34 WM. MITCHELL L. REV. 635, 637 (2008).
119. *See, e.g.*, Fazekas, *supra* note 35, at 267 (listing factors that "indicate deviations from standard competitive tendering at various stages of the tendering process").
120. *See* Dahlström et al., *supra* note 51, at 660–661; Fazekas, *supra* note 35, at 272–275; Krause & Zarit, *supra* note 51, at 525–528.
121. For a similar proposal, see Fazekas, *supra* note 35, at 277.
122. *See, e.g., Casino Ass'n of La. v. State ex rel. Foster*, 820 So.2d 494, 508 (La. 2002) ("[Regulated] gaming is associated with political corruption...."); *Petition of Soto*, 565 A.2d 1088, 1104 (N.J. App. Div. 1989) ("[C]rime and corruption are inherent in the [licensed] casino industry....").
123. *See, e.g., Casino Ass'n*, 820 So .2d at 496; *Petition of Soto*, 565 A.2d at 1092; *Schiller Park Colonial Inn, Inc. v. Berz*, 349 N.E.2d 61, 64–65 (Ill. 1976).
124. *See, e.g., Casino Ass'n*, 820 So .2d at 510; *Petition of Soto*, 565 A.2d at 1106; *Schiller Park Colonial Inn*, 349 N.E.2d at 69.
125. *See* Maria M. Correia, *Political Connections and SEC Enforcement*, 57 J. ACCOUNT. & ECON. 241, 250, 258 (2014).
126. *See* Sarah Fulmer et al., *Negation of Sanctions: The Personal Effect of Political Contributions*, 58 J. FIN. & QUANT. ANAL. 2783, 2795 (2023).
127. *See* Sanford C. Gordon & Catherine Hafer, *Flexing Muscle: Corporate Political Expenditures as Signals to the Bureaucracy*, 99 AM. POL. SCI. REV. 245, 254 (2005).
128. *See* Ran Duchin & Denis Sosyura, *The Politics of Government Investment*, 106 J. FIN. ECON. 24, 26 (2012).
129. *See* Mara Faccio et al., *Political Connections and Corporate Bailouts*, 61 J. FIN. 2597, 2614 (2006).
130. Mearns, *supra* note 2.

CHAPTER 11

1. *McKee v. Cosby*, 139 S. Ct. 675, 676 (2019).
2. Asawin Suebsaeng, *"Super PAC" Makes It into the Dictionary*, MOTHER JONES (Nov. 29, 2009), https://www.motherjones.com/politics/2012/11/super-pac-added-merriam-webster-dictionary/.
3. *See, e.g.*, Christopher Wolfe, *Originalist Reflections on Constitutional Freedom of Speech*, 72 SMU L. REV. 535, 535 (2019) ("pretty clear that the original intent of the First Amendment is much narrower than the modern

understanding of free speech that has developed since the clear and present danger opinion of Justice Oliver Wendell Holmes Jr. in *Schenck v. United States* and *Gitlow v. New York*")(citations omitted); Jud Campbell, *Natural Rights and the First Amendment*, 127 YALE L.J. 246 (2017). Some have read that gap as an aspiration. *See, e.g.*, Geoffrey R. Stone, *The Story of the Sedition Act of 1798*: "*The Reign of Witches*," in FIRST AMENDMENT STORIES 13, 23 (Richard W. Garnett & Andrew Koppelman eds., 2012) (the First Amendment is "an aspiration, to be given meaning over time"). Tyler Broker rejects that there is a gap, arguing that changed circumstances (one could have said "translation") explain the changing application of the principle. See *Free Speech Originalism*, 81 ALBANY L. REV. 45 (2018).
4. *Smith v. California*, 361 U.S. 147, 157 (1959) (Black, J., concurring).
5. *United States v. O'Brien*, 391 US 367 (1968); *Tinker v. Des Moines Indep. Cmty. Sch. Dist.*, 393 U.S. 503 (1969) (Black, J., dissenting). Eugene Volokh argues powerfully that symbolic speech would have received the same protection as expressive speech. Eugene Volokh, *Symbolic Expression and the Original Meaning of the First Amendment*, 97 GEORGETOWN L. REV. 1057 (2009).
6. *Va. Pharmacy Bd. v. Va. Consumer Council*, 425 U.S. 748, 781 (1976) (Rehnquist, J., dissenting).
7. *Buckley v. Valeo*, 424 U.S. 1 (1976).
8. *See* the insightful discussion in Genevieve Lakier, *The First Amendment's Real Lochner Problem*, 87 U. CHI. L. REV. 1241 (2020).
9. Caroline Mala Corbin argues effectively against embracing First Amendment originalism. *See Free Speech Originalism*: *Unconstraining in Theory and Opportunistic in Practice*, 92 GEO. WASH. L. REV. 633 (2024). Yet the question—for an originalist—remains: why not here?
10. Alexander M. Bickel, THE LEAST DANGEROUS BRANCH: THE SUPREME COURT AT THE BAR OF POLITICS 16 (1962) ("The root difficulty is that judicial review is a counter-majoritarian force in our system").
11. Amul Thapar makes a similar point in *Smith, Scalia, and Originalism*, 68 CATH. U. L. REV. 687, 694 (2019), *available at* https://scholarship.law.edu/lawreview/vol68/iss4/10 ("Modern originalism emerged largely as a reaction to the perceived excesses of the Warren Court. Originalists of that mold, such as Justice Scalia and Judge Robert Bork, cared deeply about religious liberty. But they believed that such protections would primarily come from the legislature, not the courts. These first-generation originalists worried most about the Court encroaching on democracy's role. Where a judge had 'no basis other than his own values upon which to set aside . . . community judgment,' he had no basis to intervene. The answer, for these originalists, was judicial restraint, giving the political branches the benefit of the doubt").
12. *See generally* Lawrence B. Solum, *What Is Originalism? The Evolution of Contemporary Originalist Theory*, GEO. L. FAC. PUBL'NS & OTHER WORKS

8 (2011) ("Bork, Rehnquist, Berger, and Meese did not develop anything that approaches a full-blown constitutional theory, but their views suggested something like the theory we now call 'original intentions originalism,' the view that the original intentions of the Framers should guide constitutional interpretation"); RANDY E. BARNETT & EVAN D. BERNICK, THE ORIGINAL MEANING OF THE 14TH AMENDMENT: ITS LETTER AND SPIRIT 2–5 (2021) (discussing the intellectual origins of modern originalism).
13. *See generally* BARNETT & BERNICK, *supra*, at 4–5; Solum, *supra*, at 15–21.
14. CHARLES FRIED, ORDER AND LAW: ARGUING THE REAGAN REVOLUTION—A FIRSTHAND ACCOUNT 62 (1991).
15. *Id.* at 65.
16. Lawrence B. Solum, *Originalist Methodology*, 84 U. CHI. L. REV. 269–270 (2017) (noting that the two commitments of originalists are the "Fixation Thesis," which imbues words with a fixed meaning, and the "Constraint Principle," which restricts constitutional practice and interpretation).
17. Antonin Scalia, *Originalism: The Lesser Evil*, 57 U. CIN. L. REV. 849, 863 (1989).
18. *McDonald v. City of Chicago*, 561 U.S. 742, 803–804 (2010) (Scalia, J., concurring).
19. *NetChoice, LLC v. Bonta*, 692 F. Supp. 3d 924 (N.D. Cal. 2023), *aff'd in part, vacated in part*, No. 23-2969, 2024 WL 3838423 (9th Cir. Aug. 16, 2024).
20. *Marbury v. Madison*, 5 U.S. (1 Cranch) 137 (1803).
21. *McCutcheon v. Fed. Election Comm'n*, 572 U.S. 185, 232 (2014) (Breyer, dissenting).
22. *Dobbs v. Jackson Women's Health Org.*, 142 S. Ct. 2228, 2300 (2022) (Thomas, J., concurring) ("The idea that the Framers of the Fourteenth Amendment understood the Due Process Clause to protect a right to abortion is farcical") (citations omitted).
23. *See again* Corbin, *supra*.
24. Federal Election Campaign Act of 1971, 86 Stat. 3, as amended by the Federal Election Campaign Act Amendments of 1974, 88 Stat. 1263. The limitation on contributions was added in 1974, 90 Stat. 487.
25. *See* 18 U.S.C. § 608(e) (1970 ed., Supp. IV), reproduced at *Buckley v. Valeo*, 424 U.S. 1, 194 (1976) (per curiam).
26. 424 U.S. 1 at 47.
27. *Citizens United v. FEC*, 558 U.S. 310 (2010).
28. 558 U.S. 310, 360. Justice Scalia, in concurrence, advanced the argument that the case did not turn on the character of the speaker, but rather on the nature of the speech being regulated. To him, whether or not a corporation was a "person," the speech being regulated was political speech, and the question under the First Amendment was whether Congress had the power to regulate political speech. This approach was drawn into doubt shortly after

Citizens United was decided. In *Bluman v. Fed. Election Comm'n*, the DC Circuit (with Judge Kavanaugh writing the opinion) upheld limitations on independent spending by legal immigrants. 800 F. Supp. 2d 281 (D.D.C. 2011). Though the speech being regulated was political speech, the fact that it was uttered by non-citizens mattered to whether it was constitutionally protected. Justice Stevens flagged this inconsistency in a lecture at the University of Arkansas. Calvin Sloan, *Justice Stevens: A Crack in the Foundation of the* Citizens United *Majority Opinion Is Inevitable*, PEOPLEFOR.ORG (June 1, 2012), https://www.peoplefor.org/blog-posts/justice-stevens-a-crack-in-the-foundation-of-the-citizens-united-majority-opinion-is-inevitable.

29. *SpeechNow v. FEC*, 599 F.3d 686, 694–695 (2010) (en banc), *cert. denied sub nom. Keating v. FEC*, 562 U.S. 1003 (2010). The government did not seek review of the holding. In a letter explaining the government's decision, the attorney general did not express agreement with the DC Circuit's holding but mistakenly predicted that the SpeechNow ruling would "affect only a small subset of federally regulated contributions." Letter from Eric Holder, Attorney Gen., to Harry Reid, Senate Majority Leader (June 16, 2010), *available at* perma.cc/G9KL-MHMS. The plaintiffs in SpeechNow asked the Supreme Court to review a distinct portion of the DC Circuit's decision upholding certain disclosure requirements. The Court denied certiorari on that question.

30. *N.Y. Progress and Protection PAC v. Walsh*, 733 F.3d 483 (2d Cir. 2013); *Texans for Free Enter. v. Tex. Ethics Comm.*, 732 F.3d 535 (5th Cir. 2013); *Wis. Right to Life State PAC v. Barland*, 664 F.3d 139 (7th Cir. 2011); *Farris v. Seabrook*, 677 F.3d 858 (9th Cir. 2012); *Thalheimer v. City of San Diego*, 645 F.3d 1109 (9th Cir. 2011); *Long Beach Area Chamber of Com. v. City of Long Beach*, 603 F.3d 684 (9th Cir. 2010); *Republican Party of N.M. v. King*, 741 F.3d 1089 (10th Cir. 2013).

31. Albert W. Alschuler, Laurence H. Tribe, Norman L. Eisen, and Richard W. Painter, *Why Limits on Contributions to Super PACs Should Survive* Citizens United, 86 FORDHAM L. REV. 2299 (2018), *available at* https://ir.lawnet.fordham.edu/flr/vol86/iss5/2.

32. Motion to Dismiss No. 9, *United States v. Menendez*, Crim. No. 2:15-cr-00155, D. NJ (2015).

33. 424 U.S. 1 at 27–28.

34. But not always. At the start of his career, McConnell viewed money in politics as a "cancer." Ella Nilsen, *Mitch McConnell's Dark Secret: He Used to Support Campaign Finance Reform*, VOX (Feb. 15, 2019), *available at* https://www.vox.com/2019/2/15/18224850/mitch-mcconnell-campaign-finance-reform-hr1.

35. Al Weaver, *Hawley Sparks McConnell Battle over Push to Gut Citizens United Ruling*, THE HILL, *available at* https://thehill.com/homenews/senate/4288563-hawley-mcconnell-battle-gut-citizens-united-ruling/.

36. 139 S. Ct. 675 (2019).
37. 376 U.S. 254 (1964).
38. 139 S. Ct. at 676 (Thomas, J., dissenting).
39. *Id. See also Coral Ridge Ministries Media, Inc., v. S. Poverty L. Ctr.*, 142 S. Ct. 2453 (2022) (opinion dissenting from denial of certiorari) (slip op., at 3) (arguing for reconsideration of *Sullivan*); *Berisha v. Lawson*, 141 S. Ct. 2424, 2425 (2021) (opinion dissenting from denial of certiorari) ("lack of historical support for this Court's actual-malice requirement is reason enough to take a second look at the Court's doctrine").
40. 141 S. Ct. 1220, 1223–1224 (2021) (Thomas, J., concurring).
41. *See* Jud Campbell, *Natural Rights and the First Amendment*, 127 YALE L.J. 246, 256, 313–314 (2017).
42. *See United States v. Sineneng-Smith*, 140 S. Ct. 1575, 1584 (2020) (Thomas, J., concurring) ("[T]here is no evidence from the founding indicating that the First Amendment empowered judges to determine whether particular restrictions of speech promoted the general welfare") (citations omitted). *Accord* Letter from James Madison to Spencer Roane (Sept. 2, 1819), in 1 THE PAPERS OF JAMES MADISON: RETIREMENT SERIES 500, 501 (David B. Mattern et al. eds., 2009) (stating that questions "of mere expediency or policy" are not amenable to judicial resolution).
43. Jud Campbell, *Republicanism and Natural Rights at the Founding*, 32 CONST. COMMENT. 85, 104 (2017).
44. *Id.*; *see also* Jack N. Rakove, ORIGINAL MEANINGS: POLITICS AND IDEAS IN THE MAKING OF THE CONSTITUTION 333 (1996) ("[A] national bill of rights would have [no] great practical value"); *id.* at 335 ("Madison did not expect the adoption of amendments to free judges to act vigorously in defense of rights"); Hortensius [George Hay], AN ESSAY ON THE LIBERTY OF THE PRESS 38 (Philadelphia, 1799) (First Amendment would "amount precisely to the privilege of publishing, as far as the legislative power shall say, the public good requires"); *see generally* Jud Campbell, *Judicial Review and the Enumeration of Rights*, 15 GEO. J. L. & PUB. POL'Y 569 (2017).
45. THE FEDERALIST Nos. 52, 57 (Madison).
46. *See Bluman v. FEC*, 800 F. Supp. 2d 281, 288 (D.D.C. 2011) (Kavanaugh, J.), *aff'd*, 565 U.S. 1104 (2012) (upholding restrictions on non-citizens' participation in the political process).
47. *See* Lawrence B. Solum, *Originalist Methodology*, 84 U. CHI. L. REV. 269, 269–270 (2017) (noting that the two commitments of originalists are the "Fixation Thesis," which imbues words with a fixed meaning, and the "Constraint Principle," which restricts constitutional practice and interpretation).
48. 491 U.S. 110 (1989) (plurality opinion) (interpreting the scope of "due process").
49. *Id.* at 127 n.6.

50. *New York State Rifle & Pistol Ass'n, Inc. v. Bruen*, 142 S. Ct. 2111, 2129 (2022).
51. *See* Zephyr Teachout, *The Anti-Corruption Principle*, 94 CORNELL L. REV. 341, 352 (2009).
52. *Alaska Pub. Offs. Comm'n v. Patrick*, 494 P.3d 53 (Sep. 3, 2021), *cert. denied*, 142 S. Ct. 779 (2022).
53. *Patrick v. Interior Voters*, No. 3AN-18-05726CI (Nov. 4, 2019), *available at* perma.cc/YLW2-KHRJ.
54. Respondents' Excerpts of Record, Supreme Court of Alaska, S-17649 (2020).
55. *See* Brief for Constitutional Accountability Center as Amicus Curiae Supporting FEC, *McCutcheon v. FEC*, 572 U.S. 185 (2014) (12–536) (56% of uses identified discussed corruption of institutions, not individuals; 69% of "improper dependence" references were references to an entity, not an individual), *available at* perma.cc/6KLW-7DB8. *See also* Database of Framing References to Corruption, *available at* perma.cc/YG4C-GTC5.
56. 1 THE RECORDS OF THE FEDERAL CONVENTION OF 1787 at 386 (Max Farrand ed., 1911).
57. 2 FARRAND'S RECORDS at 218.

CHAPTER 12

1. 424 U.S. 1 (1976) (per curiam).
2. *FEC v. Nat'l Conservative Pol. Action Comm.*, 470 U.S. 480, 497 (1985).
3. *See* Samuel Issacharoff & Pamela S. Karlan, *The Hydraulics of Campaign Finance Reform*, 77 TEX. L. REV. 1705 (1999).
4. *See generally* Nathaniel Persily & Kelli Lammie, *Perceptions of Corruption and Campaign Finance: When Public Opinion Determines Constitutional Law*, 153 U. PA. L. REV. 119 (2004) (finding that perceptions of corruption derive to some extent from (1) position in society (race, income, education level), (2) opinion of the incumbent President and performance of the economy over the previous year, (3) attitudes concerning taxation and "big government," and (4) propensity to trust people).
5. *See Regents of the Univ. of Cal. v. Bakke*, 438 U.S. 265, 311–312 (1978).
6. 548 U.S. 230, 262 (2006).
7. *See, e.g.*, CHRISTOPHER J. ANDERSON ET AL., LOSERS' CONSENT: ELECTIONS AND DEMOCRATIC LEGITIMACY 142 (2005); Cecile Tobin et al., *Losing Predicts Perceptions That Elections Were Decided by Fraud, but Margin of Loss and Candidate Race Do Not* (2024), https://bpb-us-e1.wpmucdn.com/sites.dartmouth.edu/dist/5/2293/files/2024/02/house-fraud-perceptions-31bd2505dabcd0fb.pdf.
8. Scott Conroy, *Obama, Romney Getting Cozier with Super PACs*, CBS NEWS (Feb. 14, 2012), https://www.cbsnews.com/news/obama-romney-getting-cozier-with-super-pacs/.

9. 558 U.S. 310 (2010).
10. *Cost of Election*, OPENSECRETS, https://www.opensecrets.org/elections-overview/cost-of-election (last visited Oct. 13, 2024) [hereinafter *Cost of Election*].
11. *See* Stephen Ansolabehere & James M. Snyder, Jr., *Soft Money, Hard Money, Strong Parties*, 100 COLUM. L. REV. 598, 614–615 (2000).
12. *See id.* at 606–607 (roughly 15% held back by state parties); PETER REUTER & EDWIN M. TRUMAN, CHASING DIRTY MONEY: THE FIGHT AGAINST MONEY LAUNDERING 36 (2004) ("Experienced investigators refer to a general price range of 7% to 15% for laundering for drug dealers, but some reports are inconsistent with such estimates").
13. Bipartisan Campaign Reform Act of 2002, Pub. L. No. 107-155, 116 Stat. 81; Robert Kelner & Raymond La Raja, Opinion, *McCain-Feingold's Devastating Legacy*, WASH. POST (Apr. 11, 2014), https://www.washingtonpost.com/opinions/mccain-feingolds-devastating-legacy/2014/04/11/14a528e2-c18f-11e3-bcec-b71ee10e9bc3_story.html.
14. 540 U.S. 93, 224 (2003).
15. Between 2000 and 2008, independent expenditures in the federal domain increased by at least 325%. In the 2000 election cycle, the Center for Responsive Politics reports that independent expenditures totaled $33,777,718 across all federal elections. The 2008 total was $143,659,091, representing a 325% increase. *Total Outside Spending by Election Cycle, Excluding Party Committees*, OPENSECRETS, https://www.opensecrets.org/outside-spending/by_cycle (last visited Oct. 8, 2024) [hereinafter *Total Outside Spending*].
16. Joseph Fishkin & Heather K. Gerken, *The Two Trends That Matter for Party Politics*, 89 N.Y.U. L. REV. ONLINE 32, 35 (2014).
17. *Total Outside Spending*, *supra* note 16.
18. *See Cost of Election*, *supra* note 11.
19. *See* Douglas M. Spencer & Abby K. Wood, *Citizens United, States Divided: An Empirical Analysis of Independent Political Spending*, 89 IND. L. J. 315, 318, 342 (2014).
20. *See* Spencer & Wood, *supra* note 20, at 345–347 (presenting evidence that independent expenditures from corporations increased nominally at most in states where *Citizens United* struck down regulations on independent expenditures, suggesting that *Citizens United* did not causally increase independent expenditures from corporations). *See also, e.g.*, Fredreka Schouten, Christopher Schnaars & Gregory Korte, *Individuals, Not Corporations, Drive Super PAC Financing; But Critics Say Donors' Goal to Buy Influence Is the Same*, USA TODAY, Feb. 2, 2012, at A7 ("less than $1 out of every $5 flowing into super PACs' coffers came from corporations").

21. *Ten Years Later*: *What Citizens United Has Wrought* 9-11 (2020) PUBLIC CITIZEN, https://www.citizen.org/wp-content/uploads/citizens-united-retrospective.pdf.
22. Karl Evers-Hillstrom, *More Money, Less Transparency*: *A Decade Under* Citizens United 21 (2020), OPENSECRETS, https://www.opensecrets.org/news/reports/a-decade-under-citizens-united.
23. *See* Spencer & Wood, *supra* note 20, at 345–347.
24. *See, e.g.*, *Corporate Contributions to Outside Groups*, OPENSECRETS, https://www.opensecrets.org/outside-spending/corporate-contributions/2020 (last visited Apr. 13, 2024) (offering evidence that the largest corporate contributions to super PACs concentrated in the fossil-fuel extraction industry).
25. *See, e.g.*, *Political Action Committees (PACs)*, OPENSECRETS, https://www.opensecrets.org/political-action-committees-pacs/2020 (last visited Oct. 13, 2024) (offering evidence that the largest PACs, as opposed to super PACs, are closely aligned with a specific corporation or industry).
26. *Compare id.* ($536.4 million spent by PACs in 2020), *with 2020 Outside Spending, by Super PAC*, OPENSECRETS, www.opensecrets.org/outside-spending/super_pacs/2020?chrt=2024&disp=O&type=S (last visited Apr. 13, 2024) ($2.1 billion spent by super PACs), *with Cost of Election*, *supra* note 11 ($15.1 billion spent overall in 2020).
27. Stephen Ansolabehere, John M. de Figueiredo & James M. Snyder Jr., *Why Is There So Little Money in U.S. Politics?*, 17 J. ECON. PERSPECTIVES 105 (2003). *See also id.* at 110–111 (reasoning that, given the relatively small amount corporations donate relative to the amount of federal spending, one would expect far higher amounts of corporate donations).
28. EVERS-HILLSTROM, *supra* note 23, at 3.
29. *Id.*
30. Ian Vandewalker & Mariana Paez, *4 Takeaways About Money in the Midterms*, BRENNAN CTR. FOR JUST. (Nov. 16, 2022), https://www.brennancenter.org/our-work/analysis-opinion/4-takeaways-about-money-midterms.
31. *Id.*
32. Michael Beckel, *Outsized Influence*, ISSUEONE, 1 (2021), https://www.issueone.org/wp-content/uploads/2021/04/Issue-One-Outsized-Influence-Report-final.pdf.
33. *See* PUB. CITIZEN, *supra* note 22, at 9.
34. *See, e.g.*, *Super PACs*: *How Many Donors Give*, OPENSECRETS, https://www.opensecrets.org/outside-spending/donor-stats/2020?type=B (last visited Apr. 14, 2024).
35. Conroy, *supra* note 9.

36. Colleen Long & Chris Megerian, *Biden Raises Record $26 Million at Star-Studded New York Campaign Event*, PBS (Mar. 29, 2024), https://www.pbs.org/newshour/politics/biden-raises-record-26-million-at-star-studded-new-york-campaign-event.
37. Fredreka Schouten & Alayna Treene, *Trump Campaign Announces Record $50.5 Million Haul at Florida Fundraiser*, CNN (Apr. 7, 2024), www.cnn.com/2024/04/06/politics/trump-fundraiser-florida-rnc/index.html.
38. Seth Masket & Hans Noel, Political Parties 176–177 (2021); Daniel Schlozman & Sam Rosenfeld, The Hollow Parties: The Many Pasts and Disordered Present of American Party Politics 8 (2024).
39. *Colo. Republican Fed. Campaign Comm. v. FEC* (*Colorado Republican I*), 518 U.S. 604 (1996).
40. *FEC v. Colo. Republican Fed. Campaign Comm.* (*Colorado Republican II*), 533 U.S. 431 (2001).
41. Joseph A. Schumpeter, Capitalism, Socialism & Democracy 250 (2003) (1943).
42. *See Colorado Republican I*, 518 U.S. at 608.
43. *Id.* at 613–615.
44. *See Colorado Republican II*, 533 U.S. at 465.
45. *Id.* at 438; Eric L. Richards, Federal Election Commission v. Colorado Republican Federal Campaign Committee: *Implications for Parties, Corporate Political Dialogue, and Campaign Finance Reform*, 40 A.M. Bus. L.J. 83, 98 (2008).
46. *Colorado Republican II*, 533 U.S. at 450–452.
47. *Id.* at 451–452.
48. *Id.* at 452.
49. *See Colorado Republican I*, 518 U.S. at 614 (recognizing protection of party independent expenditures so long as not coordinated with any candidate).
50. *See Colorado Republican II*, 533 U.S. at 453 (2001).
51. *See id.* at 465.
52. V. O. Key, Jr., Politics, Parties and Pressure Groups 163, 166–167 (5th ed. 1964).
53. *See* Samuel Issacharoff, *Outsourcing Politics: The Hostile Takeover of Our Hollowed-Out Political Parties*, 54 Hous. L. Rev. 845, 858–861 (2017).
54. Seth E. Masket, The Inevitable Party: Why Attempts to Kill the Party System Fail and How They Weaken Democracy 18 (2016).
55. *Colorado Republican I*, 518 U.S. at 629 (Kennedy, J., concurring).
56. *Id.* at 629–630 (concluding that party activity and spending on behalf of candidate is the heart of party political engagement).
57. *Nat'l Republican Senatorial Comm. v. FEC*, No. 24-3051 (6th Cir. argued June 12, 2024).
58. *See* Franita Tolson, *Republicanism Redefined: The Constitutional Status of Political Parties After the Ratification of the Twelfth Amendment*, in

RESEARCH HANDBOOK ON THE POLITICS OF CONSTITUTIONAL LAW 2023, at 310, 310–312 (Mark Tushnet & Dimitry Kochenov eds., 2023).
59. *See* 376 U.S. 254, 279–280 (1964) (holding that the First Amendment protects the publication of all statements by public officials, except when statements are made with "actual malice"); *see also Gertz v. Robert Welch, Inc.* 418 U.S. 323, 348 (1974) (clarifying that this standard of proving "actual malice" only applied to public figures and not private individuals); *Hustler Mag., Inc. v. Falwell*, 485 U.S. 46, 56 (1988) (reaffirming that *Sullivan* applies to offensive or outrageous satire).
60. *See Walker v. Tex. Div., Sons of Confederate Veterans, Inc.*, 576 U.S. 200, 207 (2015) ("[T]he Free Speech Clause helps produce informed opinions among members of the public, who are then able to influence the choices of a government...").
61. *See, e.g.*, Robert Post, *Participatory Democracy and Free Speech*, 97 VA. L. REV. 477, 482 (2011); James Weinstein, *Participatory Democracy as the Central Value of American Free Speech Doctrine*, 97 VA. L. REV. 491, 493–497 (2011); Robert H. Bork, *Neutral Principles and Some First Amendment Problems*, 47 IND. L.J. 1, 20–21 (1971); Ashutosh Bhagwat, *The Democratic First Amendment*, 110 Nw. L. REV. 1097, 1098 (2016).
62. *See* Richard H. Pildes, *Romanticizing Democracy, Political Fragmentation, and the Decline of American Government*, 124 YALE L.J. 804, 828 (2014).
63. SAMUEL ISSACHAROFF, DEMOCRACY UNMOORED: POPULISM AND THE CORRUPTION OF POPULAR SOVEREIGNTY 58 (2023).
64. *Rutan v. Republican Party*, 497 U.S. 62, 93 (1990) (Scalia, J., dissenting).
65. RAYMOND J. LA RAJA & BRIAN F. SCHAFFNER, CAMPAIGN FINANCE AND POLITICAL POLARIZATION: WHEN PURISTS PREVAIL 51 (2015).
66. *Id.* at 111.
67. Mike Norton & Richard H. Pildes, *How Outside Money Makes Governing More Difficult*, 19 ELECTION L.J. 486, 500 (2021).
68. *Id.* at 488.
69. LA RAJA & SCHAFFNER, *supra* note 66, at 104.
70. ISSACHAROFF, *supra* note 64, at 69.
71. GRUNDGESETZ [GG] [Basic Law], art. 21 (Ger.), translation at https://www.gesetze-im-internet.de/englisch_gg/englisch_gg.html.
72. *Id.*
73. FED. MINISTRY OF THE INT. & CMTY., *Funding of Political Parties*, https://www.bmi.bund.de/EN/topics/constitution/law-political-parties/funding-pol-parties/funding-pol-parties-node.html (last visited Aug. 18, 2025).
74. Press Release, THE FED. CONST. COURT, Increase of the "Absolute Limit" Applicable to State Funding of Political Parties Is Unconstitutional (Jan. 24, 2023), https://www.bundesverfassungsgericht.de/SharedDocs/ Pressemitteilungen/EN/2023/bvg23-009.html [hereinafter *Press Release*]; BVERFG, 2 BvF 2/18, Jan. 24, 2023, www.bverfg.de/e/fs20230124_2bvf000218.html.
75. *See Press Release*, *supra* note 75.

CHAPTER 13

1. *See generally* Richard H. Pildes, *Political Fragmentation in Democracies of the West*, 37 BYU J. PUB. L. 209 (2023). *See also* Pildes, *Democracies in the Age of Fragmentation*, 110 CALIF. L. REV. 2051 (2023).
2. One study found that Congress produced 166% more legislation in the least polarized congressional term compared to the most polarized term. *See* Michael J. Barber & Nolan McCarty, *Causes and Consequences of Polarization, in* SOLUTIONS TO POLITICAL POLARIZATION IN AMERICA, 15, 42 (Nate Persily ed., 2015).
3. *See* Thomas F. Schaller, *A Republican Senate in a Divided Government*, CTR. FOR POL.: SABATO'S CRYSTAL BALL (Dec. 21, 2023), https://centerforpolitics.org/crystalball/a-republican-senate-in-a-divided-government/ (highlighting that government has been unified 30% of the time from 1969–2023); JAMES M. CURRY & FRANCES E. LEE, THE LIMITS OF PARTY: CONGRESS AND LAWMAKING IN A POLARIZED ERA (2020) (highlighting the need for bipartisan support during unified government).
4. *See, e.g.*, Richard H. Pildes, *Combatting Extremism*, 76 FLA. L. REV. 1583(2025) (2024 Dunwoody Lecture).
5. In political science, *see* RAYMOND J. LA RAJA & BRIAN F. SCHAFFNER, CAMPAIGN FINANCE AND POLITICAL POLARIZATION: WHEN PURISTS PREVAIL (2015); *see also* Barber & McCarty, *supra* note 3, at 33 (mentioning that "data suggest there may be a direct connection between the rise in individual contributions and polarization in American politics"). Among legal scholars, the issue is mentioned in Michael S. Kang, *Campaign Finance Deregulation and the Hyperpolarization of Presidential Nominations in the Super PAC Era, in* THE BEST CANDIDATE 260, 262 (Eugene D. Mazo & Michael R. Dimino eds., 2020).
6. *See generally* ALAN I. ABRAMOWITZ, THE DISAPPEARING CENTER: ENGAGED CITIZENS, POLARIZATION, AND AMERICAN DEMOCRACY (2010) (discussing polarization among "the engaged public").
7. This figure is from LA RAJA & SCHAFFNER, CAMPAIGN FINANCE AND POLITICAL POLARIZATION.
8. David Broockman & Neil Malhotra, *What Do Partisan Donors Want?*, 84 PUB. OP. Q. 104 (2020).
9. *See* Joseph Bafumi & Michael C. Herron, *Leapfrog Representation and Extremism*: *A Study of American Voters and Their Members in Congress*, 104 A.M. POL. SCI. REV. 519 (2010) ("Insofar as members of Congress are also extreme, we suggest that a contributing factor for this may be the relative extremism of donating voters"); Joshua D. Clinton, *Representation in Congress*: *Constituents and Roll Calls in the 106th House*, 68 J. POL. 397 (2006).
10. Seth J. Hill & Gregory A. Huber, *Representativeness and Motivations of the Contemporary Donorate*: *Results from Merged Survey and Administrative Records*, 39 POL. BEHAV. 3, 5–6 (2017).

11. Michael J. Barber, *Ideological Donors, Contribution Limits, and the Polarization of American Legislatures*, 78 J. POL. 296, 306 (2016).
12. *See* Michael J. Barber et al., Donors and Dollars: Comparing the Policy Views of Donors and the Affluent (July 2024) (unpublished manuscript, on file with author).
13. *See McConnell v. FEC*, 540 U.S. 93, 124 n.12 (2003).
14. *See* Michael J. Barber & Nolan McCarty, *Causes and Consequences of Polarization*, in SOLUTIONS TO POLITICAL POLARIZATION IN AMERICA, 15, 33 (Nathaniel Persily ed., 2015).
15. *See* Sarah Bryner, *The Nationalization of Political Contributions and the Rising Role of Out-of-State Donations*, OPENSECRETS (June 1, 2023), https://www.opensecrets.org/news/reports/out-of-state-donations. The percentages are similar for incumbents, challengers and open-seat candidates.
16. *Id.*
17. *Id.*
18. *See* James G. Gimpel, Frances E. Lee & Shanna Pearson-Merkowitz, *The Check Is in the Mail: Interdistrict Funding Flows in Congressional Elections*, 52 AM. J. POL. SCI. 373 (2008).
19. *In-District vs. Out-of-District*, OPENSECRETS, https://www.opensecrets.org/elections-overview/in-district-vs-out-of-district?cycle=2020&display=M (last visited July 30, 2024).
20. *See* Joseph Bafumi & Michael C. Herron, *Leapfrog Representation and Extremism: A Study of American Voters and Their Members in Congress*, 104 AM. POL. SCI. REV. 519 (2010); Michael J. Barber, *Representing the Preferences of Donors, Partisans, and Voters in the US Senate*, 80 PUB. OP. Q. 225 (2016); Anne E. Baker, *Getting Short-Changed? The Impact of Outside Money on District Representation*, 97 SOC. SCI. Q. 1096 (2016); Michael J. Barber, Brandice Canes-Wrone & Sharece Thrower, *Ideologically Sophisticated Donors: Which Candidates Do Individual Contributors Finance?*, 61 AM. J. POL. SCI. 271 (2016); Brandice Canes-Wrone & Kenneth M. Miller, *Out-of-District Donors and Representation in the US House*, 47 LEGIS. STUD. Q. 361 (2022) [hereinafter *Out-of-District Donors*].
21. *See Out-of-District Donors, supra* note 21.
22. As of August 2024, 57% of donors to the 2024 elections were men, who donated about 70% of the money. *Donor Demographics*, OPENSECRETS, https://www.opensecrets.org/elections-overview/donor-demographics (last visited Aug. 18, 2024).
23. *See* Adam Bonica & Jacob M. Grumbach, Old Money: Campaign Finance and Gerontocracy in the United States (June 23, 2024) (unpublished manuscript, on file with author).
24. *See* Ilyana Kuziemko, Nicolas Longuet-Marx & Suresh Naidu, *"Compensate the Losers?" Economic Policy and Partisan Realignment in the US* (Nat'l Bureau of Econ. Rsch., Working Paper No. 31,794, 2023).

25. Lawrence Lessig, *We the People, and the Republic We Must Reclaim*, TED (Feb. 2013), https://www.ted.com/talks/lawrence_lessig_we_the_people_and_the_republic_we_must_reclaim.
26. ANTHONY J. CORRADO ET AL., REFORM IN AN AGE OF NETWORKED CAMPAIGNS: HOW TO FOSTER CITIZEN PARTICIPATION THROUGH SMALL DONORS AND VOLUNTEERS (2010), https://www.brookings.edu/wp-content/uploads/2016/06/0114_campaign_finance_reform.pdf.
27. ADAM SKAGGS & FRED WERTHEIMER, EMPOWERING SMALL DONORS IN FEDERAL ELECTIONS (2012), BRENNAN CTR. FOR JUST., https://www.brennancenter.org/sites/default/files/legacy/publications/Small_donor_report_FINAL.pdf.
28. *See* Richard H. Pildes, *Small-Donor-Based Campaign-Finance Reform and Political Polarization*, 129 YALE L.J.F. 149 (2019) [hereinafter *Small-Donor-Based Campaign-Finance Reform*]; Pildes, *Participation and Polarization*, 22 U. PA. J. CONST. L. 341 (2020); Pildes, *Small Dollars, Big Changes*, WASH. POST (Feb. 6, 2020), https://www.washingtonpost.com/outlook/2020/02/06/small-dollars-big-changes/.
29. DAVID B. MAGLEBY, JAY GOODLIFFE & JOSEPH A. OLSEN, WHO DONATES IN CAMPAIGNS? THE IMPORTANCE OF MESSAGE, MESSENGER, MEDIUM, AND STRUCTURE (2018).
30. *See* RICHARD H. PILDES & FRANCES E. LEE, TASK FORCE ON INSTITUTIONAL REFORMS TO COMBAT EXTREMISM, REPORT: CAMPAIGN FINANCE (forthcoming 2025).
31. *See* Laurent Bouton et al., *Small Campaign Donors* (Nat'l Bureau of Econ. Rsch., Working Paper No. 30050, 2022), https://sciencespo.hal.science/hal-03878175/file/2022_bouton_cage_dewitte_pons_small_campaign_donors.pdf.
32. *See* Zachary Albert & Raymond J. La Raja, *Small Donors in US Elections*, 35 POLITIQUE AMÉRICAINE 15 (2020); Tyler Culberson, Michael P. McDonald & Suzanne M. Robbins, *Small Donors in Congressional Elections*, 47 AM. POL. RSCH. 970 (2019).
33. *See* Richard H. Pildes, *Romanticizing Democracy, Political Fragmentation, and the Decline of American Government*, 124 YALE L. J. 804 (2014) [hereinafter *Romanticizing Democracy*].
34. Julie Bykowicz, *Why Big-Money Donors Can't Reel in GOP Rebels*, WALL ST. J. (Jan. 6, 2023), https://www.wsj.com/articles/why-big-money-donors-cant-reel-in-gop-rebels-11673012291.
35. *Id.*
36. Mike Norton & Richard H. Pildes, *How Outside Money Makes Governing More Difficult*, 19 ELECTION L. J., 486 (2020).
37. Kevin Breuninger, *Trump Campaign Raises Record $34.8 Million in Donations after Guilty Verdict*, CNBC (May 31, 2024), https://www.cnbc.com/2024/05/31/trump-campaign-donations-record.html.

38. Steven Shepard & Sarah Ferris, *Omar Rakes in Cash Online as Controversies Pile Up*, POLITICO (April 15, 2019), https://www.politico.com/story/2019/04/15/online-donors-ilhan-omar-1277273.
39. Jonathan Allen, *"You Lie!" Worth $2.7M for Wilson*, POLITICO (Oct. 15, 2009), https://politi.co/3SI6mVQ.
40. More precisely, we can distinguish between what might be called substantive extremism and empirical extremism. Substantive extremism refers to the specific content of the substantive positions candidates might have. Empirical extremism simply refers to those located at the poles of the parties' ideological spectrum. This chapter sometimes refers to extremism in the former sense, sometimes in the latter. In practice, these two types often overlap; those at the ideological poles are more likely to be substantive extremists. But the overlap is not perfect. Polarization without extremism in the substantive sense is possible. Extremism in either sense is not inherently problematic. Context matters; abolitionists might have been viewed as extremists, in either sense, but were morally correct. My concern is institutional design structures that reward extreme candidates even when they lack the support of a majority of the relevant general electorate. An election-financing system dominated by donors more ideologically extreme than the general electorate is one example.
41. JOHN GANZ, WHEN THE CLOCK BROKE: CON MEN, CONSPIRACISTS, AND HOW AMERICA CRACKED UP IN THE EARLY 1990S, 63 (2024) (noting "direct mail fundraising using sensational and melodramatic appeals" in the 1980s).
42. Bryan Metzger, *Republicans Are Desperate for Attention—and It's Decimating Their Ability to Govern*, BUS. INSIDER (Oct. 28, 2023), https://www.businessinsider.com/mike-johnson-speaker-fight-gaetz-mace-republicans-2023-10.
43. Pildes, *supra* note 29, at 158.
44. 424 U.S. 1 (1976) (per curiam).
45. *See Small-Donor-Based Campaign-Finance Reform*, *supra* note 28.
46. Michael Waldman, *Small Donors to Campaigns Are Not the Problem*, BRENNAN CTR. FOR JUST. (May 8, 2024), https://www.brennancenter.org/our-work/analysis-opinion/small-donors-campaigns-are-not-problem.
47. Ian Vandewalker, *Do Small Donors Cause Political Dysfunction?* (2024), BRENNAN CTR. FOR JUST., https://www.brennancenter.org/our-work/research-reports/do-small-donors-cause-political-dysfunction.
48. *Id.* at 4.
49. The Court briefly alluded to the issue in *Randall v. Sorrell*, 548 U.S. 230, 239 (2006). In striking down a provision of a Vermont statute for overly stringent limitations on campaign contributions, the Court noted that the Second Circuit had affirmed the unconstitutionality of another provision that limited contributions from out-of-state residents, a decision which the petitioner had not challenged on appeal. *See* 548 U.S. 230 at 239 ("The Act also limits

the amount of contributions a candidate, political committee, or political party can receive from out-of-state sources. § 2805(c). The lower courts held these out-of-state contribution limits unconstitutional, and the parties do not challenge that holding"). In *Vannatta v. Keisling*, 151 F.3d 1215 (2008), the Ninth Circuit in a 2–1 decision affirmed a holding that an Oregon statute's ban on out-of-district contributions violated the First Amendment. In contrast, the Alaska Supreme Court upheld against constitutional challenge an Alaska ban on out-of-state donations by political groups and a stricter contribution limit for out-of-state residents. *See State v. Alaska Civ. Liberties Union*, 978 P.2d 597, 617 (Alaska 1999). The Supreme Court denied certiorari in the Alaska case. *See Alaska Civ. Liberties Union v. Alaska*, 120 S. Ct. 1156 (2000). But the Ninth Circuit, again in a 2–1 decision, later held unconstitutional Alaska's aggregate cap limit on how much candidates could receive from out-of-state donors. *See Thompson v. Hebdon*, 909 F.3d 1027 (9th Cir. 2018). The Ninth Circuit read Supreme Court precedent to preclude justifying such a limit on the grounds that it protected Alaska's system of self-governance. The court concluded that this was a version of an "undue influence" justification and that only preventing corruption and its appearance were constitutionally permissible justifications for limiting contributions.

The Second Circuit in *Ognibene v. Parkes*, 671 F.3d 174, 193 (2d. Cir. 2011), upheld New York City's public-financing provision that matched contributions for participating candidates from residents except for "lobbyists, persons associated with lobbyists, and other individuals with business dealings with the City." In doing so, none of the judges questioned the limitation on matching funds to in-district residents.

50. *See, e.g., Rust v. Sullivan*, 500 U. S. 173, 193 (1991); *FEC v. Mass. Citizens for Life, Inc.*, 479 U. S. 238, 256, n. 9 (1986); *Regan v. Taxation with Representation of Wash.*, 461 U. S. 540, 550 (1983).
51. *Buckley v. Valeo*, 424 U.S. 23–59 (1976) (per curiam). The candidate of a party that could not meet the 5% threshold but then received more than 5% of the vote in the general election could receive post-election public funds.
52. *Buckley*, 424 U.S. at 104.
53. *See Bluman v. FEC*, 800 F. Supp. 2d 281 (D.D.C. 2011), *aff'd mem.*, 132 S. Ct. 1087 (2012).
54. *See* SEATTLE ETHICS & ELECTION COMM'N, DEMOCRACY VOUCHER PROGRAM 2023 BIENNIAL REPORT (2023), https://www.seattle.gov/documents/Departments/EthicsElections/DemocracyVoucher/Biennial%20Reports/2023%20Biennial_Report%20FINAL.pdf (noting that 30,649 residents used vouchers in 2023, compared to 48,071 in 2021).
55. *See* Chenoa Yorgason, *Campaign Finance Vouchers Do Not Expand the Diversity of Donors: Evidence from Seattle*, AM. POL. SCI. REV. 1 (2024).
56. *Id.*

57. Jennifer A. Heerwig & Brian J. McCabe, Democracy Vouchers and the Promise of Fairer Elections in Seattle 35–41 (2024).
58. In 2022, voters in Oakland endorsed a voucher program, but the mayor's budget failed to fund the program and it has not yet been used. A major issue for voucher programs, as for any form of public financing, is that they cannot limit independent spending by various groups. Indeed, in Seattle, independent spending rose significantly—and more so than in comparable jurisdictions—when the voucher system came into effect. *See id.* at 61.
59. *See, e.g.*, *Romanticizing Democracy, supra* note 34; Kang, *supra* note 6; La Raja & Schaffner, Campaign Finance and Political Polarization; Samuel Issacharoff, Democracy Unmoored: Populism and the Corruption of Popular Sovereignty (2023).
60. *See* Task Force Report, Institutional Reforms to Combat Extremism (Larry Diamond, Edward B. Foley & Richard H. Pildes eds.) (forthcoming 2025).
61. *See id.* (chapter on campaign finance, on file with author).
62. *See, e.g.*, Handbook of Political Party Funding (Jonathan Mendilow & Eric Phélippeau eds., 2018); *see also Money in Politics*, Int'l IDEA, https://www.idea.int/theme/money-politics (last visited Aug. 18, 2024).
63. *See* Richard Briffault, *A Better Financing System? The Death and Possible Rebirth of the Presidential Nomination Public Financing Program*, in The Best Candidate: Presidential Nomination in Polarized Times 235, 255–258 (Eugene D. Mazo & Michael R. Dimino eds., 2020) (citing studies). One contrary study found that public financing in Connecticut decreased the socioeconomic diversity of candidates. *See* Mitchell Kilborn, *Public Campaign Financing, Candidate Socioeconomic Diversity, and Representational Inequality at the U.S. State Level: Evidence from Connecticut*, 18 State Pol. & Pol'y Q. 296 (2018).
64. *See* Briffault, *supra* note 64 at 243–250.
65. 564 U.S. 721 (2011).
66. In the social-media context, for example, the Court recently in *Moody v. Netchoice*, 144 S. Ct. 2383, 2407–2408 (2024), relied on *Buckley v. Valeo* to hold that legislation regulating social-media platforms was unconstitutional to the extent it interfered with the platforms' own curation of speech. There the Court, relying on *Buckley*, reiterated that the government "cannot prohibit speech to improve or better balance the speech market. On the spectrum of dangers to free expression, there are few greater than allowing the government to change the speech of private actors in order to achieve its own conception of speech nirvana. That is why we have said *in so many contexts* that the government may not 'restrict the speech of some elements of our society in order to enhance the relative voice of others.' *Buckley*[.]"(emphasis added).

67. In the political-science literature, this is called affective polarization. *See, e.g.*, Diego Garzia & Frederico Ferreira da Silva, *The Electoral Consequences of Affective Polarization? Negative Voting in the 2020 US Presidential Election*, 50 AM. POL. RES. 303–311 (2022).
68. *See* Richard H. Pildes, *The Neglected Value of Effective Government*, 2023 U. CHI. L.F. 185 (2024).
69. *See Combatting Extremism*, supra note 5.

CHAPTER 14

1. WALTER DEAN BURNHAM, CRITICAL ELECTIONS AND THE MAINSPRINGS OF AMERICAN POLITICS 95–97 (1970).
2. *See generally* JOHN H. ALDRICH, WHY PARTIES?: THE ORIGIN AND TRANSFORMATION OF POLITICAL PARTIES IN AMERICA (1995) (describing parties during this era); Samuel Issacharoff, *Outsourcing Politics: The Hostile Takeover of Our Hollowed-Out Political Parties*, 54 HOU. L. REV. 845 (2017).
3. Federal Election Campaign Act Amendments of 1974, Pub. L. No. 93-443, 88 Stat. 1263 (codified as amended in scattered sections of 2 U.S.C.).
4. *See generally* ALDRICH, *supra* note 4 (tracing the historical transition from party-centric mobilization to candidate-centric media politics).
5. *See generally* Raymond J. La Raja, *Political Parties, in* GUIDE TO POLITICAL CAMPAIGNS IN AMERICA 177–198 (Paul S. Herrnson ed., 2005).
6. 424 U.S. 1, 26 (1976).
7. Michael G. Hagen & William G. Mayer, *The Modern Politics of Presidential Selection: How Changing the Rules Really Did Change the Game, in* IN PURSUIT OF THE WHITE HOUSE: HOW WE CHOOSE OUR PRESIDENTIAL NOMINEES 1, 33 (William G. Mayer ed., 2000).
8. *See, e.g., Buckley*, 424 U.S. at 26 ("The increasing importance of the communications media and sophisticated mass-mailing and polling operations to effective campaigning make the raising of large sums of money an ever more essential ingredient of an effective candidacy").
9. Walter Dean Burnham, *The Reagan Heritage, in* THE ELECTION OF 1988: REPORTS AND INTERPRETATIONS 1, 24 (Gerald M. Pomper ed., 1989).
10. *See generally* MARTIN P. WATTENBERG, THE DECLINE OF AMERICAN POLITICAL PARTIES, 1952–1992 (1994) (assessing the nature and reasons for the decline of political partisanship in the electorate).
11. EDWARD S. GREENBERG & BENJAMIN I. PAGE, THE STRUGGLE FOR DEMOCRACY 269 (1997).
12. *See generally* Kang, *Hyperpartisan Campaign Finance*.
13. Raymond J. La Raja, *Campaign Finance and Partisan Polarization in the United States Congress*, 9 DUKE J. CONST. L. & PUB. POL'Y 223, 231 (2014).

14. Raymond J. La Raja, Small Change: Money, Political Parties, and Campaign Finance Reform 77 (2008); *see* Frank J. Sorauf, Inside Campaign Finance: Myths and Realities (1992).
15. La Raja, *supra* note 14, at 77.
16. *See id.*
17. *See, e.g.*, Aldrich *supra* note 4, at 260–274 (describing this shift); Joseph A. Schlesinger, *The New American Political Party*, 79 Am. Pol. Sci. Rev. 1152, 1163–1164 (1985); Daniel M. Shea, *The Passing of Realignment and the Advent of the "Base-less" Party System*, 27 Am. Pol. Q. 33, 41–44 (1999).
18. *McConnell v. FEC*, 540 U.S. 93, 123–124 (2003); *see* Raymond J. La Raja, *Why Super PACs: How the American Party System Outgrew the Campaign Finance System*, 10 Forum 91, 78 (2012); Laura MacCleery, *Goodbye Soft Money, Hello Grassroots: How Campaign Finance Reform Restructured Campaigns and the Political World*, 58 Cath. L. Rev. 965, 977 (2009).
19. 424 U.S. at 43–44.
20. *See* Daniel J. Galvin, *The Transformation of Political Institutions: Investments in Institutional Resources and Gradual Change in the National Party Committees*, 26 Am. Pol. Dev. 50, 57–69 (2012) (describing explosion of fundraising by political parties).
21. *See* Michael J. Malbin, *Political Parties Under the Post-McConnell Bipartisan Campaign Reform Act*, 3 Election L.J. 177, 177 (2004).
22. The Bipartisan Campaign Reform Act of 2002, Pub. L. No. 107-155, 116 Stat. 81 (codified in scattered sections of 2 U.S.C., 18 U.S.C., 28 U.S.C., 36 U.S.C., and 47 U.S.C.).
23. See Richard Briffault, *The 527 Problem . . . and the* Buckley *Problem*, 73 Geo. Wash. L. Rev. 949 (2005).
24. 558 U.S. 310 (2010).
25. *See generally* Michael J. Malbin, *A Neo-Madisonian Perspective on Campaign Finance Reform, Institutions, Pluralism, and Small Donors*, 23 U. Pa. J. Const. L. 907, 926–931 (2021).
26. *See generally* Kang, *supra* note 12; Kang, *Hyperpartisan Gerrymandering*, 61 B.C. L. Rev. 1379 (2020).
27. *See, e.g.*, Julia Azari, *Weak Parties and Strong Partisanship Are a Bad Combination*, Vox, Nov. 3, 2016 (summarizing this view).
28. 424 U.S. at 25–29, 38.
29. 558 U.S. 310 (2010).
30. *See* Michael S. Kang, *The Year of the Super PAC*, 81 Geo. Wash. L. Rev. 1902 (2013).
31. *See generally* Michael S. Kang, *The End of Campaign Finance Law*, 98 Va. L. Rev. 1 (2012).
32. Mark Schmitt, *Note to the Last* Citizens United *Denier: It Really Did Change Money in Politics*, Next New Deal, July 19, 2012. *See also* Jessica Piper, *Super PACs Keep Testing the Limits of Campaign Finance Law*, Politico,

Apr. 8, 2024 (describing recent super-PAC gambits that further challenge current legal limits).

33. *See, e.g.*, Adam Bonica, *Ideology and Interests in the Political Marketplace*, 57 AM. J. POL. SCI. 294, 301–308 (2013); Michael J. Barber et al., *Ideologically Sophisticated Donors: Which Candidates Do Individual Contributors Finance?*, 61 AM. J. POL. SCI. 271, 285 (2017); Joseph Bafumi & Michael C. Herron, *Leapfrog Representation and Extremism: A Study of American Voters and Their Members in Congress*, 104 AM. POL. SCI. REV. 519, 519 (2010); Walter J. Stone & Elizabeth N. Simas, *Candidate Valence and Ideological Positions in U.S. House Elections*, 54 AM. J. POL. SCI. 371, 381 (2010).

34. *See* Michael Barber, *Donation Motivations: Testing Theories of Access and Ideology*, 69 POL. RSCH. Q. 148, 152–156 (2016).

35. *See Donor Demographics*, OPENSECRETS, https://www.opensecrets.org/elections-overview/donor-demographics?cycle=2016&display=A (last visited Aug. 19, 2024) (reporting FEC figures for individual contributions of $200 or more during the 2015–2016 and 2019–2020 cycles).

36. *See id.*

37. *See* David Broockman & Neil Malhotra, *What Do Partisan Donors Want?*, 84 PUB. OP. Q. 104, 108–111 (2020).

38. *See generally* Richard H. Pildes, *Participation and Polarization*, 22 U. PA. J. CONST. L. 341 (2020) (surveying the rise of small donors).

39. *See, e.g.*, La Raja, *supra* note 13 at 250–252; Wesley Y. Joe et al., *Do Small Donors Improve Representation? Some Answers from Recent Gubernatorial and State Legislative Elections*, CAMPAIGN FIN. INST. 2 (2008).

40. *See, e.g.*, Piper, *supra* note 33.

41. *See* Richard H. Pildes, *Why the Center Does Not Hold: The Causes of Hyperpolarized Democracy in America*, 99 CALIF. L. REV. 273, 277 (2011).

42. *See, e.g.*, Alan I. Abramowitz & Steven W. Webster, *Negative Partisanship: Why Americans Dislike Parties but Behave Like Rabid Partisans*, 39 ADVANCES POL. PSYCH. 119, 119–120 (2018).

43. *See, e.g.*, Nolan D. McCaskill, *Pew Study: Partisan Divide Widest in 25 Years*, POLITICO, June 22, 2016. *But see* James N. Druckman et al., *(Mis)estimating Affective Polarization*, 84 J. POL. 1106 (2022).

44. *See, e.g.*, RAYMOND J. LA RAJA & BRIAN F. SCHAFFNER, CAMPAIGN FINANCE AND POLITICAL POLARIZATION: WHEN PURISTS PREVAIL (2015); Nathaniel Persily, *Stronger Parties as a Solution to Polarization*, *in* SOLUTIONS TO POLITICAL POLARIZATION IN AMERICA 123–135 (Nathaniel Persily ed., 2015).

45. Richard H. Pildes, *Romanticizing Democracy, Political Fragmentation, and the Decline of American Government*, 124 YALE L.J. 804 (2014).

46. *Id.* at 839.

47. *Id.* at 838–839.

48. *Id.* at 829.

49. The first contributors to take advantage of the expanded opportunities to donate to the party committees under the Cromnibus provisions included Sheldon Adelson, David Koch, and Henry Kravis. *See* Kenneth P. Doyle, *Big GOP Donors Giving to New Accounts Congress Created to Help Political Parties*, BNA DAILY REPORT, May 26, 2015, at A-6.
50. *See* Hannah Hess, *Campaign Finance Provisions Causing 'Cromnibus' Heartburn*, ROLL CALL (Dec. 10, 2014), http://blogs.rollcall.com/hill-blotter/campaign-finance-provisions-causing-cromnibus-heartburn/ [http://perma.cc/LQK2-Q27L].
51. *See, e.g.*, Clyde Wilcox et al., *With Limits Raised, Who Will Give More? The Impact of BCRA on Individual Donors*, in LIFE AFTER REFORM: WHEN THE BIPARTISAN CAMPAIGN REFORM ACT MEETS POLITICS 61, 69–79 (Michael J. Malbin ed., 2003) (reporting the ideological motivations of the wealthy donors affected by regulation of party campaign finance).
52. *Compare* Pildes, *supra* note 41, at 832 (arguing that party leadership comprises ideological middlemen) *with* Bernard Grofman et al., *Congressional Leadership 1965–96: A New Look at the Extremism Versus Centrality Debate*, 27 LEGIS. STUD. Q. 87, 98 (2002) ("[P]arty leaders (in both parties) tend to be drawn from the part of the ideological spectrum where the greatest concentration of their members lies, the area beyond the median toward the party mode"); *see also* Eric Heberlig et al., *The Price of Leadership: Campaign Money and the Polarization of Congressional Parties*, 68 J. POL. 992, 993–995 (2006) ("[B]oth the elected leadership itself and the farm system for elected leaders are increasingly populated by ideologues"); A. J. McGann et al., *Why Party Leaders Are More Extreme Than Their Members: Modeling Sequential Elimination Elections in the U.S. House of Representatives*, 113 PUB. CHOICE 337, 351–352 (2002) (finding that "party leaders tend to be more extreme that their median members. . . ."). For a neutral assessment, see Douglas B. Harris & Garrison Nelson, *Middlemen No More? Emergent Patterns in Congressional Leadership Selection*, 41 PS: POL. SCI. & POL. 49, 51 (noting that leaders from the 107th to 110th Congress were equally likely to be middlemen as extremists) (2008); Stephen Jessee & Neil Malhotra, *Are Congressional Leaders Middlepersons or Extremists? Yes*, 35 LEGIS. STUD. Q. 361, 380–384 (2010) (finding that elected leaders are usually close to their party's ideological median, but also display extremist tendencies). *See also* Stephanie Stamm, *Paul Ryan Would Be the Most Conservative House Speaker in Recent History*, NAT'L J., Oct. 21, 2015 (reporting that new House Speaker Paul Ryan has the most polarized DW-NOMINATE score among the last eleven Speakers and ranks in the top quintile for conservatism in the House).
53. *See* Michael J. Ensley, *Individual Campaign Contributions and Candidate Ideology*, 138 PUB. CHOICE 221, 227 (2009) (finding that Republican and Democratic candidates could raise more money if they deviated from their respective parties' ideological centers); Heberlig, *supra* note 53; Bertram

Johnson, *Individual Contributions: A Fundraising Advantage for the Ideologically Extreme?*, 38 AM. POL. RES. 890, 903–906 (2010) (noting the advantages candidates can obtain from appealing to ideologically extreme individual donors); Walter J. Stone & Elizabeth N. Simas, *Candidate Valence and Ideological Positions in U.S. House Elections*, 54 AM. J. POL. SCI. 371, 380–382 (2010) (finding that candidates have an electoral incentive to move ideologically away from their districts and speculating that this finding is linked to campaign contributions by ideologically extreme individual contributors).

54. *See* Heberlig, *supra* note 53, at 1002–1004.
55. *See generally* THOMAS E. MANN & NORMAN J. ORNSTEIN, IT'S EVEN WORSE THAN IT LOOKS: HOW THE AMERICAN CONSTITUTIONAL SYSTEM COLLIDED WITH THE NEW POLITICS OF EXTREMISM 51–59 (2012) (criticizing the Republican Party's rightward shift and developing this argument).
56. *See* DAVID W. ROHDE, PARTIES AND LEADERS IN THE POSTREFORM HOUSE 105 (1991).
57. *See* MANN & CORRADO, *supra* note 52, at 14 ("Parties today are strong in the electorate, strong in their vast organizational networks, and strong in government"); *see also id.* at 18 ("Inadequate resources are among the least important problems facing party leaders in Congress on either side of the aisle"). It may be that advocates of stronger party leadership today are simply nostalgic for bygone postwar bipartisanship that was itself historically exceptional. *See* Hahrie Han & David W. Brady, *A Delayed Return to Historical Norms: Congressional Party Polarization After the Second World War*, 37 BRIT. J. POL. SCI. 505, 507–512 (2007).
58. *See* Morris P. Fiorina, *An Era of Divided Government*, 107 POL. SCI. Q. 387, 408 (1992) ("In obscuring responsibility for government actions and the results thereof, divided control exacerbates the already serious problems of responsibility that are inherent in American politics").
59. *See* Seth Masket, *Mitigating Extreme Partisanship in an Era of Networked Parties: An Examination of Various Reform Strategies*, 13 CTR. FOR EFFECTIVE PUB. MGMT. AT BROOKINGS INST. (2014) ("[T]here is little reason to believe that a change in the campaign finance system would substantially hurt or help parties or change the voting behavior of the politicians they nominate").
60. *See, e.g.*, Shane Goldmacher & Nick Corasaniti, *Inside the G.O.P.'s State Party Problem*, N.Y. TIMES, Feb. 22, 2024; Andy Kroll, *Scenes from a MAGA Meltdown: Inside the "America First" Movement's War over Democracy*, PROPUBLICA, May 22, 2024; Isaac Arnsdorf et al., *MAGA-Dominated State Republican Parties Plagued by Infighting, Money Woes*, WASH. POST, Nov. 16, 2023; David Smith, *"It's Endemic": State-Level Republican Groups Lead Party's Drift to Extremism*, GUARDIAN, Jan. 31, 2021.
61. Goldmacher & Corasaniti, *supra* note.

62. *See* Craig Mauger, *Separate Michigan GOP Group Votes to Keep Kristina Karamo as Chairwoman*, DETROIT NEWS, Jan. 13, 2024.
63. *See* Margery A. Beck, *The Nebraska GOP Is Rejecting All Republican Congressional Incumbents in Tuesday's Primary Election*, ASSOC. PRESS, May 13, 2024.
64. Smith, *supra* note (quoting Tim Miller).
65. *See* Thomas E. Mann & Anthony Corrado, *Party Polarization and Campaign Finance*, 17, CTR. FOR EFFECTIVE PUB. MGMT. AT BROOKINGS INST (2014); Joseph R. Fishkin & Heather K. Gerken, *The Two Trends That Matter for Party Politics*, 89 N.Y.U. L. REV ONLINE 32, 39–46 (2014).
66. *See, e.g.*, BENJAMIN I. PAGE, JASON SEAWRIGHT & MATTHEW J. LACOMBE, BILLIONAIRES AND STEALTH POLITICS (2018); Jaime Lowe, *With "Stealth Politics," Billionaires Make Sure Their Money Talks*, N.Y. TIMES MAG., Apr. 6, 2022.
67. *See* LARRY M. BARTELS, UNEQUAL DEMOCRACY: THE POLITICAL ECONOMY OF THE NEW GILDED AGE 257–265 (2008); MARTIN GILENS, AFFLUENCE AND INFLUENCE: ECONOMIC INEQUALITY AND POLITICAL POWER IN AMERICA (2012); JACOB S. HACKER & PAUL PIERSON, WINNER-TAKE-ALL POLITICS: HOW WASHINGTON MADE THE RICH RICHER—AND TURNED ITS BACK ON THE MIDDLE CLASS (2010); *see also* Nicholas Stephanopoulos, *Aligning Campaign Finance Law*, 101 VA. L. REV. 1425, 1425 (2015) (summarizing this literature and proposing campaign finance law be directed toward aligning policymaking with public opinion).
68. Martin Gilens & Benjamin I. Page, *Testing Theories of American Politics: Elites, Interest Groups, and Average Citizens*, 12 PERSP. ON POL. 564, 572 (2014).
69. Michael S. Kang, *Party Campaign Finance and Partisan Polarization*, *in* THE BEST CANDIDATE: PRESIDENTIAL NOMINATION IN POLARIZED TIMES (Eugene D. Mazo & Michael R. Dimino eds. 2020).
70. 548 U.S. 230 (2006).
71. *Citizens United v. FEC*, 558 U.S. 310 (2010); *SpeechNow.org v. FEC*, 599 F.3d 686 (2010).
72. 572 U.S. 185 (2014).
73. *See* LA RAJA, *supra* note 14; Pildes, *supra* note 41.
74. 424 U.S. at 78.
75. 533 U.S. 431 (2001).
76. *See Nat'l Republican Senatorial Comm. v. FEC*, No. 1:22-cv-639, 2024 U.S. Dist. LEXIS 9998 (S.D. Ohio Jan. 19, 2024).
77. First Brief of Plaintiff-Appellants Nat'l Republican Senatorial Cmte, J.D. Vance, and Steven Chabot at 4, *Nat'l Republican Senatorial Comm. v. FEC*, No. 1:22-cv-639 (6th Cir. Mar. 4, 2024).
78. A similar proposal is raising limits on the party committees' own contributions to their candidates, which La Raja and Schaffner specifically associate

with lower polarization at the state legislative level. LA RAJA & SCHAFFNER, *supra* note 40. Professor Tabatha Abu El-Haj expresses sympathy for removal of the federal ban on party soft money as a way to strengthen party grass-roots networks. Tabatha Abu El-Haj, *Networking the Party: First Amendment Rights and the Pursuit of Responsive Party Government*, 118 COLUM. L. REV. 1225 (2018). Former FEC Commissioner Lee Goodman argues for the deregulation of party voter-registration drives and volunteer activities such as mail drives, phone banking, and literature distribution. Lee Goodman, *A Time to Revive the Party*, WASH. EXAMINER, Nov. 16, 2015. Professor Allison Hayward argues along similar lines for simplification of the federal rules for Levin funds to encourage state and local parties currently crowded out by the national parties in election activity. Allison R. Hayward, *Revisiting the Fable of Reform*, 45 HARV. J. LEGIS. 421 (2008).

CHAPTER 15

1. *See* Federal Election Campaign Act Amendments of 1974, Pub. L. No. 93-443, 88 Stat. 1263 (1974) (codified as amended at 52 U.S.C. § 30101 *et seq.* (2018)).
2. FRANK J. SORAUF, INSIDE CAMPAIGN FINANCE: MYTHS AND REALITIES 7–8 (1992).
3. *Cf.* Mariano-Florentino Cuéllar & Matthew C. Stephenson, *Taming Systemic Corruption: The American Experience and Its Implications for Contemporary Debates*, WORLD DEV., July 2022, at 1, 8–19.
4. *See* Warren Weaver Jr., *'72 Election Set Spending Record*, N.Y. TIMES (Apr. 25, 1976), https://www.nytimes.com/1976/04/25/archives/72-election-set-spending-record-137-million-went-for-major-parties.html.
5. Joel L. Fleishman, *The 1974 Federal Election Campaign Act Amendments: The Shortcomings of Good Intentions*, 1975 DUKE L.J. 851, 865–866.
6. *See* Federal Election Campaign Act Amendments of 1974, 88 Stat. 1263.
7. *See* Pub. L. No. 62-32, 37 Stat. 25 (1911) (codified as amended in scattered sections of 15 U.S.C.).
8. 424 U.S. 1 (1976).
9. *See id.* at 26.
10. *See id.* at 143.
11. Samuel Issacharoff, *On Corruption*, 124 HARV. L. REV. 118, 119–120 (2010).
12. Guy-Uriel E. Charles, *Corruption Temptation*, 102 CALIF. L. REV. 25, 26 (2014).
13. *See* Pub. L. 107-155, 116 Stat. 81 (2002) (codified as amended at 52 U.S.C. § 30101 *et seq.* (2018)).
14. *See, e.g.*, RICHARD L. HASEN, PLUTOCRATS UNITED: CAMPAIGN MONEY, THE SUPREME COURT, AND THE DISTORTION OF AMERICAN ELECTIONS (2016); LAWRENCE LESSIG, REPUBLIC, LOST: HOW MONEY CORRUPTS

CONGRESS—AND A PLAN TO STOP IT (2011); Michael S. Kang, *Hyperpartisan Campaign Finance*, 70 EMORY L.J. 1171 (2021) [hereinafter Kang, *Hyperpartisan Campaign Finance*]; Tabatha Abu El-Haj, *Beyond Campaign Finance Reform*, 57 B.C.L. REV. 1127 (2016).

15. *See, e.g.*, Pamela S. Karlan, *Citizens Deflected: Electoral Integrity and Political Reform*, in CITIZENS DIVIDED: CAMPAIGN FINANCE REFORM AND THE CONSTITUTION 143 (Robert C. Post ed., 2014) (noting that "[t]he pernicious kinds of political spending we now have are shaped not only by the law of campaign finance but also by a range of other factors").
16. Federal Election Campaign Act Amendments of 1974, Pub. L. No. 93-443, 88 Stat. 1263 (1974) (codified as amended at 52 U.S.C. § 30101 *et seq.*); *see also* Federal Election Campaign Act of 1971, Pub. L. No. 92-225, 86 Stat. 3 (1972) (codified as amended at 52 U.S.C. § 30101 *et seq.*).
17. Kenneth J. Levit, Note, *Campaign Finance Reform and the Return of* Buckley v. Valeo, 103 YALE L.J. 469, 471 (1993).
18. *Buckley v. Valeo*, 519 F.2d 821, 831 (D.C. Cir. 1975).
19. *Id.* at 907.
20. *Id.*
21. *Id.*
22. *Cf., e.g.*, Spencer A. Overton, *The Participation Interest*, 100 GEO. L.J. 1259, 1261–1262 (2012).
23. *Buckley v. Valeo*, 424 U.S. 1, 39 (1976).
24. *Id.*
25. *Id.*
26. 435 U.S. 765 (1978).
27. *See id.* at 786.
28. *Id.* at 788–789 (cleaned up).
29. *See id.* at 788–790.
30. 494 U.S. 652 (1990).
31. *Id.* at 660–662.
32. *Id.*
33. *McConnell v. Fed. Election Comm'n*, 540 U.S. 93, 224 (2003).
34. *Id.*
35. 558 U.S. 310 (2010).
36. *Id.* at 363–365.
37. *Id.* at 359.
38. *See, e.g.*, Michael S. Kang, *After Citizens United*, 44 IND. L. REV. 243 (2010); Richard L. Hasen, Citizens United *and the Illusion of Coherence*, 109 MICH. L. REV. 581 (2010); Ganesh Sitaraman, *Contracting Around* Citizens United, 114 COLUM. L. REV. 755, 757–759 (2014); Robert Yablon, *Campaign Finance Reform Without Law*, 103 IOWA L. REV. 185, 187 (2017); Deborah Hellman, *Money Talks but It Isn't Speech*, 95 MINN. L. REV. 953, 954 (2011); Nicholas Almendares & Catherine Hafer, *Beyond* Citizens United,

84 FORDHAM L. REV. 2755, 2758 (2016); Michael S. Kang, *The Brave New Word of Party Campaign Finance Law*, 101 CORNELL L. REV. 531, 532 (2015).

39. *See, e.g.*, Deborah Hellman, *Defining Corruption and Constitutionalizing Democracy*, 111 MICH. L. REV. 1385, 1388 (2013).
40. *See, e.g.*, Nicholas O. Stephanopoulos, *Campaign Finance and "Real" Corruption* in Chapter 10 of this volume.
41. *See, e.g.*, Abhay P. Aneja et al., *Financial Inclusion in Politics*, 97 N.Y.U. L. REV. 566 (2022); Abby K. Wood, *Learning from Campaign Finance Information*, 70 EMORY L.J. 1091 (2021); Note, *Drowning Out Democracy*, 137 HARV. L. REV. 2386 (2024).
42. *See, e.g.*, Erin Kesler & Corey Goldstone, *Supreme Court Leaves Seattle's Democracy Voucher System in Place*, CAMPAIGN LEGAL CTR. (Mar. 30, 2020), https://campaignlegal.org/update/supreme-court-leaves-seattles-democracy-voucher-system-place.
43. *See id.*
44. *See, e.g.*, Spencer A. Overton, *Matching Political Contributions*, 96 MINN. L. REV. 1694, 1694–1696 (2012).
45. *See, e.g.*, JACOB S. HACKER & PAUL PIERSON, LET THEM EAT TWEETS: HOW THE RIGHT RULES IN AN AGE OF EXTREME INEQUALITY (2020) [hereinafter HACKER & PIERSON, LET THEM EAT TWEETS].
46. *See, e.g., id.* at 139–151; Jason Lange & James Oliphant, *Republicans Have Taken Sharp Populist Turn in the Trump Era*, REUTERS (Mar. 21, 2024), https://www.reuters.com/world/us/us-republicans-have-taken-sharp-populist-turn-trump-era-reutersipsos-data-shows-2024-03-21/.
47. *See* Peter Overby, *Every Position Donald Trump Has Taken on How He Is Funding His Campaign*, NPR (July 14, 2016), https://www.npr.org/2016/07/14/485699964/every-position-donald-trump-has-taken-on-how-he-is-funding-his-campaign.
48. *See* Isaac Arnsdorf, *Trump Won with Half as Much Money as Clinton Raised*, POLITICO (Dec. 8, 2016), https://www.politico.com/story/2016/12/trump-clinton-campaign-fundraising-totals-232400.
49. *See* HACKER & PIERSON, LET THEM EAT TWEETS, *supra* note 45, at 139–140.
50. *See* Paul Pierson, *American Hybrid: Donald Trump and the Strange Merger of Populism and Plutocracy*, 68 BRIT. J. SOCIO. 106, 112 (2017).
51. Jeffrey Kucik, *How Trump Fueled Economic Inequality in America* (Jan. 21, 2021), https://thehill.com/opinion/finance/535239-how-trump-fueled-economic-inequality-in-america/.
52. *See* William G. Gale et al., *Effects of the Tax Cuts and Jobs Act: A Preliminary Analysis*, BROOKINGS (June 13, 2018), https://www.brookings.edu/articles/effects-of-the-tax-cuts-and-jobs-act-a-preliminary-

analysis; Robert Pear et al., *In Major Defeat for Trump, Push to Repeal Health Law Fails*, N.Y. TIMES (Mar. 24, 2017), https://www.nytimes.com/2017/03/24/us/politics/health-care-affordable-care-act.html.

53. *See, e.g.*, Thomas Stratmann, *Some Talk: Money in Politics. A (Partial) Review of the Literature*, 124 PUB. CHOICE 135, 136 (2005).

54. *See* Kate Conger & Lauren Hirsch, *Elon Musk Completes $44 Billion Deal to Own Twitter*, N.Y. TIMES (Oct. 27, 2022), https://www.nytimes.com/2022/10/27/technology/elon-musk-twitter-deal-complete.html.

55. *See* Kate Conger, *Trump Returns to X in Victory for Elon Musk*, N.Y. TIMES (Aug. 12, 2024), https://www.nytimes.com/2024/08/12/technology/donald-trump-elon-musk-x.html.

56. *See* Kate Conger, *Elon Musk Is Using X to Push His Views, and Donald Trump*, N.Y. TIMES (Aug. 12, 2024), https://www.nytimes.com/2024/08/12/technology/elon-musk-political-views.html.

57. *See* Anthony Cuthbertson, *Elon Musk Appears to Have Tweaked X's Algorithm to Promote Trump, Study Claims*, INDEPENDENT (Nov. 4, 2024), https://www.independent.co.uk/tech/elon-musk-trump-x-algorithm-bias-b2640976.html.

58. *See* Theodore Schleifer & Susanne Craig, *Trump's Victory Is a Major Win for Elon Musk and Big-Money Politics*, N.Y. TIMES (Nov. 6, 2024), https://www.nytimes.com/2024/11/06/us/elections/trump-musk-america-pac.html.

59. *Id.*

60. *Id.*

61. *Id.*

62. *Id.*

63. *Id.*

64. *See Coronavirus: Musk Defies Orders and Reopens Tesla's California Plant*, BBC (May 12, 2020), https://www.bbc.com/news/technology-52627744.

65. *See* Eric Lipton, *Wildlife Protections Take a Back Seat to SpaceX's Ambitions*, N.Y. TIMES (July 7, 2024), https://www.nytimes.com/2024/07/07/us/politics/spacex-wildlife-texas.html.

66. *See* Chris Isidore, *Tesla Just Got Snubbed by Biden's Electric Vehicle Summit*, CNN (Aug. 5, 2021), https://www.cnn.com/2021/08/05/business/tesla-snub-white-house-event/index.html.

67. *See* Paul A. Eisenstein, *Opposites Attract? Why Musk and Trump Are Having a Bromance*, NBC NEWS (Jan. 27, 2017), https://www.nbcnews.com/business/autos/opposites-attract-why-musk-trump-are-having-bromance-n713046.

68. *See* Kyle Chayka, *How Elon Musk Rebranded Trump*, NEW YORKER (Nov. 13, 2024), https://www.newyorker.com/culture/infinite-scroll/how-elon-musk-rebranded-trump.

69. *See* Dan Lips, *What Could a Trump-Musk Government Efficiency Commission Solve?*, THE HILL (Aug. 21, 2024), https://thehill.com/opinion/4837212-government-efficiency-commission/.
70. *See* Maggie Haberman, *Trump Put Musk on Phone with Zelensky During Call*, N.Y. TIMES (Nov. 8, 2024), https://www.nytimes.com/2024/11/08/us/politics/trump-musk-zelensky.html.
71. Farnaz Fassihi, *Elon Musk Met with Iran's U.N. Ambassador, Iranian Officials Say*, N.Y. TIMES (Nov. 14, 2024), https://www.nytimes.com/2024/11/14/world/middleeast/elon-musk-iran-trump.html.
72. *See, e.g.*, Lee Fang, *The Kochs' Ground Game*, THE NATION (Sept. 26, 2012), https://www.thenation.com/article/archive/kochs-ground-game/.
73. Kang, *supra* note 15.
74. *See* JOSEPH C. HARSCH, ROLE OF POLITICAL PARTIES U.S.A. 23 (1955).
75. *See* Geoffrey C. Layman & Thomas M. Carsey, *Party Polarization and "Conflict Extension" in the American Electorate*, 46 AM. J. POL. SCI. 786, 786 (2002) ("[T]he elections of Ronald Reagan in 1980 and a Republican congressional majority in 1994 repolarized party debate on the social welfare issues that have structured party conflicts since the New Deal").
76. *See, e.g.*, Greg D. Adams, *Abortion: Evidence of an Issue Evolution*, 41 AM. J. POL. SCI. 718, 735 (1997) (finding both mass and elite shifts between the 1970s and 1990s that made Democrats more distinctly pro-choice).
77. *See* Layman & Carsey, supra note 75, at 789.
78. *See* Drew DeSilver, *U.S. Income Inequality, on Rise for Decades, Is Now Highest Since 1928*, PEW RSCH. CTR. (Dec. 5, 2013), https://www.pewresearch.org/short-reads/2013/12/05/u-s-income-inequality-on-rise-for-decades-is-now-highest-since-1928/.
79. *See* Juliana Menasce Horowitz et al., *Trends in Income and Wealth Inequality*, PEW RSCH. CTR. (Jan. 9, 2020), https://www.pewresearch.org/social-trends/2020/01/09/trends-in-income-and-wealth-inequality/.
80. *See* NOLAN MCCARTY, POLARIZATION: WHAT EVERYONE NEEDS TO KNOW 15 (2019) (noting that evidence suggests voter polarization and partisan sorting began in the 1990s—although the partisan sorting of party elites began fifteen to twenty years earlier).
81. *See* Geoffrey C. Layman et al., *Party Polarization in American Politics: Characteristics, Causes, and Consequences*, 9 ANN. REV. POL. SCI. 83, 84 (2006) (summarizing the literature); *see also* Keith T. Poole & Howard Rosenthal, *The Polarization of American Politics*, 46 J. POL. 1061, 1073 (1984); BARBARA SINCLAIR, PARTY WARS: POLARIZATION AND THE POLITICS OF NATIONAL POLICY MAKING (2012).
82. *See, e.g.*, THOMAS E. MANN & NORMAN J. ORNSTEIN, IT'S EVEN WORSE THAN IT WAS: HOW THE AMERICAN CONSTITUTIONAL SYSTEM COLLIDED WITH THE NEW POLITICS OF EXTREMISM 31–43, 47 (2016); John E. Owens, *The Onward March of (Asymmetric) Political Polarisation in the*

Contemporary Congress, in ISSUES IN AMERICAN POLITICS: POLARIZED POLITICS IN THE AGE OF OBAMA 98 (John W. Dumbrell ed., 2013); Edward G. Carmines, *Review Symposium: Class Politics, American-Style*, PERSPS. ON POLS., Sept. 2011, at 645; JACOB S. HACKER & PAUL PIERSON, OFF CENTER: THE REPUBLICAN REVOLUTION AND THE EROSION OF AMERICAN DEMOCRACY 25–44, 135–162 (2005); *cf. also* Adam Lovett, *The Ethics of Asymmetric Politics*, 22 POL., PHIL. & ECON., Feb. 2023, at 3.

83. *See generally, e.g.*, Shanto Iyengar et al., *The Origins and Consequences of Affective Polarization in the United States*, 22 ANN. REV. POL. SCI. 129 (2019).
84. HACKER & PIERSON, LET THEM EAT TWEETS, *supra* note 45, at 1.
85. *Id.* at 6–9.
86. *Id.* at 2–4.
87. *See id.* at 1–10; *see also* Kang, *Hyperpartisan Campaign Finance*, *supra* note 15, at 1191.
88. HACKER & PIERSON, LET THEM EAT TWEETS, *supra* note 45, at 7–15.
89. Kang, *Hyperpartisan Campaign Finance*, *supra* note 14, at 1188.
90. *Id.* at 1192–1193.
91. *See id.* at 1193–1207.
92. Abu El-Haj, *supra* note 14, at 1130.
93. *E.g.*, CORNELIUS P. COTTER & BERNARD C. HENNESSY, POLITICS WITHOUT POWER: THE NATIONAL PARTY COMMITTEES (2009).
94. *Cf. e.g.*, Richard Pildes, *How to Fix Our Polarized Politics? Strengthen Political Parties*, WASH. POST (Feb. 6, 2014), https://www.washingtonpost.com/news/monkey-cage/wp/2014/02/06/how-to-fix-our-polarized-politics-strengthen-political-parties/; Seth Masket, *Our Political Parties Are Networked, Not Fragmented*, WASH. POST (Feb. 14, 2014), https://www.washingtonpost.com/news/monkey-cage/wp/2014/02/14/our-political-parties-are-networked-not-fragmented/.
95. *Cf., e.g.*, Christopher Hare & Keith T. Poole, *The Polarization of Contemporary American Politics*, 46 POLITY, July 2014, at 411; RACHEL BLUM, HOW THE TEA PARTY CAPTURED THE GOP: INSURGENT FACTIONS IN AMERICAN POLITICS (2020); Jack M. Balkin, *The Last Days of Disco: Why the American Political System Is Dysfunctional*, 94 B.U. L. REV. 1159 (2014).
96. *See, e.g.*, TIM ALBERTA, AMERICAN CARNAGE: ON THE FRONT LINES OF THE REPUBLICAN CIVIL WAR AND THE RISE OF PRESIDENT TRUMP (2019).
97. For other proposals broadly contemplating the importance of reinvigorating parties, see, e.g., Richard H. Pildes, *Romanticizing Democracy, Political Fragmentation, and the Decline of American Government*, 124 YALE L.J. 804, 825 (2014); Samuel Issacharoff, *Outsourcing Politics: The Hostile Takeovers of Our Hollowed-Out Political Parties*, 54 HOUS. L. REV. 845, 862 (2017).
98. Democratic National Committee Fundraising Overview, 2024 Election Cycle, OPEN SECRETS, https://www.opensecrets.org/political-parties/

DNC/2024/summary?name=democratic-national-committee (last visited Nov. 20, 2024).

99. Shane Goldmacher & Maggie Haberman, *Kamala Harris Has Raised $1 Billion Since Entering 2024 Presidential Race*, N.Y. TIMES (Oct. 9, 2024), https://www.nytimes.com/2024/10/09/us/politics/harris-billion-dollar-fundraising.html.
100. April Rubin, *Harris' Campaign Shares $24.5M with Down-Ballot Democratic Races*, AXIOS (Sept. 3, 2024), https://www.axios.com/2024/09/03/harris-campaign-finance-democrat-races-state-congress.
101. Democratic Senatorial Campaign Committee Fundraising Overview, 2024 Election Cycle, OPEN SECRETS, https://www.opensecrets.org/political-parties/DSCC/2024/summary?name=democratic-senatorial-campaign-cmte (last visited Nov. 20, 2024).
102. Jared Gans, *Brown Raises Close To $31M in Competitive Ohio Senate Race*, THE HILL (Oct. 2, 2024), https://thehill.com/homenews/campaign/4912441-brown-raises-close-to-31m-in-competitive-ohio-senate-race/.
103. Republican National Committee Fundraising Overview, 2024 Election Cycle, OPEN SECRETS, https://www.opensecrets.org/political-parties/RNC/2024/summary?name=republican-national-cmte (last visited Nov. 20, 2024).
104. Donald Trump (R) Winner, OPEN SECRETS, https://www.opensecrets.org/2024-presidential-race/donald-trump/candidate?id=N00023864 (last visited Nov. 20, 2024).
105. *See Contribution Limits*, FEC.gov, https://www.fec.gov/help-candidates-and-committees/candidate-taking-receipts/contribution-limits/; *cf. also* Michael S. Kang, *Party-Based Corruption and* McCutcheon v. FEC, 108 N.W. L. REV. ONLINE 240, 244 (2014).
106. *See* Julia Azari, *Weak Parties and Strong Partisanship Are a Bad Combination*, VOX (Nov. 3, 2016), https://www.vox.com/mischiefs-of-faction/2016/11/3/13512362/weak-parties-strong-partisanship-bad-combination.
107. *See* Michael S. Kang, *The Year of the Super PAC*, 81 GEO. WASH. L. REV. 1902, 1904, 1915, 1920 (2013); *see also Citizens United*, 558 U.S. 310, 360 (2010).
108. 533 U.S. 431, 437 (2001).

CHAPTER 16

1. 588 U.S. 684 (alteration in original) (citations omitted).
2. *Id.* at 691–692.
3. 588 U.S. 684.
4. *Citizens United v. Fed. Election Comn'n*, 558 U.S. 310, 350 (2010) (quoting *Buckley v. Valeo*, 424 U.S. 1, 48 (1976)).
5. *Rucho*, 588 U.S. at 701.
6. *Id.*

7. The Elections Clause provides: "The Times, Places and Manner of holding Elections for Senators and Representatives, shall be prescribed in each State by the Legislature thereof; but the Congress may at any time by Law make or alter such Regulations, except as to the Places of chusing Senators." U.S. Const. art. I, § 4, cl. 1. The Seventeenth Amendment, providing for the popular election of senators, modified the Elections Clause as to senators.
8. *Rucho*, 588 U.S. at 691.
9. *See, e.g., Rucho*, 588 U.S. at 701.
10. *Moody v. NetChoice*, 144 S. Ct. 2383, 2402 (2024).
11. The Twenty-Fourth Amendment to the Constitution forbids poll taxes in federal elections, and the Supreme Court held, in *Harper v. Virginia State Board of Elections*, 383 U.S. 663 (1966), that a state poll tax violated the Equal Protection Clause.
12. *Citizens United v. Federal Election Comm'n*, 558 U.S. 310, 350 (2010) (quoting *Buckley v. Valeo*, 424 U.S. 1, 48 (1976)).
13. 424 U.S. 1, 48–49 (1976).
14. *Id.*
15. *Rucho*, 588 U.S. at 707 (citing sources).
16. *Id.* at 721 (Kagan, J., dissenting).
17. *Id.* at 718 (majority opinion) (citation omitted).
18. *Id.*
19. *See, e.g., id.* at 707, 710 (holding that to be justiciable, courts require "a limited and precise standard that is judicially discernible and manageable").
20. Lee C. Bollinger Jr., *Freedom of the Press and Public Access: Toward a Theory of Partial Regulation of the Mass Media*, 75 MICH. L. REV. 1 (1976), suggests another possible example: what was then a difference in the treatment of printed and electronic media.
21. *See, e.g., Carter v. Carter Coal Co.*, 298 U.S. 238 (1936); *A.L.A. Schechter Poultry Corp. v. United States*, 295 U.S. 495 (1935); *Hammer v. Dagenhart*, 247 U.S. 251 (1918); *United States v. E.C. Knight Co.*, 156 U.S. 1 (1895).
22. *See, e.g., Perez v. United States*, 402 U.S. 146 (1971); *Katzenbach v. McClung*, 379 U.S. 294 (1964); *Heart of Atlanta Motel v. United States*, 379 U.S. 241 (1964); *Wickard v. Filburn*, 317 U.S. 111 (1942); *United States v. Darby*, 312 U.S. 100 (1941).
23. *See United States v. Morrison*, 529 U.S. 598 (2000); *United States v. Lopez*, 514 U.S. 549 (1995).

CHAPTER 17

1. *See generally* RICHARD J. EVANS, ALTERED PASTS: COUNTERFACTUALS IN HISTORY (2013).
2. 424 U.S. 1 (1976) (per curiam).
3. SAMUEL ISSACHAROFF ET AL., THE LAW OF DEMOCRACY: LEGAL STRUCTURE OF THE POLITICAL PROCESS 787 (6th ed. 2022).

4. *See, e.g.*, Samuel Issacharoff & Pamela S. Karlan, *The Hydraulics of Campaign Finance Reform*, 77 TEX. L. REV. 1705 (1999); Karlan, *Answering Questions, Questioning Answers, and the Roles of Empiricism in the Law of Democracy*, 65 STAN. L. REV. 1269, 1279–1288 (2013); Karlan, *Foreword: Democracy and Disdain*, 126 HARV. L. REV. 1, 30–41 (2012) [hereinafter Karlan, *Democracy and Disdain*]; Karlan, *New Beginnings and Dead Ends in the Law of Democracy*, 68 OHIO ST. L.J. 743, 746–754 (2007).
5. *See* LAWRENCE LESSIG, REPUBLIC, LOST: HOW MONEY CORRUPTS CONGRESS—AND A PLAN TO STOP IT (2015); Bertrall L. Ross II, *Addressing Inequality in the Age of* Citizens United, 93 N.Y.U. L. REV. 1120, 1139–1146 (2018) (summarizing, but then critiquing, the arguments about the link between the campaign finance regime and economic inequality).
6. *Buckley*, 424 U.S. at 48.
7. Issacharoff & Karlan, *supra* note 4, at 1718.
8. 18 U.S.C. § 608(e)(1) (1970 ed., Supp. IV).
9. *Buckley*, 424 U.S. at 45.
10. Issacharoff & Karlan, *supra* note 4, at 1718.
11. *Id.* at 1713.
12. *See, e.g.*, SAMUEL POPKIN, CRACKUP: THE REPUBLICAN IMPLOSION AND THE FUTURE OF PRESIDENTIAL POLITICS 22 (2021); Richard H. Pildes, *Romanticizing Democracy, Political Fragmentation, and the Decline of American Government*, 124 YALE L.J. 804, 834–836 (2014) [hereinafter Pildes, *Romanticizing Democracy*].
13. *See* BRUCE CAIN, DEMOCRACY MORE OR LESS: AMERICA'S POLITICAL REFORM QUANDARY (2015); Mike Norton & Richard H. Pildes, *How Outside Money Makes Governing More Difficult*, 19 ELECTION L.J. 486 (2020); Nathaniel Persily, *Stronger Parties as a Solution to Polarization*, in SOLUTIONS TO POLITICAL POLARIZATION IN AMERICA 123 (Nathaniel Persily ed., 2015).
14. Scott Bomboy, *A Brief History of Presidential Primaries*, NAT'L CONST. CTR. BLOG (Mar. 1, 2024), https://constitutioncenter.org/blog/a-brief-history-of-presidential-primaries.
15. Stephen Gardbaum & Richard H. Pildes, *Populism and Institutional Design: Methods of Selecting Candidates for Chief Executive*, 93 N.Y.U.L. REV. 647, 663 (2018).
16. V. O. KEY, JR., POLITICS, PARTIES, & PRESSURE GROUPS 164–165 (5th ed. 1964) (identifying this framework).
17. *See, e.g.*, Alexander Burns, Maggie Haberman & Jonathan Martin, *Inside the Republican Party's Desperate Mission to Stop Donald Trump*, N.Y. TIMES (Feb. 27, 2016), https://www.nytimes.com/2016/02/28/us/politics/donald-trump-republican-party.html.
18. Gardbaum & Pildes, *supra* note 15, at 666.

19. The Democratic Party responded to a series of electoral setbacks by creating a cadre of "superdelegates" drawn from the first two categories (denominated "party leaders and elected officials"). But after rules changes in 2018, those delegates can vote only after the first ballot, which means they have influence only if the primary electorate is divided among multiple candidates. *See also* Samuel Issacharoff, *Outsourcing Politics: The Hostile Takeover of Our Hollowed-Out Political Parties*, 54 HOUS. L. REV. 845, 875, 878–879 (2017) (describing how "taking nominations away from the party . . . weakens the hold of the party on not just candidates but on elected officials" as well).
20. BILL BISHOP, THE BIG SORT: WHY THE CLUSTERING OF LIKE-MINDED AMERICA IS TEARING US APART (2008). On top of the Big Sort, there has been a "Great Alignment": In contrast to the mid-20th century, today a range of socioeconomic characteristics—from race, to religion, to the nature of one's work, to geographic location, to ideology—all align. ALAN I. ABRAMOWITZ, THE GREAT ALIGNMENT: RACE, PARTY TRANSFORMATION, AND THE RISE OF DONALD TRUMP (2018). Various important aspects of individual identity are "fusing together" and "stacking atop one another" to create "mega-identities" that get aligned with partisanship. EZRA KLEIN, WHY WE'RE POLARIZED 37 (2020).
21. Alexander Kustov et al., *The Rise of Safe Seats and Party Indiscipline in the U.S. Congress* (2021), https://jackson.yale.edu/wp-content/uploads/2022/08/Kustov-et-al.-2021.pdf; see also Pildes, *Romanticizing Democracy, supra* note 12, at 831 (pointing to "the unprecedented power that senators in their first year in power have in relation to their party leaders and consequently over our politics" that makes it difficult for party leaders "to stop one or a few individual senators, or a minority faction" from "shutting down the government and threatening to default" even though that "would be destructive to the party's interests").
22. WILLIAM L. RIORDON, PLUNKITT OF TAMMANY HALL: A SERIES OF VERY PLAIN TALKS ON VERY PRACTICAL POLITICS 13 (1963).
23. 427 U.S. 347 (1976).
24. *See Rutan v. Republican Party*, 497 U.S. 62 (1990) (hiring, transfer, and promotion decisions); *O'Hare Truck Serv., Inc. v. City of Northlake*, 518 U.S. 712 (1996) (government contracts).
25. *See* Issacharoff, *supra* note 19, at 870–875 (describing the link between patronage and party strength and the series of events and decisions that weakened that link); Ronald N. Johnson & Gary D. Libecap, *Courts, A Protected Bureaucracy, and Reinventing Government*, 37 ARIZ. L. REV. 791, 794 (1995) (suggesting that "by prohibiting the remaining controls available to elected officials through political patronage," the Court's decisions contributed to the problem of bureaucracy" being unresponsive to "new electoral mandates").

26. Samuel Issacharoff & Daniel R. Ortiz, *Governing Through Intermediaries*, 85 VA. L. REV. 1627, 1629 (1999).
27. Eben Moglen & Pamela S. Karlan, *The Soul of a New Political Machine: The Online, the Color Line and Electronic Democracy*, 34 LOY. L.A. L. REV. 1089, 1106 (2001).
28. Pildes, *Romanticizing Democracy, supra* note 12, at 834. For discussion of the connection between the Internet and populist distrust of mediating institutions, see NATHANIEL PERSILY, THE INTERNET'S CHALLENGE TO DEMOCRACY: FRAMING THE PROBLEM AND ASSESSING REFORMS (2019).
29. *Buckley v. Valeo*, 424 U.S. 1, 25 (1976) (per curiam).
30. *Id.* at 48–49.
31. 383 U.S. 663 (1966).
32. *Id.* at 667.
33. *Id.* at 668. The principle that access to processes where the government exercises its key sovereign powers should not "depend[] on the amount of money [an individual] has" informed the Warren Court's criminal-justice jurisprudence as well. *See, e.g., Griffin v. Illinois*, 351 U.S. 12, 19 (1956); *Douglas v. California*, 372 U.S. 353, 355 (1963).
34. 411 U.S. 1 (1973).
35. *Id.* at 114 (Marshall, J., dissenting).
36. 494 U.S. 652 (1990).
37. *Id.* at 660.
38. 558 U.S. 310, 365 (2010).
39. *Id.* at 361.
40. *Id.* at 362 (quoting *First Nat'l Bank v. Bellotti*, 435 U.S. 765, 794 (1978)). For a discussion of just how difficult it would be to pursue those procedures and how federal tax law regarding retirement savings "as a matter of effective mandate, forces Americans to turn over their wealth to institutions that are permitted to use it for expressive purposes that they do not support," see Leo E. Strine, Jr., & Nicholas Walter, *Conservative Collision Course: The Tension Between Conservative Corporate Law Theory and Citizens United*, 100 CORNELL L. REV. 335, 341–342 (2015).
41. Press Release, Bureau of Lab. Stats., DOL, Union Members—2023 (Jan. 23, 2024), https://www.bls.gov/news.release/pdf/union2.pdf.
42. 567 U.S. 298 (2012).
43. 585 U.S. 878 (2018).
44. Strine & Walter, *supra* note 40, at 342.
45. 504 U.S. 428 (1992).
46. *Id.* at 432.
47. *Id.* at 433.
48. *Id.* at 434 (citing *Anderson v. Celebrezze*, 460 U.S. 780, 788–789 (1983)).
49. *Id.* (quoting *Norman v. Reed*, 502 U.S. 279, 289 (1992)).
50. *Id.* (quoting *Anderson*, 460 U.S. at 788).

51. *Crawford v. Marion County Election Bd.*, 553 U.S. 181 (2008).
52. *Shelby County v. Holder*, 570 U.S. 529 (2013).
53. *Brnovich v. Democratic Nat'l Comm.*, 594 U.S. 647 (2021).
54. *Rucho v. Common Cause*, 588 U.S. 684 (2019).
55. Karlan, *Democracy and Disdain*, *supra* note 4, at 32.
56. AINA GALLEGO, UNEQUAL POLITICAL PARTICIPATION WORLDWIDE 193 (2014). By contrast, "[t]here are no differences in the turnout rates of highly and less educated citizens in elections in countries such as Spain, Denmark, or South Korea." *Id.*
57. Randall Akee, *Voting and Income*, ECONOFACT (Feb. 7, 2019), https://econofact.org/voting-and-income.
58. Bruce E. Cain, *Moralism and Realism in Campaign Finance Reform*, 1995 U. CHI. LEGAL F. 111, 116.
59. Ross, *supra* note 5, at 1151.
60. Karl Evers-Hillstrom, *Most Expensive Ever: 2020 Election Cost $14.4 Billion*, OPEN SECRETS (Feb. 11, 2021), https://www.opensecrets.org/news/2021/02/2020-cycle-cost-14p4-billion-doubling-16/.
61. Issacharoff et al., *supra* note 3, at 927.
62. *See* Charles Stewart III, *The Cost of Conducting Elections* 3 (2022), https://electionlab.mit.edu/sites/default/files/2022-05/TheCostofConductingElections-2022.pdf ("[A] consensus exists within the election administration community that elections are underfunded nationwide, even if they are more underfunded in some places than others").
63. AM. ENTER. INST. & MIT ELECTION DATA + SCI. LAB, LESSONS LEARNED FROM THE 2020 ELECTION: REPORT TO THE U.S. ELECTION ASSISTANCE COMMISSION 84 (2021), https://electionlab.mit.edu/sites/default/files/2021-09/Lessons-Learned-in-the-2020-Election.pdf.
64. Wendy Underhill, *Democracy Is Priceless, but Elections Cost Big Bucks*, NAT'L CONF. STATE LEGISLATURES (Apr. 20, 2022), https://www.ncsl.org/state-legislatures-news/details/democracy-is-priceless-but-elections-cost-big-bucks.
65. Issacharoff & Karlan, *supra* note 4, at 1732.

CHAPTER 18

1. Bipartisan Campaign Reform Act of 2002, Pub. L. No. 107-155, 116 Stat. 81.
2. 558 U.S. 310 (2010).
3. Samuel Issacharoff & Pamela S. Karlan, *The Hydraulics of Campaign Finance Reform*, 77 TEX. L. REV. 1705 (1999).
4. *McConnell v. FEC*, 540 U.S. 93, 224 (2003).
5. *See generally* Nathaniel Persily, *Introduction* to SOLUTIONS TO POLITICAL POLARIZATION IN AMERICA (Nathaniel Persily ed., 2015).
6. Pub. L. No. 107-155, 116 Stat. 81 (2002).

7. Arthur D. Santana, *Virtuous or Vitriolic: The Effect of Anonymity on Civility in Online Newspaper Reader Comment Boards*, 8 JOURNALISM PRAC. 18, 18–33 (2013).
8. *See* Richard H. Pildes, *Small-Donor-Based Campaign-Finance Reform and Political Polarization*, 129 YALE L.J. F. 149, (2019) [hereinafter Pildes, *Campaign-Finance Reform and Political Polarization*].
9. Drew DeSilver, *The Polarization in Today's Congress Has Roots That Go Back Decades*, PEW RSCH. CTR. (Mar. 10, 2022), https://www.pewresearch.org/short-reads/2022/03/10/the-polarization-in-todays-congress-has-roots-that-go-back-decades/.
10. Michael J. Barber & Nolan McCarty, *Causes and Consequences of Polarization*, in SOLUTIONS TO POLITICAL POLARIZATION IN AMERICA 15, 32 (Nathaniel Persily ed., 2015).
11. Pub. L. No. 93-443, 88 Stat. 1263 (1974) (codified as amended in scattered titles of the U.S.C.).
12. 424 U.S. 1 (1976).
13. Pub. L. No. 107-155, 116 Stat. 81 (2002) (codified as amended in scattered titles of the U.S.C.).
14. Barber & McCarty, supra note 11, at 33.
15. *See* RAYMOND J. LA RAJA & BRIAN F. SCHAFFNER, CAMPAIGN FINANCE AND POLITICAL POLARIZATION: WHEN PURISTS PREVAIL 100–105 (2015); Raymond J. La Raja, *Richer Parties, Better Politics? Party-Centered Campaign Finance Laws and American Democracy*, 11 FORUM 313 (2013).
16. *See* Thomas E. Mann & Anthony Corrado, *Party Polarization and Campaign Finance*, CTR. FOR EFFECTIVE PUB. MGMT. AT BROOKINGS (2014), https://www.brookings.edu/wp-content/uploads/2016/06/Mann-and-Corrad_Party-Polarization-and-Campaign-Finance.pdf.
17. 533 U.S. 431 (2001) (upholding limits on party-coordinated contributions against a facial challenge).
18. 540 U.S. 93 (2003) (upholding the ban on soft money).
19. *See* NELSON W. POLSBY, CONSEQUENCES OF PARTY REFORM (1983).
20. *See* Nathaniel Persily, *Soft Parties and Strong Money*, 3 ELECTION L.J. 315 (2004).
21. *See* NATHANIEL PERSILY, BENJAMIN L. GINSBERG & ROBERT F. BAUER, CAMPAIGN FINANCE IN THE UNITED STATES: ASSESSING AN ERA OF FUNDAMENTAL CHANGE 33 (2018); DIANA DWYRE, POLITICAL PARTIES AND CAMPAIGN FINANCE: WHAT ROLE DO THE NATIONAL PARTIES PLAY? (2017), https://bipartisanpolicy.org/download/?file=/wp-content/uploads/2019/05/Political-Parties-and-Campaign-Finance-What-Role-Do-the-National-Parties-Play.-Diana-Dwyre.-Diana-Dwyre.pdf.
22. Christopher Hickey, *How a McConnell-Linked Group Is Closing the Ad Spending Gap with Democrats in Key Senate Races*, CNN (Oct. 17, 2022),

https://www.cnn.com/2022/10/17/politics/senate-republican-super-pac-ad-spending/index.html.
23. Isaac Arnsdorf et al., *MAGA-Dominated State Republican Parties Plagued by Infighting, Money Woes*, WASH. POST (Nov. 16, 2023), https://www.washingtonpost.com/politics/2023/11/13/republican-state-parties-struggles-maga/ ("In each of these states, cultivating center-right voters is key for a Republican to win the presidency. But the activists who overwhelmingly embrace Trump's false election claims, demand fealty to him and want to purge the party of Trump . . . have largely taken over").
24. Allan Smith & Megan Lebowitz, *RNC Chair Ronna McDaniel Announces Her Resignation*, NBC NEWS (Feb. 26, 2024), https://www.nbcnews.com/politics/2024-election/rnc-chair-ronna-mcdaniel-resignation-rcna137347.
25. One important limitation and oversight in this chapter (due to space constraints) is the topic of asymmetric polarization: the fact that polarization is occurring primarily through the rightward movement of Republicans and not the leftward movement of Democrats. For a complete treatment of this topic, see Jacob S. Hacker & Paul Pierson, *Confronting Asymmetric Polarization*, in SOLUTIONS TO POLITICAL POLARIZATION IN AMERICA 59 (Nathaniel Persily ed., 2015). The rightward ideological tilt and the deterioration of party-imposed constraints among Republicans, which can be seen not only in the election of Donald Trump but also in the insurrection against and deposing of Kevin McCarthy as Speaker of the House, is not paralleled on the left. However, the rise of Bernie Sanders and the "Squad," let alone fissures over Israel and Gaza, have demonstrated that centrifugal pressures (in the population and in the legislative caucus) are not limited to Republicans. Nolan McCarty finds that, at the state level, weaker party organizations explain the rightward shift of the Republican Party, but he does not find a similar effect for Democrats. See Nolan McCarty, *Reducing Polarization by Making Parties Stronger*, in SOLUTIONS TO POLITICAL POLARIZATION IN AMERICA (Nathaniel Persily ed., 2015).
26. 558 U.S. 310 (2010).
27. *See* PERSILY ET AL., *supra* note 22, at 4; Adam Bonica, *Avenues of Influence: On the Political Expenditures of Corporations and Their Directors and Executives*, 18 BUS. & POL. 367 (2016).
28. COMM. FOR ECON. DEV., THE LANDSCAPE OF CAMPAIGN CONTRIBUTIONS: CAMPAIGN FINANCE AFTER *CITIZENS UNITED* 4 (2017).
29. 599 F.3d 686 (D.C. Cir. 2010) (en banc).
30. *Buckley v. Valeo*, 424 U.S. 1 (1976).
31. 581 F.3d 1 (D.C. Cir 2009); *see also Cal. Med. Ass'n v. FEC*, 453 U.S. 182, 202–203 (1981) (Blackmun, J., concurring in part and concurring in the judgment); *FEC v. Mass. Citizens for Life, Inc.*, 479 U.S. 238 (1986).

32. *2020 Outside Spending, by Super Pac*, OPEN SECRETS, https://www.opensecrets.org/outside-spending/super_pacs/2020?chrt=2024&disp=O&type=S (last visited Oct. 26, 2024).
33. DIANA DWYRE & ROBIN KOLODNY, THE FUNDAMENTALS OF CAMPAIGN FINANCE IN THE U.S.: WHY WE HAVE THE SYSTEM WE HAVE, fig. 5.2 (2024), https://doi.org/10.3998/mpub.9813302.
34. *See* Paul S. Herrnson et al., *The Impact of Associational Ties on the Financing of Super PACs*, 13 INT. GRPS. & ADVOC. 43 (2023).
35. Pildes, *Campaign-Finance Reform and Political Polarization*, supra note 9, at 161; Pildes, *Participation and Polarization*, 22 U. PA. J. CONST. L. 341 (2020).
36. *See* Sandra González-Bailón et al., *Asymmetric Ideological Segregation in Exposure to Political News on Facebook*, 381 SCIENCE 392 (2023); Pablo Barbera, *Social Media, Echo Chambers, and Political Polarization*, in SOCIAL MEDIA AND DEMOCRACY: THE STATE OF THE FIELD AND PROSPECTS FOR REFORM 34 (Nathaniel Persily & Joshua Tucker eds., 2020).
37. CASS R. SUNSTEIN, REPUBLIC: DIVIDED DEMOCRACY IN THE AGE OF SOCIAL MEDIA (2017).
38. Nathaniel Persily, *The Campaign Revolution Will Not Be Televised*, AM. INT. (Oct. 10, 2015), https://www.the-american-interest.com/2015/10/10/the-campaign-revolution-will-not-be-televised/.
39. Dustin Volz and David Ingram, *U.S. May Need New Law to Address Russian Ad Buys on Facebook—Senator*, REUTERS (Sep. 6, 2017), https://www.reuters.com/article/technology/u-s-may-need-new-law-to-address-russian-ad-buys-on-facebook-senator-idUSKCN1BI2X7/.
40. *See* Stephanie Lai, *Campaigns Pay Influencers to Carry Their Messages, Skirting Political Ad Rules*, N.Y. TIMES (Nov. 2, 2022), https://www.nytimes.com/2022/11/02/us/elections/influencers-political-ads-tiktok-instagram.html.
41. *See* Sean J. Miller, *Media Buyers Warn of Inventory Price Spike as Late Money Floods into Midterm Races*, CAMPAIGNS & ELECTIONS (Oct. 12, 2022), https://campaignsandelections.com/industry-news/media-buyers-warn-of-inventory-price-spike-as-late-money-floods-into-midterm-races/.
42. SASHA ISSENBERG, THE VICTORY LAB: THE SECRET SCIENCE OF WINNING CAMPAIGNS (2012).
43. Ben Smith, *Joe Wilson's Tally Since "You Lie" Rises to $2.7 Million*, POLITICO (Oct. 8, 2009), https://www.politico.com/blogs/ben-smith/2009/10/joe-wilsons-tally-since-you-lie-rises-to-27-million-021968. So-called viral moments have become common fodder for digital fundraising ads targeting small donors. *See, e.g.*, Jasmine Crockett, META AD LIBR. (May 24, 2024), https://www.facebook.com/ads/library/?id=758638983125301 (following a viral confrontation with Rep. Taylor Greene in a House Oversight Committee meeting); Ron DeSantis, META AD LIBR. (Sept. 10, 2022),

https://www.facebook.com/ads/library/?id=619548696551348 (inviting would-be donors to vote on which state to send the next bus of migrants to, in reference to an earlier campaign stunt).
44. Zach Montellaro, *Matt Gaetz Deposed Kevin McCarthy and the Donations Came Pouring In*, POLITICO (Feb. 1, 2024), https://www.politico.com/news/2024/02/01/matt-gaetz-donations-00139182.
45. *Donor Demographics*, OPEN SECRETS, https://www.opensecrets.org/elections-overview/donor-demographics?cycle=2020&display=A (last visited Oct. 26, 2024) ("Only a tiny fraction of Americans actually give campaign contributions to political candidates, parties or PACs"). Of note is the fact that FEC records report only those who give more than $200, inherently making this harder to track.
46. Adam Hughes, *5 Facts About U.S. Political Donations*, PEW RSCH. CTR. (May 17, 2017), https://www.pewresearch.org/short-reads/2017/05/17/5-facts-about-u-s-political-donations/.
47. Laurent Bouton et al., *Small Campaign Donors* (Nat'l Bureau of Econ. Rsch., Working Paper No. 30050, 2022), http://www.nber.org/papers/w30050. *See also* Ollie Gratzinger, *Small Donors Give Big Money in 2020 Election Cycle*, OPEN SECRETS (Oct. 26, 2020), https://www.opensecrets.org/news/2020/10/small-donors-give-big-2020-thanks-to-technology/
(noting that small donors made up 22% of 2020 fundraising, up from 15% at the same point in 2016); Pildes, *Campaign-Finance Reform and Political Polarization*, supra note 9 (highlighting that, from 2014 to 2018, on ActBlue—the Democrats' predominant small-dollar fundraising platform—donations increased by 80%). In surveys following the 2016 election, the majority of Americans who gave a donation say they gave less than $100. *See* Hughes, *supra* note 47.
48. *See* Individual Contributions, FEC, https://www.fec.gov/data/receipts/individual-contributions/?two_year_transaction_period=2004&min_amount=1000 (last visited Oct. 26, 2024).
49. *Compare* Pildes, *Campaign-Finance Reform and Political Polarization*, supra note 9 (noting that Republicans who voted to reject the 2020 Electoral College vote received more than three times as much money in small-donor contributions as those who voted to accept Biden's victory); *with* Thomas B. Edsall, *For $200, a Person Can Fuel the Decline of Our Major Parties*, N.Y. TIMES (Aug. 30, 2023), https://www.nytimes.com/2023/08/30/opinion/campaign-finance-small-donors.html; David Byler, *Small-Dollar Donors Didn't Save Democracy. They Made It Worse*, WASH. POST (May 1, 2023), https://www.washingtonpost.com/opinions/2023/05/01/small-donors-political-campaign-spending. *Compare also* Jonah Goldberg, *How Small Donors Have Become a Destructive, Dividing Force in American Politics*, L.A. TIMES (Aug. 15, 2023), https://www.latimes.com/opinion/story/2023-08-15/small-donors-polarization-politicians-ideology-democracy, *with*

Ian Vandewalker, *Do Small Donors Cause Political Dysfunction?*, BRENNAN CTR. FOR JUST. (2024), at 2.

50. *See, e.g.*, Michael J. Barber et al., *Ideologically Sophisticated Donors: Which Candidates Do Individual Contributors Finance?*, 61 AMER. J. POL. SCI. 271 (2017).
51. David Broockman & Neil Malhotra, *What Do Partisan Donors Want?*, 84 PUB. OP. Q. 104 (2020).
52. *Large Versus Small Individual Donations, 2020*, OPEN SECRETS, https://www.opensecrets.org/elections-overview/large-vs-small-donations?cycle=2020&type=M (last visited Oct. 26, 2024). This trend has continued, with Reps. Taylor Greene, Ocasio-Cortez, Jordan, Schiff, and Porter each raising over $10 million mostly from small-dollar donations in the 2022 cycle. *See Large Versus Small Individual Donations, 2022*, OPEN SECRETS, https://www.opensecrets.org/elections-overview/large-vs-small-donations?cycle=2022&type=M (last visited Oct. 26, 2024).
53. See Schaffner & La Raja, *Campaign Finance and Political Polarization*, *supra* note 16, at 71.
54. Michael J. Barber, *Ideological Donors, Contribution Limits, and the Polarization of American Legislatures*, 78 J. POL. 296 (2016).
55. There are those, such as Professor Lawrence Lessig, who argue that a public finance voucher system that creates close to 100% participation would not produce the same kind of polarization as one dependent on those willing to give their own money, which admittedly is an unrepresentative and more ideological substratum of the population. But if the problem is "people," who are more likely to be mobilized to give based on ideological appeals, then we should not expect even broad participation to make much of an impact. That does not mean all public financing would have those effects. Indeed, a system that guarantees public money to candidates and parties could reduce the impact of money given for ideological reasons coming from any source.
56. *See* Barber & McCarty, *supra* note 11.
57. Richard H. Pildes, *Democracies in the Age of Fragmentation*, 110 CAL. L. REV. 2051 (2022).

CHAPTER 19

1. ANN SOUTHWORTH, BIG MONEY UNLEASHED: THE CAMPAIGN TO DEREGULATE ELECTION SPENDING 32–33 (2024).
2. *See, e.g.*, BRUCE ACKERMAN & IAN AYRES, VOTING WITH DOLLARS: A NEW PARADIGM FOR CAMPAIGN FINANCE (2002).
3. The German Constitutional Court has held that tax deductions for campaign contributions are permissible "only as long as the contributions remain within a range which is accessible to those with average incomes." CHRISTIAN BUMKE & ANDREAS VOSSKUHLE, GERMAN CONSTITUTIONAL LAW:

INTRODUCTION, CASES, AND PRINCIPLES § 1554 (2019) (quoting 85 BVerfGE 264 (Party Financing II)).
4. Alexander Meiklejohn, *"Everything Worth Saying Should Be Said"*: *An Educator Says We Talk of Free Speech, but Hedge That Freedom with Too Many Restrictions*, N.Y. TIMES MAGAZINE, July 18, 1948, at 8–9, 32.
5. ALEXANDER MEIKLEJOHN, FREE SPEECH AND ITS RELATION TO SELF-GOVERNMENT 26 (1948).
6. Nonetheless, this is a common approach around the world, perhaps because it's easy to understand and administer. In Germany, for example, parties that meet a relatively low threshold (0.5% of the vote in a national election) receive a subsidy for each vote received and a separate subsidy equal to the amounts the party raised through small individual contributions. Germany doesn't limit spending on campaigns; the subsidies are supplemented by whatever else the parties can raise on their own.
7. The Supreme Court of Canada upheld legislation limiting third-party spending to $3,000 per district and a national total of $150,000. *Harper v. Canada*, 2004 SCC 33, [2004] 1 SCR 827. In response to a decision by the European Court of Human Rights, the British Parliament increased the limit on independent expenditures from £5 per person (!) to £500.
8. 523 U.S. 666 (1997).
9. *See* Mark Tushnet, *The Possibilities of Comparative Constitutional Law*, 108 YALE L.J. 1225, 1257–1264 (1999).
10. For a discussion, *see* MARK TUSHNET, THE NEW FOURTH BRANCH: INSTITUTIONS FOR PROTECTING CONSTITUTIONAL DEMOCRACY 174 (2021).
11. MANUEL JOSÉ CEPEDA ESPINOSA & DAVID LANDAU, COLOMBIAN CONSTITUTIONAL LAW: LEADING CASES 130–131 (2017) (quoting Sentencia C-1153/05, Gaceta de la Corte Constitucional [G.C.C.] (Colom.)).
12. *Id.* (internal quotation marks omitted) (quoting Sentencia C-1153/05).
13. *Id.* at 129.
14. CEPEDA ESPINOSA & LANDAU, *supra* note 12, at 130–131 (internal quotation marks omitted) (quoting Sentencia C-1153/05). I refer to non-US jurisprudence for the ideas the materials cited express, not knowing whether the cited decisions reflect current law in the several nations.
15. GRUNDGESETZ arts. 21, 38 [GG] [Basic Law], translation at http://www.gesetze-im-internet.de/englisch_gg/index.html.
16. *Id.*
17. DONALD P. KOMMERS & RUSSELL A. MILLER, THE CONSTITUTIONAL JURISPRUDENCE OF THE FEDERAL REPUBLIC OF GERMANY 666, 672 (3d ed. 2012) (first citing 7 BVerfGE 377 (1958); then citing 53 BVerfGE 138 (1980)).
18. CONSTITUCIÓN POLÍTICA DE COLOMBIA [C.P.] art. 264, 232. Canada's system is administered by Elections Canada, headed by a commissioner

appointed by the House of Commons, which appears to follow a norm of nonpartisanship in selecting the commissioner.

19. For an overview of election administration in the United States, *see* Kathleen Hale, Robert Montjoy & Mitchell Brown, Administering Elections: How American Elections Work 27–51 (2015).

Index

For the benefit of digital users, indexed terms that span two pages (e.g., 52–53) may, on occasion, appear on only one of those pages.

A

advertisements, 20, 26, 81, 86–87, 127, 150, 161, 213, 230, 249–250, 281–282
   dark-money, 100–101, 106–109
   role of advertisers, 32–33, 101–102
   targets of, 98, 105, 109
Alito, Samuel, 6–7, 23, 63, 128
American Israel Public Affairs Committee (AIPAC), 45–46
Americans for Prosperity v. Bonta, 79–80, 118
Arizona Citizens Clean Election Act, 64–65
Arizona Free Enterprise Club v. Bennett, 8, 24–25, 223
artificial intelligence, 82, 121–123, 132, 134–135, 136–138, 308–309, 319
   emergence of, 124–126
Austin v. Michigan Chamber of Commerce, 5–6, 8–9, 39, 62–63, 74–77, 128, 143, 288–289

B

battleground states, 238–239, 248, 253 254
BCRA. *See* Bipartisan Campaign Reform Act
Bickel, Alexander M., 85–86, 181–182
Biden, Joseph R., 121, 201–202, 303
Bipartisan Campaign Reform Act, 6–7, 19, 20–21, 74–79, 127–128, 199–200, 231, 297–299
   millionaire's amendment, 7, 20–21
Blackmun, Harry, 14, 21–22, 25
Bollinger, Lee C., 1–2, 5, 10, 13–14, 69, 85–86, 121–122, 143, 159–160, 195–196, 281–282
Brennan, William J., 179, 204

Breyer, Stephen, 6–9, 23, 26–27, 39–40, 63, 129, 183
bribery, 42–43, 81, 116, 133, 146, 168–169, 190, 204, 271–272. *See also* corruption
Buckley v. Valeo, 5–6, 13–14, 21–22, 26–30, 87, 123, 130–131, 139–143, 177–180, 184–186, 191–197, 198–199, 202–203, 245, 281–284, 305–306

C

campaign finance regime, 14, 148, 152–153, 199, 221, 226, 258, 284, 285, 290, 292
campaign-related spending. *See* expenditures
Care Act, 96–97, 253
cash-for-votes, 127–129
Charles, Guy-Uriel E., 242–244
Citizens United v. FEC, 31, 68, 70–71, 76, 79–85, 87, 115–116, 117–118, 128–129, 144, 184–185, 200–201, 232–233, 240, 250–251, 304–306
climate change, 258, 319
Clinton, Hillary, 76, 128, 252
collective-action problems, 204–205, 258
Colorado Republican Federal Campaign Committee, 241, 261, 301
Colorado Republican I, 18, 26, 203, 204–206, 241–242
Colorado Republican II, 18, 22–23, 26, 31–32, 203–205
commerce, interstate, 277
concentration of benefits, 160–161, 169–170, 176–178
constitutional courts, foreign, 209–210, 316–317, 325, 327–329

contributions, 13–14, 15–16, 17–18, 19–23, 25–29, 30–31, 32–33, 37–38, 46–47, 55–58, 59–60, 73–74, 164–166, 186, 203–205, 241
   aggregation of, 8, 23–24, 26–27, 240
   application of limits, 240–242
   corporate, 31, 37, 54, 61, 94, 166, 167–168, 200
   made post-election, 24, 162, 166–167
   soft-money, 35–36, 44, 161
   unlimited, 127, 188, 305–306
   upholding limits on, 38, 42–43, 126, 249
   violations of limits on, 55, 74
corporate spending, 61–63, 66, 74–75, 117, 127, 305–306
corruption, 128–129, 139–146, 148–149, 151–153, 159–162, 171–175, 183–184, 186, 188–191, 196–197, 250–251, 315
   anticorruption measures, 2, 4, 13, 15–16, 29, 31–32, 35, 38, 42–43, 52–53, 77, 127–128, 161, 174–175, 185–186, 281–284, 305
   appearance of, 2, 8, 13, 15–16, 29, 52–53, 58–59, 77, 128–129, 181, 196, 281–284
   compelling-interest corruption, 145–148, 150–153, 156–157
   defined, 52, 143, 144–145, 146–148, 152–153, 156–157
   in government contracting, 160, 163–169, 172, 174–175, 177–178
   institutional, 189–191
   quid pro quo, 42–43, 130, 143–144, 152–153, 159–160, 161–162, 167–177, 184–186, 189–191, 241, 250–251
Count Binface, 322–324
Czech Republic, 159–160, 166, 323

D

dark money, 63–64, 95, 98–100, 109, 117–118, 123, 132–134, 137, 284
   groups, 99–100, 115, 129, 133, 138
Davis v. FEC, 7, 20–21, 23–24, 67
deepfakes, 82, 121–123, 134–136, 138
deregulation, 67, 93–98, 103, 114, 233, 235–240, 242
disclaimers, 77–78, 79–80, 136–137, 297–298
DISCLOSE Act, 114, 119, 132–133, 137

disclosure requirements, 3–4, 55, 70, 74, 77–78, 79–80, 94–95, 98, 101, 109, 114, 130–132, 136–137, 186
   targets of advertising, 98, 100, 105–106
discrimination, racial, 124, 271, 279
disinformation, 95, 98, 100–101, 102–103, 105–106, 123, 134–136, 138
distorting effects of money, 2–3, 5–6, 9, 61–62, 143, 250
districting, 269–271, 274–276, 311, 330
District of Columbia Circuit Court of Appeals, 56, 126, 185, 220, 249, 305–306
donor class, 96, 102–103, 208, 234, 236–237, 239, 244, 257, 262, 310
Due Process Clause, 20, 61, 189

E

electioneering communications, 6, 74–76, 250
Elections Clause, 71, 270
electoral administration, 124, 198, 229
electoral campaigns (generally), 36–37, 42, 43–44, 45–46, 83–84, 87, 95–96, 100, 104–105, 106–109, 191–192, 198–199, 216–217, 222–223, 230, 234, 243–244, 252–254
equality, 95, 106–109, 154–155, 272–276, 280, 318, 321
Equal Protection Clause, 71, 103–104, 279
expenditures, 3–4, 13–23, 25–31, 47, 59–61, 66, 74–75, 77–78, 161–162, 196, 203–204, 248
   coordinated, 17–18, 31–32, 240–242
   corporate, 9, 39, 60–61, 62–64, 66, 143, 200–201, 305
   independent, 4, 18–19, 44, 105, 185, 186, 200, 203, 321, 324
   limitations, 14–16, 20–22, 25–27, 38–39, 47–48, 55–58, 73, 126, 249, 259
   unlimited, 62, 209, 305–306
extremism. *See* ideological extremism

F

fairness doctrine, 3, 40, 88–89
FCC. *See* Federal Communications Commission
FEC. *See* Federal Election Commission
FECA. *See* Federal Election Campaign Act

INDEX

FEC v. Beaumont, 22–23, 61
FEC v. Ted Cruz for Senate, 8, 24, 27–28, 30–31, 162, 166–168, 174–175
Federal Communications Commission, 3, 40, 82, 88, 100, 121–122, 206, 332
Federal Election Campaign Act, 3–4, 5–6, 13, 14–15, 17–18, 21–22, 71–74, 94, 98, 184, 195–196, 198–199, 228, 243, 244–245, 248–249, 261
  amendments to, 13, 126, 299
Federal Election Commission, 6–8, 19–25, 62–63, 67, 94, 127, 128–129, 143–144, 161–162, 184–185, 241–242, 294–295, 301, 305–306
Feingold, Russ, 6, 123, 127
First Amendment (generally), 1–2, 9–10, 14–16, 29–30, 38, 39–40, 51–52, 66–67, 68–69, 72–74, 79–80, 82–83, 84–88, 183, 191, 270–272, 331–332
First National Bank of Boston v. Bellotti, 60–61, 249–250
Fourth Circuit Court of Appeals, 123–124
fragmentation, 241–242, 295
freedom of expression, 14–15, 20–21, 22–23, 66–67, 73, 202–203, 206, 273, 321, 324–325
  quantity of expression, 14–15, 56, 72–73, 87
Freedom to Vote Act, 123–124, 132–133, 137
fundamental rights, 56–57, 71, 84

G

German constitutional law, 197–198, 209–210, 319–320, 327–328
gerrymandering, 95, 267–268, 269–271, 274–276, 279–281, 311
Ginsburg, Ruth Bader, 6–7, 9, 26, 63, 129
Green Party, 319, 323
Grundgesetz, 197–198, 209–210, 319–320, 327–328

H

Harris, Kamala, 45, 69, 122
Hawley, Joshua, 186–187
Hellman, Deborah, 139–143
hydraulic argument, 196, 198–199, 202–203, 285, 296

I

ideological extremism, 208–209, 212, 215–216, 218, 222, 234–235, 237–238, 295, 296–297, 300–301
  extremist rhetoric, 211–212, 217, 225–226
inequality, 247–248, 252–253, 257, 262, 284, 288
interest-group pluralism, 320–321, 328–330
interstate commerce, 277
Issacharoff, Samuel, 191–192, 195–196, 244–245, 284, 291

K

Kagan, Elena, 8, 24, 53, 65, 129, 224
Kang, Michael S., 227–228, 257–258
Karlan, Pamela S., 196, 281–282
Kennedy, Anthony, 9, 20, 26–27, 71, 76, 89, 128–129, 131, 144, 184, 205

L

Lessig, Lawrence, 177–179

M

marketplace of ideas metaphor, 2, 35, 37, 38–41, 45–46, 60, 62–63, 82, 272, 331
Marshall, Thurgood, 5–6, 9, 17, 26, 28, 62, 204, 288
McCain, John, 6, 45, 117–118, 123, 127, 252
McCain-Feingold. *See* Bipartisan Campaign Reform Act
McCarthy, Kevin, 286, 309
McConnell, Mitch, 87, 127
McConnell v. FEC, 6–7, 9, 44, 62–63, 67, 74–75, 127–129, 143, 161, 301
McCutcheon v. FEC, 8, 23–24, 26–28, 30–31, 39–40, 67, 129–132, 136–138, 183, 240
McDonnell v. United States, 149–150, 153, 155–156
McGovern, George, 195–196, 290–291
megadonors, 37, 45–46, 237
Meiklejohn, Alexander, 321
Michael H. v. Gerald D., 189, 191
Musk, Elon, 122, 208, 242–244, 248, 253–256, 258, 262

N

National Republican Senatorial Committee, 205, 241–242
New York Times Co. v. Sullivan, 179, 187, 191–192, 206
New York Times Co. v. United States, 1–2, 85–86
New York Times organization, 69, 77, 238–239
Nixon, Richard, 3, 86, 88, 94, 125–126
Nixon v. Shrink Missouri Gov't PAC, 22–23, 26–27, 127–129, 243

O

Obama, Barack, 45, 164–165, 201–202, 217, 252, 290–291, 308–309
Ocasio-Cortez, Alexandria, 216, 310
O'Connor, Sandra Day, 6–7, 63, 127–128
originalism, 65–66, 116, 179–180, 181–182, 183–184, 186–191
out-of-district donors, 214–215, 224

P

PACs, 3–4, 21–22, 75, 83, 113, 129–130, 159–160, 164–165, 167, 175–177, 180, 184, 185–186, 187–188, 191, 214, 229–230, 285, 310
  donations to, 162, 164
pay-to-play, 160, 173–175
Peale, Farris, 242–244
Pentagon Papers. See York Times Co. v. United States
Persily, Nathaniel, 292–294
personal funds, 7, 26
Pildes, Richard H., 210, 211–212, 236–237, 241–242
playing field metaphor, 54, 119, 312, 315–316, 317–318, 320–322, 323–324, 326–329
plutocracy, 248, 256–259, 262
polarization, 211–212, 218, 224–226, 235–236, 257, 294–295, 296–302, 304–305, 307–308, 311–312
  asymmetric, 257, 260
  causes, 212, 218, 221, 227, 239, 300, 302
  definitions of, 296–297
  dimensions of, 242, 296–297, 299–300, 306–307

hyperpartisanship, 217–218, 227, 231–232, 234–236, 239, 242, 260, 263
  by party, 231–232, 235–240, 247
Political Action Committees. *See* PACs
political culture, 53, 211, 217–218, 225, 284, 316, 320, 324–325, 328–329
political dysfunction, 293–295, 312
political ideology, 213–214, 234, 258, 303, 305, 312
political parties, 17–18, 169–171, 203–207, 208–210, 213–214, 221–222, 227–242, 259–260, 285–287, 299–304, 322–324
  leadership, 44, 114, 170–171, 216–217, 221, 227–228, 236–238, 240, 259–260, 286, 302–303
  loyalty, 171, 227–228, 286–287
  responsiveness, 104, 239
political question doctrine, 263, 267–269, 275–276, 278–279
polling, 54, 135, 227–228, 243, 254
populism, 252–253, 257, 262, 293–294
Powell, Lewis, 60
primary elections, 62–63, 76–77, 95, 207, 213–214, 219, 228, 238–239, 252, 285–286, 290–291, 295–296, 306–307, 312
privacy, 74, 79–80
procurement, 159–160, 165–168, 170, 173, 176
proportionality test, 321, 325
public funding, 4, 21–22, 64–65, 67, 104–105, 222–224, 251, 290–291, 318
public goods, 187–188, 316, 319–321, 329
public opinion, 39–40, 171, 331–332
  voter confidence, 4–5, 25–26, 139
public subsidies, 219–220, 223–224, 323–324

R

Randall v. Sorrell, 23–24, 26–27, 30–31, 47, 197, 240
Red Lion Broadcasting Co. v. FCC, 3, 332
Rehnquist, William H., 63, 71, 180, 291–292
Republican National Committee, 254, 260, 301–303

Roberts, John, 23–24, 26–28, 63, 128, 130, 131–132, 168–169, 197
Roberts Court, 9, 54, 161–162, 174–175, 233, 241–242, 289–290
Rucho v. Common Cause, 269–271, 275–276, 279–282

S

Scalia, Antonin, 6–7, 26, 66, 182, 189, 191, 204, 207
scrutiny, 16, 22–23, 38, 66–67, 76, 80, 94, 106, 196–197
  closely drawn, 22–24, 31–32, 38
  compelling interest, 9, 22, 62, 63–64, 76–77, 109, 250
  exacting, 14–16, 74, 78, 80
  intermediate, 55–57
  narrowly tailored, 31–32
  strict, 22, 27–28, 31–32, 38, 55–56, 57–58, 76–78, 288–290
Second Circuit Court of Appeals, 27, 86
self-funding, 7, 45, 223
self-government, 246–247, 249, 252, 263
Sixth Circuit Court of Appeals, 31–32, 205, 241–242
small donors, 33, 45–46, 201, 211–212, 215–218, 225–226, 234, 296–298, 309–310
social media, 1–2, 46, 81–82, 95, 98, 100–101, 105–106, 123, 217, 248, 306–308, 333
soft money, 13–14, 21, 27, 44, 161, 198–199, 230–234, 237, 305
Sotomayor, Sonia, 9, 63, 129
Souter, David, 6–7, 23, 26
speech, 15, 28–29, 37–38, 51–52, 55–58, 60–61, 65, 66–67, 71–72, 80, 81–82, 85–86, 87–88, 115–116, 145–147, 272–273
  content neutrality, 18–19, 38, 77–78, 80, 84, 123, 125, 134, 135, 307–308
  corporate, 39, 62, 76–77, 78–79, 99, 131, 149, 288–289
  examination of, 80–81
  by proxy, 15, 26–28
  regulation of, 5, 60, 71–72, 144, 147, 180–182, 187–188, 270, 272–273
SpeechNow v. FEC, 44, 94, 98–100, 185–186, 191, 305–306

spending
  coordinated, 222, 240–241
  direct, 128, 320, 324
  limiting, 14–15, 18, 20–21, 24–25, 27, 86, 126, 251, 317, 318, 324, 327
standard of review, 15–16, 20–22, 26, 30–31, 106–109, 281–282, 288, 291–292
state legislatures, 27, 126, 132, 155–156, 269–271, 278, 299–300, 306–307
Stephanopoulos, Nicholas O., 156–157, 159–160
Stevens, John Paul, 6–7, 9–10, 26, 56–57, 59, 61, 63, 65, 78–79, 127, 129, 137–138, 204
Stone, Geoffrey R., 1–2, 13–14, 69, 85–86, 121–122, 143, 159–160, 179, 195–196, 211–212, 281–282
Strauss, David A., 263, 267–268
super PACs, 32–33, 36–37, 44–46, 47–48, 113–114, 137, 191, 201–202, 232–234, 235–236, 253–254, 261, 302, 306

T

television, 3, 32–33, 36–37, 40, 42, 46, 88, 100, 124–125, 228, 230, 297
Thomas, Clarence, 6–7, 26–27, 59–60, 78–79, 131, 179, 183, 187–188, 191–192, 204
Tillman Act, 3, 94
Trump, Donald, 45, 69, 121, 124, 201–202, 208, 216–217, 248, 252–254, 257, 286, 303, 308–309
  presidential campaigns of, 248, 254, 260–261
Tushnet, Mark, 61, 312, 315, 331–332

U

undue influence, 35, 41–43, 45, 109, 124, 138
unions, 60, 62–63, 74–76, 78, 82–83, 153, 206–207, 289, 298, 327
  membership, 75, 83, 289
United Kingdom, 321, 325
United States v. O'Brien, 55–57

V

voluntary associations, 66, 68, 82
vote dilution, 95, 103–104

voting behavior, 163, 208, 231–232, 272, 299–300
  cohesion, 208
  turnout, 290
  voters of color, 93, 94–95, 96–97, 99, 101–103, 106–110
voting rights, 272–273, 290
Voting Rights Act, 103–104, 106–109, 124, 289–290, 291–292

W

Watergate, 94, 123, 125–126, 243
wealth gap, 93, 95–97
western democracies, 211, 215, 326–327
White, Byron, 4–5, 25–26, 72–73, 80
Whitehouse, Sheldon, 110, 113–114, 132–133
wholly foreign dictum, 39, 275–276, 280
Wood, Diane P., 68–69